NOTABLE WOMEN OF CHINA

NOTABLE WOMEN OF CHINA

SHANG DYNASTY TO THE EARLY TWENTIETH CENTURY

EDITOR-IN-CHIEF

BARBARA BENNETT PETERSON

ASSOCIATE EDITORS

HE HONG FEI   WANG JIYU

HAN TIE   ZHANG GUANGYU

AN EAST GATE BOOK

M.E.Sharpe
Armonk, New York
London, England

An East Gate Book

Library of Congress Cataloging-in-Publication Data

Notable women of China : Shang dynasty to the early twentieth century
/ editor-in-chief, Barbara Bennett Peterson : associate editors,
Zhang Guangyu . . . [et al.].
    p.   cm.
    "An East gate book."
    Includes bibliographical references and index.
    ISBN 0-7656-0504-X (cloth : alk. paper)
    1. Women—China Biography.   2. Women—China—History Biography.
I. Peterson, Barbara Bennett, 1942– .   II. Zhang, Guangyu.
HQ1767.5.A3N67   1999
305.4'092'251—dc21   99-30322
[B]   CIP

Printed in the United States of America

The paper used in this publication meets the minimum requirements of
American National Standard for Information Sciences
Permanence of Paper for Printed Library Materials,
ANSI Z 39.48-1984.

BM (c)   10   9   8   7   6   5   4   3   2   1

To citizens of the world—may we understand one another's cultures and appreciate our diversity

Contents

PART V. THE SONG AND YUAN DYNASTIES REVITALIZE CHINA • 243

PART VI. THE MING AND QING DYNASTIES AND THE COMING OF THE OPIUM WARS • 285

Editorial Board

Chief Executive Editor

Barbara Bennett Peterson, Fulbright Senior Scholar and professor of history, Wuhan University, and professor emeritus of World and American history, University of Hawaii; adjunct fellow of East-West Center, USA

Associate Editors

Han Tie, professor of American history, Wuhan University, Wuchang, China

He Hongfei, professor of modern and contemporary history, Wuhan University, Wuchang, China, and fellow, Yenching Institute, Harvard University

Wang Jiyu, chairman, English department, and head of graduate studies, Wuhan University, Wuchang, China

Zhang Guangyu, former vice-chairman, History department, head of research, and professor of history, Wuhan University, Wuchang, China

Advisory Board

Uwe Baur, professor of German literature, Institut für Germanisuk, Universität Graz, Graz, Austria

Betty Chandler, editor, English department, Foreign Languages Press, Beijing, China

Chen Qing, professor, department of English, Sichuan University, Chengdu, China

Michaelyn P. Chou, head of public services and special collections, Hawaii/Pacific Collection, Hamilton Library, University of Hawaii, Honolulu, Hawaii, USA

Dina Choulajeva, professor of Russian, Wuhan University, Wuchang, China

Godwin C. Chu, emeritus fellow, East-West Center, former assistant director and research associate, Institute for Culture and Communications, East-West Center, Honolulu, Hawaii, USA

Dong Shuri, associate professor of history, Tianjin University, China

Elizabeth R. Eames, professor of philosophy, Southern Illinois University, Carbondale, Illinois, USA

Gu Xuejia, professor of history and deputy-director, American Studies Center, Sichuan University, Chengdu, China

Donald Holzman, director, Ecole des Hautes Etudes en Sciences Sociales, and director, Institut des Hautes Etudes Chinoises, Paris, France

Huang Dianqi, president of the Tianjin Dramatic Museum; member of China's People's Arts and Crafts Council; director of the Tianjin Folk-lore Society; member of the Chinese Artists Association, Tianjin, China

Florence Karlstrom, professor of sociology, Northern Arizona University, Flagstaff, Arizona, USA

Gloria Kern, Chinese cultural specialist, Honolulu, Hawaii, USA

Nadine LaPorte, visiting professor of French literature, Wuhan University, Wuchang, China

Mark Larsen, Academic Exchanges, second secretary, Press and Cultural Section, American embassy, Beijing, China

Li Shidong, emeritus professor of American history, Wuhan University, Wuchang, China; former vice-president and secretary-general of the American History Research Association of China

Liang Maoxin, professor of Chinese history, Hebei Normal College, Shijiazhuang, China

Liu Xuyi, professor of American history, Wuhan University, Wuchang, China; international contributing editor to the *Journal of American History* (USA), and former vice president and secretary-general, American History Research Association of China

H. Nishioka, professor of Chinese literature, Shinshu University, Matsumoto, Nagano, Japan

Takashi Oka, professor of Japanese, Wuhan University, Wuchang, China

David Perry, professor of English literature, Wuhan University, Wuchang,

China; former professor of English, Simmons College, Boston, Massachusetts, USA

Shi Fengyan, research fellow, Chinese Academy of Social Sciences, Beijing, China

Song Ruizhi, professor of Chinese history, Hubei University, Wuhan, China

Robert D. Stueart, dean and professor of library and information sciences, Graduate School of Library and Information Sciences, Simmons College, Boston, Massachusetts, USA

Tan Junjiu, professor of international politics, department of political science, Wuhan University, Wuchang, China; member of the directorate and vice-secretary-general of the American History Research Association of China; Fulbright Scholar, Yale University, New Haven, Connecticut, USA, 1990–91

Wang Jianglin, associate professor, director, department of International Relations Studies and secretary-general of the American Studies Center of the Foreign Languages University, Luoyang, China

Wang Tingzhi, professor of world history, department of history, Sichuan University, Chengdu, China

Karen Wei, Chinese librarian, associate professor of library administration, Asian Library, University of Illinois, Champaign-Urbana, Illinois, USA

Xia Qing, professor, department of English, Sichuan University, Chengdu, China

Xie Fang, professor, department of History, Sichuan University, Chengdu, China

Xu Meifeng, professor of journalism, Wuhan University, Wuchang, China

Yang Qinde, head of the Foreign Affairs Office, president of the univer-

Preface

Notable Women of China is a biographical reference work that offers new knowledge about Chinese women's contributions throughout the long history of their country. The criteria used for inclusion are the same as those used for *Notable American Women* (Cambridge: Harvard University Press, [vols. 1–3, 1971; vol. 4, 1980]) and *Notable Women of Hawaii* (Honolulu: University of Hawaii Press, 1984): "The individual's influence on her time and field; the importance and significance of her achievement; the pioneering or innovative quality of her work; and the relevance of her career for the history of women." Using these criteria, the editorial and advisory boards, composed primarily of faculty from Wuhan University in China, selected the notable Chinese women included in this book. As chief executive editor, I also received suggestions from some of the most outstanding scholars teaching in China. All of them gave me good advice, which I took to heart. My interest in doing a book on *Notable Women of China* began as the idea for a research project to be completed during the year I would spend as a Senior Fulbright Scholar in the People's Republic of China. I had been invited to Wuhan University in part because the faculty liked my idea. Almost as soon as I arrived, the chairman of the history department, Professor Zhu Lei organized the rest of the faculty to collaborate with me and to write individual biographies for inclusion in this book. I am indebted to him for his kindness. Our efforts will greatly change the face of Chinese scholarship because the book offers the history of women during each period of Chinese history, a feat of value to scholars in China and the rest of the world alike.

Throughout the world, the search for role models for young women has become increasingly urgent, along with an increasing interest in women's history and their contributions. For young Chinese women who want to be "modern" and break out of the old stereotypes, the book offers examples of those who have gone before them, whose strengths they may seek to emulate. This volume traces the history of famous Chinese women from the Shang dynasty to the end of the Qing dynasty as it highlights notable women as, for example, empresses, court ladies-in-waiting, scientists, teachers, singers, dancers, poets, mother models, craftswomen, politicians, writers, and diplomatic envoys. Their history is as intriguing as it is valuable.

Notable Women of China is arranged chronologically and has introductory historical sections to explain the ebb and flow of Chinese dynasties. The organization of the entries within each section is also strictly chronological by the birth date of the subject.

Each biography contains information about the subject's life (the life span dates, when known, family background, education, marital status, children), a summary of her career or significance, and a bibliography. Throughout, the titles of Emperors are given with their reign title, and their personal names are so indicated. Empresses' and other royalty's titles are given in the same way with imperial titles used, with personal or original names being indicated as well.

In addition to its value as a reference work, this volume might also be used as a textbook on the history of China as seen through the lives of its famous women. Women's history allows us to double our vision of ourselves—to place in tandem the known lives of great men with the little-known lives of its outstanding women. This is the purpose of *Notable Women of China*—to double China's vision of its own history by including women and to make that history known to readers outside China.

Traditionally the stereotypes of Chinese women depict them as delicate and powerless creatures, controlled by their fathers, husbands, or sons. This book breaks new ground by refuting that stereotype: There were always strong Chinese women, but their story has been inadequately told. The real history of China with a more accurate depiction of women's contribution to society, which made possible harmony within the modern family, has been lacking. Men and women often worked together to accomplish great tasks, and they both deserve respect as well as appreciation for their roles in society. Chinese women in these pages are revealed as wise empresses and community leaders, able rulers, worthy advisers, military warriors, scholarly writers, expert business women, articulate poets, lovely artists and calligraphers, thoughtful wives and mothers, and inspirational role models for young women. Chinese women's history is a treasure trove for new discoveries as their stories are revealed from ancient sources, stone carvings, diaries, court histories, poetry, songs, ancient rites and literature, and genealogical records. Many of these sources are newly translated and became accessible in the 1970s, after relations between the United States and China were re-established. Further new technology has allowed the source material to be more widely disseminated than ever before, making possible studies such as this one in both Chinese and English. Included is a table indicating the dates of each dynasty as well as the significant subperiods.

I thank the history department at Wuhan University for its contributions to this book, whether writing, research, or translation. In particular I am grateful to the department chairman, Zhu Lei, for encouraging his department to collaborate with me on this project. The project benefited from having as associate editors the late Zhang Guangyu, former vice-chairman of Wuhan's history department and head of research; He Hongfei, who taught modern history, and who was my teaching assistant who went on to attend Yenching Institute at Harvard upon my recommendation; Han Tie, who taught American history at Wuhan and then came to the United States to teach East Asian History at Central Connecticut State University; and Wang Jiyu, chairman of the English department at Wuhan, who supervised necessary translation work. This proved a formidable team, with which I worked very well.

The editorial board of Chinese history specialists formed by Yang Fanzhong, Wang Chengren, Yang Debin, and Wu Dehua deserves my gratitude as well for identifying those women from the past who should be included and for contributing entries. These professors contributed names of biography subjects in their specialty areas such as ancient, classical, or modern Chinese history. The members of the advisory board, which included outstanding China scholars, is likewise due my appreciation for their helpful advice. Likewise, my husband, Dr. Frank L. Peterson, emeritus professor of geology, University of Hawaii, deserves special respect and credit for encouraging me to complete this project as a major contribution to new themes and ideas in the field. It is my hope that this project, which gave me so much pleasure, will aid future research and scholarship on China.

Barbara Bennett Peterson
East-West Center, University of Hawaii

Acknowledgments

I would like to thank the United States Fulbright International Exchange Program for sending me to the People's Republic of China as a Senior Fulbright Scholar, 1988–89, and for the opportunity to research and compile this book. I would like to thank the Office of Research, University of Hawaii, for a grant to translate several of the biographies from Chinese into English. Parvin Fellows in Journalism at the East-West Center were used for several translations that had not been completed earlier in China. I would like to thank the library staffs of Hamilton Library at the University of Hawaii, Manoa—the Asian and Hawaii Pacific Collections—both for their resources and their assistance. I would like to thank the East-West Center for granting me an Adjunct Fellowship to direct the activities of the Hawaii chapter of the Fulbright Association and the opportunity to coordinate final details of this book.

I would like to thank Doug Merwin, Patricia Loo, Angela Piliouras, and Debra Soled at M.E. Sharpe for their efforts in making this book such a success, and Laura Cabayan at the University of Hawaii for her assistance in typing the manuscript. All the editors and advisors deserve special thanks and pride for sharing the vision and wisdom to create *Notable Women of China.*

B.B.P.

Chinese Dynasties

Neolithic Period:
      5000–200 B.C.   Yanshao Culture
      300/2500–1500 B.C.   Longshan Culture
      2000–1500 B.C.   Xia dynasty

Shang 16th century–11th century B.C.

Zhou:
      Western 11th century–771 B.C.
      Eastern: 770–256 B.C.
            Spring and Autumn Period   770–476 B.C.
            Warring States Period   475–221 B.C.

Qin 221–207 B.C.

Han:
      Western 206 B.C.–24 A.D.
      Eastern 25–220 A.D.

Three Kingdoms:
      Wei 220–265 A.D.
      Shu Han 221–263 A.D.
      Wu 222–280 A.D.

Jin:

>   Western 265–316 A.D.
>   Eastern 317–420 A.D.

Northern and Southern Dynasties:

Southern:		Northern:	
Song	420–479 A.D.	Northern Wei	386–534 A.D.
Qi	479–502 A.D.	Eastern Wei	534–550 A.D.
Liang	502–557 A.D.	Northern Qi	550–577 A.D.
Chen	557–589 A.D.	Western Wei	535–556 A.D.
		Northern Zhou	557–581 A.D.

Sui   581–618 A.D.

Tang   618–907 A.D.

Five Dynasties:

Later Liang	907–923 A.D.
Later Tang	923–936 A.D.
Later Jin	936–946 A.D.
Later Han	947–950 A.D.
Later Zhou	951–960 A.D.

Song:

>   Northern 960–1127 A.D.
>   Southern 1127–1279 A.D.

Liao   916–1125 A.D.

Jin   1115–1234 A.D.

Yuan   1271–1368 A.D.

Ming   1368–1644 A.D.

Qing   1644–1911 A.D.

Republic of China   1912–1949 A.D.

People's Republic of China   1949–Present

Source: Based on "A Brief Chinese Chronology," *The* Pinyin *Chinese-English Dictionary* (Beijing: The Commercial Press, 1979) 972.

NOTABLE
WOMEN
OF CHINA

Part I

Ancient Chinese Civilization: An Orientation to the Xia, Shang, and Zhou Dynasties

According to legendary and scientific information, the birthplace of Chinese civilization and culture was in the central plain of Henan province. In ancient times this area was called Yu, which means "hunting elephants," and indeed today one can find unearthed elephant fossil remains that date back 480,000 years. Paleolithic humanoid ancestors date back to 500,000 to 600,000 years ago in Henan, and Mesolithic remains found here date to ten thousand years ago. On this North China plain, more than three hundred Neolithic villages have been found dating to around eight thousand years ago, and these areas are dotted with cave homes and bone and stone artifacts, making careful dating possible. The western region of the Funiu and Taihang mountains are especially abundant in artifacts, offering archaeologists, ecologists, and anthropologists material for study. Early China developed along the Yellow river (Huang he), which carries *loess,* or yellow silt. It is within the river's basin that civilization began, based on the cultivation of millet, soybeans, and wheat. The headwaters of the Yellow river are in the Himalayas of Tibet and flow eastward across China toward the Pacific. Chinese people regulated the river and irrigated arid land to extend their developing culture. China's southern river, the Yangzi, also flows from the mountains of Tibet. Along its banks developed a culture that depended on wet-rice cultivation.

One of the earliest cultures in ancient China is known as Peiligang culture, which predates the Longshan and Yangshao pottery. Peiligang, revealed through recent digs in the Xinzheng and Mixian regions, offers some of the best and earliest evidence of Neolithic culture in China. Peiligang culture was discovered in the 1970s on the south side of the Yellow river between Zhengzhou and Kaifeng. A similar site was found at about the same time at Cishan, in Hebei province, north of the river. Using carbon-14 dating techniques, archaeologists place Peiligang culture at 5500–5100 B.C. The red pottery site of Yangshao (named after Yangshao village, Mianchi county, Henan province), which dates back to the latter part of the new stone age, and the later black pottery site of Longshan (2300–1800 B.C.) had earlier been thought to be China's earliest sites. At Peiligang, pit houses and storage caves were found, as well as tombs for ancestors. Red pottery was also found at Peiligang, and so were water jars, bowls, and two-handled jars, along with pestles and stone mortars for grinding grains such as wheat and millet. Sharpened stone implements such as saws, picks, and sharpened plough shares were also discovered there. The evidence points to an early division of labor between the sexes: The heavier, planting tools were found in the men's tombs, while the processing tools were found in those of the women, which indicates that as tools became heavier, agricultural planting was taken over by men. This probably had much to do with the emergence of a patrilineal society over the initial matriarchal society. The tools also indicate that sedentary agriculture had begun to supplement the primary activities of hunting, foraging, and fishing. Primitive societies in China were based on communal ownership of property, and men and women worked together to find sufficient food to sustain the group.

Henan was the cradle of China's early civilization.[1] In this region arose the tale of Nu Wa, who is illustrated in Daoist scripture from the Han period as a beautiful woman, sometimes with a snake or dragon body. The tale explains the mythological origin of all living things, which has been passed down from the Han dynasty's collection of ancient legends compiled by

Ying Shao entitled *The Constant Rule of Customs*. One legend, similar to the biblical story of Genesis, states that the goddess Nu Wa gathered some earth and molded it into human figures and gave them life. Day after day she worked, making the arms, legs, heads, and bodies. She finally thought of a way to make them faster by adding ropes made from straw and mixing it with the clay. From this mixture, numerous people were formed when she pulled the rope through the clay. As the legend goes, China's official class came from her figures of pure clay, while China's poor peasantry came from the straw. Nu Wa established the customs of marriage; thereafter, men and women began to reproduce and thus Nu Wa created the human race. In other legends, Nu Wa was featured holding up the sky and repairing the leaky heavens.[2] She stopped the deluge that had caused a great flood, mended cracks in the earth, and brought safety and comfort again to the Chinese.

In the absence of written records in prehistoric societies, oral legends and myths retold by generations preserved these early beliefs and explanations of the cosmic order. The legend of Nu Wa offered evidence of a matriarchal society in early China. In later times, she was referred to as Emperor Wa or Emperor Earth, a reminder of a period in which women ruled the earth. Archaeologists and anthropologists believe that the introduction of heavier agricultural implements may have been the reason for the shift in power originally based upon women as food providers to men. In early Chinese primitive societies women enjoyed high status as food providers and wielded enormous power based on economics.[3] They would later cede this status as metal tools supplanted wooden implements.

In primitive cave societies or among the tree-dwelling *nest people,* as they were called, communal sexual intercourse was practiced, making it difficult to establish parentage and family blood lineage of the children. Children born were viewed as children of the community, but it was primarily the mother's responsibility to raise and protect her progeny. Children knew their mothers, but often not their fathers; hence in early communities property passed from mother to daughter, or along matrilineal lines. Children took the surnames of their mothers. Slightly later in these matriarchal communities, if a woman married outside her family or clan, she brought her spouse to live in her home. The discovery of fire and the use of the campfire contributed to a sense of kinship groups and eventually to the family. Numerous legends sprang up to explain conception: A woman became fascinated with a spirit with a dragon's head, and later gave birth to the emperor Shen Nong; the mother of the emperor Fu Xi was blessed with a child after stepping into the footprint of a giant; the emperor Huangdi was conceived after his mother saw a streak of lightning; Qing Du gave birth to Yao after mating with a dragon; and the mother of emperor Da Yu bore him after swallowing a pearl.

Beyond procreation and food production, clothing and shelter were important in early survival. As in other areas of the world, in China the earliest forms of clothing were made from animal skins. However, early artifacts in China indicate the use of textiles, even if primitive. Among artifacts found in a cave on a hillside near Zhoukoudian, about 48 kilometers (1 mile = 1.6093 kilometers) from Beijing, were a bone sewing needle, which indicated that clothing was made as early as the latter part of the old stone age, or 10,000 to 50,000 years ago. At the Yangshao pottery site, a stone spinning wheel was found—evidence of the use of natural fibers such as cotton in producing clothing. Sericulture, or silkworm cultivation, developed in China as early as the new stone age, or about 4,000 years ago. At an archaeological excavation in Wuxing county, Zhejiang province, East China, fragments of silk clothing, ribbons, and thread were found in bamboo baskets. By the time of the Zhou dynasty, the silkworm had become a venerated creature, and its image decorated many of the bronzes of the time. The *Shi jing* (Classic of Songs), recorded in the Zhou dynasty, contains a poem celebrating sericulture:

> *Orioles sing merrily*
> *In the bright spring sunshine;*
> *Women, baskets in hand or slung on poles,*
> *Move along the paths in a steady stream;*
> *They are on their way*
> *To pick tender mulberry leaves for their silkworms.*

Initially, the silk dress was decorative and ceremonial. Common people even in the Zhou period usually wore clothing made of hemp. Even the minority groups in Southwestern China wore clothing made from hemp. But the cultivation of silk led to the development of weaving and its related technology. By the time of the Han dynasty, the silk industry had progressed to include the making of brocade, damask, satin, and gauze.

Cotton was another fiber used early on in Chinese clothing production. As early as 1 A.D. tree-grown cotton from Guangdong in South China was utilized for making clothing. Herbaceous cotton was imported over land from Central Asia and raised in Xinjiang, as well as imported by sea from Southeast Asia and raised around Guangdong, Guangxi, and Fujian. By the time of the Song dynasty, cotton raising had spread from its concentration in the south, northward across the Yangzi and Huai rivers into Central China. Extensive cotton weaving dates back to the Southern Song dynasty with the Li people on Hainan island.[4]

New technology was developed in toolmaking at the same time weaving of textiles was improving. The discovery of a new toolmaking process—the casting of bronze—allowed the production of more advanced implements for agriculture, and may have ushered in the shift from a matriarchal to a patriarchal social system by ca. 1500 B.C. Agricultural tools such as plow blades could now be made sharper, since they were fashioned from bronze rather than wood or stone. The new tools gave an advantage to men with greater physical strength, who took over food-producing tasks and began to have more of a say in administering common property. The technological knowledge of bronze making was a closely guarded secret and may also have been an increasing source of political power. Under the patrilineal system, upon marriage a woman joined her husband's household and took her husband's surname, and property descended first from father to younger brother, and then later from father to son. The son's succession to power and titles increasingly made men the center of society. The patriarchal system influenced the family: The father performed the rituals of ancestor worship on behalf of his family and practiced the agricultural rites to ensure productivity. Gradually clan or communal ownership of property was replaced by individual or private ownership. Private property was controlled by the male head of the family, and wives and children gradually became viewed as property. Inequality now appeared within the family, as depicted by Xu Shen in *Shuiwen* written during the Han dynasty. He defined *father* as ''head of the family and a great, esteemed man who controls and educates the family and can beat whomever he choses.''[5]

Bronze technology and the utilization of draft animals enabled the accumulation of food surpluses. These food surpluses sustained extra population and now prisoners captured in war were no longer killed but compelled to do forced labor. Female prisoners of war were taken as concubines and passed down as property from father to son. A selection from the *Yi jing* (Classic of Changes) vividly portrays the fears of a young woman as she heard horses' hooves clattering because she knew she could be swept away and abused at will if captured by the enemy. Mercenary buying and selling of women appeared in these early societies, with the common unit of exchange in bartering for women being deerskins. Initially clan military leaders divided the spoils of war with their clan, but gradually military warriors began to hoard their trophies and prizes; class divisions appeared, and for the defeated, impoverishment and slavery. Thus the so-called slave society arose within the earliest dynasties. The early communal clan traditions rooted in equality and common ownership of property disintegrated and were replaced by the patriarchal, stratified class structure based on the slave labor.

New historical and archaeological evidence has continued to push China's earliest dynasties back to earlier and earlier dates. Not so long ago, it was believed in the West that the Shang dynasty was the first *real* dynasty, and that an earlier dynasty known as the Xia was merely mythical. New archaeological evidence shows that the Xia dynasty did exist, that it was a bronze age culture, and its earliest capital was in Henan province. Myths, songs, legends, and historical references had reported that the Xia existed 4,000 years ago with its first capital at Yangcheng, the capital of Yu the Great, the flood-controller and founder of the dynasty. North of the Yellow river and half a kilometer northwest of Gaocheng, Yangcheng has finally been discovered by archaeologists. Part of the city's eastern wall remained, and the foundations of a house was found with skeletons buried beneath them. Using radioactive carbon dating on charcoal used for fuel, archaeologists dated this site to 2000 B.C., a date compatible with the traditional dates for the Xia dynasty.

The Xia period was a bronze age culture; for example, bronze *yue* (jue), or drinking cups, dating from the earliest periods, were characteristic of the period. Bronze—the symbol of power, class, and ritual—was used in burial practices and ancestor worship, for functional household items, for weaponry, and as a symbol of state authority. Cups found at Erlitou in 1975 A.D. dated to the second millennium B.C. The design of bronze vessels also found in 1975 A.D. indicated an origin in Neolithic prototypes, and their complicated piece-mold construction, not known in the Middle East, argues for the indigenous discovery of bronze making and casting in China rather than its importation. Ertilou vessels also seemed to point to the early presence of a Xia aristocracy, previously thought to have been developed only later during the Shang dynasty. The excavations that turned up these items also revealed palatial foundations for palaces and burial sites decorated with jades and bronze weapons, cinnabar, and pottery inscribed with early Chinese characters.

Contemporary researchers believe that the Xia dynasty was overthrown by the Shang dynasty. The ancestors of the Shang had lived in the lower Yellow river valley. The Shang dynasty moved its capital six times; five of the Shang capitals are thought to have been in Henan. The last capital of the Shang was discovered by archaeologists near Anyang in northern Henan. Royal tombs have been found, including the previously undiscovered and untouched burial chamber of Fu Hao, consort of King Wuding. She distinguished herself as a bronze age queen, leading her countrymen in battle, after receiving the military commission from her husband. Fu Hao is the subject of the first entry. The quality of the bronzes and the number of objects found in her tomb indicate she was of very high rank, as the refined workmanship of the artifacts was rarely found elsewhere.

Another significant site has been found at Pingliangtai in Huaiyang county, East-Central Henan. It is believed that this was an early Shang capital before its people conquered the Xia dynasty. Archaeological excavations reveal that Pingliangtai, a walled city with northern and southern gates, was approximately 700 meters (39.37" = 1 meter) around the perimeter and formed the shape of a square. The Shang culture was distinguished by its casting of bronze, as shown by the remains of slag from bronze casting found here. This site contained the earliest example of a sewage system: three pottery pipes located inside the southern gate. Another capital of the Shang was discovered at Xibo in Yanshi county, approximately 30 kilometers east of Luoyang in western Henan. Three sides of the city remain—the north, the east, and the west. The south section of the walls guarding the city was washed away by floods. Another middle-period Shang capital, then called Ao or Aodu, 7 kilometers in area was discovered in 1955 A.D. at Zhengzhou. In addition to bronze artifacts, valued ivory and jade objects were unearthed there. Until recently, the excavations at Anyang, from which at least fourteen of the thirty Shang kings ruled, had led scholars to believe that the Shang power was concentrated in the Yellow river valley. New evidence discovered in the 1970s widened the Shang domain considerably. Some archaeologists speculate that Zhengzhou was an early Shang capital and that another site, Panlongcheng, Hubei province, far to the south, was modeled after Zhengzhou. Various artifacts were found at Anyang and the other Shang sites, including tortoise shells and bone scapulae with early Chinese characters, which are viewed as some of China's first writings.

By the end of the Shang dynasty, China had established an early writing system based on pictograms and evolving characters, ancestor worship, and oracle bone divination or scapulimancy through which the gods could be asked for advice or assistance in significant issues such as planting crops. Their gods were nature gods such as the river god He or the sky god Tian (T'ien.) Shamans were used to communicate with these nature gods and the Shang kings performed rituals and sacrifices on behalf of the community. The Shang bronzes, cast in a variety of shapes, often displayed the *Tao Tie* (*T'ao Tieh*), or animal mask design, indicating a close relationship maintained with nature.

The institution of exogamy was practiced by which one married outside one's clan name *Xing* (*hsing*) and this had the effect of ever-enlarging the familial networks within Chinese society and thereby too the areas of political control. The Shang dynasty had established the lunar calendar based on a cycle of sixty days, and during the Shang a ten-day week was practiced, although this changed during the Zhou dynasty to a seven-day week.

The Zhou dynasty which followed the Shang extended from 1027–256 B.C. and is divided into the Western Zhou from 1027 to 771 B.C. with the capital at Xi'an and the Eastern Zhou 771 to 256 B.C. with the capital at Luoyang. During this period the idea of the Mandate of Heaven to rule was proclaimed by the victorious Zhou rulers who had been former vassals of the Shang kings, revolted, and toppled the Shang, proclaiming that the Shang had lost the Mandate of Heaven to rule. During this period, also a bronze age culture, feudalism continued to envolve through the vassalization of subordinate rulers of various regions loyal to the Zhou king. Wu Wang was the first Zhou king and politically and socially many of the former institutions of the Shang culture were taken over intact. The Zhou kings retained much of the Shang kings' religious authority, making rituals on behalf of society.

During the Eastern Zhou, Confucius (551–479 B.C.) began his teachings in the region of Lu, and eventually his thoughts were written down in the *Lunyu* (Analects) and eventually gave rise to the five Confucian Classics—the *Yi jing* (Classic of Changes or Book of Divination), which contains popular omen lore, the *Shu jing* (Classic of Documents or Book of History), containing stories and speeches from the early Zhou, *Shi jing* (Classic of Songs or Book of Poetry), which contains poems from the early Zhou, *Li ji* (Record of Rituals or Book of Rites), which explains proper conduct and philosophy, and the *Chun qiu* (Spring and Autumn Annals), which is a collection of significant events between 722 and 481 B.C. in Confucius' native region of Lu. These *Classics* became the basis for the cultivated gentry ruling class of early China and later formed the basis for the examination system, which evaluated candidates for high governmental positions. Confucius was monumentally important in the teaching of ethics as he taught that the ruler should lead by virtuous example and all of society should understand the importance of mutual respect within the five basic human relationships—ruler and subject, father and son, elder brother and younger brother, husband and wife, friend and friend. These relationships formed the basis for filial piety within the family. An individual who displayed the Confucian virtues, practiced proper decorum called *li*, and became thereby a *junzi* (*chun-tzu*), a cultivated individual.

During this great age of philosophy in the Eastern Zhou, Daoism, which literally means "the road" or the way," also evolved and emphasized "going with the flow" blending into the harmony of nature, and rebelling against the rigid teachings of the Classics. The school of the Naturalists developed around 300 B.C. with its emphasis upon *yang* and *yin*, which explained the nature of the cosmos by explaining that all physical elements were composed of both *yang*—male, light, hot, and positive, and *yin*—female, black, cold, and negative. Thus the early Chinese came remarkably close to explaining positive and negative atoms in nature centuries before the atomic theory was explained. They believed that nature was composed of five basic elements—wood, metal, fire, water, and earth. The school of the Naturalists continued the Chinese interest in astrology and alchemy. Out of this school too, would come the concepts and practices of acupunture and holistic medicine. The Zhou dynasty was highly structured and feudalism continued its expansion. Its arts and philosophy perhaps are its trademark and continue to impact China down through the ages.

Thus, these early Chinese dynasties, the Xia, the Shang, and the Zhou, which were early bronze age cultures, developed early Chinese writings, religions, ethics, governmental institutions, familial rites, societal art forms, and economic bases. The heritage of these three dynasties would be passed on through the ages with enduring resilence.

The women who distinguished themselves during China's early bronze age are the subjects of the first section. Their lives and accomplishments demonstrate a great deal about early China and its values.

B. B. P.

Notes

1. An Jinhuai, "Henan: Birthplace of Chinese Civilization," *China Reconstructs* (October 1984), pp. 65–67.

2. Liu An, *Huai nan zi*, written in the Han dynasty, contains the legend of Nu Wa repairing the sky (Repr. Shanghai: Zhonghua shuju, 1927–35; Taibei: Zhonghua shuju, 1988).

3. Tian Jiaying, "Women in Prehistoric China," part 1, in *Women of China* (January 1981), pp. 16–17.

4. Cheng Hong and Zhao Yuannian, "Legend and Facts about Clothing in China," *Women of China* (May 1980), pp. 40–41.

5. Tian Jiaying, "Women in Prehistoric China," part 2, in *Women of China* (February 1981), p. 29; and part 3, in *Women of China* (March 1981), pp. 18–19.

Fu Hao (ca. 1040 B.C.) was the earliest female general of the Shang dynasty and queen consort of Emperor Wuding. Her tomb was unearthed during the winter of 1976 A.D. in the ruins of the Shang dynasty capital situated on the outskirts of Anyang in Henan province. The tomb held more than a hundred funerary objects, including bronze dagger axes, bows and arrows, and, of greatest significance, four bronze *yue,* or drinking vessels, which were the symbols of both royal and military power. On these *yue* were written the characters "Fu Hao." One of the *yue* weighed 9 kilograms (2.2. pounds = 1 kilogram), another weighed 8.5 kilograms. These bronzes suggest class, royalty, and power, indicating that this was the tomb of a person of great importance, unusual for a woman in ancient China. In addition to Fu Hao's sarcophagus, the tomb, discovered intact, contained the remains of sixteen slaves who had been buried alive with her to attend to her after death; 440 smaller bronze vessels, bells, mirrors, and weapons; 560 hairpins and arrowheads made of bone; 700 pieces of jade; and several articles of opal, ivory, and stone amid pieces of pottery. Many of the bronze vessels were inscribed with Fu Hao's name and were probably cast to hold offerings made in her honor at her burial. Of the more than twenty different bronze vessel types found in the tomb, seventy of these objects of various shapes are inscribed with either her given name or her temple name, the name by which her descendants would remember her.

The jade carvings were reminders of China's Neolithic past, when man depended heavily upon animals for food, and used them as protective totems signifying the nature gods. The jade figurines are of dragons, eagles, elephants, and phoenix, images that held cosmological significance. In addition, there were human figurines carefully depicting the facial features and dress of the Shang upper class, which held a monopoly on bronze military technology.

Archaeologists who studied this burial site concluded that Fu Hao was China's earliest woman general, but her name had been left out of the ancient classics of later periods, beginning with the Zhou. This burial find explained the frequent appearance of the words Fu Hao on Shang tortoise shells and ox bones used in oracle bone divination, or scapulimancy, of this period. Some of the inscriptions refer to Fu Hao as a royal consort, some as a military leader with the rank of general, and others title her a feudal vassal. Some divinations undertaken on her behalf also included questions concerning childbirth, the success of her religious rituals, and her military enterprises. The venerated name Fu Hao appeared on the oracle bones prepared by the Shang king Wuding, the fourth Shang king to make his capital at Anyang. She was his wife and also, remarkably, his general in the battlefield. He empowered her by awarding her the *yue* given at the time of commissioning her for a battle or protracted military campaign. At the Gulbenkian Museum of Oriental Art and Archaeology in Britain, there is a tortoise shell inscription recording that Lady Hao led a force of 3,000 and commanded one of two columns that fought against a regional enemy.

Fu Hao was one, but not the only, female militarist of Shang China, as oracle bones of the period indicate more than a hundred women by name who were active in military campaigns. Comparing the oracle bone inscriptions from the Shang with those of the later Zhou, it appears that Shang aristocratic women enjoyed much higher status than Zhou women, possibly because of the Confucian doctrines introduced in the Zhou, which reduced and subordinated women's status. It has been estimated from oracle bone inscriptions that at least thirty kings ruled during the Shang dynasty and the last fourteen ruled from Anyang, Henan province. At this time there was not yet a tradition of naming the king's wife queen, hence Fu Hao is referred to as wife or consort. Recent archaeologists have increased their estimates of the extent of the Shang dynasty's control much beyond the area of the Yellow river to include Zhengzhou, believed to have been an earlier Shang capital. Shang control may possibly have extended as far south as Panlongcheng, Hubei, in the Yangzi river valley, as artifacts similar to those of Zhengzhou have been found there.

Wuding's father was Di Xiaoyi and his grandfather, Di Xiaoxin. Wuding was forced into mourning for three years following his father's death. During this time he toured the countryside with Fu Hao, inspecting crops and irrigation systems and meeting the people. Wherever they traveled, they called together the local officials, who in turn called forth a meeting of the villagers and held an inquest after the state of public and private affairs. During this period, the Shang dynasty was faced by reverses in agricultural productivity and challenges from the barbarians, the *xiongnu*, on the dynasty's northern frontiers. At one of their inquiries, the commoners recommended an intelligent slave, Fu Yue, for service at the king's court. Fu Yue was brilliant at making walls for defense. Eager to bring him to the imperial court, Wuding feared that the elite court members would look down upon a slave. Hence Wuding concocted the story that he had had a vision in which Heaven (Tian) had spoken to him in a dream, telling him that a man named Fu Yue who lived in a sage's cave would save the country. He related that the wise Fu Yue had great virtues and knowledge of politics, both of which proved true after Fu Yue had joined courtly circles.

While they had been in mourning on tour of the provinces, Wuding and Fu Hao had left a court official Tian Guanqin in charge of national affairs, but, after the return from the countryside, they again took charge, making the clever Fu Yue premier and honoring him with the name Father of a Dream. Fu Yue prepared the defenses of the Shang territories to ward off a hostile tribe of northern barbarians called the Tu Fang. A boundary dispute broke out with the Tu Fang at a time when two leading Shang military commanders had previously been sent out from the capital, one to the southeast and one to the southwest. Realizing the emergency, Fu Hao herself stepped forward and asked to lead a military campaign against the Tu Fang. She had received military training in her youth and, as she grew up, was introduced to more sophisticated arts of war. She had gained firsthand knowledge of the geography of the countryside while on her three-year tour with her husband. Above all, she was respected as a military leader.

Wuding knew his wife's capabilities and was persuaded, after consulting with Fu Yue, to grant Fu Hao a bronze *yue*, a symbol of empowerment for a military campaign. A diviner, brought in to see whether the omens were favorable, wrote questions on tortoise shells and they were answered in the affirmative. Fu Hao was commissioned to fight. Marching with her troops northward to battle the Tu Fang, she fought at the head of her troops. Off the battlefield, she nursed the wounded and raised morale. The Tu Fang were badly beaten and would never again challenge the Shang's military power.

Subsequently, another tribe, the Qiangfang, threatened war in the northwest. Again Fu Hao asked for a *yue* and a military commission. Again her troops were victorious: The cavalry units of the Qiangfang barbarians were routed. Exhausted upon her return to the capital Anyang, she did not rest. She responded to yet another threat as she led a third force against the Yifang, who threatened Shang power from the southeast and southwest. Again she was triumphant. A fourth and final campaign against the Bafang tribe in the southwest gained Fu Hao yet another *yue*; this time, sharing command of the army, she fought beside her husband. Wuding attacked a neighboring tribe allied with the Bafang, and when the Bafang moved to aid them, they fell into a trap laid by Fu Hao. Again the Shang forces were victorious and Fu Hao was celebrated as the most outstanding military leader of the country. Shortly after returning to Anyang, however, she fell ill from exhaustion. While she was ill, her only son, Xiaoyi, died, and she herself died shortly thereafter. The *yue* with which she had been honored were buried with her. A remarkable woman warrior, Fu Hao will forever illuminate the Shang culture with her feats of daring, courage, and skill.

Barbara Bennett Peterson and Wang Guorong

Fang Hong, trans.

Sources

Peter Neill, ''New Light On China's Oldest Civilizations.'' *Asia*, May–June, 1980, 30–32. ''Fu Hao,'' in *Famous Women In Chinese History*. Shanghai: Shanghai People's Press, 1988, (translated from Chinese by Fang Hong); Danielle Elisséeff, *La Femme au Temps des Empereurs de Chine*, Paris:

Stock/L. Pernoud, 1988, in French. Adapted and reprinted by permission from the publishers of *Women in History* (Waterford, CT: Yorkin Publications).

Xu Mu (b. ca. seventh century B.C.) was the earliest poet of note in Chinese history. She was born in the Wei kingdom during the Spring and Autumn period within the Eastern Zhou. She was the daughter of Duke Wei Xuan and the younger sister of Duke Wei Yi, the ruler of Wei. In the seventh century B.C., the ancient Wei kingdom was located in Qixian county, Henan province. Xu Mu had two other brothers who would also rule as Dukes Dai and Wei Wen. The time of the Wei kingdom was a period of limited centralized authority with a multiplicity of small rival states and kingdoms. It was a time when the use of the horse made the pastoral nomadic tribes in the north a great military threat.

The well spring of Xu Mu's beautiful poetry was the natural beauty of her homeland and the political confrontations the Wei kingdom would experience during her lifetime. From her poetry emerged the image of a deeply patriotic woman who rose to the occasion and saved her kingdom in time of crisis. Her poetry recalled the loveliness of her homeland with its mountains, waterfalls, bamboo groves, and the Qi river and recalled youthful events such as river boating with other maidens, all of them wearing twinkling jewelry.

The turbulent times of the Spring and Autumn period honed her political acumen. She was married to Duke Mu of the neighboring kingdom of Xu, hence her name, Xu Mu. She had disagreed with her parents' choice of husband, but they persisted—with disastrous results. When she became eligible for marriage, representatives from the two neighboring and competing kingdoms Xu and Qi visited the Wei court. Persuaded by rich gifts from the Xu kingdom, her parents selected their duke as her future husband. But she believed Xu to be a weak state, unable to rise to the defense of Wei or to be an effective ally. She saw no advantage militarily or politically in her marriage of alliance with Xu and preferred the Qi kingdom as it was closer to Wei and had larger military forces. Nonetheless she became Madam Xu Mu. She moved to her husband's kingdom and, as poetry was an art form for cultivated young ladies, she wrote "Bamboo," several lines of which reveal her nostalgia:

> *With a long and slender bamboo,*
> *I fished by the shores of Qi;*
> *Can't help thinking of that river,*
> *And the land so far from me.*

> *On the left the fountain gushes,*
> *On the right the river flows.*
> *Far away the girl has traveled*
> *From parents, brothers and home.*

In 660 B.C. the kingdom of Wei was attacked by uncivilized people to the north called the Di. This savage tribe struck using mounted horsemen in a terrorizing assault. The local ruler, Duke Wei Yi, was no match for their prowess, as he was a dilettante who indulged himself with raising cranes and had even given some of his prized crane birds important places at court. Duke Wei Yi went so far as to have his pet cranes ride in carriages, an honor usually reserved for high court officials. As his indulgence led to depletion of financial resources, he levied a special crane tax on the peasants, which was considered unjust. Hence, when the Di tribe attacked, the citizen forces did not rise up en masse to repel the invaders. Wei Yi's forces crumbled, and he died in the fighting. His body was mutilated and cut to pieces by the invaders.

The kingdom of Wei was pillaged, its capital burned, causing the inhabitants to flee across the Yellow river to its southern bank; they resettled in Caoyi, which is modern-day Huaxian county. Caoyi was small town originally on the southern edge of the kingdom of Wei. This point of retreat became a refugee camp, but after Wei inhabitatants who had fled slowly regathered their strength and attracted new military forces as allies, Caoyi would become the staging point for a comeback to rebuild the kingdom.

Madam Xu Mu, saddened by the reports of these events, which she had foreseen, wrote the poem "Fountain" from her husband's homeland:

The sparkling fountain rushes on,
It flows into the river Qi.
Not a day passes without thoughts of home
The home I shall never see.

When I think of the dear fountain,
I heave a sigh in vain;
When I think of Xuyi and Caoyi,
My heart flies far away.

Despondent after Wei's defeat, Xu Mu called upon her husband to send reinforcements to Caoyi and drive the invaders out. Her husband was unmoved by her pleas and would not risk involving his forces. Xu Mu left the kingdom of Xu and went directly to Caoyi to meet with her brother Duke Dai, who led the Wei people in exile there, and discussed the rebuilding of the kingdom. Much-needed supplies, food, and necessities brought by Xu Mu were distributed. She rekindled hope and immediately recommended enrolling more troops from the surrounding area close to Caoyi, thus expanding the army to 4,000 men. The citizen-soldier tradition was reactivated. She also recommended asking the strong kingdom of Qi, which she had originally desired to join for marriage and alliance purposes, to send troops to be allied with Wei to recover their lost territories.

At this juncture, representatives from her husband's realm arrived asking her not to interfere in the plans to rebuild Wei. Some called her rash and meddlesome. Others ridiculed her for attempting a task they considered impossible. Still others attacked her for taking a strong leadership role in public, an action some conservatives viewed as incompatible with the dignity and virtues of a woman in feudal society, while many secretly admired her vital stand.

She rose to defend herself in her most famous poem, ''Speeding Away,'' written during this time, which illustrated her patriotism:

The wheels turn fast, the horse trots on,
I return to my brother in Wei.
A long, long way the carriage has come,
To Caoyi, my homeland to stay.

The lords who follow me, far and long,
Have caused no little dismay.

Harshly though you may judge me,
From my course I will not veer.
Compared to your limited vision,
Do I not see far and clear?

Harshly though you may judge me,
My steps you never can stay.
Compared to your limited vision,
Am I not wise in my way?

I've climbed the heights of A Qiu,
Gathered herbs on the slope alone.
All women are prone to sorrow—
Each follows a path of her own.
The people of Xu still blame me,
Such ignorance has never been known.

I walk the land of my fathers,
The wheat fields are green and wide.
I'll tell the world of my sorrow,
All friends will be at our side.
O listen, ye lords and nobles,
Blame not my stubbornness so!
A hundred schemes you may conjure,
None match this course that I know.

Xu Mu refused to be diverted from her cause to rebuild her homeland. Duke Dai died of illness. A third brother of Xu Mu then came from the kingdom of Qi, where he had been well received and well treated, to rule as Duke Wei Wen. The Qi kingdom was persuaded by the entreaties of Xu Mu and her brother to help resurrect Wei. It's leader, Duke Qi Huan, gave the Wei leadership three hundred battle chariots and three thousand soldiers committed to fight for Wei as proof of support from the Qi Kingdom. He also personally gave the Wei leaders three hundred pairs each of cattle, oxen, pigs, hens, and dogs. He gave Duke Wei Wen a magnificent horse on which he would lead his forces in recovering the regions formerly held by the

Wei kingdom. Duke Wei Wen, who dressed simply and frugally and refused to be adorned in silk finery, was a more able ruler than his brothers who had previously reigned. After two years of fighting, the Wei leaders had recaptured most of its lost territories and re-established a capital at Chuqiu. The Wei kingdom had been saved.

The Wei people remembered Xu Mu for bringing needed supplies, securing military aid, and passionately inspiring the rebuilding of her state. Remembered best as a patriotic poet, Xu Mu wrote moving words that recalled China's Spring and Autumn period, with its small state rivalries.

Barbara Bennett Peterson

Sources

Cai Lei, "Patriotic Poetess of the Spring-Autumn Period," in *Famous Women of Ancient Times and Today*, edited by *Chinese Woman Magazine*, published by Hebei People's Publishing House, 1986; Ah Yuan, "First Patriotic Woman Poet in Chinese History," *Women of China*, vol. 8, August 1984, 40–41; for background of the Spring-Autumn Period (722–481 B.C.) see Edwin O. Reischauer and John K. Fairbank, *East Asia, the Great Tradition*. Boston: Houghton-Mifflin Company, 1989.

Qi Jiang (b. ca. 658 B.C.), also called Jiangshi, lived during the Spring and Autumn period of the Eastern Zhou dynasty. A member of the royal family of the king of Qi, she was born in the Qi capital somewhere northeast of the modern city of Zibo, Shandong province. Her future husband, Chong'er, had lived the life of a political refugee. To escape persecution by a powerful concubine married to his father, the king of Jin, he had left his native state of Jin for the kingdom of Di. He was accompanied by his uncle Huyanjiou and his trusted adviser Zhangshui. Chong'er remained for twelve years with little improvement in his affairs with the Di, whom he had hoped to convince to aid him in recovering his royal position in the Jin kingdom. Hence he decided to go to the kingdom of the Qi, where he met and married Qi Jiang. She was quick-witted and decisive and had been educated in the classics extremely well, qualities that he admired. King Huan of Qi had introduced them and authorized their marriage in 644 B.C.

The following year King Huan died and the princes of the realm fought over the throne in a civil war. The country was weakened by a siege that ended when a usurper named Xiao, supported by other regions, proclaimed himself king of Qi. Chong'er, presuming that Qi forces were now too weak to assist him in his political restoration in Jin, became dispirited in his ambition. His associates Jiufan and Zhaozui, noting this change, conspired in 639 B.C. beneath a mulberry tree to force Chong'er to leave Qi and reclaim the kingdom of Jin. One of Qi Jiang's maids overheard the plotters' discussion while sitting in the mulberry tree picking leaves. She told Qi Jiang what she had overheard.

Qi Jiang told Chong'er about the plot and advised him to leave Qi as soon as possible. She examined the political situation in the Jin kingdom, saying that Jin had not had a strong king since the demise of Chong'er's father. Other possible claimants had now died, leaving Chong'er the sole heir to the kingdom. She encouraged him to act swiftly. Chong'er, now in his sixties, knew his wife was right, but preferred the safe and stable life of the Qi kingdom and refused to heed her advice. Qi Jiang cited lessons from history, attempting to convince Chong'er to reclaim his title to the throne and reward his friends and followers who had been faithful to him during his years of exile. She appealed to his love for her and his own sense of pride and dignity, but to no avail; he refused to leave Qi.

Qi Jiang now conspired with Chong'er's friend and associate, Jiufan. They first made Chong'er drunk, then Jiufan carried him away in the direction of Jin in a wagon. When he regained his senses, Chong'er became angry. He picked up a spear and chased Jiufan as he attempted to shout explanations. Soon realizing the pursuit was pointless, Chong'er decided to go on to Jin to reclaim his proper inheritance. They went through the kingdoms of Zhao and Qin, which gave them military escorts back to Jin, where Chong'er was proclaimed king. Chong'er then sent for Qi Jiang, the architect of the successful scheme. Qi Jiang was proclaimed the fifth of Chong'er's nine queens.

Chong'er successfully made alliances with other regional kings, promising reciprocal protection.

Qi Jiang was praised in her lifetime for being a successful kingmaker and for her modesty in accepting the position of fifth queen. Poems celebrated her virtues:

> *Selfish Qi Jiang was not,*
> *Justice she always upheld,*
> *and the king became king of kings,*
> *as the queen had laid the foundation.*

Luo Yunhuan
Zhu Binzhong, trans.

Sources

History of Zao Qiuming; Sima Qian (Ssu-ma Ch'ien), *Shi ji* (Records of the Historian).

Zhuang Fanji (b. ca. 625 B.C.) lived during the Spring and Autumn period of the Eastern Zhou. She came from a family named Ji that lived in the ancient region of Fan. In 614 B.C. Mu, the king of Chu, died, and his son Xionglu succeeded to the throne as King Zhuang the following year. Fanji and Zhuang were married in 611 B.C., and she became his queen. Fanji was never jealous of his concubines and displayed the proper ethics and decorum in every circumstance. In previous courts, intrigues and jealousies plagued the back palace, but the reverse was true under Fanji's management. Seeking additional beautiful girls for King Zhuang, she sent envoys to the regions of Zhen and Wei. Two of the girls they found were more beautiful than Fanji, but she remained selfless in allowing these young women opportunities to show their virtues and talents. Under her direction, court relations remained amicable and tranquil, and this freed the king from worries and frustrations.

During the first years of his rule, Zhuang spent his time hunt-

ing and traveling, forgetting his duties at court. Fanji repri-
manded him for the indulgence of eating meat (which he often
brought home from his hunts), and she gradually persuaded him
to remain at court, pay more attention to his official duties, and
govern more diligently. King Zhuang had selected Yu Qiuzi as
his prime minister, but Yu had failed to make the Chu kingdom
prosperous. Fanji noticed that Zhuang relied on and trusted his
chief minister too much. When Zhuang told her how much he
enjoyed talking with Yu and how capable he was, Fanji disagreed. Giving herself as an example, she reminded her husband
that she had willingly sought lovely women as his concubines
and never concealed their strong points from him. She pointed
out that Yu had never recommended anyone to him who had
merit, talent, and virtue. Further, the minister had not dismissed
subordinates of low morality and incompetence. Yu had deceived the king, she attested, as he kept those of talent and
morality away from the king so that they had no opportunities
to show their talents at court. Yu was shown, through comparison with the queen, to be neither loyal nor able. Taking his
wife's advice, King Zhuang forced his chief minister to resign
and appointed in his place Shu Aosun, who was known for his
morality and ability. Under the leadership of Shu, the kingdom
of Chu rose to great prominence and, within three years, had
formed alliances with other kingdoms that recognized King
Zhuang as their titular head. King Zhuang and his kingdom respected Fanji for having assisted in these results. In 601 B.C.,
when King Zhuang died, her son Xiong Shen took the throne.

Fanji's efforts to mend the ways of her husband and to manage the queen's court had allowed Chu to rise to become one
of the five "Lord Powers" in the Spring and Autumn period.
The Lord Powers followed one another in influencing the policies of neighboring realms. The official historians of the Chu,
writing on bamboo, recorded that "Zhuang was able to lord it
over others because Fanji made all the effort."

Fanji's fame and influence were recorded in many poems and
essays. Zhang Shen, prime minister of the Tang dynasty, composed the poem "To Fanji's Tomb on Climbing Jin Li Tai," in
which he wrote, "Chu became the lord, Fanji did the work."

Details of her later life are unknown, but her tomb remains

in Jiangling county. Surrounded by many shade trees, it is 14 meters high and 388 meters in circumference. Yu Jifeng, an administrative inspector during the Qing dynasty, wrote on Fanji's tomb that she was "A Virtuous Lady of Ability."

Luo Yunhuang
Zhu Binzhong, trans.

Sources

Stories of the Han Shi, Book 2; Du Yu of the Jin (Chin) dynasty, *Explanations of the Book on the Spring and Autumn Period*; Yun Hanluo, *A Study of the Queens and Concubines of the Chu Kingdom.*

Xi Shi (b. ca. 500 B.C.), who lived during the Spring and Autumn period of the Eastern Zhou dynasty, was the most famous of the four great beauties in Chinese history responsible for the collapse of various Chinese kingdoms or states and the downfall of their rulers. Her name became synonymous with beauty in China, especially in Jiangsu and Zhejiang provinces. Xi Shi was born in a village in Zhuji county, Zhejiang. Most of the inhabitants of her region shared the same surname, Shi, and, as her village was on the western slope of a mountain, she was given the name Xi (western) Shi. Her father was a woodcutter, and she contributed to family finances by washing silk in a stream near her home.

Near the end of the Spring and Autumn period, two great kingdoms emerged south of the Yangzi river: Wu, with its capital in modern-day Suzhou, Jiangsu province, and Yue (or Chu), with its capital in modern-day Shaoxing county, Zhejiang province. These rival kingdoms eventually declared war during which Fu Chai, king of Wu, and Gou Jian, king of Yue, sought to dominate the region. In 494 B.C., the kingdom of Wu defeated the kingdom of Yue and made it a tributary state. King Gou Jian and his queen were made to work for three years as slaves in the kingdom of Wu, after which they returned to the king's homeland and set upon a course of revenge. He steeled himself to future encounters by sleeping on a pallet of brush and wood in a thatched hut and tasting gall before each meal and before bedtime, giving up all luxuries and comforts of his former life. To build up the peasants' strength, he issued a decree to farmers in his region exempting them from in kind taxes that normally were paid to him for his sustenance. He employed as his aide and confidante Fan Li, who had attended him while he had been a slave, and General Wen Zhong.

Planning a course that would weaken the king of Wu and realizing his penchant for beautiful women and his tendency to dissipation and extravagance, Fu Li suggested that Gou Jian send Fu Chai a gift of an enticing woman. Gou Jian agreed, and Fan Li set about dressed as a merchant on a quest to find the loveliest girl in the kingdom of Yue.

In this way Xi Shi was discovered and then taken to the court of Gou Jian for extensive training by Fan Li in court etiquette and seductive arts. After three years, she was viewed as competent for her mission of vengeance. Xi Shi and Fan Li had fallen in love, but put aside their personal feelings for each other, and she was commissioned as the tributary gift to the king of Wu, who had earlier crushed their kingdom.

Fu Chai, as hoped, became completely infatuated with Xi Shi. He spent all his time with her and created extravagant entertainment to please her. Xi Shi cleverly encouraged him, using her influence to secure the dismissal of the capable minister Wu Zixu, who was later ordered to commit suicide. Fu Chai built for her the Guanwa Palace in an imperial park on the slope of Lingyan hill, about 15 kilometers (1 mile = 1.6093 kilometers) west of Suzhou. The palace was said to be so luxurious that it had pearl strands hanging to shade the windows. Next to this palace, Fu Chai built the Promenade of Musical Shoes. Under the marble floors were thousands of earthenware jars, which sounded like chimes when she walked or danced on them. For Xi Shi, he dug a special river and erected upon its banks pavilions where musicians and dancers performed.

In 482 B.C., when Fu Chai traveled north of the Yangzi for a conference of rulers to discuss control of China's central area, the kingdom of Yue launched a surprise attack on the kingdom of Wu, inflicting heavy casualties. Nine years later, realizing the weakened state of Wu, the leaders of Yue attacked again and won a decisive victory. Gou Jian exiled Fu Chai to an island off China's coast; Fu Chai, in shame, cut his throat.

There are two sequels to the story of Xi Shi. One version holds that she threw herself into a swift river and was drowned; another legend portrays Xi Shi and Fan Li as reunited lovers after her mission was successfully accomplished. Fan Li became a merchant near Lake Tai, where they shared their lives. Today, there are two caves named for Xi Shi and Fan Li in Yixing, Jiangsu province, where, the legend related, they lived together in seclusion. Many stories and plays recall the story of Xi Shi, and she often appeared in the Chinese classics. One of the best-known reminiscences is by Liang Chenyu, *The Girl Who Washes Silk*, which recalls the tragic love affair between Xi Shi and Fan Li, who sacrificed their own happiness to avenge their kingdom.

Xu Kaichang

Sources

Bai Shouyi, ed., *An Outline and History of China*, Sima Guang, *History as a Mirror*.

Mother Meng (ca. 400–350 B.C.) was the mother of Meng Ke, or Mengzi, known in the West as Mencius (ca. 371–289 B.C.). Mother Meng, who lived during the Warring States period, was famous in Chinese history for educating her son and as a mother role model. She was also known by the surname Zhang, although some historians say Li was her maiden name. Her husband, Meng Ji, also known as Gongyi, was a descendant of Madam Meng, whose family, named Sun, had been members of a noble clan in the state of Lu.

At the time of their marriage, Meng's family position was declining, and they were forced to live in the state of Zou, the birthplace of Mencius, in what is now Fu village, Qufu county, 12 kilometers (1 mile = 1.6093 kilometers) north of Zou county, Shandong province. In about 371 B.C., Madam Meng gave birth to Mencius in this small state bordering on the state of Lu. Three years after Mencius's birth, Meng Ji died. Forced to rear the boy on her own, Madam Meng attached great importance to her son's education. It was said that she had begun to train her child during her pregnancy: She would not sit on a straw cushion improperly or eat a piece of meat cut irregularly. Thus she taught her child in the womb through her example, a technique now called "prenatal education." They lived first near a cemetery, so Mencius played among the graves and imitated the mourners and burial officials. Considering this environment unfavorable, Madam Meng moved to a neighborhood near a marketplace, now marked with a stone tablet that identifies "Mother Meng's Second Residence." Here Mencius began to imitate peddlers hawking their wares along the street. Disapproving, Mother Meng again relocated their household to another suburb of the town, close to a school just outside the town's southern gate. Influenced by Confucian teachers near the school, Mencius learned the ceremonies of arranging *zu* (rectangular sacrificial utensils) and *dou* (oval sacrificial utensils with long legs); the rites of *yi* (bowing with hands clasped) and *rang* (extending a polite invitation and declining an invitation); and social graces such as *jin* (how to enter properly), and *tui* (how to retreat properly).

Madam Meng was pleased with their third location. Young Mencius, at the beginning of his formal schooling, was not doing well and was often a truant. To teach him a lesson, Mother Meng took a knife and cut off the fabric being woven on her loom, comparing giving up school to breaking the loom that gave them their livelihood. Realizing that without an education one could hardly survive, the now-enlightened Mencius applied himself diligently. This was passed down as Mother Meng's lesson of "duan ji quan xue" (breaking the loom to illustrate to the child that the learning process should not be interrupted).

[In 1832 A.D., during the Qing dynasty, Meng Guangjun, the seventieth grandson of Mencius erected a tablet with the inscription: The Place Where Mother Meng Broke the Loom. Today, the old house near the school where they had lived is gone, but the tablet was removed and stands in the Temple of Mencius in Zou county.] After teaching the value of scholarly diligence and perseverance, Mother Meng instructed her son in the value of truthfulness and the importance of keeping one's word. When young Mencius saw a neighbor killing a hog and asked his mother why he was doing so, she had answered absentmindedly that it was for his sake, but she soon regretted what she had said in haste as she had not intended to buy any pork. Thinking of the bad influence on her child, should she fail to keep her word, she decided to carry out her ruse and bought pork for her son from the neighbor. By her example, she illustrated the importance of keeping promises and never telling lies. This famous lesson of Mother Meng's was known as "sha tun bu qi zi" (not deceiving the son as to the true reason for butchering the swine).

Upon coming of age, Mencius married and brought his wife back to his mother's house to live. One day Mencius found his wife squatting (it was considered impolite to squat in the presence of an elder or superior) alone in the bedroom (some say she was naked down to the waist). Mencius was very displeased. The young couple quarreled; he vowing never to enter the bedroom again and to seek an immediate divorce, she demanding to return to her own family. Mother Meng interceded, pointing out the right and the wrong. Whoever enters the house, she said, especially the sitting room or the bedroom, should keep his or her eyes downward and not take people by surprise. To enter without forewarning means intentionally to catch others in disgrace. She criticized her son for his rudeness; realizing his error, Mencius apologized to his wife, and they remained happily married. This lesson of Mother Meng was known as "Meng mu bu shu chu fu" (Mother Meng did not allow the daughter-in-law to go away).

In his prime, Mencius was a scholar and champion of Confucianism who traveled from state to state teaching his doctrines. He was destined to become one of China's most revered and illustrious intellectuals, and by the twelfth century his book *Mencius* was elevated to the status of a classic, second only to the *Analects* of Confucius. He countered the views of the scholar Mozi and the Daoist hedonist Yang Zhu. Mencius and his retinue, which included his wife, Mother Meng, and his numerous followers, appear to have been graciously received at the various courts, especially in the principality of Qi. One day, when Mencius was discussing moving on to another state but was concerned over his mother's health and ability to travel, Mother Meng offered one of her last lessons. She announced that she was determined to move on and help her son fulfill his aspirations. This lesson became known as "Meng mu chu qi" (Mother Meng went along with her son).

Mencius was her only child, and Mother Meng never remarried. She died in Qi, but her body was brought back to the state of Lu for burial by Mencius. In the temple of Mencius there is a statue of Mother Meng reputed to have been carved by Mencius himself at the time of her death, but later proved to be the work of an imitator.

Mother Meng has been revered in China for more than two thousand years. To honor her memory, one hall was built in the temple of Mencius for her alone; another hall honored her and her husband with their pictures on an altar. Among the numerous tablet inscriptions in memory of Mother Meng, one written between 1912 and 1949 on the western side of the temple hall devoted to her summarized her import best: "Mother and Teacher Both in One." In 1316, during the Yuan dynasty, her husband was posthumously granted the title duke of the state of Zou, and she the title Lady Xuanxian of the state of Zou.

From her fine family background, Mother Meng was well versed in traditional etiquette and knew well the Confucian virtues of womanhood. She has historically been viewed as the epitome of the mother model in China. Her attention to prenatal education has proved significant, as have her instructions for cultivating neighbors, keeping promises, maintaining one's convictions, and molding a child's character. Chinese history credits Mother Meng with inspiring Mencius's virtues, which enabled him to become a scholar on a par with Confucius.

Luo Yunhuan and Ma Jianjun

Sources

Mencius, *Gongsun chouxia*, extensively quoted in Arthur Waley, *Three Ways of Thought in Ancient China*. London: G. Allen and Unwin, 1939; and *The Biographies of the Chinese Women Martyrs*.

Qin Xuan (ca. 324–265 B.C.), also known as Hua Bazi, was queen dowager of the Qin court. She was born in the Chu kingdom and lived during the Warring States period. Known early in life as Hua Bazi, she was an imperial concubine of King Hui Wen and the mother of Ce, who became King Zhao Xiang of the Qin kingdom. In 311 B.C. the heir apparent, Dang, whose mother was a court favorite, succeeded his father Hui Wen as king, with the royal name King Wu. He was fond of martial arts activities and contests of physical strength. During a contest of physical prowess in 307 B.C., he lifted a heavy *ding* (an ancient bronze cooking vessel regarded as a symbol of authority), but miscalculated, dropping the huge vessel, breaking his shin bones, and thus causing his death. As he had no sons, his brothers were his heirs, and they fought for the throne, generating chaos and turmoil.

Hui Bazi now sought the throne for her son Ce, and she solicited the aid of her stepbrother Wei Ran—who was a high court official in the imperial courts of Kings Hui Wen and Wu—in accomplishing her purpose. Ce was elevated through his mother's political manipulations and became King Zhao Xiang. With her son's ascension to the throne, Hua Bazi obtained the royal title Queen Dowager Xuan, and in this role she ruled over the court.

Although Queen Dowager Xuan succeeded in making her son the king, the brothers of the late King Wu would not accept him on the throne. Prince Zhuang rebelled in 305 B.C. against his nephew King Zhao Xiang. Queen Dowager Xuan, Wei Ran, and their capable ministers sent troops to suppress the rebellion; the potential usurper was killed and the widow of King Wu was sent to her native Wei kingdom. Queen Dowager Xuan and Wen Ran became known far and wide for consolidating their power (using her son-king as a puppet), and they worked closely in a triumvirate with the prime minister, Chu Liji, who had been appointed by the late King Wu before his death.

Because the queen dowager's birthplace was in the Chu kingdom, throughout her rule she maintained a foreign policy friendly to Chu. In 306 B.C., when the Chu kingdom invaded the Han kingdom, Queen Dowager Xuan refused to send troops to aid the Han when they requested military assistance. In 305 B.C. she forced her son to marry a Chu princess and make her his queen. The following year, King Zhao of Qin had a conference with King Huai of Chu at Huangji (northeast of Xinye county, Henan province), and they established an alliance ensuring friendly relations. The kingdom of Qin also returned the previously conquered region of Shangyong (modern-day Zhushan county and a neighboring area in Hubei province) to the kingdom of Chu as a gesture of good will. These harmonious relations continued until 302 B.C., when Prince Heng of Chu, who was held as a Qin hostage (a general practice between friendly countries at that time to ensure peace), murdered a Qin minister in order to return to his native Chu.

Queen Dowager Xuan also controlled policies through her charms and appeal. To the northwest of Qin lived a nomadic tribe, the Yiqurong, which in ancient China lived around modern-day Qingyang and Jingchuan counties in Gansu province. This tribe presented a constant military threat to the Qin. But when the king of Yiqu came to the Qin court to congratulate King Zhao on his succession to the throne, Queen Dowager Xuan beguiled him and had an affair with him, and thus was he conquered. This relationship, which produced two sons, was an effective means of conciliation and collaboration and eased the tensions between their rival countries. Yet the queen dowager placed the welfare of her kingdom above everything else. Realizing that the king of Yiqurong had lost his vigilance against the Qin, she seized the opportunity in 272 B.C. to have him assassinated in her Ganquan Palace. She then dispatched the imperial troops to exterminate the Yiqurong people. Thus the nomadic threat to her kingdom had been removed and her borders strengthened.

Using nepotism, the queen dowager administered with an iron hand by placing her kinsmen in important posts at court. She gave her two younger brothers positions: Wei Ran as an official of Xiang, and Hua Rong as governor of Huayang. Wei Ran was also granted the title of general and later appointed prime minister, an office he held for twenty-five years. Hua Rong also received the title and rank of general and was given the post of ''left-hand'' prime minister, a position of lesser authority. The queen dowager's two younger sons were Xian, who was appointed governor of Gaoling, and Li, who became governor of Jiangyang. The populace considered the two brothers and the younger two sons of Queen Dowager Xuan the four major politicians, or principal influences, at court. The queen dowager made state decisions without consulting King Zhao, and the four major politicians neither asked for instructions nor submitted reports to the king for his approval, seconding the queen dowager's will. Suddenly, in 266 B.C., in the forty-first year of his reign, King Zhao cut off Queen Dowager Xuan's power and replaced prime minister Wei Ran with Fan Sui. The king banished the queen dowager's other brother, sons, and aides at court, ending her rule.

By the next year, Queen Dowager Xuan had fallen seriously ill. As she was dying, she asked to be buried with a *mianshou*—a handsome man who was made to offer sexual services to a woman who enjoyed high social status and great power, usually a widowed queen. Minister Yong Rui dissuaded the queen dowager from this demand. After she died, King Zhao ordered her burial on Mount Li, to the west of modern-day Lintong county, Shanxi province.

Although modern standards of morality may condemn Queen Dowager Xuan, in her time she was viewed as an astute politician, although she ultimately lost power because of her duplicity. For forty years, Qin Xuan had administered the state politics of the Qin kingdom, and she was thought worthy of the title "outstanding stateswoman."

Luo Yunhuan
Chen Yuchun, trans.

Sources

Strategy Developed During the Warring States Period; *History of the Later Han*; *Books of Historians* (Warring States period).

Ru Ji (b. ca. 276 B.C.) was summoned to the palace to serve the court of the king of the Wei kingdom by King Wei Anli, who ruled from 276 to 243 B.C. She lived during the Warring States period, a time of chaos caused by constant warfare among the feudal states of Qin, Chu, Qi, Yan, Zhao, Han, and Wei

administered by princes or dukes attempting to annex one another's territory or to overthrow the Zhou ruling dynasty. In 206
B.C., the kingdom of Qin sent its senior general, Bai Qi, and his
troops to eliminate the forces of the kingdom of Zhao in
Changping, located in the modern-day northwestern region of
Gaoping county, Shanxi province. General Bai Qi was victorious
over the Zhao forces and buried alive more than 400,000 of
those captured. In September of the next year, Qin forces were
sent under the generalship of Wang Ling to attack Handan, the
capital of the Zhao kingdom. They encountered stiff resistance
from the Zhao army, and Handan did not fall. But the Qin forces
did not pull back. The generalship of the Qin troops was
changed, and fresh recruits sent to besiege Handan, encircling
the capital for almost two years. The citizens of Handan were
running out of food and basic necessities, and the kingdom of
Zhao verged on collapse. The kingdom of Wei was a friendly
neighbor to the Zhao people, and the royal family had intermarried. Zhao Shen, Zhao's prime minister, Ping Yuan, was the
uncle of the king of Zhao, and his wife, was the sister of Xinling,
the duke of Wei. Cognizant of their interdependent alliance, Wei
Anli sent General Jinbi, commanding 100,000 troops, to aid the
besieged Zhao capital, Handan. Meanwhile, Qin's king was informed of Wei's intentions to aid Zhao and sent a message to
the king of Wei not to send assistance upon threat of attack.
King Wei Anli was frightened into submission and inaction. He
ordered General Jinbi to halt his movement toward reinforcing
Handan and stationed the Wei troops in Yuye (modern-day
Tangying in Henan province), to observe the developments between the two belligerents. The Zhao court, through Ping Yuan,
sent urgent messages to the Wei palace and asked for immediate
aid and protection for the sister of Xinling, who faced almost
certain death, should Handan fall. Xinling himself urged that the
Wei troops be moved quickly to protect Handan, but, upon receiving no encouragement from Wei Anli, decided to take a few
personal troops to reinforce the Zhao capital. Just before his
departure, Xinling was advised by a friend, Hou Ying, that his
sacrifice would be meaningless as he surely would be defeated
by the powerful Qin forces. It would be like throwing meat
before a tiger. Hou Ying suggested a clever plan to get the other

Wei troops released to fight the Qin threatening the kingdom of Zhao. He recommended that Ru Ji, because of her family's history, assist them. Ru Ji would be asked to get a military credential from the king of Wei so that they could give it to Xinling, who thereby would be empowered to replace General Jinbi.

Some time before, Ru Ji's father had been killed by enemies, causing her much grief. She had vowed to avenge him and had asked Xinling and his forces to hunt down the murderer. Xinling would become the new commander and lead the Wei troops toward Handan. Xinling did not disappoint her. He found the enemy, beheaded him, and presented his head to the grateful Ru Ji. Now Ru Ji wanted to repay Xinling by becoming a willing accomplice, even though she risked her life in the plan to steal the military authorization to move the Wei troops to aid Zhao. Her debt of gratitude to Xinling would be fully repaid should she succeed. It would be no easy task to get the military credential illegally. But the military credential was the only means through which the Wei troops could be activated and moved. If the king gave an order to mobilize an army, he sent the order in the form of a military credential to the commanding general, who would check the signature with the one he brought with him, and, if there was no mistake, he would implement the military operations. Because of the need for security, the credentials were usually kept by the king himself. All the military credentials of King Wei Anli were kept in his bedroom. As Ru Ji was one of the king's favorites and frequently was invited to his bedroom, she knew where they were kept. Aware of the danger to herself, Ru Ji proceeded with caution, convinced of the righteousness of Xinling's mission to aid Zhao. Finally, Ru Ji stole the credential with the king's authorization and gave it to Xinling, who rushed to take control of Wei forces. When General Jinbi balked at the new order, Xinling had him killed and then moved eighty thousand well-trained troops northward to save the Zhao kingdom, which was fighting against the Qin forces. Simultaneously, the kingdom of Chu also sent forces to aid Zhao against the Qin. The troops of Wei under Xinling and the troops of Chu under Jingyang squeezed the Qin forces between them and, aided by the Zhao army in Handan, destroyed the Qin army and forced the surrender of its commander, Zheng Anping. Zhao had turned from the brink of defeat to victory because it received aid from the Wei troops. And the Wei forces had been set in motion through the military credential stolen by the brave Ru Ji.

The consequences of her actions are unrecorded, but her noble and virtuous behavior was well remembered by contemporaries and historians alike. Guo Moruo, a well-known historian and writer in modern China, wrote a play called ''The Military Credential,'' which recounted the act of courage of Ru Ji. This play was immensely popular during the period of Chinese resistance against Japan in the 1930s and gave heart to the Chinese in Chongqing then resisting Japanese aggression. Today, the play is frequently staged, giving life again to her heroism.

Yang Fanzhong
Zhu Zhongliang, trans.

Sources

"The Biography of the Duke of Wei." Sima Qian, *Shi ji* (Records of the Historian), vol. 77; "The Biography of Ping Yuan," *Shi Ji*, vol. 76; "The Biography of Fan Sui," *Shi ji*, vol. 79.

Part I Sources

Ah Yuan. "First Patriotic Woman Poet in Chinese History." (Xu Mu) *Women of China*, vol. 8 (August 1984), pp. 40–41.

Analects. Translated under the title *The Sayings of Confucius*. New York: Mentor Books, 1955.

The Analects of Confucius. London: G. Allen and Unwin, 1938.

The Book of Songs. London: G. Allen and Unwin, 1937.

Cheng, L., Furth, C. and Bon-ming, Yip. *Women in China*. Berkeley: Institute of East Asian Studies, 1984.

Cheng Te-k'un. *Archaeology in China*. Cambridge, England: Heffen, vol. 1, 1959.

Dubs, Homer H., trans. *The History of the Former Han Dynasty by Pan Ku*. Baltimore: Waverly Press, vol. 1, 1938; vol. 2, 1944; vol. 3, 1955.

Elisséeff, Danielle. *La Femme au Temps des Empereurs de Chine*. Paris: Stock/L. Pernoud, 1988. (in French)

"Fu Hao," in *Famous Women in Chinese History*. Shanghai: Shanghai People's Press, 1988.

Cai Lei, "Patriotic Poetess of the Spring-Autumn Period" (Xu Mu) in *Famous Women of Ancient Times and Today,* ed. *Chinese Woman Magazine* (Hebei People's Publishing House, 1986).

Hanshu, vol. 31.

Hanwei, vol. 2, annotated by Yu Guan-ying. Beijing: Renming Chubanshe.

History of the Later Han

History of Zao Qiuming

Hulsewe, A.F.P. *Remnants of Han Law*. Leiden: Brice, 1955 (information on Queen Lu).

Li Zhi. *The Beginnings of Chinese Civilization: Three Lectures Illustrated with Finds at Anyang*. Seattle: University of Washington Press, 1957.

Li Zhi, *Shigang Pingyao,* vol. 5.

Liu An. *Huai nan zi*. Repr. Shanghai: Zhonghua shuju, 1927–35; Taibei: Zhonghua shuju, 1965.

Mencius. *Gongsun chouxia,* extensively quoted in Arthur Waley, *Three Ways of Thought in Ancient China,* London: G. Allen and Unwin, 1939.

Meschel, S.V. "Teacher Keng's Heritage, A Survey of Chinese Women Scientists," *Journal of Chemical Education,* vol. 69, no. 9, Sept. 1992, pp. 723–730.

Neill, Peter. "New Light on China's Oldest Civilizations." *Asia* (May-June 1980), pp. 30–32.

O'Hara, A.H. *The Position of Women in Early China*. Taiwan: Mei Ya Publications, 1971.

Qinghau shi, vol. 1, ed. Lu An-mian. Shanghai: Shanghai Guji Chubanshe.

Reischauer, Edwin O., and John K. Fairbank. *East Asia, the Great Tradition*. Boston: Houghton-Mifflin Co., 1989.

Shiji, vols. 6 and 7.

Sidel, R. *Women and Child Care in China*. Baltimore: Penguin, 1972.

Sima Guang. *History as a Mirror*.

Sima Qian. *Shi ji* (Records of the Historian); the last 70 chapters are "Biographies."

Stories of the Han Shi, Book 2.

Tao te ching (The Way and Its Power). London: G. Allen and Unwin, 1934.

Watson, Burton. *Ssu-ma Ch'ien: Grand Historian of China*. New York: Columbia University Press, 1958. Includes information of Lu Zhi (Queen Lu).

Wolf, M., and Witke, M., eds. *Women in Chinese Society*. Palo Alto: Stanford University Press, 1975.

Wei, K.T. *Women in China*. Westport, CT: Greenwood Press, 1984.

Yun Hanluo. *A Study of the Queens and Concubines of the Chu Kingdom*.

Part II

The Decline of the Zhou, the Period of the Warring States, and the Formation of the Qin and Han Dynasties

Internal political and economic weaknesses caused the Zhou dynasty to decline gradually, and China entered what is known as the period of the Warring States. The period of the Warring States began around 403 B.C. and ended in 221 B.C. with the unification of China under the Qin dynasty (221–206 B.C.). The period of the Warring States followed the Spring and Autumn period at the end of the Eastern Zhou dynasty. The "warring states" were the regions of Qin, Chu, Qi, Zhou, Wei, and Han which vived for territories, with the first three being the major contenders for power. During this period, a grisly practice of sacrificing young women was adopted to appease the river god, Ho. The annual flooding of the Yellow river (Huang Ho) fell upon Yexian county (near modern-day Linzhang county, Hebei province) in the kingdom of Wei. With an eye to averting future disaster, local officials selected the community's most beautiful young virgin to be ceremoniously "married" to the river god to pacify him. As a supposed dowry, these same officials would extort large sums of money from the populace. This cruel practice became more and more onerous, causing many families to leave the region to protect their beautiful daughters. An enlightened king of Wei sent an emissary, Ximen Bao, to become head of the county, and he vowed to stop the annual sacrifice. Ximen

Bao wanted to ferret out those responsible for perpetuating the cruel practice and called for the annual ceremony in early October as had been the usual custom. Several cult priestesses appeared beside the young woman who, it was thought, was to be sacrificed to the river god. The barge on which she was to be tied was at the river bank, and, as the ceremony was about to begin, she wept softly. As the ceremony started, Ximen Bao suddenly called a halt. He commanded that several of the cult priestesses be thrown into the river instead of the young woman, thus ending the torturous ceremony of marriage to the river god.

His wisdom was once more proved when Ximen Bao organized flood-control and irrigation projects. His forces dug twelve ditches, which gradually tamed the Yellow river, and the county continued to prosper under his direction and guidance. He built temples with funds earned during fruitful times, and today inscriptions from the Song, Ming, and Qing dynasties remain on the temples he erected, as testimony to his leadership in ending the cruel practice.[1]

The Qin Dynasty

The three warring political kingdoms of the Warring States period were Qin in the north, Chu in the south in the Yangzi valley, and Qi on the Shandong peninsula. The Qin, led by Shi Huangdi, emerged from the struggle victorious and proclaimed a new dynasty from which the word China came. He ruled from Xianyang (Xi'an), where 120,000 of the richest and most powerful families in the empire were transported to live. Taking the title First August Emperor, Qin Shihuangdi had used mounted cavalry instead of war chariots in his campaigns and once in power made great agricultural advances by introducing the iron-tipped plow. Discarding Confucianism in favor of the autocratic philosophy of Legalism, his regime became one of ruthless militarism, ruled by the will of the king. It became a crime to possess a Confucian text, although Qin Shihuangdi carefully stored one copy of each of the Confucian classics in his state library. Confucian scholars, to thwart the emperor, memorized entire books to keep the knowledge alive for future generations.

In 215 B.C. Qin Shihuangdi dispatched General Meng Tien to

build the Great Wall to protect China from the invasions of the northern barbarians, called the *xiongnu*. The Great Wall was built with conscripted laborers and political prisoners numbering 300,000; often, if one of them died at the construction site, his body was put into the wall. The wall is nearly 3,000 miles long with 25,000 watchtowers within signaling distance of one another, so that fires could be lit to call for reinforcements, and each tower garrisoned a hundred men. The emperor standardized weights and measures, such as the axle lengths of chariots used on the wall so that two chariots could pass one another going full tilt.

The Qin emperor had the Chinese characters simplified and standardized to ensure the mutual intelligibility of written communication throughout the country. He had divided China into thirty-six military districts, later these were expanded to forty-one after his annexations of Fujian, Guangdong, and Guangxi. In 210 B.C. Qin Shihuangdi was assassinated by a Daoist magician who claimed to offer an elixir of life guaranteeing immortality, which in reality was poison, and the empire collapsed soon thereafter in 206 B.C.[2]

Formation of the Han Dynasty

Out of the turmoil following the end of the Qin came the Han dynasty. The Han was founded by Liu Bang, a commoner whose charisma controlled the generals who carried him to victory over Xiang Yu, a nobleman. Two prominent women during this period are Empress Lu, the wife of Liu Bang, and Yu Ji (also called Beauty Yu), the favorite concubine of Xiang Yu. Liu Bang named his dynasty Han after the Han, or Heavenly, river and established his capital at Chang'an in the same vicinity as the old Qin capital Xianyang (Xi'an). He divided his conquered kingdom into fiefdoms as he passed them to his generals and relatives in exchange for their promise of military service.[3] But soon these generals became a threat, and he retook the lands. He passed an edict declaring that henceforth there would be no divisions of the kingdom except to the members of the royal family. This centralization of power would continue through the time of Emperor Wudi (ruled 141–87 B.C.) when former vassals had lost all vestiges of autonomous power. Wudi, the martial emperor, was so named because he fought against the *xiongnu*, and he ended the former tribute of appeasement through gifts of Chinese princesses in marriage and rolls of silk, which had pacified these northern tribes. Wudi also sent a trusted officer, Chang Jian, westward to negotiate agreements of peace and friendship with Central Asian tribes so that the Silk Route could be opened. Trade between Chang'an, now Xi'an, and the Mediterranean Middle East dominated by Rome along the Silk Route became the basis of the Han dynasty's prosperity. In 124 B.C., Wudi established the Imperial University in Chang'an and based its curriculum on the Confucian classics.[4]

Life in Chang'an was very pleasant. The wealthy lived in two-story houses with a central courtyard and decorated with carved or inlaid screens and silk embroidered cushions. Bedrooms had carved wooden beds, privacy screens, draperies, and lacquered chests and ornaments. Upper-class women dressed in silks, fox furs, silk and leather shoes, jade pendants, and rings. At parties, musical troupes played flutes, stringed instruments, bells, and drums; youthful choirs sang. Life for the poor was less luxurious: they typically wore clothing made of coarse hemp and furnished their houses with animal skins or coarse mats. But at the markets they watched puppet shows, jugglers and acrobats, cock fighting and magicians. The upper classes ate a variety of meats (pork, liver, dog, wild game, and fish) relatively frequently, while the lower classes ate rice and vegetables for their regular meals and reserved meat for festival days.

Wudi established a colony in North Korea through which Chinese culture spread to Japan and dispatched military expeditions to control Yunnan province and what is now North Vietnam. The Chinese military campaigns were expensive and drained Wudi's imperial treasury. The emperor turned to extorting additional taxes from merchants, currency debasement, government monopolies on wine, salt, and iron making, which in turn dampened incentives and caused declining tax yields. In the end, deficit and rebellion hastened Wudi's death.

By the end of the first century B.C. Han prosperity had vanished, and in 9 A.D. Wang Mang, nephew of the late empress Wang Zhengjun whose family had controlled politics since

Wudi's death, usurped the throne. One of the great reformers in Chinese history, he attempted to redistribute land and ease tax burdens through his self-proclaimed Xin dynasty, which he desired to build into a model Confucian state. His reforms failed, and numerous revolts broke out, including that of the Red Eyebrows, and Wang was assassinated in the year 23 A.D.[5]

The Han throne was restored two years later by the Illustrious Martial Emperor, Guang Wudi, whose capital was at Luoyang. He ushered in the Eastern (Later) Han, but soon after his reign began the old financial difficulties returned. Intrigues by the palace eunuchs and the empresses combined with numerous economic dislocations caused the end of the Han and produced disunity in China that lasted nearly four hundred years.

In spite of these shortcomings, the Han was so successful that today modern Chinese often call themselves men or women of Han. The histories of Sima Qian mark this period, as do the accomplishments of Ban Zhao, the first woman historian of China, who completed the *Han shu* (History of the Han Dynasty). Under the Han, there were many inventions, including that of paper, an early seismograph, and the water-powered mill.[6] Metallurgy was largely devoted to iron craftsmanship beginning in the first century A.D. with about fifty state-administered foundries smelting crude iron ingots and distributing them to be fashioned into tools, plowshares, and weapons, including a metal crossbow, which predated by far the crossbow of Western Europe. However, bronze was still used for ornaments, household items, coinage, and polished mirrors. Carriage wheels were crafted of bronze and wood, and sculptured bronze appeared in the forms of censers for incense and oil lamps.[7] There were also remarkable advances in the healing arts; for example the publication of the physician Ching Chi's *Treatise on Fevers*. The physician Hua Duo discovered a drug that, when combined with wine, would render unconscious a patient about to undergo surgery. Han astronomers like Chang Heng understood the earth to be round rather than flat.

Between the first century B.C. and the first century A.D., Buddhism also permeated Chinese culture, sweeping in from the Kushan empire, which shared a border with the Han empire west of the Tarim basin. A merchant class began to develop in China, although their status was below that of the *literati* scholars, no-bles, statesmen, and the farmers (whose profession of tilling the soil was viewed as more honorable than the art of winning prof-its). Merchants built stalls in the city markets that were licensed and policed by the government officials; the markets were also used as the site of public executions to scare would-be offenders. The merchants traveling the Silk Route used Bactrian, or two-humped, camels and rested along the way in caves decorated with Buddhas or in private inns of the major cities. The exten-sion of rule to southern China allowed the development of trade with India, Vietnam, Cambodia, and Malaya, both overland through the rivers of Vietnam and Burma to ports on the Bay of Bengal and directly by sea. The glories of the Han represented the first great age of empire in Chinese history, and many no-table women rose to prominence during this period.

B.B.P.

Notes

1. Chu Nan, "River God's Wife," *Women of China* (April 1982), pp. 4–43.

2. Derk Bodde, *China's First Unifier: A Study of the Ch'in Dynasty as Seen in the Life of Li Ssu (ca. 208 B.C.)*, 1958; P. Nancarrow, *Early China and the Wall*, 1978.

3. Pan Ku, *The History of the Former Han Dynasty*, trans. Homer H. Dubs, 3 vols. (Baltimore: Waverly Press, 1938–55).

4. C. Chang, *The Development of Neo-Confucian Thought*, 1957; Ho Ping-ti, *Cradle of the East*, 1975.

5. M. Loewe, *Everyday Life in Early Imperial China*, 1968.

6. W. Zhongshu, *Han Civilization*, 1982.

7. Burton Watson, *Records of the Grand Historian of China*, 1961, and, *Ssu-ma Ch'ien: Grand Historian of China*. (New York: Columbia University Press, 1958); N.L. Swann, *Pan Chao: Foremost Woman Scholar of China*. New York and London: The Century Company, 1932, reprinted 1950.

Lu Zhi (241–180 B.C.), or Empress Lu, was the politically astute first wife of Liu Bang, who founded the Western Han dynasty. Lu Zhi, also called Lu Hou or Lu Erju, was born in Shangfu county, Shandong province, during the Qin dynasty. Her father moved his family to Pei county to escape a personal enemy and met Liu Bang, who was then a local magistrate. Soon afterward, Lu Zhi and Liu Bang were married. As the Qin dynasty came to an end, there were uprisings all over the country. A commoner of peasant origin, Liu Bang was one of the influential leaders behind the rebellion, and he captured the Qin capital, Xianyang. Liu Bang was challenged by his rival for power Xiang Yu, an aristocratic general descended from warlords in the state of Chu. They warred for control of most of Central China for four years, during which time Lu Zhi and her parents were captured and held hostage by Xiang Yu. They were released in 226 B.C., after Xiang Yu was defeated and returned to Liu Bang.

By 202 B.C., Liu Bang held supreme power over Han China, and after 206 B.C. he ruled as the Han emperor. Lu Zhi reigned as his empress in the new capital, Chang'an. They had one son, Liu Ying, who succeeded Liu Bang as Emperor Xiaohui, and a daughter, Lu Yuan. Lu Zhi had two brothers, who aided in the formation of the Han dynasty as generals; one became an official in Zhou, the other in Jiancheng. The success of the new ruling family of Han owed largely to political shrewdness. Empress Lu excelled in political astuteness and played a vital role in assisting Liu Bang in removing the nobility with surnames other than Liu and Lu. In 196 B.C., she plotted against and had killed Han Xin and Peng Yue, along with their entire families, as they were the two figures who had contributed to the establishment of the Han dynasty. This was part of a general cashiering of former aides and reclaiming their lands in order to centralize effective power.

The distinguished historian Sima Qian later wrote: "The Empress Lu was a resolute and steadfast woman. She assisted (Emperor) Han Gaozhu in establishing control over the country and had much more responsibility for eliminating the members of the nobility.'' At the beginning of their reign, Liu Bang and Lu Zhi retreated from the former Qin system of centralized power. They developed a feudal system under which trusted general-vassals would administer the remote area in the emperor's name. They had worked hard to retain the loyalties of the military leaders and collateral branches of the imperial family. But once secure in power, the new Han rulers began to liquidate these potential challengers to centralized power. Demanding fewer taxes and less forced labor, Liu Bang and Lu Zhi dealt more fairly with the peasant class. They tolerated diversity of opinions other than those of the Qin legalists. Coming from common backgrounds, they sympathized with the peasants, who, at least in the beginning, accepted the new Han rulers as holders of the mandate of heaven.

Liu Bang had taken a beautiful concubine, Qi Zi, who bore him a son, named Ru Yi. Liu Bang favored Ru Yi and considered naming him his heir, while Empress Lu favored the elevation of their son Liu Ying. The empress and the prime minister, Zhang Liang, worked through various political factions at court to preserve the throne for Liu Ying. On April 25, 195 B.C., Liu Bang died, but Empress Lu did not immediately announce his death. She conspired with her confidant Shen Yiji to control the generals in the provinces, ensured the succession of her son and finally announced her husband's passing three days later.

Although Liu Ying, now the Emperor Xiaohui, technically ruled for seven years, the real power and authority was lodged in the hands of his mother, now known as Empress Dowager Lu. Before his death, Liu Bang had established only members of his own imperial family as his vassal kings and determined by law that no one else was to hold this title or rank. He had divided his territories into kingdoms and marquisettes, but controlled them so that they were never a threat to centralized authority. Empress Lu continued to whittle away at the powers and possessions of the remaining familial vassal-kings' powers, and elevated her own Lu family members, using nepotism to further entrench herself. Liu Bang had eight sons by Empress Lu and various concubines, each of whom had been given the title of king: Liu Fei, King Qidi; Liu Ying, King (later Emperor) Xiao-hui; Ru Yi, king of Zhao; Liu Heng, king of Dai; Liu Hui, king of Liang; Liu You, king of Huaiyang; Liu Chang, king of Huainan; and Liu Jian, king of Yan. Empress Lu attempted to rule through several of these sons or eliminated them if they challenged her authority. After the death of her husband, Empress Lu conspired first against Lady Qi and her son Ru Yi because they had previously enjoyed great honors and affection.

Empress Lu assassinated Ru Yi using poisoned wine and persecuted Lady Qi: Empress Lu had Lady Qi's hands and feet chopped off, eyes dug out, and ears burned and forced upon her a medicine that made her dumb. The unfortunate Lady Qi was enclosed in a pigsty where she was mocked as "the human-shaped pig." Emperor Xiaohui was called by Empress Dowager Lu to view Lady Qi; he wept bitterly and afterward seldom administered the affairs of state, leaving all important decisions to his mother.

The imperious empress dowager repeatedly used terror and intimidation to maintain her influence and power. In 193 B.C., she called both Emperor Xiaohui and Liu Fei, the king of Qi, to a banquet. Xiaohui sat next to Liu Fei, to show his respect; this infuriated Empress Dowager Lu, who thereupon ordered two cups of poisoned wine to be placed before Liu Fei. She then asked that he toast to her good health, and, as he lifted his glass, Xiaohui took the other cup. The empress dowager was astonished and knocked the emperor's poisoned cup away, saving them both. As a show of gratitude, Liu Fei respectfully offered the region of Chengyang to Princess Lu Yuan, which greatly pleased Empress Dowager Lu, who then allowed him to return to his own palace.

In 192 B.C., Mao Dun, chief of the *xiongnu*, asked the empress dowager to marry him, as they were both now widowed. She gently acknowledged his offer of marriage with respect and gifts, but did not accept his proposal. Nonetheless, through her clever diplomacy, the two remained good friends and peaceful allies during her reign. Mao Dun sent her numerous swift horses as imperial gifts, and she sent him many carriages.

Emperor Xiaohui died in 188 B.C., and his heir, known as

King Shao, was elevated to the throne as Emperor Shao. To avoid a civil war over the throne, Empress Lu carefully placated the other sons of Liu Bang by granting them prestigious commissions as commanders in southern China. The new emperor was rumored not to be the natural son of Xiaohui. It was said that his wife had not been able to conceive a son; she had deceived the emperor by taking another beauty's son, putting the natural mother to death, and pretending the child was hers with Xiaohui. After Emperor Shao was told of the circumstances of his birth and parentage, he swore to seek vengeance.

Because of these circumstances, Empress Dowager Lu carefully administered the powers of state. By 187 B.C., she had consolidated all power in her own hands and refused to allow any affairs of state to be administered by Emperor Shao, saying he was too ill. She removed the ministers at court who had served Liu Bang, replaced them with her own, and conferred the title of king on many members of her own family. Chen Ping and Shen Yiji were elevated as her right and left prime ministers. She eventually removed Emperor Shao and established the king of Changshan, Wang Yi, as puppet emperor. She promoted Zhi Houchao as king of Changshan. She imprisoned the king of Zhao, Liu You (who had been elevated to that position after the death of Ru Yi), for plotting treason, even though she suspected that he had been falsely accused by his wife, a member of the Lu clan, who was jealous of his love for a concubine. She later had Liu You killed and was responsible for the death of the subsequent king of Zhao, Liu Hui.

The empress dowager continued her policy of marrying female members of her own Lu family to the royal Liu heirs and conferred titles upon them. At one point it was feared that she would usurp the throne for her own family. She continued her imperious despotic ways until her death on July 30, 180 B.C., when there was a conservative reaction against her Lu supporters. The Liu royal family members reasserted their powers, reclaimed the Lu family's titles and privileges, and massacred the key members of the Lu clan. Liu Bang's son, Liu Heng, was elevated to the throne, and was known as Wen Di, the cultured emperor.

The empire that Liu Bang and Lu Zhi founded lasted for more

than two centuries with little interruption; then, after a temporary break, the Han dynasty continued for another two centuries as the Eastern Han dynasty. The two Han periods paralleled the Roman empire in the West in historical grandeur. Empress Lu came to be viewed in Chinese history as a cruel politician, who improved the condition of the common people, lowered taxes, increased state revenues, and promoted peace, despite her despicable acts of cruelty and torture. Some Chinese historians, such as Jian Bozhan, regard her as the first female emperor of China, although she never formally took the title. She seized and used power and governed efficiently to continue the legacy of her husband Liu Bang and ensured the continuance of the Han dynasty. She encouraged the Chinese to "recuperate and multiply" after the civil wars that had brought Liu Bang and her to power. She had sections of the Great Wall rebuilt for common defense, neutralized the barbarians, and ended family blood feuds through centralized courts of justice. She had wielded power at court as no other woman had previously done, and ruled over more people than the Caesars of Rome.

Song Ruizhi
Liu Zhenyun, trans.

Sources

Burton Watson, *Ssu-ma Ch'ien: Grand Historian of China*. New York, Columbia University Press, 1958; Homer H. Dubs (translation), *The History of the Former Han Dynasty by Pan Ku*. Baltimore: Waverly Press, vol. 1, 1938, vol. 2, 1944, vol. 3, 1955; A.F.P. Hulsewe, *Remnants of Han Law*. Leiden: Brill, 1955.

Yu Ji (ca. 224–202 B.C.), known in Chinese history as Beauty Yu, was the most famous concubine of Xiang Yu, the rival of Liu Bang, the founder of the Han dynasty (see Lu Zhi). Yu Ji, who was viewed as the most beautiful woman in China at the end of the Qin dynasty, followed Xiang Yu throughout his struggles to capture power and establish a new dynasty in China. General Xiang Yu, known as Xichu Bawang, or the Conqueror, was descended from aristocrats in the state of Chu. As the leader of the state of Chu, he was a natural rival to the growing power of the Han forces led by Liu Bang; in 202 B.C. war broke out anew between the two to determine which was the stronger. Liu Bang took precautions to reinforce himself with additional troops from General Han Xin, Ying Bu, and Peng Yue. Yu Ji was in the city of Pengcheng (now Xuzhou, Jiangsu province) with Xiang Yu when he was attacked, surrounded, and trapped in Hexia by the Han forces of Liu Bang. The Chu army was exhausted from fighting and further demoralized by the Han army's singing of a nostalgic song about the Chu homeland.

One evening, as Chu morale sank ever lower, Xiang Yu and Lady Yu Ji sat together drinking wine and recalling the glorious days of his previous conquests. He remembered his favorite horse, Wuzhui, which he had ridden to many victories, and re-told stories of his shared happiness with Yu Ji in days gone by. His spirit moved him to recite a poem on his current circumstance, now known as "Hexia ge" (Song in Hexia):

> *My strength could move mountains,*
> *My spirit is peerless anywhere;*
> *But the weather is so unfavorable,*
> *I could not ride my heroic Wuzhui;*
> *Oh, my dear Beauty Yu,*
> *What am I going to do with you?*

Lady Yu replied, saying:

> *The Han army is intruding*
> *We are besieged on all sides;*
> *So depressed is your majesty,*
> *Why should I live any longer?*

Touched by her loyalty and affection, General Xiang Yu beheld her with tears in his eyes, and his aides and subordinates lamented as Lady Yu killed herself by leaning on a sword in front of Xiang Yu.

Shortly thereafter, Xiang Yu made a desperate last attempt to escape by night, moving south with eight hundred troops. He reached the Wu river in Anhui province, but there he was cornered by the pursuing Han army. On the bank of the Wu river, following Yu Ji's example, Xiang Yu killed himself with his sword.

This tender story of love is known as "Bawang bei ji," or "Xiang Yu" (The Conqueror's Farewell to Beauty Yu). Their love for each other was a favorite historical theme in Chinese dramas, poems, and novels. "Beauty Yu" became a classification of songs in the Tang dynasty as well as a type of poetry in the Song dynasty. Yu Ji's tomb, erected in Dingyuan county, Anhui province, is called Meiren Mu (tomb for a beauty).

Zhao Xiaoming
William Cheng, trans.

Sources

Shi ji, Xiang Yu Benji, vol. 7; *Shi ji*, Gaozu Benji, vol. 6; *Han shu*, Gaodi Ji, vol. 1; *Han shu*, Cheng Sheng, Xiang Ji Zhuan, vol. 31; *Zizhitongjian*, Gaodi, vol. 31; *Shigang Pingyao*, Gaozu, by Li Zhi, vol. 5; *Hanwei* Liuchao Shixun, vol. 2, annotated by Yu Guan-ying, published by Renming Chubanshe; *Qinghan Shi*, vol. I, by Lu An-mian, published by Shanghai Guji Chubanshe; Gushi Yuan by Sheng De-yuan, published by Zhonghua Shuju.

Empress Dowager Dou (ca. 200–135 or 129 B.C.) was a Han ruler who maintained order through advocating Daoism as an antidote to Legalism and Confucianism. She was born in Guanjin village in Qinghe county (modern-day eastern Hengshui), Hebei province, and named Yi. The wife of the Cultured Emperor, Emperor Xiaowen (r. 180–157 B.C.), and the mother of Emperor Jingdi, she was historically known as Empress Dowager Dou.

She lost her parents when she was very young, but had two older brothers, Dou Jian, known as Changjun, and Dou Guangguo, called Shaojun. Her youth was spent in a tumultuous era of incessant warfare that offered little solace for commoners. Seeking a position, she was called to the imperial palace by the Han court officials to become a servant to Empress Lu (see Empress Lu). Shortly thereafter, she was made a concubine to one of five vassal kings loyal to the Han empire. Dou Yi told a palace eunuch that she desired to be sent to the kingdom of Zhao because her hometown, Guanjin, was nearby. The eunuch failed to assist her, and along with four other young women she was sent to the kingdom of Dai, whose king, Liu Heng, would later become Emperor Xiaowen of the Western (Former) Han dynasty. After Empress Lu died, her family relatives were replaced in positions of influence within the court. Members of the Liu family nominated the king of Dai to succeed her, and thus he began his reign as emperor.

When Dou Yi entered the Dai court, she won the king's immediate favor and was granted the rank of an elevated concubine; she bore him a daughter, named Piao, and two sons, Qi and Wu. The king's imperial concubine, Madam Wang, had earlier had four sons, and Dou Yi, who understood her place, trained her children to defer to their half-brothers. But the imperial concubine and her four sons had died before Liu Heng became emperor, thus opening the way for Dou Yi and her sons. In 179 B.C., the prime minister and other officials signed a petition to the emperor requesting that an heir be designated. Liu Heng, now Emperor Xiaowen, repeatedly declined the proposal, until a second petition arrived, after which he named Qi as his successor. At the same time, with the encouragement of his mother, Empress Dowager Bo, Liu Heng named Dou Yi as his empress. Their daughter Piao was named the princess of Guantao and Wu was confirmed as king of Huaiyang. Dou Yi's parents were posthumously granted titles: her father as duke of Anchen, and her mother as Madam Anchen. Large tombs were constructed to rebury her deceased parents, and her brother Changjun received large grants of farmland.

But at the time, the whereabouts of Shaojun were not known, because he had been abducted at the age of four and sold to a number of households in succession. Dou Yi's brother Shaojun worked as a charcoal burner in the mountains; one evening the side of the mountain collapsed, killing more than a hundred, and Shaojun alone survived. He then went to a fortune teller, who told him that he would soon become an imperial duke. When Shaojun arrived in Chang'an, he learned that the new empress was named Dou and that she was from Guanjin. Despite the many intervening years, he could still remember his family name, birthplace, and early events of his life, and he recalled having fallen from a mulberry tree while he was picking the fruit with his elder sister, with a scar to prove it. With this evidence, he presented himself to the imperial officials, seeking to be reunited with his sister. Having read the report and consulted with her husband, Dou Yi invited him to the palace. What Shaojun told her was consistent with her own childhood memories. He told her that when his elder sister had left for the capital, she had bade him farewell after begging some food for him. At this remark, Empress Dou began to weep and grasped his hand in recognition. The emperor bestowed gifts upon Shaojun and permitted him to live in Chang'an. When Zhou Bo, the prime minister, and Guan Ying, the highest-ranking imperial minister in charge of military affairs, received the news, they worried that the Dou family would emulate Empress Lu's family in its attempt to control affairs of state. The ministers found wise tutors for the Dou brothers, and the emperor refused to confer any official positions upon them. Empress Dou herself had learned from the former Lu intrigues, and she maintained a respectful position at all times, cognizant of her humble birth and subsequent good fortune. Her brothers grew to be gentlemen of virtue and taste. Empress Dou lost her sight during an illness, and the affections of the emperor shifted to concubines Madam Handan and Ji, but neither bore any children.

When Emperor Xiaowen died in 157 B.C., Crown Prince Qi ascended the throne as Emperor Xiaojing (Jingdi), and Dou was made empress dowager. Her brothers were elevated in reputation; after Changjun died, his son, Pengzhu, was named Duke Nanpi, Shaojun was made Duke Zhangwu, and Hou Ying, a cousin of Empress Dou, was named Duke Wei for his military accomplishments. Dou Yi became grand empress dowager in 141 B.C., when the Emperor Wudi ascended the throne upon the death of Jingdi.

Empress Dou is famous in Chinese history for maintaining an interest at court in Daoism, especially the ruling philosophy of "wu wei er zhi," or "governing by doing nothing (that goes against nature)." By this the Daoists meant doing what comes naturally, not inaction. Empress Dou, a follower of the teachings of Laozi, believed the universe operated according to its own harmonies and the efforts of humankind to interfere simply upset those harmonies. Accomplishments should be spontaneous; if one goes with the flow, one will have no failures. The ideal political state for Empress Dou and her supporters was unsophisticated and simple, without elaborate rituals and etiquette; the emperor should rule as a Daoist sage over a passive peasantry. At the same time, the court also supported Confucian academicians, so there were often intellectual arguments over the virtues of Confucianism versus Daoism.

The empress trained her son Jingdi in Daoist theories, and they remained the guiding principles during his reign. The *Laozi,* also called *Dao de jing* (The Way and Its Power), was widely circulated in court circles, as was the venerated *Zhuangzi,* which contained poems and parables. Both Daoist texts were from the third century B.C., as was another favorite, the *Liezi.* The person who transcended ambition, desire for power, and control and blended with nature became one with the Dao and was beyond all harm. Daoists such as Empress Dou were reacting against Confucian rigidities, but not Confucian ethics or the ideals of virtue.

When the Emperor Wudi took the throne, he made Dou Ying, then Duke Weiqi, prime minister, and Tian Jie, then Duke Wuan, the military affairs minister—both of them were Confucians. Next he appointed Zhao Wan, another disciple of Confucianism, as senior official in charge of the archives, and Wang Zhang as imperial officer in charge of logistics and palace security. These officials suggested that Wudi establish a special place where Confucianism could be worshipped; they put forward their teacher Shen Pei to take charge of the planning. These same officials advised Wudi not to look to Empress Dou for guidance, knowing that she favored Daoism.

Empress Dou secretly investigated the new officials and made her findings known to the emperor, who thereupon decided against establishing the temple and eventually dismissed his new Confucian appointees, Zhao Wan and Wang Zhang. The deposed Confucians committed suicide. Henceforth, Empress Dou would permit no advances in the acceptance of Confucianism.

That the general public had widely accepted Daoism at the time is recounted by the *bo shu* (old writings on silk) excavated in the Han tombs at Mawangdui in Changsha. It appears that Daoist ideas were accepted widely to replace the tyrannical Legalism prominent during the Qin dynasty. In addition to eliminating corruption from the Qin dynasty, this philosophy also served as a stimulus to economic vitality and social freedoms, which contributed to the early health of the Han dynasty. From early Daoism there continued strong beliefs in alchemy, seeking to turn base metals such as cinnabar into gold and in finding the elixir of life to guarantee immortality.

The resurgence of Daoism (which had been important earlier during the Zhou dynasty) in Empress Dou's lifetime also supported the Naturalists' school of thought, which taught the concepts of the *yin* and *yang*. (The universe or nature was composed of yin (the female principle) and yang (the male principle); yin was dark, earth, and negative, while yang was bright, hot and positive). Nature was a balance of these two forces. So strong was the influence of revived Daoism under her patronage that in 110 B.C. Emperor Wudi was persuaded to perform a sacrifice to heaven on the summit of Mount Tai in Shandong and perform similar ceremonies at the mountain's base honoring the earth. When Dou Yi died, she was buried with her husband in Shuangling (Shuang mausoleum). Her personal wealth, treasures, and wardrobe were bestowed upon her daughter, Princess Piao. She will always be remembered as a politician who used Daoism to keep China unified.

Zhao Xiaoming
Zhu Zhongliang, trans.

Sources

Ban Zhao (Pan Chao), *The History of the Han Dynasty*. Central Chinese Publishing House, 1962; Repr. Beijing: China Publishing House, 1988. "The Biography of Emperor Wen Di," vol. 4; "The Biography of Emperor Jing Di," vol. 5; "The Biography of Wu Di," vol. 6; "The Biography of Empress Dou," vol. 97, Book one; "The Archives of Art and Culture," vol. 30; "The

Archives of Ceremonies and Rites," vol. 22; "The Biography of Tian Jie," vol. 52; "The Biography of Dou Ying," vol. 52; "The Biography of Dou Bo," vol. 40; "The Biography of Dailing," vol. 88; "The Biography of Yuan Gu." vol. 88; all volumes published by China Publishing House, Beijing: 1988, edition; Sima Qian (Ssu-ma Chien), *The History* (*Shi ji*, usually translated as Records of the Historian), vols. 10, 11, 12, 49, 57, 58, 63, 111, 120, and 170, China Publishing House, Beijing, 1988 edition; Sima Guang (Ssu-ma Guang), *Zizhi tongjian*. Beijing: China Publishing House, 1988 edition; Li Zhi, Xu Tianling, *The Major Events of Western Han Dynasty: The Emperors* (Book Two), vol. 2, Shanghai: People's Publishing House 1986. Xiong Tieji, *The Brief Review of the New Taoist of Qin and Han Dynasties*. Shanghai: People's Publishing House, 1988; Xu Tianling, *The Major Events of the Western Han Dynasty: The Rites* (Book Five), vol. 11, Shanghai People's Publishing House; Wu Guang, *The General Survey of Huang Lao Theory*. Zhejiang: People's Publishing House, 1989.

Chunyu Tiying (b. ca. 190 B.C.), who secured an end to cruel corporal punishments, was born in Lingzhi (modern-day Zhibo), Shandong province, during the Western (Former) Han dynasty. Her father, Chunyu Yi, was the chief of the imperial warehouse for the kingdom of Qi, in charge of storing grain. She was the youngest of five daughters. Her mother's name is unknown.

Chunyu Yi had an interest in medicine and studied how to make medical prescriptions while a youth. In 180 B.C. he began studying medicine under Yang Qing, a well-known physician, and later under Doctor Gongsun Guang, from whom he learned to diagnose and treat diseases. He was given copies of books related to pulse reading by Leaders Huangdi and Bian Que and learned to make diagnoses by observing the patient and measuring the pulse. Chunyu Yi began to practice medicine, compiling *Medical Archives,* the first book of medical cases in Chinese history, in which he described his treatments in detail. His book played an important role during the formative period of Chinese medicine. He developed his skills rapidly, achieving fame for treating those assumed to be incurable. He traveled far and wide to serve patients, and more and more individuals sought his treatment. Perhaps because of his rapid rise to fame, he began to take on pretentious airs, alienating many families that he now refused to treat.

In 176 B.C. Chunyu Yi was accused of malpractice because of his failure to treat the sick and sentenced to prison in the capital, Chang'an (modern-day Xi'an). Seeing their father arrested, the five daughters were distressed. He asked them to do something about his plight. Chunyu Tiying, out of compassion for her father, offered to accompany him to Chang'an. Upon their arrival, she took care of her father's daily needs and began writing a report to be submitted to the imperial court, pleading her father's case. In this report, she volunteered to be a servant girl to atone for her father's misdeeds. She wrote: "When my father was a low-ranking official in the kingdom of Qi, the local people considered him as an honest and fair official. Now he is accused of breaking the law, which accordingly will sentence him to corporal punishments such as having his nose, toes, or kneecaps chopped off, if he is not put to death. I feel very sad about it, for a person can never live again if he is killed, and the chopped off parts will not be again linked to the body. Even though the criminal desires to mend his ways, it is already impossible. Considering the serious consequences for my father, I have decided to volunteer my services as a servant in the court to atone for my father's crime. Let him correct his errors and make a fresh start." Her report reached the Emperor Wendi, who was moved by her sincerity and filial piety. At this time, the Emperor Wendi himself found these corporal punishments too harsh. More lenient punishments were more conducive to stability and the development of a harmonious society. Therefore, the emperor gave an order to reverse her father's sentence; he had been convinced by Chunyu Tiying's persuasive report.

Corporal punishment was abolished throughout the country. No longer was a criminal branded on the face with a Chinese character identifying him as a criminal. Punishments of having limbs or the nose cut off were reduced to flogging. Emperor Wendi's edict had wide repercussions, as many criminals now escaped the cruel tortures and maiming. The law was now considered more just, even though some dispassionate officials still exerted great energy in flogging. Emperor Wendi had reformed feudal policies of the Han, reducing oppression, which in turn revitalized the populace, increasing production.

Chunyu Tiying had risen from an unknown figure to a national heroine overnight. The story that she had submitted a report to the imperial court, offering to be a servant in the palace to atone for her father's crime, and that Wendi had been so moved that he reduced the penalty previously given her father, spread widely. Her story was recorded in history as an outstanding example of filial piety, courage, and benevolence. Ban Gu, the famous historian of the Eastern (Later) Han composed a poem called "Chanting the History," telling the story of Chunyu Tiying's heroism and noble virtue.

Yang Yi
Zhu Zhongliang, trans.

Sources

The History: the 105th vol., the biographies of Bian Que; Ban Zhao, *History of the Han Dynasty.* Central Chinese Publishing House, 1962; repr. Beijing: Chinese Publishing House, 1988, vol. 23, the Records of Punishments and Laws; *The History of Chinese Medicine.* Shanghai: Science and Technology Publishing House, 1972, 18.

Zhuo Wenjun (ca. 179–118 B.C.), a talented poet who lived during the Western (Former) Han dynasty, was noted for her love affair with scholar-writer Sima Xiangru (179–118 B.C.). She was born in Linqiong county, Sichuan province, to a wealthy industrialist's family. Her father, Zhuo Wangsun, operated an iron mine and became the richest man in the region. Zhuo Wenjun lived with her widowed father, whose household included another daughter and a son by another wife. Wenjun was considered attractive and entertained her father by playing the seven-stringed zither.

While still young, she married into the wealthy Chen family, and soon discovered that her husband was an invalid; there was no love between them, and he died not long afterward. Wenjun became a widow at seventeen. She longed to return to the home of her father, but it was forbidden by feudal ethics of the time. In her despair, she devoted herself to reading books, becoming especially attached to one written by Sima Xiangru, whom she greatly admired. After many months, Wenjun finally left the confines of her deceased husband's family after what was deemed an appropriate period of mourning and re-entered the home of her father, although there was now a distance between them.

Sima Xiangru, a native of Chengdu, Sichuan province, excelled in writing prose-poems that developed out of songs from the state of Chu. His best-known work includes various styles of prose including "Zi xu fu" and "Shang lin fu," both considered prose masterpieces in Western Han scholarship. Sima Xiangru had served Emperor Jindi's younger brother, Liu Wu. But after Liu Wu's death, he lost his post and decided to return home via Linqiong. His friend Wang Ji, head of the county, hosted him and introduced him to Zhuo Wangsun, who invited them both for dinner. Since it was well known that Zhuo had a lovely and well-read daughter, the invitation was accepted. Sima Xiangru, a bachelor leading an itinerant scholarly life, welcomed the opportunity. Zhuo Wangsun gave a sumptuous banquet and had placed Wenjun's zither in the reception room. Sima Xiangru noticed the instrument, picking it up to play. One of his songs was "Courting of the Phoenix," in which he revealed his admiration for a beautiful woman. This conjuring melody reached Wenjun, and she tried to see from where the music was emanating. Peering from behind a magnificent screen, she watched Xiangru play; he appeared masterful and elegant, and she fell in love with him at first sight. Sima Xiangru noticed her and wrote a note to her professing his admiration; that night she joined him. Early the next day she, accompanied by her maid, and Sima Xiangru left for Chengdu. They had eloped, causing a scandal throughout the country. Her father, realizing what had happened, told no one. After reaching Chengdu, the couple spent their days writing poetry together and playing the zither. But as Sima Xiangru was rather poor, the couple soon returned to Linqiong, where they opened a small wine shop in which Wenjun heated and served the wine and Sima, taking off his scholar's robes, washed the cups and dishes. Her father, upon hearing this, could not tolerate such a standard of living for his daughter, believing she disgraced him. Zhuo Wangsun presented them with a hundred servants, a million copper coins, and the dowry from her first marriage. Overnight the young couple became wealthy, and they returned to Chengdu to purchase land, houses, and possessions.

Shortly thereafter, one of Sima Xiangru's rhapsodic poems on hunting was read by the new emperor, Wudi, who invited Sima Xiangru to the palace as a court official. The young couple enjoyed their success at court in Chang'an. Later Sima Xiangru was named commander of the imperial bodyguards in Chengdu and was dispatched there to represent the emperor. Wenjun was proud of her husband, and her father, pleased to have such a son-in-law, bestowed additional riches upon them. Sometime later, Sima Xiangru resigned his official post as he suffered from diabetes and returned with Wenjun to Maolin, near Chang'an.

Now middle-aged, the couple suffered personal setbacks. Sima Xiangru fell in love with an attractive young girl and determined to marry her; Wenjun, in her despair, took to writing poetry to lift her spirits. Her moving poem, "White Hair," has been retold down through the centuries:

> White as the snow on the mountain,
> Pure as the moon in the sky
> But I know you now love another,
> I bid you a last goodbye.
>
> Today the good wine flows freely,
> Tomorrow to the ditch I go.
> In short steps by the ditch I wander,
> In silence the waters flow.
>
> O Sorrow, is there need in wedlock
> For tears to well from the heart?
> I wish I had a true lover,
> In old age never to part.

Deeply touched by Wenjun's poem, Sima Xiangru felt ashamed and gave up the idea of marrying the younger woman; he stayed with Wenjun until he died. Although some scholars now have doubts about the authorship of this poem, Zhuo Wenjun and

Sima Xiangru remain famous as the first couple in China's history in which both partners were talented and brilliant. Zhuo Wenjun's elopement served as a role model for modern Chinese young women who defiantly challenged old feudal marriage customs in which bonds were arranged by matchmakers. Wenjun has been celebrated as a strong, talented poetess, who used the power of her pen to win back the affections and attentions of the man she loved.

Yang Fanzhong
Xu Kaichang, trans.

Sources

Records of the Historian, 117; Ban Zhao, *History of the Han Dynasty*, Central Chinese Publishing House, 1962; repr. Beijing: China Publishing House, 1988. vol. 57; Liu Dai-Ji, *History of China's Literature*.

Queen Wei (ca. 148–91 B.C.) was queen and consort to Liu Che, known as Wudi, the martial emperor (r. 141–87 B.C.). Born in Linfen city, Xi'an province, she was originally named Wei Zifu, the third child born to parents of humble background. Her father died when she was a child, and her mother was a servant in Princess Pingyang's (see Princess Pingyang) household. Princess Pingyang was the elder sister of Liu Che. Wei Zifu studied singing, music, chess, painting, and calligraphy, and became artistically accomplished. In March 139 B.C., Emperor Wudi went to the northern suburb of Chang'an (modern-day Xi'an) to offer sacrifices to the gods and his ancestors and stopped at Princess Pingyang's home. During a banquet there, the emperor was entertained by lovely young women, including Wei Zifu, who sang and danced; he was immediately attracted to her. Princess Pingyang, seeking to please her brother, ordered Wei Zifu to the emperor's palace upon his request, and the young dancer soon became a court favorite.

Wei Zifu was thrust into the power struggles within the royal circle, as the emperor's noble-born wife, Queen Chenjiao, had produced no male heir. Wei Zifu was viewed by the queen as a serious rival for the emperor's affections. The emperor, realizing this rivalry, did not desire at this point to break with the queen. He temporarily set Wei Zifu aside, and she became lonely within the palace. But just as she was about to be released to return to her former position in the home of Princess Pingyang, she was invited to an audience with the emperor, who, moved by her tears which rekindled his love for her, persuaded her to remain with him. Wei Zifu once again attracted the jealousy of Queen Chenjiao, who now conspired to get rid of her. The queen's plot was discovered by the emperor, and he moved swiftly to protect Wei Zifu. The queen's rage was undiminished, however, and she decided to kill Wei's entire family. The emperor, disgusted with the queen's behavior, designated Wei Zifu as a high-ranking concubine. Now Lady Wei, she became even more popular at court, singing, and dancing; she bore the emperor three daughters—Weichang, Yangshi, and Zhuyi—and a son, Liuju.

In 130 B.C., Emperor Liu Che charged his queen with attempted murder and had her formally deposed and imprisoned. Two years later he formally bestowed the title of queen on Wei Zifu and named their son, the seven-year-old Liuju, the crown prince. Although Wei Zifu had been declared queen, as time passed and her beauty faded, other rivals and their sons thrust themselves forward coveting the throne. Nonetheless, Queen Wei was able to elevate members of her own family to high positions: her elder brother, Wei Changju, held an official's rank, and her elder sister, Wei Junru, was married to Gong Shunhe, the prime minister. Wei Zifu's younger sister married court official He Zhongru and their son He Qiubin became a famous general. But in 91 B.C., Wei Zifu's nephew, Gong Shun Ji Shen, took over his father's post as prime minister, and was accused of graft. The emperor ordered all of Gong Shun's family to be killed. The Princesses Yangshi and Zhuyi were forced to commit suicide because they had close links with the accused; this become known as the Gong Shun affair. Her elder sister, sister-in-law, and nephew were also killed, which dealt a further blow.

Queen Wei was besieged with troubles from another source soon thereafter, when the envoy Jiang Chong falsely accused her and the crown prince of sorcery and treason, charging them in an attempt to assassinate the emperor. This campaign against Queen Wei continued as the emperor fell ill, and the slanderous court faction produced a forged document in which the crown prince had supposedly admitted his guilt. Moving swiftly to counterattack, the crown prince arrested the scheming Jiang Chong, but he could not regain the emperor's trust. Wudi ordered the arrest of the crown prince, but Liuju fled and later hanged himself. Queen Wei understood that she too was now doomed, and at age fifty-seven, she followed her son in death by suicide, hanging herself from a beam. She was buried beside the Tongbao Pavilion in the southern section of Chang'an. Of humble origin, she had risen through her talents, only to become a victim of palace intrigues. Queen Wei is remembered in China as one of Wudi's great loves.

Song Ruizhi
Ma Li, trans.

Sources

"Wu Di," in Ban Zhao, *History of the Han Dynasty* (in Chinese). Beijing: Central Chinese Publishing House, 1962 repr. Beijing: China Publishing House, 1988; *Dictionary of Famous Women in China*. Beijing: Hua Xia Publishing House, 1988; *The Death of Queen Mother (Wei)* (in Chinese), Hai Tian Publishing House, 1987.

Queen Xiaowu (ca. 135–106 B.C.), a court dancer, also known as Queen Hanwu and Lady Li, became one of the favorite wives of Liu Che, the Emperor Han Wu or Wudi (r. 141–87 B.C.). She was born north of Zhongshan, in modern-day Ding county, Hebei province, during the Western (Former) Han dynasty. Her parents were singers and dancers, and she and her brothers and sisters were trained and skilled in these arts. Queen Xiaowu's brother, Li Yannian, was a famous musician who had been castrated as punishment for a crime and had once been reduced to feeding the emperor's hounds. Nonetheless Li Yannian was allowed to sing and dance periodically for Emperor Wudi, who liked him. Li Yannian was often called upon to sing a special song:

There is a beautiful lady in the north
She is the most attractive in the world
The more you see her, the more you love her
She is so rarely found that you would give up
Everything for a glance at her.

Li Yannian was asked by Wudi to identify this girl; the emperor discovered her identity to be Li's sister and soon summoned her to join his court. So beautiful and skilled in dancing was she that Wudi fell in love with her and married her, naming her his fourth wife.

Now called Madam Li, she was a favorite of the emperor, and Li Yannian became more prominent. In 120 B.C. Emperor Wudi established a music institution, naming Li Yannian as his senior official in charge of musical affairs. This position was equal in status to the rank of a magistrate in a province. Li Yannian performed his duties with competence and distinction. Madam Li grew ever closer to the emperor and bore him a son, called Liu Bo.

Sometime later, Madam Li contracted a serious disease and was confined to her bed. Emperor Wudi went to visit her, but she had covered herself with a quilt, refusing to let him see her during her illness. She was reproached by her sisters for refusing his visit and failing to ask him for special favors on behalf of her brothers. Madam Li explained to them that the emperor missed her beauty. She had won his affections through her appearance, and if she revealed herself to him now, he would neither miss her nor sympathetically employ her brothers. She believed that she had safeguarded their interests by allowing Wudi to hold on to his memories of her. In his mind, she was still as lovely as ever, and when she died, the emperor gave her a state funeral and ordered her portrait painted for the Ganquan Palace. After the death of Wudi, his will provided that Madam Li posthumously be granted the title of Queen Xiaowu. A commemorative memorial service was held for her along with the funeral services for Wudi in the same temple.

The *History of the Han Dynasty* contains a section on the queen's relatives that includes an account of how Emperor Wudi had employed Shao Weng, a sorcerer, to use magic to bring back the spirit of Queen Xiaowu, because he missed her so much. He commissioned her brother Li Guangli as a general to conquer Er Shi (now Mapxamat); in 101 B.C. General Li Guangli was granted the title of marquis of Xexi. When Li Yannian was sentenced to death for crimes committed at court, his relatives were spared thanks to the emperor's affectionate respect for Queen Xiaowu. In 97 B.C., Liu Bo was named Prince Ai of Chengyi. But in 90 B.C., General Li Guangli's forces were defeated in the north by the barbarian *xiongnu*. He was forced to surrender and because of this disgrace, his clan was later eliminated.

Three years later, Emperor Wudi died. His eight-year-old son by his concubine surnamed Zhao mounted the throne as Emperor Zhao. When Emperor Zhao died thirteen years later, he left no sons; his general, Huo Guang, and court officials supported Liu He, the son of Liu Bo. Unfortunately, Liu He was a fatuous emperor, who led a dissipated life; twenty-seven days after he assumed the throne, he was deposed.

Queen Xiaowu protected her beauty to maintain her relatives' position of influence at court. She thus ensured that her own grandson would have a chance, however brief, to rule China.

Luo Yunhun
Tan Mingxia, trans.

Sources

Wang Xian Qian, *Biography of Lady Li and Her Relatives*; Ban Zhao, *History of the Han Dynasty*. Central Chinese Publishing House, 1962; repr. Beijing: China Publishing House, 1988. The sections on Lady Li and her family, and the biography Li Yan Nian; Fengchan, *Records of Empress Xiao Wu*.

Liu Xijun (ca. 124–87 B.C.) was a Western Han princess who married a king of Wusun, leader of one of the northern minorities, in order to ally Han China with Wusun against the *xiongnu,* fierce northern nomads and thereby protect the Silk Route and its trade, so vital to Han's China vitality. Liu Xijun was born in Jiangdu (modern-day Yangzhou, Jiangsu province) during the early Han dynasty. The Liu family was of imperial lineage. Her grandfather Liu Fei was the son of Liu Qi, who ruled as Emperor Jindi. Liu Fei had distinguished himself by leading forces to quell the Disturbance of the Seven States (the central Han government eliminated the powers of several kings or marquises not directly related to the Han dynasty's royal line) when he was fifteen, leading the emperor to confer upon him the title of prince of Runang. Later Liu Fei was made prince of Jiangdu by the Emperor Wudi, and the Liu family continued to rule this area after Liu Fei's death in 127 B.C. Liu Jian, Xijun's father, inherited power and title over the area; since he took several wives and concubines, it is not known who Xijun's natural mother was.

Xijun was born during a time of great prosperity for the Western Han dynasty. The Emperor Wudi, who would open the famous Silk Route between China and cities of the Middle East, desired to safeguard the northern routes through alliances with nomadic barbarian tribes. An alliance with the peoples who inhabited Dayuezhi and Wusun, in modern-day Central and Western Asia and parts of Xinjiang, would allow the Han Chinese to converge on the area of the dreaded *xiongnu*. Wudi sent Zhang Qian as an envoy to the western regions to negotiate alliances in 138 B.C. and in 126 B.C.; these trips resulted in the opening of the Silk Route and the development of political, economic, and cultural ties between East and West—Han China and the Roman world—overland. Trade goods moved from Chang'an (modern-day Xi'an), through Dunhuang, Congling, and Anxi, to present-day Iran, to Dagin, in what is now Rome. But these two trips did not result in a military alliance against the *xiongnu*.

The kingdom of Wusun was viewed as pivotal for protecting the Silk Route and bolstering the prosperity of the Han Chinese. Located in what is now northwestern Xinjiang and Kazakhstan, Wusun had its capital in Chigu (now called Yishitike). Its people were nomads led by their chief, Dakunmo, who was recognized by the Han Chinese as the king of Wusun. Threatened previously by the fierce *xiongnu*, the Wusun nomads recognized the advantage of a military alliance with the Han during the second visit of special envoy Zhang Qian. Presents including a dozen prize horses were dispatched from Wusun to accompany Zhang Qian home as a sign of good faith to Wudi that the Wusun sought an alliance against the *xiongnu*.

The Wusun representatives also asked for the hand in marriage of a Han princess to seal the pact of friendship. The Emperor Wudi agreed, and the two sides began to exchange betrothal gifts in 110 B.C. Liu Xijun, a granddaughter of the Emperor Wudi with the title of princess, after a careful search was finally chosen as the bride for Lie Jiaomi, who now ruled Wusun. Liu Xijun assumed her political mission, traveling with an escort to Wusun for her marriage accompanied by several hundred servants laden with an enormous dowry of clothes, carts, and gifts. When the *xiongnu* heard of this marriage, they also dispatched a young woman to Wusun. Not wishing to offend them, Lie Jiaomi also married this *xiongnu* woman, naming her as his "left-hand" lady, while Liu Xijun became his "right-hand" lady. Princess Xijun was not accustomed to living in a yurt or eating raw meat and cheese, so she built a palace of her own in Chinese architectural style and imported furnishings. Usually she lived here with her retinue, meeting her husband on special occasions such as festivals. Thus passed their life together, as he enjoyed annual nomadic migrations with the tribal herds, and she maintained the household awaiting his return. Through her marriage, Xijun did a great deal to enhance diplomatic relations between the two countries. Her efforts also spread the culture of Han China through the stimulation of trade and the maintenance of peaceful borders. However, Xijun was occasionally lonely for her own surroundings and wrote poems expressing her nostalgia for Han China, such as this one, which appears in "The Story of the Western Regions," in *The History of the Han Dynasty:*

> *I was forced to marry Wusun*
> *Who lives in a land far away from Han,*
> *Sheltered in the yurt, eating raw meat and cold cheese,*
> *I suffered from homesickness and sadness,*
> *If only I could fly like a swan,*
> *Back to my homeland.*

This expression of her sense of isolation from her homeland and family was conveyed to the Emperor Wudi, who every year sent her additional necessities—mosquito netting, brocade, elegant clothes, and personal items.

Her husband, Lie Jiaomi, was considerably older than she was; he wanted to marry her to his grandson so that she would be protected after his death. She felt this was unethical and appealed to the Han Emperor Wudi to intervene. The emperor, however, asked that she follow Wusun customs in order to maintain friendly relations. Thus Liu Xijun was married to Jun Xumi, the king's grandson, and they had a daughter named Shaofu. She shared the life of the new king for many years before her death in 87 B.C.; the mission of friendship through diplomacy she had begun between the Han and Wusun peoples would be carried on by Princess Jie You (see Jie You). Xijun's contributions to cultural exchange and understanding have often been retold in Chinese history, plays, and songs and speak of the efforts of the Han Chinese to use skillful diplomacy and intercultural marriage to achieve peace.

Yang Fanzhong and Barbara Bennett Peterson
Cao Jun, trans.

Sources

Ban Zhao, *History of the Han Dynasty*. Central Chinese Publishing House, 1962; repr. Beijing: China Publishing House, 1988. "Story of the Western Regions," vol. 96; "Story of Zhang Qian," vol. 61; "Records of the Historians," vol. 110; "Biographies of Xiongnu," vol. 14.

Jie You (ca. 121–49 B.C.) was a princess during the reign of Emperor Wudi (141–87 B.C.) of the Western (Former) Han dynasty, who helped establish good relations between the Western Han and the minorities living northwest of the Great Wall, now in Central Asia. Through her marriage to Jun Xumi, king of Wusun, Princess Jie You was able to neutralize or "cut off the right arm" of the *xiongnu* tribes that threatened Chang'an and to establish friendly relations between them and the Wusun kingdom in the region of present-day Xinjiang. She, like her lady-in-waiting Feng Liao (see Feng Liao) did much to lengthen the life of the Han dynasty through her marriage and diplomacy between the Han court and the nomadic peoples south of the Tianshan mountains. The *xiongnu* kingdoms, which threatened the Han dynasty from the north, extended beyond the Great Wall north to Lake Baikal, east to the Liao river, and west to Congling. This enormous region was largely an open grassland through which the nomadic *xiongnu* tribes migrated with their animals. The *xiongnu* often conducted terrorizing raids across the wall, captured Chinese inhabitants, pillaged their properties, and sought food, captives, and supplies. Seeking a means of defeating the *xiongnu,* Wudi sent an envoy, Zhang Qian, westward into Central Asia to make contact with the Wusun kingdom at the western extremity of the *xiongnu.* He hoped a treaty of alliance might be made with the Wusun leaders so that, working together, the Wusun kingdom and the Han empire could attack the *xiongnu* from two sides in a pincer movement. By this alliance, Wudi planned to neutralize or subdue the barbarians. His stated policies were to "pacify the minority nationalities nearby externally, and proceed with large-scale economic construction at home."

After the completion of envoy Zhang Qian's second trip, an alliance was formed with the Wusun kingdom located near Lake Balchao, in the region of the Yili river. The nomadic Wusun kingdom comprised 12,000 families totaling 630,000 inhabitants and had flourishing animal husbandry. The kingdom's leaders could put 180,000 mounted horsemen into the combat field, and the kingdom was probably the only one of Central Asia strong enough to challenge the *xiongnu* in conjunction with the Han Chinese to the south. In strength, the kingdom of Wusun alone roughly balanced the forces of the barbarians, but the *xiongnu* cleverly kept the individual western kingdoms divided and off-balance through diplomacy and raids. Now combined, Wusun and the Han were a formidable match for the marauding *xiongnu.* Representatives from Wusun had accompanied Zhang Qian back to Chang'an, bringing dozens of horses as symbolic gifts to pledge their faith in the new military alliance, concluded before 115 B.C. The *xiongnu,* upon hearing of this alliance, announced an immediate attack on the Wusun kingdom to crush the Wusun-Han pact. The king of Wusun, feeling the need to reinforce the alliance agreement, sent emissaries to the Han court laden with additional gifts and horses and asked for protection and marriage to a Han princess to consummate the alliance.

Wudi decided to affirm his friendly intentions, and in 105 B.C., he gave Liu Xijun (see Liu Xijun), the daughter of Liu Jian, in marriage to the king of Wusun, Lie Jiaomi. As custom dictated, the weak and elderly Lie Jiaomi gave Xijun in marriage also to his grandson, Jun Xumi, the heir to the throne. Xijun had one daughter by Jun Xumi. When Xijun died in 87 B.C., the beautiful and bright princess Jie You was sent by Wu Di to marry the widowed Jun Xumi, bringing treasures and silks, a large marriage portion, and bodyguards. Since she was some-what younger than her husband, it was expected that she would outlive him. Hence, Jie You would marry her husband's younger brother and heir, Weng Guimi; this union yielded three sons and two daughters. Yuan Guimi, the eldest of their sons, would later inherit the Wusun throne. Thus, through her marriage alliance, Princess Jie You effectively counterbalanced the *xiongnu,* keeping them pacified and Wusun friendly to Han China.

In the year 75 B.C., the joint forces of Wusun and the Western Han, totaling 200,000 troops, assailed the *xiongnu* from both east and west in a successful two-pronged attack. The *xiongnu* were severely weakened, and their influence greatly reduced, especially in the region of East-Central Asia. Subsequently, the *xiongnu* peoples would be split in two: one part ventured west-ward, pushing the other tribes before them—a mixture that would later yield the Huns in Western Europe; the other part moved south of the Great Wall and intermingled with the Han Chinese.

When Princess Jie You's second husband died, she again mar-ried the heir to the throne, as custom dictated—this time her stepson Nimi, who was the son of Jun Xumi and his *xiongnu* wife. Throughout her marriages, Jie You had positioned herself and remained the superior wife, and hence ruled as queen to ensure peace.

To her credit, Princess Jie You, who became queen-consort to three Wusun kings, used her cultivated skills of diplomacy to maneuver her own sons and daughters into greater positions of power than the *xiongnu* wife of each of her respective mates. This skill alone secured her a place in history. The art of diplomacy was raised to a high level by Jie You, who triumphed over multiple wives, foreign living conditions, three subsequent husbands, and the social distance from the civilized court of Han China to preserve diplomatic peace and friendship.

Jie You and her third husband, Nimi, however, fell out with each other near the end of his life, and she conspired to have him assassinated at a banquet. Nimi was only wounded in this attempt on his life, and subsequently his son, Xi Shenshou (by another wife), tried to avenge him after surrounding Jie You in a city and threatening to take it by storm. The pressure on the city was relieved when Jie You was assisted by a military official from the Han dynasty, who, with her son, defeated Xi Shenshou. Nimi was later killed in a rebellion led by Jioutu, the son of Weng Guimi and his *xiongnu* wife. Jioutu temporarily became king of Wusun after Nimi's death. This news caused a great stir in the court at Chang'an. The new rebel king was viewed as a potential threat because he was the child of the *xiongnu* wife; this was seen as a means for the *xiongnu* to control the Wusun kingdom. Hence, once more the diplomacy of a woman came into play as Feng Liao, a lady-in-waiting to Princess Jie You, was called upon to mediate the situation. Fifteen thousand Han troops were sent to the border and placed on alert, in case her negotiations with Jioutu failed. Feng Liao had been married to a high ranking Wusun general who was a close friend of the rebel king. She soon convinced the rebellious Jioutu that it was in his best interests to relinquish the throne to the rightful heir, Yuan Guimi. Jioutu, cognizant of the Han forces on alert, decided to acquiesce in Feng Liao's request and abdicated in favor of Yuan Guimi, who became king. Jioutu was named a subordinate king. Feng Liao presented both of them with seals of Han officials. The Han military forces, knowing the threat to their influence in the Wusun region was over, then withdrew.

Throughout her life, Jie You maintained contact with the court at Chang'an, as most of her children were educated there. Her eldest daughter, Dishi, studied Han literature, culture, and music in the capital for three years. Later, she became the Empress Guizi, of the kingdom of Guizi, an ally of Wusun and the Western Han. Jie You's younger daughter married Ruohu Linhou, a nobleman in Wusun, and this alliance further strengthened Jie

You's and Han influence with the minority population of Wusun. Her second son, Wan Nian, was also educated in Chang'an; he was beloved by the king of Shache, another king friendly toward one of the western tribes, who adopted him and later made him the king of Shache, thus strengthening his mother's grip on the western minorities even more, as Shache became allied with Wusun.

Thus the art of alliance making and diplomacy was carried to an extraordinary level by both Jie You and her lady-in-waiting, Feng Liao. They cultivated relations with minorities on the fringe of China that would become loyal to the Han, thus enlarging and amplifying Chinese influence and culture. In 51 B.C. Jie You sent a letter to Emperor Xuan Liuxun asking return home to Chang'an, and the emperor consented. Her children accompanied her to the capital, where she was given a beautiful home surrounded by farmland. She died two years later.

Princess Jie You made a significant contribution to the development of western China. Despite hardship and danger, she helped foster friendly relations between Han Chinese and the minority nationalities in the northwestern regions of China.

Barbara Bennett Peterson and Yang Zhong
Wang Defang, trans.
Fang Hong, trans.

Sources

Ban Zhao, *History of the Han Dynasty*. Central Chinese Publishing House, 1962; repr. Beijing: China Publishing House, 1988, vols. 8, 14, 61, 94, 96. Li Hu, "The Gemini in the History of Good Relations Between Western Han and the Minorities," *Famous Women of Ancient Times and Today*, ed. *Chinese Woman Magazine*, Beijing: Hebei People's Publishing House, 1986; Xin Tianshou, "China's First Woman Diplomat," in *Women of China*, March, 1981, 16–17; for background of the Han dynasty consult Edwin O. Reischauer and John K. Fairbank, *East Asia, the Great Tradition*. Boston, Houghton-Mifflin, 1960, 1984; *Famous Women in Chinese History*. Shanghai: People's Press, 1988.

Feng Liao (ca. 110–50 B.C.), a diplomat and ambassador for Han China, was a close friend and lady-in-waiting to Princess

Jie You, who had married the king of Wusun, in present-day Xinjiang, in 87 B.C. in order to improve relations with the minority tribes of Central Asia. Feng Liao had accompanied Princess Jie You on her bridal journey from Chang'an, traveling northward to Wusun. Acting as a diplomatic envoy, Feng Liao stayed for fifty years in Wusun, promoting unity and friendship between the Han Chinese and the minority peoples living south of the Tianshan mountains.

Feng Liao was well educated and understood the history and customs of the people in the Wusun region. She was also astute about political affairs in Chang'an and displayed great skill in diplomacy and negotiation as the princess's envoy. She toured the areas south of the Tianshan mountains bearing gifts and made peaceful overtures to these states. She was admiringly called Madam Feng. This entire western region was under the influence of the *xiongnu,* and many tribal chieftains dared not antagonize them. Feng Liao was courageous as she tried to influence Han culture and communicate with these people to win their loyalty and friendship.

Her diplomacy was in marked contrast to *xiongnu* tactics: She brought tasteful gifts offering peace, while the barbarians often offered brutal domination and plunder. Wusun itself was divided between those who supported contact with Han China and those who advocated support for the *xiongnu.* Feng Liao and Princess Jie You (see Princess Jie You) maneuvered to protect Han interests. Feng Liao had married a Wusun general who was a close friend of the rebel king Jioutu. Wu had attempted to seize the throne from Princess Jie You's son, Yuan Guimi his half brother, as Jioutu was the son of Weng Guimi by his *xiongnu* wife. The Han court saw the rebel king as a threat and hoped to install Yuan Guimi as Wusun king. Feng Liao was given the task by the Han court of persuading Jioutu to step down. With her husband's influence, as well as the threat of military force stationed on the border sent by Han Emperor Xuandi and her own powers of reason and acumen, she convieced the rebel to withdraw his claim to the throne and Yuan Guimi was elevated. A bargain had been struck, which allowed the rebel king to hold a subordinate king's or duke's title while the real power was in Yuan Guimi's hands. Thus Feng Liao acted as a go-between for the Han court when the trouble in the Wusun kingdom started over the line of succession. After this episode, the descendants of Jie You who were part Han Chinese always ruled in Wusun, thus circumventing the power of the *xiongnu*. In this way, through intermarriage and diplomacy, the Western Han court had been able to "cut off the right arm of the *xiongnu*," or remove the threat from northern barbarians who had terrorized Han interests and protected the safe passage of caravans on the Silk Route to maintain Han prosperity. When Yuan Guimi died, his son Xinmi became king of Wusun. Because of his youth he relied on Feng Liao for advice. Feng Liao had returned briefly to Chang'an after Yuan Guimi became king, but when Xinmi came to power she asked the Han court to permit her to return to Wusun to assist the young leader in her adopted land. Arriving as an ambassador, she worked with the new king to promote good relations among tribes of West-Central Asia and the Western Han. Because she had lived with them for most of her life, she spoke the language of the northern tribes and was able to help maintain the political balance in favor of the Han dynasty in the region.

A later poem commemorated her accomplishments as an ambassador for the Western Han court during the time of Emperors Wudi and Xuandi:

> *A warm send-off for the royal caravan*
> *moving westward through the pass.*
> *Resourceful and talented,*
> *   the woman envoy*
> *Studied history and emulates*
> *Ambassador Su Wu.*
> *Her sage, heroic deeds will be famous*
> *down through the ages.*

Feng Liao was likened to Su Wu, a Han envoy sent to the western region of Central Asia in about 100 B.C., who was captured by the *xiongnu* and held by force for nineteen years. He remained faithful to his mission and was allowed to return to Chang'an following a reconciliation between the Han and the *xiongnu* around 81 B.C. Feng Liao and Princess Jie You willingly married into the Wusun nomadic tribe and adopted their way of life, gaining respect for their diplomatic efforts to promote the interests of their beloved Han China.

Barbara Bennett Peterson

Sources

Li Hu, "The Gemini in the History of Good Relations Between Western Han and the Minorities," in *Famous Women of Ancient Times and Today*, (translated from Chinese by Fang Hong), ed. *Chinese Woman Magazine*. Beijing: Hebei People's Publishing House, 1986; Xin Tianshou, "China's First Woman Diplomat," in *Women of China*, March, 1981, pp. 16–17; "Feng Liao," in *The Famous Women in Chinese History*. Shanghai: People's Press, 1988.

Wang Wengxu (ca. 110–91 B.C.), an imperial court dancer, became the wife of Emperor Wudi's grandson, Shi, during the Western (Former) Han dynasty and the mother of Liu Xun, Emperor Xuandi. She was born in Guangwang county, Zhao prefecture (modern-day Wangdou county, Hebei province). Her mother, Wang Ren, came from a long line of farmers; at fourteen she married Wang Gende, her fellow villager. Several years later, he died of disease and her mother was remarried, to Wang Naishi; Wengxu was their daughter. Wengxu's parents had two sons, but their ages are unknown.

Wengxu's family was poor and had difficulty making a living. Despite these hardships, she grew to be beautiful and bright, and when she reached the age of eight or nine, her parents entrusted her to Liu Zhongqiu, a distant imperial kinsman, who adopted her. Liu Zhongqiu proved to be farsighted and calculating. He knew that Wengxu, young as she was, would develop into a lovely woman with appropriate training. Believing she might be beneficial to him, he sent her to dance school, hoping she could be trained to become a court favorite. Wengxu enjoyed dancing and worked very hard to make rapid progress. By her early teens, she had become highly skilled in both dancing and singing.

Liu Zhongqiu, whose noble family had suffered political and

economic decline, saw an opportunity to sell Wengxu as a rare and valuable commodity. Jia Chang'er, a businessman in Handan, sought dancers for the imperial court. Liu Zhongqiu planned to sell Wengxu and five other young women to him at a handsome profit. When Wengxu became aware of these plans, she ran away to her parents and told them of his dishonorable intentions. Her parents were shocked and hid Wengxu in her grandmother's home. Liu Zhongqiu, determined not to let his profits vanish, came after his adopted ward, threatening her parents if they continued to harbor her. Liu Zhongqiu was confronted by Wengxu's mother, who asked: "Since my child went to your family, we've never accepted any pay for services she performed for you. Why do you now want to sell my daughter?" "It is not true," lied Liu Zhongqiu. Several days after taking Wengxu back, Liu Zhongqiu sold her to Jia Chang'er. The carriage that was carrying her to the palace passed by the home of her parents and she cried out, "I have been sold to Jia Chang'er. Now I am going to Liusu." Upon hearing this, her parents followed her to Liusu, where, reunited, they cried in each other's arms. Her mother begged Jia Chang'er for mercy, but Wengxu said it was unnecessary. "It is useless to ask for mercy," she continued, "I will live on wherever I go."

Her parents were heartbroken, and determined to buy her back. They followed her to Lunu, Zhongshan (modern-day Ding county, Hebei province), where her father stayed with her, while her mother attempted to borrow money to redeem her freedom. But once more, Wengxu was placed in transit bound for Handan. Her parents could no longer follow and they lost contact with her.

Wengxu and the five other young women arrived in Handan, the capital of the Zhao state during the Han dynasty. By chance, the household manager for Prince Houming, a son of Emperor Wudi, was in Handan to select dancing girls for the court at Chang'an. Through an introduction arranged by Jia Chang'er, Wengxu and the five other dancers met Houming. He was impressed by Wengxu's gracious behavior and talent and paid a high price for the group of dancers. Wengxu entered Houming's palace around 96 B.C., when the Emperor Wudi was nearly seventy. After Wang Wengxu entered the palace of the crown prince, she became a regular actress and dancer in the imperial court. Because of her beauty and outstanding dancing skill, she attracted the attentions of Liujin, the son of Prince Liuju, Houming's brother. An elegant young man of seventeen or eighteen whose mother was a concubine surnamed Shi, Liujin fell in love with her. Soon they were betrothed and then married.

In 91 B.C. Wengxu gave birth to a son, Liuxun. Just as everything in her life seemed perfect, it was rumored that someone had secretly cursed Emperor Wudi using witchcraft and attempted to kill him. The emperor, who was growing superstitious in his old age, ordered an inquiry. Jiang Chang, a minister at court, held grievances against Liuju and implicated him unjustly in the incident. The minister, under the pretense of enforcing the law to safeguard the emperor, had Prime Minister Gongsun and his son killed, and then exterminated Liuju's sisters, Zhuyi and Yangshi. Gaining in confidence from these deeds, Jiang Chang now charged Liuju directly with high crimes against the state. Liuju was forced to battle in the city of Chang'an against the new prime minister, Liu Qumao, a pawn of Jiang Chang. Upon hearing this news, Emperor Wudi, living in a temporary palace outside the city, sent troops to suppress the fighting. The forces of Liuju were defeated, and he and Liujin were arrested and put to death. Subsequently, all members of Liuju's family were put to death, including Wengxu, who was not yet twenty. She, her husband, and their imperial relatives were buried in Guangming Garden.

Only Wengxu's son Liuxun, not yet a year old, survived. Thereafter he lived in the countryside with his great-grandmother, Zhen Jun, the mother of the concubine Shi. Eighteen years later, Emperor Zhaodi, son of former Emperor Wudi, passed away, leaving no heirs. Liuxun was proclaimed Emperor Xuandi. Although his mother Wengxu's life was short, she had risen by her talents and hard work as a dancer to marry Emperor Wudi's grandson and to bear a future emperor of the Han dynasty.

Yang Fanzhong
Cao Jun, trans.

Sources

Ban Zhao, *History of the Han Dynasty*. Central Chinese Publishing House, 1962; repr. Beijing: China Publishing House, 1988, vols. 6, 7, 63; Sima Qian, *Records of the Historian*, vol. 49.

Wang Zhengjun (ca. 71 B.C.–13 A.D.), a politician at court, was the wife of Emperor Yuandi (r. 48–33 B.C.) in the Western (Former) Han dynasty and aunt of Wang Mang, who from 8 to 23 A.D. usurped the throne and proclaimed himself emperor. She was also known as Empress Xiaoyuan or Empress Yuan. Wang Zhengjun was of noble lineage: Her grandfather Wang He was an imperial envoy under Emperor Wudi (r. 141–87 B.C.) and her father, Wang Jin, who had studied law, was a judge. Her mother was from the Li family of Wei county, but was deserted by Wang Jin, who married several times, begetting eight sons and four daughters. The second eldest child, Wang Zhengjun had two siblings born of the same mother: Wang Feng and Wang Chong. Zhengjun was born in Dongpinlin to the east of modern-day Jinan, Shandong province, and later moved to Weisuili, Wei county, Hebei province.

Wang Zhengjun had a formal education specializing in history and music. She was brought to the palace by Emperor Xuandi in about 57 B.C. and was later granted the title of princess. The concubine of Liu Shi, the crown prince, Wang Zhengjun in 51 B.C. gave birth to a son whom the emperor named Liu'ao. The name Ao (galloping steed) reflected the emperor's ambition for his grandson to carry and expand the Han empire. In 49 B.C. Emperor Xuandi died and the crown prince ascended the throne as Emperor Yuandi. As the mother of the heir to the throne, Wang Zhengjun became Empress Xiaoyuan. Because of her stature, Wang Jin and Zhengjun's uncle, Wang Hong, were given high-ranking positions at court; after her father's death in 42 B.C., her brother Wang Feng succeeded him as a marquis, with responsibility for ensuring the security of the palace. Wang Feng was later appointed grand general, the highest official post in charge of military and civilian administration in the entire Han empire.

In 33 B.C. Zhengjun's son, Liu'ao, ascended the throne as the

Emperor Chendi, and Zhengjun became the empress dowager. She now began to direct the affairs of state as the powerful and political mother of the reigning emperor. Further entrenching her power, Zhengjun secured positions for her younger brother, Wang Chong, who was made the marquis of Achen, and her stepbrother Wang Tang received a lesser title but also received large grants of land. Eventually all of her surviving brothers— Wang Tan, Wang Shang, Wang Li, Wang Geng, and Wang Fengshi—were granted vast territories as vassals of the emperor; they came to be known as the "Five Vassals." The children of these vassals also gained power through their posts as ministers and advisers to the emperor. Every significant office of the state administration was filled by the empress dowager with her Wang relatives. Although these members of the Wang family were elevated to high stations, none of them became as distinguished as the empress dowager herself. The emperor remained a figurehead with no functional powers to make decisions; he allowed Wang Feng to make all important decisions with the empress dowager's approval. Wang Feng was intimidating and corrupt, but the emperor was too weak and incompetent to challenge his authority, or his mother's, and he acquiesced in the condemnation of more honest officials when they criticized court politics. Fear dominated the court.

The Wangs now controlled the Li family, which had established the Han dynasty (see Lu Zhi). They extorted money and grain from the peasants, accepted bribes, lived in luxury surrounded by concubines and maids, and led lives of gradual dissipation in their stately villas, hillside pavilions, and lovely gardens, which all required scarce resources such as water from the local people. When the tyrannical Wang Feng died, the dowager empress gave his position to his cousin Wang Ying. One of the empress dowager's brothers, Wang Man, had died before the emperor had made her other brothers vassals. The empress dowager wanted to assist Wang Man's son, named Wang Mang, as he felt that he too should be as titled and propertied as his cousins. At her urging, the emperor posthumously granted Wang Man the title of vassal, and this title now passed to Wang Mang, as vassal of Xindu. Wang Mang's sister, Chun Yuchang, was also granted titles and properties in Dinling. Wang Mang's fortunes eventually elevated him to the powerful post of grand general, after the death of the empress dowager's brothers who had previously held the position. Nevertheless, as the empress dowager's nephew, Wang Mang studiously secured her approval for all decisions in military and civilian government. Wang Mang, however, was much more ambitious than his uncles who had held the post before him; he cultivated the empress dowager, while eliminating his rivals for power.

In 7 B.C. Dowager Empress Xiaoyuan's son, the childless emperor, died, and Liu Xin, the son of the emperor's brother, was selected to ascend to the throne as Emperor Aidi (r. 7–1 B.C.). Wang Zhengjun knew that her power was now challenged by the collateral relatives of the new emperor; hence she enlisted support from Wang Mang. To heighten his appeal at court, she had her trusted aides praise the virtues of Wang Mang, seeking to stem the influence of her potential rivals, the new emperor's mother and grandmother. Behind the scenes, the supporters of Emperor Aidi withdrew the titles and lands from the Wang family's relatives, entrusting these confiscated lands to their own supporters, and removed all Wangs from courtly prominence. In 2 B.C. there was a solar eclipse, which Wang Zhengjun sought to have interpreted as a sign from heaven that the Wangs should not have been removed from power. In these superstitious times, Emperor Aidi was greatly moved by the eclipse and restored Wang Mang as well as Wang Zhengjun to positions of influence. The empress dowager had effectively countered the first challenge to her influence.

In 1 B.C. Emperor Aidi died, leaving no heirs, which gave the Wang family a further opportunity to regain their power over military and civilian affairs. Now age seventy, Grand Empress Dowager Wang Zhengjun refused to step down from the political stage and again appointed Wang Mang as grand general and installed Liu Xian, the nine-year-old prince of Zhongshan, as Emperor Pingdi (r. 1 B.C.–6 A.D.). Acting as regent, Wang Zhengjun openly seized power, consolidating all control in her own hands. Wang Mang, as his aunt's grand general, had risen to power during a time when state revenues had declined because most peasants lived on the estates of large landowners who were untaxed, while the remaining peasants, who were taxed, had to undertake a heavier burden. The population had grown, so every peasant regardless of residence had less land to cultivate. Some twenty years earlier, there had been revolts among the slave laborers of the government's iron works. This prefigured a period of economic collapse, and Wang Mang viewed himself as a leader in the virtuous Confucian model to re-establish the old values and Han power.

Wang Mang planned to take over the throne by monopolizing power, building a cadre of supporters, and eliminating dissidents. He cleverly bribed the supporters of Wang Zhengjun to praise him before her and arranged excursions for her to the countryside. For these efforts he was rewarded with greater latitude in determining court affairs and given the title of *an Han gong* (great man stabilizing the Han). In 4 A.D. Wang Mang's son was appointed prime minister and his daughter was named as empress. In 5 A.D. Emperor Pingdi turned fourteen, and would soon reach the age at which he could determine policies in his own name; hence, the following year Wang Mang poisoned him to death and installed Liu Ying, the two-year-old great-great-grandson of Emperor Xuandi, and the great-grandson of Wang Zhengjun, on the throne. Wang Mang openly usurped the throne in 8 A.D. and endeavored to wrest all remaining power from his aunt. Wang Zhengjun disapproved of her nephew's seizure, but it was too late. Wang Mang changed the name of the Han dynasty to the Xin dynasty and regained control of the imperial seal from Wang Zhengjun, who now lost her title.

Beginning his program of economic reform, he made agricultural loans available to the peasants, debased the currency, and in 9 A.D. ended the private ownership of large estates, nationalizing all land with the intention of redistributing it to taxpaying peasants and abolishing privately held slaves. He would soon lose support of the noble families who had brought the original Han emperor, Gaozu, to power. Thereupon followed the revolt of the Red Eyebrows, and then an invasion of northern barbarians. Wang Mang died in the capital at the hands of rebels in 23 A.D..

In the fifth year of Wang Mang's rule, in 13 A.D., Wang Zhengjun died at the age of eighty-four. For nearly fifty years, she ruled Han China; after 25 A.D., her descendant Lui Xiu would restore the Han throne and revive the Han name as the Eastern (Later) Han dynasty.

Yang Fanzhong and Barbara Bennett Peterson
Chen Gengduo, trans.

Sources

Ban Zhao, *History of the Han Dynasty*. Central Chinese Publishing House, 1962; repr. Beijing: China Publishing House, 1988, vol. 9, "Stories of Emperor Yuan Di"; vol. 10, "Stories of Emperor Chen Di"; vol. 11, "Stories of Emperor Ai Di"; vol. l2, "Stories of Emperor Ping Di"; vol. 97, "Stories of the Relatives"; vol. 98, "Stories of Empress Yuan"; vol. 99, "Stories of Wang Mang."

Ban Jieyu (ca. 48–6 B.C.) was a poet during the Western (Former) Han dynasty. Ban was her surname, and Jieyu was a title for ladies-in-waiting. Her real first name is unknown. She was born in Loufan (modern-day Su county, Shanxi province), and her father, Ban Kuang, was an officer in the imperial army. Ban Jieyu's nephew, Ban Biao, became a noted historian who began the *Han shu* (History of the Han Dynasty). This famous book would later be supplemented by Ban Biao's son, Ban Gu, and it was completed by his daughter, Ban Zhao (see Ban Zhao).

Ban Jieyu was gifted and well read. In 33 B.C., she was chosen by the emperor's court to work as a librarian in the palace. The Emperor Chengdi loved her fervently and gave her the title Jieyu. She gave birth to a son, who unfortunately lived for only a few months. Ban Jieyu was well liked by the empress dowager for her modesty, her adherence to feudal traditions and Confucian ethics, and her suggestions of frugality made to the emperor. In time, the emperor's attentions and affections turned to younger women at court, and she would lose her position through palace intrigue.

Ban Jieyu was vilified, as was Empress Xu, by the two newly arrived and beautiful Zhao sisters (see Zhao Feiyan) who lied to the emperor, saying Jieyu and the empress had cursed the emperor in secret through witchcraft. Empress Xu was deposed because of this slander, but Ban Jieyu stood up to the emperor, proclaimed her innocence and loyalty, and was not punished. She knew that the two childless Zhao sisters were jealous of her because she had previously borne a child. Hence, she petitioned the emperor to be moved to the Changxin palace, to wait upon the empress dowager. Here she lived a secluded and reflective life, enjoying her spare moments devoted to writing poetry. Many of her poems express her sorrows of unrequited love. Her one surviving poem "The Autumn Fan," won her an everlasting place in Chinese literature; it was translated into English in various ways:

O fair white silk, fresh from the weaver's loom,
Clear as the frost, bright as the winter snow—
See! Friendship fashions out of thee a fan,
Round as the round moon shines in heaven above;
At home, abroad, a close companion thou,
Stirring at every move the grateful gale;
And yet I fear, ah me, that autumn chills,
Cooling the dying summer's torrid rage,
Will see thee laid neglected on the shelf,
All thought of bygone days, like them bygone.

Of fresh new silk all snowy white,
And round as harvest moon;
A pledge of purity and love,
A small but welcome boon.
While summer lasts, borne in the hand,
Or folded on the breast;
'Twill gently soothe thy burning brow.
And charm thee to thy rest.
But ah, when autumn frosts descend,
And winter winds blow cold,
No longer sought, no longer loved,
'Twill lie in dust and mould.
This silken fan then deign accept,
Sad emblem of my lot;
Caressed and fondled for an hour,

Glazed silk, newly cut, smooth, glittering, white,
As white, as clear, even as frost and snow.
Perfectly fashioned into a fan,

> *Round, round like the brilliant moon,*
> *Treasured in my lord's sleeve, taken out, put in—*
> *Wave it, shake it, and a little wind flies from it.*
> *How often I fear the autumn season's coming*
> *And the fierce, cold wind which scatters the blazing heat,*
> *Discarded, passed by, laid in a box alone;*
> *Such a little time, and the thing of love cast off.*

In Chinese classics, autumn was a metaphor for middle age, and an autumn fan was an emblem of a forsaken sweetheart. Ban Jieyu wrote metaphorically of her own love for the emperor being cast off, as he became infatuated with younger women later in life, such as the Zhao sisters. Ban Jieyu was like ''The Autumn Fan,'' once treasured and loved, her virgin purity taken away, only later to be cast away and replaced by other favorites at court. She was one of the few well-educated concubines able to leave a literary legacy.

Zhao Xiaoming
Xu Kaichang, trans.

Sources

Ban Gu and Ban Zhao, *History of the Han Dynasty*. Central Chinese Publishing House, 1962; repr. Beijing: China Publishing House, 1988. Li Zhi, *The Life of Han Cheng Di,The Life of Ban Jie Yu, The Life of Zhao Fei-yian* (in Chinese); all published in Beijing: China Publishing House, 1988.

Huan Shaojun (ca. 35 B.C.–30 A.D.), a moralist and mother model during the turbulent period between the Western and Eastern Han dynasties, was born in Bohai prefecture (now Cangzhou, Hebei province). According to available records, her father was a Confucian scholar with substantial property who established a school in his home. The school gained a wide reputation, attracting outstanding students, including Bao Xuan from a poor family in Gaocheng (modern-day Yanshan county, Hebei province). Displaying diligence and ambition, Bao Xuan studied very hard and was recognized as an outstanding scholar of remarkable integrity and ability. Huan Shaojun's father betrothed her to this outstanding pupil.

As his family was poor, Bao Xuan had no money to marry, but Shaojun's parents gave her a sumptuous dowry so that the couple could live well. Bao Xuan felt embarrassed by this gift, saying to his wife, "You are from a rich family and have lived a luxurious life. It is quite natural for you to accept this large dowry. But, as you know, I am a poor man with low status. How can I accept your parents' gift?" Shaojun realized her husband's desire not to rely upon her parents, replying, "My parents married me to you only because they appreciate your fine qualities and competence. Now that I am your wife, I will respect your views." Bao Xuan rejoiced at his wife's decision to return the gift of several servants and the dowry to her family. Shaojun took to wearing coarse clothing and pushed a cart with her husband back to his native region.

Upon reaching Bao Xuan's hometown, she gave up her aristocratic habit of not performing domestic chores. She was never haughty and displayed modesty in his parents' home and in the homes of his siblings. Her virtue as an excellent wife spread afar, as Bao Xuan concentrated on his Confucian studies and learned how to administer. Upon completing his studies, he became an official in his village, was soon promoted to a post as a county official, then was elevated to become an army commander, and later became a magistrate of his prefecture. An honest and upright official, he was concerned about the plight of the poor. He promoted the beneficial and eradicated what was harmful, and gained the respect of the community.

In 2 B.C., Bao Xuan attracted the attention of Emperor Aidi (r. 7–1 B.C.), who made him an imperial censor upon the recommendation of He Wu, minister of public works (see Wang Zhengjun). He took up a post as an administrator in the state of Yu for a brief period and returned to court as a minister investigating crimes committed by central government officials. As a minister-censor, Bao Xuan paid great attention to court policy and examined accusations of misadministration, regularly reporting to Emperor Aidi any wrongdoing he uncovered. He pointed out that it was the political corruption of the imperial court, the wantonness of both landlords and bureaucrats, and the tyranny of the officials that caused the starvation and misery of the poor peasants. In saying these things, he exposed the severe crisis in leadership in the later Western Han. His advice to the emperor to reform the official administration, and to put the wise into important positions and dismiss the sycophants, made him famous throughout the court. During his career, he was ably advised by his wife. Under Emperor Aidi's successor, Emperor Pingdi (1 B.C.–6 A.D.), Bao Xuan did not conspire with Wang Mang, who later usurped the throne. Wang Mang feared Bao Xuan and exiled him from the court, but Bao Xuan and his wife refused to be intimidated by threats of force or be seduced by rank or wealth. The sons of Bao Xuan and Huan Shaojun, Bao Yong and Bao Sheng, were raised to emulate the high standards of their parents. Bao Xuan was assassinated by the forces of Wang Mang, and Bao Yong, a well-educated scholar, sought to avenge his father by participating in the Lu Lin army rebellion in 17 A.D. (see Madam Lu). Wang Mang was eventually overthrown, and in 25 A.D. Liu Xiu established the Eastern Han dynasty. Bao Yong was appointed the administrator first over Lu prefecture and then over Yanzhou prefecture.

Huan Shaojun followed her husband's rise and fall from political power, encouraging her sons to administer as their father had and rejoicing when her grandson was named administrator of Gaodu county. She continuously instructed her progeny not to seek luxury and pleasure, but to remain vigilant and disciplined while serving the state. Her grandson once remarked to her, "Grandma, you are old and we are now prominent. Why do you recall the old times when you pushed a small cart with my grandpa?" Shaojun replied that her mother had instructed her "not to forget death when alive, nor danger when safe." The virtues of Bao Xuan and Huan Shaojun became respected moral models, as Confucian scholar Ma Rong's daughter during the Eastern Han stated to her husband, Yuan Kai: "If you follow the fine qualities of Bao Xuan, I will learn from Shaojun," believing that through ethics one could lead a good and productive life.

Yuang Fengzhun
Tan Mingxia, trans.

Sources

Ban Zhao, *History of the Han Dynasty*. Central Chinese Publishing House, 1962; repr. Beijing: China Publishing House, 1988, vol. 72; *History of the Late Han*, vols. 79 and 84; Li Zhi, *Book Collection*, vol. 64.

Zhao Feiyan (32 B.C.–1 A.D.) was a court dancer who became Empress Xiaocheng of the Western (Former) Han dynasty. Originally named Feng Yizhu, she was the child of poor residents of Chang'an who abandoned her shortly after her birth. After she survived three days of exposure, her parents were shamed into taking her back. As a youth, she roamed the streets with her younger sister He De looking for food; they were taken in by Zhao Lin, who raised them as his own daughters. Later Feng Yizhu worked as a servant in the home of Yang Azhu, where she eagerly learned singing and dancing. Because of her slender figure and superior performances, she became known as Feiyan (flying swallow).

In 18 B.C., Emperor Cheng met Zhao Feiyan while on a visit to the Yang home. Taken with her beauty, the emperor brought Feiyan and her sister to the palace and soon appointed her as an imperial concubine. The beauty of the Zhao sisters was remarked upon throughout the court. They were sent to visit the back palace (women's quarters), whose female leader jealously remarked, ''They are bound to bring calamity upon the country.'' The emperor indulged the lovely Zhao sisters, while his wife, Empress Xu, and imperial concubine Ban Jieyu (see Ban Jieyu) fell from favor. Feiyan capitalized on her position as the emperor's favorite.

Various clashes had broken out at court to intensify the deteriorating relationships. Wang Feng, the chief general and Emperor Cheng's uncle, who presided over court affairs, opposed Empress Xu because her sister Xu Ye had used witchcraft to curse Madam Wang, who was pregnant. Having gained the affectionate ear of the emperor, Feiyan Zhao reported the plot to him and also accused Empress Xu and concubine Ban Jieyu in this scandal, saying they had secretly cursed the emperor with witchcraft. Xu Ye was tortured and put to death, Empress Xu was sent away, and her relatives were forced to return to their native Shanyang. Ban Jieyu, when interrogated, convinced the emperor that she was blameless and escaped punishment.

In 16 B.C., Emperor Cheng desired to elevate Feiyan to empress, but Empress Dowager Fu resisted because of Zhao's humble origins. The emperor continued his negotiations with the back palace through Chun Yuchang, the empress dowager's nephew, and eventually prevailed. He issued an imperial edict naming Feiyan's adoptive father marquis of Chengyan, thus elevating her status. The court ministers complained, and Liu Fu, the opposition leader, was thrown into prison for complaining that Feiyan could not become the empress "simply because of her humble birth." Liu Fu was exempted from death only through the intercession of the ministers, who pleaded on his behalf. All challenges now evaporated, and Feiyan was proclaimed empress in June 16 B.C. No sooner had Feiyan been crowned than the emperor's desire for her ebbed and he began showering affection on her sister, He De, to whom he bestowed the resplendent Shaoyan Palace.

During the years when the Zhao sisters were the emperor's favorites, neither gave birth to heirs. To maintain her position, Feiyan committed adultery with numerous courtiers and attendants, hoping to conceive a child. Her sister protected her virtue, telling the emperor to ignore the rumors and slanders on Feiyan's character. Being childless, Feiyan resented the imperial concubines who succeeded in becoming pregnant. She forced many of them into having abortions and killed any living offspring. As a result, Emperor Cheng had no heirs.

In 9 B.C., Liu Xing, King Zhongshan, the youngest brother of Emperor Cheng, and Liu Xin, King Dingtao, his son, came to the imperial palace with Empress Dowager Fu. The dowager empress bribed the Zhao sisters and General Wang Gen to enable Liu Xin to be named heir to the throne. The following year the emperor, finding the Zhao sisters still barren, consented and named Liu Xin his crown prince. In 7 B.C., Emperor Cheng suddenly died, even though he had never been seriously ill. The day before his death, he had held several large going-away parties for kings of his realm, Yan, King Chu'en, and Li, King Liang, and had sworn in General Kong Guang as prime minister.

The death of the emperor aroused great suspicion, and investigations were held. Shortly thereafter, when Liu Xin ascended the throne as Emperor Aidi, Empress Dowager Fu became the grand empress dowager and Feiyan became empress dowager. Zhao Qin, Feiyan's younger brother, was named marquis of Xincheng, and his son became marquis of Chengyan.

In 6 B.C., soon after he was crowned, the new emperor received a memorial stating that the Zhao sisters had been responsible for the death of the children of former Empress Xu and other concubines. Feiyan's brother and nephew now lost their royal posts, and their families were sent to Liaoxi as punishment. Emperor Aidi did not look into the Zhao sisters' involvement because he owed his own position to them. This exemption of the Zhao sisters from investigation caused great dissatisfaction at court, especially among Wang Mang and his supporters within the royal clan.

In 1 B.C., Emperor Aidi died, leaving no heirs. He was succeeded by Liu Xian, the prince of Zhongshan, now Emperor Pingdi, who ascended the throne at age nine and would remain in office until 6 A.D. The grand empress dowager acted as his regent; however, gradually power fell into the hands of Wang Mang, who slowly removed Feiyan as empress dowager and eventually stripped her of her titles. In shame and humiliation, Feiyan committed suicide.

To maintain her position at court, Zhao Feiyan had become sinister and ruthless; still, her reputation remained as an accomplished dancer during the Han dynasty, and her beauty was praised by later generations. The saying "Huan fei, Yan shou" (plump Huan and slender Yan) exemplifies her continued influence: "Huan" refers to Yang Yuhuan, who was the favorite of Emperor Ming during the Tang dynasty because of her plumpness; "Yan" refers to Zhao Feiyan, who won the favor of Emperor Cheng because of her slenderness. The idiom was originally used to describe the figures of charming Chinese girls. But later it was used figuratively to refer to different yet equally effective literary styles which were either verbose or sparse in language.

Zhao Xiaoming
Hu Yanchu, trans.

Sources

Ban Gu and Ban Zhao, *History of the Han Dynasty*. Central Chinese Publishing House, 1962; repr. Beijing: China Publishing House, 1988, which includes the life stories of Emperor Cheng and Zhao Feiyan; other biographies include Li Zhi, *The Life of Han Cheng Di, The Life of Ban Jie Yu*, and *The Life of Zhao Feiyan* (in Chinese); all published in Beijing: China Publishing House, 1988.

Madam Lu (ca. 20 B.C.–17 A.D.) was an aristocratic leader of a peasant uprising against the usurper Wang Mang, who ruled from 8 to 23 A.D. (see Wang Zhengjun). The first female leader of a peasant uprising in China, she was a native of Langxiehaiqu (now Rizhao in Shandong province) and came from a wealthy family.

The Western (Former) Han had been brought down under tumultuous circumstances when the nephew of Dowager Empress Wang Zhengjun, Wang Mang, seized the throne and attempted to introduce economic and social reforms that proved of little value. To divert attention from his failed domestic policies (subject to historical interpretation), Wang Mang started border wars with various minorities in China. The people were subjected to heavy taxation to support these campaigns, and men were conscripted to serve in the military.

In this atmosphere of social collapse, a number of peasant uprisings took place, the most significant one led by Madam Lu. An earlier rebellion against the failing Western Han dynasty had been launched by Madam Bi in 9 A.D., and another would be waged by Madam Chi Shaoping in 21 A.D.; the one led by Madam Lu in 17 A.D., however, would be the strongest opposition waged against Wang Mang and reflected an attempt to return to the glorious days of the Han dynasty. Madam Lu's son, a low-ranking official, had been executed by the government of Wang Mang for a misdemeanor. This unjust execution aroused public indignation. Madam Lu determined to avenge her son against Wang Mang's arbitrary sentence.

Madam Lu began her plans for vengeance by enlarging her circle of friends, using her family's wealth to set up a winery to employ local peasants. In addition to jobs and wages, she provided the young workers with clothing and other necessities, winning their loyalty. When she had nearly exhausted her financial resources, she asked her workers for their assistance in revolting against the tyranny of Wang Mang. Most of them willingly followed her. On a small island she began training her peasant military force, which numbered over a hundred. They spread the word, attracting many more to join. Madam Lu proclaimed herself the general of her rebellious army, which had grown to several thousand members. Her army recruits called themselves the "Strong Tigers." After four years of preparation, in 17 A.D., Madam Lu led her army of Strong Tigers to Haicheng, the residence of Wang Mang's government official who had ordered the execution of her son. The official was captured, and when other local officials attempted to intercede to save his life, Madam Lu replied resolutely: "My son committed only a minor crime and was not supposed to be executed, but the willful official under Wang Mang had my son killed. It is of no use to plead for his release, as my principle is 'those who kill others must die.'" She executed the official and used his head in a sacrificial offering to her dead son. Her army returned to their island base.

Her soaring prestige earned her respect, and her army dedicated to fighting oppression enlisted others by the thousands. Madam Lu nurtured good relations with the peasants of the countryside by protecting them and demanding strict discipline in her army. Her rebellious spirit echoed in other Chinese women who rebelled against exploitation and oppression. Her "eye for an eye" principle became widely popular and influenced other rebels such as Fan Chong. After Madam Lu's death, many of her soldiers joined other armies with similar goals, such as the armies of Qingdou or Tongma. Madam Lu had the courage to test authority. She clung to her values of honor and law and avenged her son after he had been killed unjustly. Her name would live on in the annals of Chinese history as a woman who spoke out for justice and the restoration of order and virtue.

Zhao Xiaoming
William Cheng, trans.

Sources

Ban Zhao, *History of the Han Dynasty.* Central Chinese Publishing House, 1962; repr. Beijing: China Publishing House, 1988, "Wang Mang Zhuan," vol. 99; Fan Ye, Hou Han shu (History of the Later Han). Beijing: Zhonghua shuju, 1965, "Liu Hezi Zhuan," vol. 11; Zizhitongjian, "Wang Mang," vol. 38; *Cangshu Liu He-zi*, by Li Zhi, vol. 57; *Hanshu xinzheng*, "Wang Mang Zhuan," vol. 69, by Chen Zhi. Tianjin: Renmin chubanshe, 1980; *Qinghan Shi*, by Lu Anmin, vol. 2, published by Shanghai: Guji chubanshe, 1987; *Ganjianyizhilu*, "Wang Mang," vol. 18, by Wu Chengquan. Beijing: Zhonghua Shuju; *Zhonggoushi Gangyao*, by Jian Bozan, published by Renmin Chubanshe, 156–159; *Gujin Zhumin Funu Renwu*, published by Hebei Renmin Chubanshe, 56–59.

Empress Yin (4–64 A.D.), whose given name was Lihua, became the empress of the first Eastern Han emperor, Liu Xiu, known posthumously as Guang Wudi, the shining martial emperor. She was born in Xinyie (now in Henan province) to a wealthy family that controlled more than 7,000 *mu* of farmland. Her father was Yin Mu, and her mother's surname was Deng. Lihua's mother and youngest brother, Yin Xin, were killed in the court battles of 33 B.C. Lihua had several surviving brothers—Yin Shi, Yin Jiu, and Yin Xing, all of whom were later appointed to important positions at court when Lihua was elevated as Empress Yin. Famous for her beauty, Lihua met the future Emperor Liu Xiu when they were both youths in Nanyang county. At that time he was beneath her status and wealth and admired her from afar. Liu Xiu studied in Chang'an, capital of the Western (Former) Han. While a student, he was impressed by the highest officer of the garrison forces and decided that if he became an officer, he would become such an officer, and if he desired to marry, he would marry Yin Lihua. Liu Xiu had loved Lihua long before he founded his kingdom as emperor of the Eastern Han.

In the fourth year of the usurper Wang Mang's reign (see Wang Zhengjun), the southern regions of the former Han empire were in the throes of starvation. A rebellious force called the Green Forest army, led by Wang Kuang and Wang Feng, broke out in Jingshan, Hebei province, and soon spread northward into Nanyang county, where Lihua lived. In 22 A.D. rebellions broke out all over the Han-controlled countryside and the Green Forest rebels were joined by uprisings in Shandong and Henan provinces. All the distant relatives of the Han dynasty's leadership, including Liu Xiu, now believed that Wang Mang should be overthrown, and the Han dynasty's leadership restored to full power. Liu Xiu joined the Green Forest army, which sought to restore the authority of the Han dynasty; thousands of peasants joined his forces to overthrow Wang Mang. Liu Xiu and his brother Liu Yan became the leaders of Green Forest armies and were joined by the brothers and clansmen of Lihua.

In 23 A.D. the Green Forest army conquered Wang Mang's imperial forces and, after a bitter series of battles, ended Wang Mang's dynasty and proclaimed the return of the Han leadership. Liu Xiu was appointed vice-general, and the rebellious Green Forest armies occupied Nanyang in Henan province. Shortly thereafter he married the nineteen-year-old Lihua, realizing his long-cherished dream. Soon after their marriage, he was dispatched to Luoyang, which he captured and controlled. Now fierce divisions arose within the forces of the rebellious armies that had successfully overthrown Wang Mang. Liu Yan had been killed, and Liu Xiu decided to retreat to Hebei province to regroup. Lihua, for safety, followed her brother Yin Shi and moved to Yunyang, where she lived in the palace of Deng Feng, the leading general of the newly proclaimed Emperor Liu Xuan. By 25 A.D., Liu Xiu had strengthened himself and his remaining troops, successfully dominated Hebei province, and marched to the city of Hao, Hebei province, and proclaimed himself rightful emperor of the Han. He later came to be known as Emperor Guang Wudi of the Eastern Han. Liu Xiu then led his army north and west, capturing Luoyang. He then sent for Yin Lihua, intending to enthrone her as his empress. Lihua joined Liu Xiu in Luoyang, but refused the noblest of positions, recommending the elevation of Guo, whom Liu Xiu had married in Hebei, as empress because she had born him a son and heir. Hence the imperial concubine Guo was named empress. Lihua remained loyal and not jealous. She was still the most beloved by Emperor Guang Wudi and served his best interests out of respect and genuine concern for his political interests.

Lihua followed the emperor on all his journeys, including his military expedition to punish the traitor Pang Chong in 28 A.D. While on this expedition, she gave birth to a son in Yuanshi, Hebei province. Thereafter, their relationship became ever more intimate. In 41 A.D. Empress Guo was dethroned in a court political struggle, and her son stripped of the title of crown prince and heir because of the Emperor's preference for Lihua and their son. Lihua was elevated as empress and their son, Liu Hong, became crown prince.

The courtly style and demeanor of Lihua, now Empress Yin, did not change, as she remained discreet and cautious in managing her administrative duties. Her brother Yin Xing was the emperor's head of imperial security, and he served them both faithfully. Empress Yin never asked for any additional ranks or positions of favor for her relatives, and she carefully nurtured the goodwill of the generals who had assisted her husband in his ascension to power. She was the example of moral integrity and virtue at court.

In 57 A.D., Liu Xiu suddenly died, having led the Eastern (Later) Han dynasty for thirty-three years. Liu Hong ascended the throne (r. 57–75 A.D.), known as the Ming emperor, the enlightened emperor. Lihua became empress dowager, but remained generous to her late husband's concubines, especially Guo and her son. Empress Yin was known in Chinese history for "treating the relatives of Yin and Guo equally," showing compassion for the other women at court and their children, many of whom were fathered by the emperor. This wise and thoughtful consideration contributed to the peace of the empire, rarely seen in other periods of Chinese feudal society when court intrigues and struggles for power were prevalent. Empress Yin died at age sixty in the palace in Luoyang and was buried with Emperor Guang Wudi.

Yang Fanzhong
Zou Jianfeng, trans.

Sources

"The Story of Emperor Guang Wu," and "The Story of the Empress," in Ban Gu, *The History of the Later Han Dynasty.* Beijing: China Publishing

House, 1988, vol. l; "The Story of the Emperor Xiaoming," vol. 2; "Stories of Yinshi," vol. 32.

Queen Ma (ca. 39–79 A.D.), the queen-consort of Emperor Ming (r. 57–75 A.D.) in the Eastern Han dynasty and a powerful force within the imperial court, was originally from Maling in Fufeng county (in the northeast section of modern-day Xinping, Shanxi). Her first name is unknown. Ma's father was Ma Yuan, a famous general during the Eastern Han dynasty. Her father's first wife had been a member of the Jia family, but she died childless while quite young; he remarried, selecting a wife from the Li family. The young girl who would grow up to become Queen Ma had one older brother, three younger brothers, and two older sisters; she was the fourth child born and the youngest daughter. Her father died when she was ten, and her older brother also died young; after their deaths, her mother's mind became disoriented, thus placing heavy family burdens on the young girl. She displayed excellent management skills and honed life skills of endurance, thrift, and strength. In her youth, she was well educated; among the books she read were the *Lushi chunqiu* (Spring and Autumn Annals of Master Lu), *Chu ci* (Elegies of Chu), and *Yi jing* (Book of Changes). She was especially fond of reading works by the great Confucian scholar Dong Zhongshu.

Ma Yuan's nephew Ma Yan recommended his cousins as possible concubines for Liu Xiu, the Emperor Guang Wudi. The emperor then sent an official to Ma Yuan's home; he selected the youngest daughter to reside at the Eastern palace. Initially, she served the empress, Yin Lihua (see Empress Yin), whose affections she won through her actions of modesty, courteousness, and tenderness. She was elevated to concubine, as her intelligence and beauty were admired by the young prince, Liu Zhuang. Empress Yin helped bring about their marriage. Ma was neutral toward the prince's other concubines, displaying neither humility nor arrogance and treating them as sisters. Toward her servants she showed generosity and concern. In February 57 A.D., Emperor Guang Wudi died and was succeeded by Prince

Liu Zhuang, known as Emperor Ming. He named Ma a middle-ranking concubine, and three years later, upon consultation with the queen mother Yin, he named her queen. Remembering her origins, and possibly the wise consuls of Queen Mother Yin, Queen Ma lived a simple life and devoted herself to weaving. She liked to wear coarse cloth, even on the first and fifteenth day of the month (which was the time for concubines to meet the emperor), when other women at court dressed beautifully. She admonished the other concubines: ''We should not live lavishly, although we are part of the imperial family. Why do I like to wear coarse clothes? Because the coarse clothes are easily dyed, but not easily faded.'' Possibly she thought of her own stature and reputation in offering this advice. In her palace, on one side, she set up a room for weaving and, on the other, she made a room for raising silkworms. She dispatched her aides to study the methods of sericulture and cloth weaving and developed a palace school in these crafts. Queen Ma was unable to have children, but she was never jealous of other concubines who could and treated all palace offspring with affection. She often remarked: ''Not every woman is able to have children, but if a woman can feed and bring up other women's children, regarding them as her own, is it not the same?'' Her older sister Jia was chosen as a concubine within the palace and bore a son, Liu Xuan. Queen Ma looked upon him as her own son and brought him up carefully; the emperor designated him as the crown prince; he succeeded to the throne of his father in 75 A.D., taking the reign title Emperor Zhang. Queen Ma was given the title empress dowager. She often advised the young emperor in matters of state, and he respected her deeply for her moral character and talents in statecraft and diplomacy. Following the prescriptions in the *Chun qiu* (Spring and Autumn Annals), she advised thrift, impartiality, and uprightness above family loyalty. She believed that if central as well as local officials could act in this manner, then government would be effective and respected. The young emperor, trusting her judgment, often passed the reigns of power to Queen Ma, allowing her to administer in his name.

Queen Ma's talent for ensuring justice was demonstrated in 70 A.D. Someone accused the king of Chu, Liu Yin, and Wang

Ping of making seals secretly to conduct imperial business fraud-
ulently, and conspiring to form a clique to overthrow the state.
The furious emperor discharged Liu Yin from his post and determined to rid himself of the remaining conspirators. More than
a thousand people were forced to join the army or sentenced to
death. All those mentioned in Liu Yin's *Book of Famous People*
were regarded as his co-conspirators and were arrested. Queen
Ma advised the emperor not to act hastily or kill people indis-
criminately if he wished to avoid popular riots. Regretting his
impetuous actions, the emperor then ordered a general amnesty.
Queen Ma's influence stabilized the state and preserved the
throne.

Emperor Ming liked to tour his empire, but Queen Ma advised
him not to stray too long from the court, the seat of central
power. Every time the emperor and his entourage of concubines
went on tour, Queen Ma stayed behind claiming to be indis-
posed, but in reality keeping a watchful eye on the government.
In this indirect way, she remained a powerful and knowledgeable force at court. She taught the palace's royal line of children
from the *Yi jing* (Classic of Changes) and wrote *The Way of
Living According to Xian Zhang,* a book on statecraft from
which the palace youth could draw lessons.

Queen Ma never exploited her key position for personal gain
or the advancement of her family's interests. Further, she was
against nepotism in general and turned down high positions for
her three brothers at handsome salaries and warned the emperor
against giving his mother's or his concubines' relatives important positions—advancement should come only through meritorious service. She further advised him that, as mother of the
state, she desired only plain tea, simple food, and coarse cloth
and wanted others at court to follow her frugal example. Once,
the emperor desired to promote his three uncles, but Queen Ma
opposed him, saying they had not yet performed notable service
in the military. She told the emperor a parable: If the root of a
tree was rotten, the tree could no longer grow. Despite her advice, in 78 A.D., a time of prosperity, the emperor promoted her
three brothers on his own, and when the news reached her, she
sighed: "Things went contrary to my wishes. I will feel eternal
regret in the netherworld." Upon hearing how she felt, her

brothers declined their appointments. But the emperor persisted, they accepted their positions reluctantly and then handed in their resignations out of respect for Queen Ma, and went back to their former official residence.

Queen Ma diligently pursued her moral course and demand for exemplary behavior from court officials and members of the imperial family. She once delivered a letter to officials at lower levels instructing them to observe her relatives, and if they violated laws or interfered with others' duties, the officials would so inform the court through a memorial (formal statement or petition) to the emperor. They were to be strictly punished if they violated the laws. Queen Ma was enforcing the Confucian idea of government by goodness or virtue, as a way to elevate the moral standards of Chinese society. When Queen Ma's mother's tomb was embellished by relatives, she promptly issued an order that it be returned to its former state. She said no one had sufficient rank or privilege to break the regulations of the court.

In early 79 A.D., Queen Ma became seriously ill. Not believing in the supernatural, she did not allow people to pray for her; she died at the age of forty. She was buried in the tomb of her husband in the tomb of Xian Jie.

Song Ruizhi
Ma Li, trans.

Sources

"Queen Ma," in Ban Zhao, *History of the Han Dynasty*. Central Chinese Publishing House, 1962; repr. Beijing: China Publishing House, 1988.

Ban Zhao (49–120 A.D.), China's first female historian, lived during the period of the Eastern Han dynasty. She was famous for completing the *Han shu* (History of the Han Dynasty), which was one of the foremost histories of China written; it became the model for writing future dynastic histories. The second volume in the twenty-four histories of China, the *Han shu* included the whole history of the Western Han dynasty and was the first period history written in the style of biographies; its methodology and style was adopted by subsequent dynasties. The *Han* *shu* consisted of 120 chapters, divided into four parts: part 1 contained the basic annals, which included twelve biographies of the emperors and the significant events of their reign; part 2 comprised eight tables, charts, and diagrams of genealogies and key events; part 3 consisted of ten treatises on a variety of subjects setting down the rules and regulations for such diverse subjects as money and taxes, music, court ceremonies, and navigation; part 4 contained seventy biographies of people important in the Han period other than the emperors.

Ban Zhao's father was Ban Biao (3–54 A.D.), who, during the transitional period between the Western and Eastern Han dynasties, had taken refuge in the home of a warlord, Rui Xiao, in what was then called Tiansui province. Dou Rong, a famous general of the Eastern Han, recommended Ban Biao to the first Eastern Han emperor, who thereupon offered Ban Biao the post of magistrate of Xu county. Shortly thereafter the emperor called him to court, but Ban Biao either refused to accept the magistrate's office or could not accept because of illness. Ban Biao later joined the court of the Emperor Guang Wudi and subsequently accepted a position as magistrate in Wangdu county, Hebei province.

Ban Zhao had twin older brothers, Ban Gu (32–92 A.D.) and Ban Chao (32–102 A.D.). Ban Gu would distinguish himself as a historian in the Eastern Han court, and Ban Chao would become a famous Chinese general. The Ban family lived in Fufenganlin, now east of Xianyang in Shaanxi province. Ban Zhao took the name Ban Huiban, or Ban Ji. At fourteen she married Cao Shou, but her husband died when she was still young; she never remarried, devoting herself to scholarship. After her husband's death, she continued to live with her sons, Cao Cheng and Cao Gu, and her daughters. Her entire family was well known for its intellectual pursuits and fine educational backgrounds. In addition to being an official, Ban Biao was a famous historian. After reading many classics and histories, especially the *Shiji* (Records of the Historian), by Sima Qian, in his childhood, her father had developed a talent for writing essays.

During the early years of the Han restoration, after the capital had been moved to Luoyang from Xian and the Eastern Han period started, Ban Biao was invited to the court as an intellectual and antiquarian. Disliking the life at court, he pleaded poor health and retired to write his histories. He had been impressed with how the *Shiji* treated China's early political dynasties, which ended midway through the Western (or Former) Han period. He found unsatisfactory successive histories written by others to continue the historical record, so he began to write a new history of the Han period himself. Using historical documents and investigating legends and sayings precisely, he began what would become the *Han shu.*

By the time he died in 54 A.D., Ban Biao had written sixty-five articles. Ban Gu immediately returned home from his studies at the Imperial College in Luoyang to make the funeral arrangements. Finding the manuscript left by his father, he decided to continue the work on this history, which was unlawful unless sanctioned by the emperor as an *official* history. Using his father's base, Ban Gu continued the full history of the Western Han dynasty. But, in 62 A.D., Ban Gu was reported by someone to the Emperor Ming for writing this private history.

Found guilty and convicted, Ban Gu was thrown into prison in the capital. All his papers and working drafts were gathered and sent to the court. His brother, Ban Chao, interceded on his brother's behalf, carrying a petition to the Emperor Guang Wudi in Luoyang to explain the situation. This eventually led to his brother's acquittal. Ban Chao by this time was an outstanding general, who extended control of China's western frontiers to the Tarim Basin, thus re-establishing China's control over Central Asia. Ban Chao had earlier tired of his own intellectual pursuits, and had decided to strive for a successful military career. After the emperor had carefully examined Ban Gu's historical papers and then released him, the emperor asked Ban Gu to write an official history and granted him the title of *Lantai linshi* (a palace scholar). This honorific title and rank gave Ban Gu access to the imperial library's books and all important previous historical records. Ban Zhao and Ban Chao at one time or another in their own careers were also granted this official title, the equivalent of a court historian. Ban Gu innovated in his writings by adding essays on law, geography, literature, and the pseudo-science of the five elements in Chinese cosmology—earth, water, wood, wind and fire. These essays actually formed a type of bibliographical essay on previous works in the imperial collection, done by a scholarly father and son team, Liu Xiang and Liu Xin. Ban Gu also retitled his own father's essay on economics "Food and Currency."

Ban Gu worked on the *Han shu* for more than twenty years. While in his mid-forties, Ban Gu became involved in political struggles that would result in his death. He joined the military staff of the general Dou Xian (the brother of the emperor's mother) and accompanied him in his victorious northern campaigns against the *xiongnu* (northern barbarians). The general was celebrated in a victory plaque inscription by Ban Gu. The young Emperor He, however, feared Dou Xian; he ordered the general to commit suicide and sent Ban Gu to prison. Ban Gu died there at the age of sixty-one, leaving his sister Ban Zhao to finish the *Han shu.*

Ban Zhao completed the eight tables left unfinished by her brother and added a treatise on astronomy. The emperor asked Ban Zhao to come to Luoyang and work in the imperial library. She worked diligently proofreading the manuscript, editing the text, adding facts, polishing the style, and checking the original sources and documents used. The position of the eight tables, which were largely the work of Ban Zhao, in relation to the entire completed book is very important. They contain genealogical charts spanning two hundred years, as well as the names and ranks of court officials and their relatives, and most significantly include the emperor's genealogy on his mother's side and the empress's side. This is important because records relating to women in Chinese history were not traditionally well kept. All the tables have accurate dates and supplement the narrative in the book. One of them, the "Table of Ancient and Current People," lists hundreds of significant individuals from ancient times to the Qin dynasty. However, despite the title, no people were included from the period in which she was writing; they all dated from before the Western Han dynasty. Although Ban Zhao was assisted in writing the treatise on astronomy, by Ma Xu, she deserves the credit for this section, which remains one of her truly remarkable additions to the original manuscript. Ban Zhao was a scholar of astronomy and mathematics in addition to being a fine historian.

Ban Zhao's completed *Han shu* became the prototype for all later dynastic histories of China, which treat either one major dynasty or a group of smaller related dynasties. It was the basis for, in the words of Edwin O. Reischauer and John K. Fairbank, the idea "that each new dynasty had the duty of continuing the record of the past by compiling an official account of the proceeding dynasty." The *Han shu* was so well done that it was accepted as one of the "standard histories" and the Emperor regarded it as the definitive study of that period. By the nineteenth century there were twenty-four standard histories.

The *Han shu,* with its emphasis on biographical entries, emphasized that the Confucian ethic of virtue should reign. The early biographies show the then current rulers as strong and just and later rulers as weak and debauched; the *Han shu* in this way analyzes the dynastic cycle by explaining that when a dynasty falls, it is because the ruler was not virtuous and lost the mandate of heaven. Thus histories like *Han shu* demonstrate the ideological base binding Chinese society over thousands of years. After completing the *Han shu* under court sanction, Ban Zhao was authorized by the emperor to teach the empress and members of the court in the imperial library. She also instructed Ma Xu's brother, Ma Rong, in the uses of the book; he thereupon assisted in publicizing its contents to the general society of scholars. The empress and high-ranking concubines so respected Ban Zhao's teaching that they called her Cao Dagu (learned or gifted one). Ban Zhao's teaching at court gained her political influence.

The ruling Empress Deng, who had come to court at the age of fifteen in 95 A.D., became well educated under Ban Zhao's tutelage and was so grateful that she made Ban Zhao a lady-in-waiting. After the emperor died, the empress's son Liu Long ascended the throne as the Emperor Shang when he was only a hundred days old. The empress, now empress dowager, aided her young son in ruling the country. As he grew up, during the day she advised him and in the evening she discussed books with Ban Zhao. The empress dowager respected Ban Zhao's keen insights and often asked her advice on court issues and affairs; she appointed Ban Zhao's son, Cao Cheng, as an official. In the spring of 113 A.D. Ban Zhao's younger son, Cao Gu, was made a county magistrate. Ban Zhao, because of her advancing age, decided to leave the court and accompany her younger son to his official post in Chengliu, where she lived out her retirement.

She described her impressions traveling to Chengliu in *Dong zheng fu* (Travel to the East). This title survives, but another of her works, the three-volume *Collected Works of Dagu,* compiled by her daughter-in-law Ding, have been lost. In addition, she also wrote many informative essays and poems, the most famous of which is "Nu shi" (Lessons for Women)—a poem directed at her daughters to educate them for polite society. This poem was used in subsequent dynasties as a treatise on the feudal rituals, in which civil duties were described and proper decorum or etiquette was explained.

After a lifetime of scholarship, Ban Zhao died; she was past seventy. Upon hearing the news of her death, the empress dowager dressed in mourning white to pay homage to the first well-known and much-respected woman historian of China.

Barbara Bennett Peterson

Sources

Fan Ye, *Hou Han Shu,* or *Post Han History,* one of the *Twenty-Four Histories of China.* Beijing: Zhonghua shuju, 1965; *Famous Women in Chinese History.* Shanghai: People's Press, 1988; Ban Zhao, in *Dictionary of Famous Women of Hua Shia* (China), Hua Shia Publishing House, Beijing, 1988, section translated from Chinese by Lucia P. Ellis. Liu Naihe, "The First Woman Historian of Our Country," in *Famous Women of Ancient Times and Today* (translated from Chinese by Fang Hong). Hebei: People's Publishing House, 1986). One can read an English translation of the Annals section of the *Han Shu* by Homer H. Dubs in his valuable *History of the Former Han Dynasty.* Baltimore: Waverly Press, vol. 1, 1938, vol. 2, 1944, vol. 3, 1955; Nancy L. Swann, *Pan Chao: Foremost Woman Scholar of China.* New York and London: The Century Company, 1950; Danielle Elisséeff, *La Femme au Temps des Empereurs de Chine.* Paris: Stock/L. Pernoud, 1988. 1988; Liu Naihe, "China's First Woman Historian," in *Women of China,* April, 1980, 40–41; Edwin O. Reischauer and John K. Fairbank, *East Asia, the Great Tradition.* Boston: Houghton-Mifflin, 1960, 1984.

Empress Dowager Dou (ca. 62–97 A.D.), who ruled China as regent for her adopted son, was the wife of Liu Da, Emperor Zhang of the Eastern Han dynasty. Dou was her family's eldest daughter, with one younger sister, one older brother, Dou Xian, and two younger brothers, Dou Jing and Dou Huan. She amazed her family with her readings and writing skills by the time she was six.

She was from a distinguished bureaucratic family in Pinling, Fufeng (northwestern Xianyang, Shaanxi province). Her great-grandfather, Dou Rong, was Wang Mang's chief archer (see Wang Zhengjun); he was later appointed chief administrator by Liu Xiu, known as Emperor Guang Wudi, the first emperor of the Eastern Han. Her grandfather, Dou Mu, was head of the palace garrisons and married Nei Huang. Her father, Dou Xun, married Princess Bi Yang, who was a granddaughter of Emperor Guang Wudi. The Dou family became one of the most famous and wealthy families in the imperial line of the Eastern Han dynasty. Her family had official mansions that rivaled those in the capital, with thousands of servants.

Despite the wealth and luxury, her life was not without problems. When she was a young girl, her father and grandfather were accused of abusing power, mistreating commoners, and conspiring at court. Liu Zhang, Emperor Ming of the Eastern Han, denounced them and dismissed them from court. Several years later, they were sentenced to death for showing resentment after their dismissal, and her family's reputation further declined. These twists and turns in life when she was very young taught her to be resourceful and manipulate power for her own ends. After the death of her father and grandfather, her family placed their hopes in her. When her family consulted fortune tellers, they unanimously flattered her, saying she had a great destiny to rise above the rest.

When an imperial order came to select beauties in her region, her family sent Dou and her sister as candidates and in 77 A.D., they were selected to join the court. Talented and beautiful, gentle and elegant, the elder Dou daughter won favor from Emperor Zhang and Queen Mother Ma. Through her astuteness and congenial qualities, she rose to a position of pre-eminence in the women's quarters or the back palace; in 78 A.D. she became the empress and her sister a concubine of the emperor.

Now fully aware of the value of power and adept at playing politics, she used her influence to remove those at court who disagreed with her. One of Emperor Zhang's favorite wives, Lady Song, had entered the palace earlier and bore a son, Liu Qing, the crown prince. Dou conspired with her supporters against Song: When Lady Song became ill and asked for medicinal herbs, Dou made it appear that Song planned to bewitch or harm the emperor. In a fury, believing the trumped-up charge, Zhang withdrew the title of crown prince from Song's son and reduced Lady Song's status. Dou convinced a court eunuch, Cai Lun, to torture Lady Song to extort a confession; Song subsequently committed suicide.

In her jealousy of another favorite wife, Lady Liang, who had bore a son, named Liu Zhao, Empress Dou ordered the writing of an anonymous letter accusing Lady Liang's father of sinister activities. He was put to death under these false charges, and Liang and her sister followed him. Empress Dou then adopted Liang's son as her own, and he was named the crown prince, From that point on, no one dared to challenge her.

Because of Empress Dou's favorable status, her brothers were also elevated to important court posts. Dou Xian was first appointed emperor's bodyguard and was soon promoted to adviser; he became general of the garrison troops. Dou Duo was made head of the back palace guards. The Dou brothers created fearsome positions for themselves, wielding such power that Dou Xian forced the emperor's sister, Princess Qin Shui, to sell her lands to him at a very low price. When this was discovered, the emperor restored her lands to her; but the intimidating presence of Dou Xian remained.

In early 88 A.D., Emperor Zhang died from an illness at age thirty-three, in the prime of his life. Liu Zhao, raised by Dou, succeeded his father as Emperor He, and Dou now became the empress dowager and regent, since the young emperor, aged only ten, could not yet rule in his own name. She immediately took measures to consolidate her power, issuing an imperial edict throughout Han China that henceforth, as regent, she would decide all vital matters of state, because of the youth and ill health of the new emperor. Dou appoint her brother Dou Xian chief minister in charge of confidential military matters, charged with defending the capital and the imperial palace; rearranging land holdings or fiefs of the major princes and dukes in the provinces, and removing them from the capital so that they could not form an armed rebellion; abolishing the government's monopoly of salt and iron production; and allowing private production, distribution and trade, which lessened resentment against the court. She cleverly appointed an old friend, Deng Biao, former defense minister, to be the emperor's tutor and concurrently to take charge of all the officials at court. Absolutely obedient to her will, he proved a great favorite because he was not a member of her family, and she was applauded for her selection, however self-serving. For a time, the court was stabilized under her rule. Dou Xian began to seize greater power, display cruelty, and eliminate enemies simply for disobedience. As numerous officials and nobles perished, outrage within and without the court called Empress Dowager Dou to counter her brothers' actions. Ever keeping a watchful eye on her power, Dou understood that she herself would be in jeopardy should she fail to discipline Dou Xian; she had him placed under house arrest awaiting further decision. Fearing that he would be put to death, Dou Xian pleaded with her to allow him to conduct a military expedition against the northern *xiongnu*. At the same time a chieftain among the southern *xiongnu* tribes that had previously sworn loyalty to the Eastern Han requested military aid in repelling the northern tribes. Seizing the opportunity to satisfy both requests, extricating her brother from his difficult position through meritorious service in battle, and making use of the southern *xiongnu* against the northern tribes to safeguard the Han borders, she ordered Dou Xian into battle. Dou Xian was appointed the expedition marshal and Geng Bing, then head of the garrison forces at the palace, was appointed vice marshal. The cavalry units directly under the court's authority in Wuxiao, Liyang, Yongying, and twelve additional counties were moved north of the Great Wall to mix with the southern *xiongnu* forces for a concerted attack on the northern scourge. By the summer of the next year, they had won decisive victories after the fierce battle at Mount Jiluo. The northern *xiongnu* were on the run, and the Han troops pursued them as far as the Siqubidi Sea (in modern-day Bayan Khongor, Mongolia). More than ten thousand enemy troops were killed, and the Han captured more than a million horses, camels, oxen, and sheep. More than two hundred thousand *xiongnu* from eighty-one tribes surrendered. To perpetuate Han prestige, Dou Xian and Geng Bing led their military forces up Mount Yanran, where they engraved their accomplishments on stones before returning in triumph to the capital at Luoyang.

Empress Dowager Dou's reputation, as well as Dou Xian's, was greatly bolstered by this expedition. She immediately dispatched a second-ranking general northward to consolidate the victories and ensure peace by carrying gifts of friendship and alliance to the subdued chief of the northern *xiongnu*. In exchange for loyalty and fidelity to the Han, the chief and his tribes would be offered amnesty and opportunity for paid commissions in the Han military forces. Empress Dowager Dou promoted her brother Dou Xian to a position as Han China's highest-ranking general, a post higher than her three chief ministers, the prime minister, the chief supervisor of the imperial household, and the minister of defense. In 91 A.D., Dou sent another expedition against the northern *xiongnu,* and again it returned victorious. Her younger brothers continued to receive elevated appointments. Dou Jing was made head of the garrison forces at the palace, and Dou Duo was made *tejin* (a palace official). But her brothers again became arrogant and abused her trust; even the brothers' servants took advantage of their own exalted positions and bullied the common people at will, imprisoning people on false charges. Neither wealthy merchants nor street vendors dared do business in their sight and ran away upon their approach as if evading bandits; no official in charge of public security dared submit a petition to the court asking redress.

Empress Dowager Dou, again reminded of her own vulnerability if others' criminal actions went unchecked, dismissed the arrogant Dou Jing from office. Yet she left too many details unchecked, and the emperor, now growing to manhood, became cognizant of the evil forces around him and determined to take action in his own name. In 92 A.D. Liu Zhao, as Emperor, launched an attack within the palace to regain authority, ordering the arrest and death of Dou Xian's henchmen, Deng Die, Deng Lei, and Guo Huang; the arrogant brothers of Empress Dowager Dou were forced to commit suicide, and all Dou relatives were dismissed and investigated. Their family relatives were exiled to what is now southern Vietnam. Emperor He regained power with the aid of trusted eunuchs such as Zhang Zhong. Empress Dowager Dou was forced to hand over the reigns of power to the emperor.

Nothing more was recorded in history books about her later years. Yet, judging from the situation at the time, she cannot have lived a happy and free life. After five lonely and depressing years, she died in 97 A.D., when she was approximately thirty-five. She was buried with her husband Liu Da, Emperor Zhang, near Luoyang.

Yang Fanzhong
Ai Xinli, trans.

Sources

Ban Zhao (Pan Chao), *The History of the Han Dynasty*. Central Chinese Publishing House, 1962; repr. Beijing: China Publishing House, 1988; "The Biography of Emperor Wen Di," vol. 4; "The Biography of Emperor Jing Di," vol. 5; "The Biography of Wu Di, vol. 6; "The Biography of Empress Dou," vol. 97, Book 1; "The Archives of Art and Culture," vol. 30; "The Archives of Ceremonies and Rites," vol. 22; "The Biography of Tian Jie," vol. 52; "The Biography of Dou Ying," vol. 52; "The Biography of Dou Bo," vol. 40; "The Biography of Dailing," vol. 88; "The Biography of Yuan Gu." vol. 88; all vols. published by China Publishing House, Beijing, 1988, edition; Sima Qian (Ssu-ma Chien), *Records of the Historian*, vols. 10, 11, 12, 49, 57, 58, 63, 111, 120, and 170, Beijing: China Publishing House, 1988; Sima Guang (Ssu-ma Guang), *Zizhi tongjian*, Beijing: China Publishing House, 1988 edition; Li Zhi, *Chang Shu*, vols. 3, 43, 61, China Publishing House, Beijing, PRC, 1988 edition; Li Zhi, *Shi Gang Ping Yao*, vols. 6, 7, Beijing: China Publishing House, 1988; Yuan Shu, *The Chronicles of Tong Jian*, vols. 1 and 6, Beijing: China Publishing House, 1988; Chen Zhi, *Hanshu Xinzheng*, The New Text Research of the History of the Han Dynasty: The Biographies of Relatives On the Empress's Side, Tianjin: People's Publishing House, 1980; Xu Tianling, *The Major Events of the Western Han Dynasty: The Emperors* (Book Two), vol. 2, Shanghai: People's Publishing House, 1986; Xiong Tieji, *The Brief Review of the New Daoist of Qin and Han Dynasties*, Shanghai: People's Publishing House, 1988; Xu Tianling, *The Major Events of the Western Han Dynasty: The Rites* (Book 5), vol. 11, Shanghai: People's Publishing House; Wu Guang, *A General Survey of Huang Lao Theory*, Zhejiang: People's Publishing House, 1989.

Xu Shu (dates unknown), a poet during the Eastern (Later) Han dynasty, was born in Longxi (modern-day northeastern Lingtao county, Gansu province). Her husband, Qin Jia, also known as Shihui, lived in the same village. Qin Jia's "Poem to My Wife" illustrated their common hard, difficult childhood, but also revealed their blissful married life, as both had an aptitude for writing.

During the reign of Emperor Huandi, Qin Jia worked as an aide to the prefectural official who prepared an annual report from the prefecture to the imperial court in Luoyang, noting the area's production and revenues. Qin Jia was asked to carry the annual report to the capital and to remain there to interpret the report for the higher government officials. Before his quick departure he had not said goodbye to his wife. So he sent a chariot to his in-laws home to pick up his wife, but Xu Shu was ill and could not travel. Instead she wrote him a farewell letter in reply:

> *Your humble wife is unwell,*
> *Sickness prevents her from returning.*
> *Lingering disease keeps her indoors,*
> *Her health situation is not stable.*
> *Imperial attendance is not worthy,*
> *Respect goes to the wrong people.*
> *You are on an official mission,*
> *Going afar to the capital.*
> *You will depart for long,*
> *But we cannot meet.*
> *Expectation and longing is intense,*
> *Waiting only makes one restless.*
> *I am missing my husband,*
> *Your looks appear in dreams.*
> *You are now on your way,*
> *Leaving me alone at home.*
> *I wish I had wings,*
> *Flying and chasing after you.*
> *All these make me sentimental,*
> *Tears wet my clothing.*

Qin Jia reread Xu Shu's letter while traveling to the capital and felt remorse at not having bid her goodbye, so he wrote a letter in reply. Xu Shu received her husband's letter and immediately sent him another; even though they were separated, they continued to write each other often, expressing their affection and longing for each other. In his "Poem to My Wife," Qin Jia wrote:

> Medical needles can be accepted, but autumn longing is intolerable.

(Although injections might cause pain, one can still tolerate them because they help cure disease, but one cannot tolerate continuous longing for loved ones.)

Qin Jia died of an illness in Luoyang. Xu Shu and Qin Jia had one natural daughter, and while he was away in the capital, she adopted a son. Xu Shu was a young and charming widow. Her brother wanted her to marry again, but she would not listen. She wrote her brother a detailed letter expressing her desire to remain a chaste widow and downplayed her looks as part of her refusal to accept a second marriage. She grieved the loss of her husband and died not long afterward.

After Xu Shu died, her adopted son returned to his birth mother's home. When the imperial court was informed of these circumstances, it issued a circular to the villages, telling the adopted son to return to his Xu Shi's home so that he could inherit the family name of Qin.

Xu Shu's poetry and prose were collected into a book, which did not survive succeeding generations. Some of her individual poems, however, appear in poetry collections. Her "Poem in Reply to Qin Jia" appears in *New Songs of the Jade Terrace*, and "A Letter of Oath to My Brother" in *Classified Collection of Literature*. Qin Jia's "Poem to My Wife" was published in *New Songs of the Jade Terrace.* "His Song of Marriage" appeared in *The Collection of Classical Literature* and his "Letter to Wife Xu Shu" and "A New Letter to My Wife" appeared in *The Classified Collection of Literature* and *Selected Readings of the Taiping.*

Xu Shu's poems reflected the affection between a husband and wife. Her poetry was sentimental and romantic, while Qin

Jia's poems expressed profound feelings with simple language. The appearance of the *ci* poetry by Xu Shu and Qin Jia marked the high point of poems with five characters in each line. Xu Shu was one of the few women poets of this era who wrote five-line poems (another one was Ban Jishu, who wrote her poems on bamboo fans).

Zhao Xiaoming
Zhu Zhongliang, trans.

Sources

Yu Guanying, *The Selected Poems of Han, Wei and the Following Six Dynasties*. Beijing: People's Literature Publishing House, 1990, 11; Shen Deqian, *The Sources of Ancient Poems*. Beijing: China Publishing House, 1988, 58; Hu Wenkai, *Textual Research on the Works By Women Writers in History*. Beijing: Commercial Publishing House, 1987, p. 3; *Notes and Commentary on the New Songs of the Jade Terrace*, Book One, China Publishing House, pp. 30–32; *Dictionary of Chinese Writers*, Book One, the section on Ancient Times, Sichuan People's Publishing House, p. 53.

Meng Guang (b. ca. A.D. 65), also known as Deju, lived during the era of Emperor Zhangdi (76–88 A.D.) of the Eastern (Later) Han dynasty. She was born in Pingling, in Fufeng, which is the northwestern section of modern-day Xianyang, Shaanxi province. Little is known of her childhood; as a young adult she grew so strong that she could lift a heavy stone mortar and was reputed to be virtuous, though fat and plain. Her father attempted to select a husband for her, but she declined his suggestions. At thirty she remained unmarried, stating: "I want to seek a fine husband like Liang Hong."

Liang Hong was born to a poor family in the same county as Meng Guang. His father, Liang Lang, was once a junior officer of the town garrison for Wang Mang (see Huan Shaojun), who usurped the throne in A.D. 8. But after Wang Mang fell from power in 24 A.D., Liang Hong's family fortunes declined, and he was forced to bury his father in only a poor mat instead of showing him honor with an expensive burial. Later Liang Hong was admitted to the very prestigious Imperial University and distinguished himself, but lacked the connections needed to advance. He was forced to make his living by tending pigs.

Once a fire caused by his carelessness damaged the house of his neighbor, and Liang Hong was forced to pay for the damage with his pigs. The neighbor remained unsatisfied, so Liang Hong agreed to be his servant to work off the debt. The village praised Liang Hong for his high-mindedness and eventually criticized the neighbor for demanding too much. The neighbor offered to return the pigs and apologized, but Liang Hong refused. His debt now paid, he returned to Fufeng.

Fellow villagers attempted to act as matchmaker for Liang Hong, but he politely declined their recommendations. He learned of Meng Guang and hearing what she had said of him in admiration, decided to marry her. She accepted his proposal of marriage, and they set a date. Meng Guang made some new plain cotton clothes and hemp shoes for herself; she gathered some farm implements, bamboo baskets and a loom. On the wedding day, Meng Guang put on heavy makeup before going to the Liang household. When Liang Hong saw her in heavy makeup, he was very unhappy and refused to talk to her for a week. Meng Guang, kneeling before her husband, asked: "Your humble woman was told that you are noble and ethical. You have harsh terms for selecting a wife and previously declined to marry several women, as I have turned down several men. Now that you have selected me for your wife, why have you not spoken to me for seven days?" Liang Hong said: "I mean to have an ordinary but physically strong woman as my wife, with whom I can live a secluded life deep in the mountains. But you are dressed now in silks and made up; this is not the wife I am looking for. How can I become close and intimate with this kind of woman?" She replied: "I am willing to live a secluded life in the mountains, to be noble and unsullied. I have prepared some clothes for that, and you should not worry about it." Then she retreated into the inner room, changed into her plain attire and hemp shoes, and reappeared before her husband, who said: "Now you are my wife and can share my interests with me." He gave her a pet name, Deju.

Liang Hong and his wife lived harmoniously after this confrontation. Some time later, Meng Guang asked him: "I was told that you want to live a secluded life to avoid trouble. Why not put your idea into practice?" He replied calmly: "I was just thinking of moving our home now." Packing their belongings, they moved to the mountains of Baling, where Liang Hong tilled the land as a farmer and Meng Guang wove cloth. They entertained one another by reciting poetry from the *Shijing* (Classic of Songs) and stories from the *Shiji* (Records of the Historian), playing the zither, painting, and doing calligraphy. They also collected stories of famous hermits in Chinese history and wrote eulogies to them, modeling their lives after them.

While briefly passing through Luoyang once on business, Liang Hong observed the luxurious palace and extravagant lifestyle of the imperial family. Expressing his sympathy for China's laboring classes, he composed a poem called "Song of the Five Oh's":

> Oh, I passed the northern mountain of Luoyang,
> Oh, I watched the emperor's forbidden city,
> Oh, It was such a luxurious palace,
> Oh, It was built on people's blood and sweat,
> Oh, Their never-ending labor and suffering.

When Emperor Zhangdi read the poem, he became very upset and wanted to punish Liang, accusing him of libel. Liang Hong had to change his name to Yao Houguang for protection. He was forced to live a secluded life with Meng Guang in the region between Wu and Lu, at the junction of modern-day Hebei and Shandong provinces.

Later, they fled to Wudi, in the area of modern-day Zhejiang province. On the way, they passed the residence of the wealthy Gao Botong, who allowed them to live in the porch area attached to the home's main hall. Liang Hong made a living as a hired hand, husking rice with mortar and pestle. Every day, Meng Guang carefully prepared a meal for her husband upon his return from work. In front of her husband, not looking at him, she held a short-legged table up to the level of her eyebrows as she kneeled, showing her respect, while he ate. When Gao Botong learned of this act, he remarked: "Liang Hong is nothing more than a hired hand, but he gains such respect from his wife that he must be an extraordinary man.'' Gao invited them to move from the porch into an inner room, supplying Liang with meals and clothing so that he could devote himself to writing.

Meng Guang's actions changed their life. Liang wrote more than ten articles, but later suffered from a serious illness. Before his death, he told his real name and circumstances to Gao Botong. After Liang's death, Botong convinced the villagers to show him further respect, saying: ''Yaoli, the warrior of the kingdom of Wu was very heroic, while Liang Hong was aloof from politics and material pursuits. Let them be buried together!'' So Liang was buried at the side of the famed Yaoli's tomb. After her husband was buried, Meng Guang returned to her ancestral home in Fufeng with their son.

Later, the four characters *ju an qi mei* (lifting the dining table to the height of one's eyebrows) came to be used as a saying to describe harmonious, respectful affection between husband and wife. Cao Xueqin, in chapter 5 of *Hong lou meng* (Dream of the Red Chamber), wrote: ''What a pity. Only now people start to believe their life is not perfect. Even though you have *ju an qi mei*, you desire more.'' In the second act of Guan Hanqing's ''Resentment of Dou E,'' a *zaju*, or opera (poetic drama set to music) during the Yuan dynasty, echoed: ''It is like the couple of the Zuo family, when the wife did the cooking and the husband did the dish washing, and it is like the *ju an qi mei* of Meng Guang.''

Meng Guang's simple dressing with a twig hairpin and coarse cloth skirt gained praise from her peers. Later generations of writers used the symbols ''twig hairpin and cloth skirt,'' ''skirt cloth and hairpin of twig,'' ''cloth attire and twig hairpin,'' and ''twig and cloth'' as standards of simple dress. And in common speech, phrases such as ''twig wife,'' ''twig woman,'' ''humble twig,'' ''mountain twig,'' and ''old twig'' were used as terms of endearment for virtuous, hardworking wives; ''deceased twig'' referred to a departed loved one. Throughout Chinese history, Meng Guang remained a symbol of Confucian virtue and model wife.

Zhao Xiaoming
Zhu Zhongliang, trans.

Sources

Ban Gu, *History of the Later Han Dynasty*. Beijing: China Publishing House, 1988. "Biographies of the Hermits;" vol. 83; Li Zhi, *Changshu* (Book Collections), "Liang Hong," vol. 67, Beijing: China Publishing House; Zhang Baorong, *Selected Explanations of Common Allusions*. Ulan Bator: Inner Mongolia People's Publishing House, 1980, 229–231; Yu Guanying, *The Selected Poems of Han, Wei and the Following Six Dynasties*. Beijing: People's Literature Publishing House, 1990, 7; Ling Geng and Feng Yuanjun, *The Selected Poetry in Chinese History*, part one, vol. 1, Beijing: People's Literature Publishing House, 1963, 101.

Empress Deng (81–121 A.D.), formerly named Deng Sui, founded an imperial palace school devoted to Confucian ethics during her reign as empress dowager and regent. Born to an aristocratic family in Xinye, Henan province, she became the wife of Emperor Liu Zhao of the Eastern (Later) Han dynasty. Her grandfather was a famous general, Deng Yu; her father was Deng Xun and her mother Yin Shi.

An excellent student with superior intellect, she loved to study as a child and by the age of six was able to read historical volumes. At twelve, she could recite the *Shujing* (Classic of Documents) and the *Lunyu* (Analects of Confucius). She often prepared difficult questions for her older brothers on the books they had read to test them. Deng Sui devoted herself to studying culture from ancient books and avoided taking part in family affairs. He mother complained that she should devote more time to sewing than to studying; henceforth, she was forced to learn sewing by day and study privately at night. Family members teasingly called her the "Confucian scholar."

Deng Sui entered the palace of the emperor when she was fifteen years old. Slender of stature, beautiful of face, generous in behavior, and elegant with words, she was an immediate favorite and highly praised. She became the wife and empress of Emperor Liu Zhao. The emperor had ascended the throne at the age of ten, and his adoptive mother Queen Mother Dou (see Queen Mother Dou) wielded excessive power at court, manipulating her son so that she ruled in his name. The power of the Dou clan steadily grew until Emperor Liu Zhao came of age, began to rule in his own name, and curtailed the authority of his Dou relatives. The emperor had his mother's older brother arrested, his seal confiscated, and forced him to commit suicide. The emperor ultimately forced all Dou family members from the palace and relied upon eunuchs in this reshuffling of powers and disbursement of political posts. Deng Sui had watched and marveled at her husband's astuteness in recapturing power from his own mother and her family and learned valuable lessons from the experience. Hence, when her husband died in 105 A.D., Deng Sui did not seek to extend the authority of her own family excessively, because this had earlier caused destructive political turmoil and power struggles. Liu Zhao's son Liu Long, only a hundred days old, became the next emperor, but died shortly thereafter. A nephew, Liu You, at age thirteen, was elevated to power. Empress Dowager Deng now took on her greater role in history as an astute politician who advised the young emperor, acting as his regent, and attempted to curtail the extravagance of court life as she introduced frugality and morality. She prohibited food delicacies formerly consumed at the palace, which were gathered at great expense from the sea and mountains. She cut in half the gifts of tribute required from the provinces; she stopped the manufacture at court of expensive handicrafts such as jade and ivory carvings and gold and silver decorations. And the frugal Empress Dowager Deng steadily eliminated the weak and incompetent from court posts; at one time she sent six hundred former superfluous palace attendants back to their villages. Concerned about the Chinese people, Deng attempted to find solutions and offer aid to peasants in areas suffering from drought, flood, or famine. She was responsive to the needs of minority nationalities, listened to their problems, and worked to offer stabilizing assistance.

In the middle of the Eastern Han, Buddhism and Daoism enjoyed a resurgence of popularity and competed with Confucianism. To counter these influences, she established a palace Confucian school, gathered about her forty children from the Liu clan and thirty children from the Deng clan, offered them classrooms, and appointed Confucian scholars to instruct them. Empress Dowager Deng supervised the examinations herself, being stricter with the children of her own family. She stated, ''The relatives at court receive sustenance from the country, wear gorgeous clothing, eat fine food, ride the best horses, and are care-free; however, they know nothing of learning and ceremony.'' Hence, she dedicated herself to teaching them the responsibilities as well as the privileges of power. In the true Confucian mold, she believed one should rule by virtuous example; if the rulers were exemplary, then the morality of the entire society would be raised. She was seconded in her efforts by Yang Zhen, her chief minister. Praised throughout subsequent Chinese history for her outstanding political skill in controlling the power of the eunuchs and reducing their tensions with other family officials, Deng undeniably reformed palace politics at an urgent moment in Han history. Most notably, she advanced Confucian ethics at court at a time when morality had ebbed. As the ''Confucian scholar'' she offered the virtuous role model advanced by Confucius in his ideas for government by goodness. She vindicated herself and her personal values based on scholarship. In 121 A.D. she died; afterward the eunuchs returned to power at court, and many of the Deng clan were put to death or committed suicide. But, for a moment, Empress Dowager Deng reestablished the virtuous ruler as benevolent example to the Chinese people.

Wang Chaizhong, Shu Aixiang, and Barbara Bennett Peterson

Sources

Fan Ye, *Hou Han shu* (History of the Later Han). Beijing: Zhonghua shuju, 1965; *The Histories of Qin, Han, Wei, Jin, Nan, and Bei Dynasties*. Beijing: Liaoning People's Press, 1984.

Empress Yan (ca. 104–134 A.D.), named Yan Ji at birth, was the wife of Emperor An, who ruled during the Eastern (Later) Han dynasty. Yan Ji's aristocratic family lived in Yengyang, Henan province, where she was born. Her grandfather was a high official at court during the reign of Emperor Ming (r. 57–75 A.D.), later promoted as an infantry officer in charge of the emperor's armies.

Yan Ji's father was an important adviser to Emperor An, who

brought her to the court at Luoyang in 114 A.D., when she was ten years old. Being well educated, from an aristocratic family, and possessing both intelligence and great beauty, she found favor with the emperor, who promoted her to imperial concubine.

The following year Yan Ji became empress. As Empress Yan, she became adept at scheming and enforcing loyalty to herself. She defended her high position in the palace, monopolized the emperor's attention and affections, and secured places for her relatives at court. Her father was appointed official in charge of supervising all imperial armies and given the title of marquis of North Yishun; 5,000 families paid taxes to him.

Empress Yan attacked the other favorite concubines in the palace. Emperor An had once bestowed great favor upon Madam Li, who bore him a son, Liu Bao, named crown prince. Out of jealousy, Empress Yan planned to poison Madam Li and dethrone Liu Bao.

Around 121 A.D., Emperor An began to rule the court personally after the death of the Empress Dowager Deng (see Empress Deng). Empress Yan secured the appointment of her four brothers, Yan Xian, Yan Jing, Yan Yao, and Yan Yan, as the commanders of the imperial armies in the capital; even her brothers' children held significant posts at court, until nearly all positions of influence were controlled by the Yan family. Next, Empress Yan proceeded with her plan to depose the crown prince. Conspiring with the eunuchs Jiang Jing and Fan Feng, who were in charge of the back palace, or the women's quarters, Empress Yan tried to have Liu Bao defamed in front of the emperor. Believing the slanderous tales, the emperor demoted Liu Bao and restored his title as Prince Jiyin.

In early 125 A.D., Emperor An and Empress Yan toured the Han empire, traveling to his hometown of Zhangling (now Zaoyang), Hubei province. On the return to the palace, however, Emperor An died of an acute disease in Yie county, Henan province. Since she was far removed from the capital, Yan feared that if the news of her husband's death became widely known, she would lose her power at court and be unable to prevent the ascendance to the throne of Liu Bao. She hurriedly returned to the capital, falsely reported that the emperor was seriously ill and had stayed in Woche. The next day, she announced the emperor's death, saying she, as empress dowager, henceforth would rule the empire.

To strengthen her position, she set about to control the army. She appointed her brother Yan Xian general commander of the imperial armies. He became one of her top three administrative advisers. Concerned about how she would hold onto power without a son, she conspired with Yan Xian to create a puppet emperor; her choice was Liu Yi, the son of Prince Jibei, then a young boy under ten. In this way she countered the criticisms of the court and secured the confidence of the people. She dominated his regency and ruled as she liked. She toppled an adversary, Geng Bao, a much-respected general, after he was viewed as opposing her dictatorship. He was impeached after false charges were introduced, accusing him of plotting with Fan Feng (head eunuch), Xie Hui (general of the garrison troops), Zhou Guang and Xie Dou (advisers to the late Emperor An), and Wang Sheng (Emperor An's former wet nurse); the general's supposed followers were either put to death or exiled and their families sent to what is now Vietnam. General Geng Bao was demoted and committed suicide. Wang Sheng and her son were exiled to Hongmen. Thus, Empress Yan rid herself of all dissident ministers and officials. Her brothers were elevated: Yan Jing was made an army officer; Yan Yao, a general; and Yan Yan, a garrison commander in the capital. After this maneuver, all the important places at court were dominated by relatives of the empress dowager.

During the reign of Empress Yan, important changes were taking place in China. Buddhism was gaining a foothold both at court and among the common peasants. It had entered China through traders traveling along the Silk Route or entering ports in South China. Buddhism began to affect Chinese architecture, as the traditional stupa construction was modified in China to become the stone, brick, or wooden pagodas that graced China's landscape. Empress Yan may have supported translation work of Buddhist scriptures (sutras) at court; certainly Buddhist writings were appreciated and duplicated.

In the autumn of 125 A.D., the young emperor became seriously ill after only two hundred days in office. After consultation with Yan Xian, Empress Yan began secretly to look for a successor. Knowing the situation would be dangerous to her if the young emperor died, Empress Yan called for the sons Prince Jibei Prince Hejian to be brought to her; she would select the next young (puppet) emperor from among them when it became necessary to prevent various factions from restoring the crown to Liu Bao. Later that month, Liu Yi died, and Empress Yan had not yet selected a successor whom she could control.

A palace revolt erupted against her, led by Sun Chen and Wang Kang, joined by seventeen others within the court. The next month, the rebels murdered the pro-empress eunuchs Jiang Jing and Liu An and their supporters. The rebels installed Liu Bao as Emperor Shun. In desperate retaliation, Empress Yan fought back, ordering General Feng Shi and Yan Cong to garrison the palace against the rebellious forces. But Feng Shi betrayed the empress's confidence, turned against her, and supported the rebels. The forces supporting the claims of Liu Bao arrested Empress Yan's brothers and routed their armies. Empress Yan was arrested and held prisoner in a secondary palace instead of being put to death. All surviving members of the Yan family were exiled to the wilderness of southern Vietnam.

The following year, Empress Yan mysteriously died while under house arrest. She had ruled Han China for twelve years and made her mark in history as an able politician, however Machiavellian. At her death, she was about thirty. Empress Yan was buried in the tomb of Emperor An, which is today in the northeastern part of Luoyang, the ancient capital of the Eastern Han.

Yang Fanzhong
Zhang Jing, trans.

Part II. Sources

Ayscough, F. *Chinese Women: Yesterday and Today.* New York: Da Capo, 1975.

Dictionary of Famous Women in China. Beijing: Huaxia, 1988.

Ban Gu, *History of the Later Han Dynasty.* Beijing: China Publishing House, 1988.

Ban Zhao, *History of the Han Dynasty*. Central Chinese Publishing House, 1962; Repr. Beijing: China Publishing House, 1988.

Bodde, Derk. *China's First Unifier: A Study of the Ch'in Dynasty as Seen in the Life of Li Ssu (280?-208 B.C.)*, 1958.

Chen Zhi. *Hanshu xinzheng* (The New Text Research of the History of the Han Dynasty: The Biographies of Relatives on the Empress's Side). Tianjin: Renmin chubanshe, 1980.

Cheng, Li, Furth, C., Bon-Ming, Yip. *Women in China*. Institute of East Asian Studies: Berkeley, 1984.

Chu Nan. "River God's Wife." *Women of China* (April 1982): 4–43.

Curtin, K. *Women in China*. New York: Pathfinder Press, 1975.

Dictionary of Chinese Writers, book 1. Chengdu: Sichuan People's Publishing House, 1986.

Elisséeff, Danielle. *La Femme au Temps des Empereurs de Chine*. Paris: Stock/L. Pernoud, 1988.

Famous Women of Ancient Times and Today. Women of China, ed. Beijing: Hebei People's Publishing House, 1986.

Famous Women in Chinese History. Shanghai: People's Press, 1988.

Fan Ye. *Hou Han shu* (History of the Later Han). Beijing: Zhonghua shuju, 1965.

Gujing zhuming funu renwu, ed. Yinguen Zhongguo Funu. Shijiazhuang: Hebei renmin chubanshe.

Guillermaz, P. *La Poésie Chinoise*. Paris: Stock/L. Pernoud, 1957.

Hanwei, vol. 2, annotated by Yu Guanying. Tianjin: Renmin chubanshe, 1980.

The Histories of Qin, Han, Wei, Jin, Nan, and Bei Dynasties. Beijing: Liaoning People's Press, 1984.

The History of Chinese Medicine. Shanghai: Science and Technology Publishing House. 1972.

Hu Wenkai. *Textual Research on the Works by Women Writers in History*. Beijing: Commercial Publishing House, 1987.

Hulsewe, A.F.P. *Remnants of Han Law*. Leiden: Brill, 1955.

Jian Bozan. *Zhongguoshi gangyao*. Beijing: Renmin chubanshe, 1980.

Li Zhi. *The Life of Zhao Feiyan*. Beijing: China Publishing House, 1988.

Li Zhi. *Cangshu* (Book Collection). Beijing: China Publishing House, 1988.

Li Zhi. *Shigang pingyao*. Beijing: China Publishing House, 1988.

Li Zhi. *The Life of Ban Jie Yu*. Beijing: China Publishing House, 1988.

Li Zhi. *The Life of Han Cheng Di*. Beijing: China Publishing House, 1988.

Ling Geng and Feng Yuanjun. *Selected Poetry in Chinese History*, part 1, vol. 1. Beijing: People's Literature Publishing House, 1963.

Liu Naihe. "China's First Woman Historian." *Women of China* (April 1980): 40–41.

Loewe, M. *Everyday Life in Early Imperial China During the Han, 202 B.C.-220 A.D.* London: Carousel Books, 1973.

Lu Anmin. *Qinghan shi*. Shanghai: Guji chubanshe, 1987.

Notes and Commentary on the New Songs of the Jade Terrace, Book 1
  Beijing: China Publishing House, 1986.
Nancarrow, P. *Early China and the Wall.* New York: Cambridge University
  Press, 1978.
Pan Ku, *The History of the Former Han Dynasty,* trans. Homer H. Dubs, 3
  vols. Baltimore: Waverly Press, 1938–55.
Preminger, Alex, ed. ''Chinese Poetry,'' in *Princeton Encyclopedia of Poetry
  and Poetics.* Princeton, NJ: Princeton University Press, 1974.
Reischauer, Edwin O., and John K. Fairbank, *East Asia: The Great Tradition.*
  Boston: Houghton-Mifflin, 1960, 1984.
Shen Deqian. *The Sources of Ancient Poems.* Beijing: China Publishing
  House, 1962.
Sheng Deyuan. *Gushi yuan.* Beijing: Zhonghua shuju, 1988.
Sima Qian. *Zizhitongjian.* Beijing: China Publishing House, 1988.
Sima Qian. *Historical Records (Shiji).* Beijing: China Publishing House,
  1988.
Swann, Nancy L. *Pan Chao: Foremost Woman Scholar of China.* New York
  and London: The Century Company, 1950.
Watson, Burton. *Ssu-ma Ch'ien: Grand Historian of China.* New York: Co-
  lumbia University Press, 1958.
Wei, K.T. *Women in China.* Westport, CT: Greenwood Press, 1984.
Wolf, M., and Witke, M., eds., *Women in Chinese Society.* Palo Alto, CA:
  Stanford University Press, 1975.
Wu Chengquan. ''Wang Mang.'' In *Ganjianyizhilu.* Beijing: Zhonghua shuju,
  1988.
Wu Guang. *A General Survey of Huang Lao Theory.* Zhejiang: People's
  Publishing House, 1989.
Xin Tianshou. ''China's First Woman Diplomat.'' *Women of China* (March
  1981): 16–17.
Xiong Tieji. *A Brief Review of the New Daoist of Qin and Han Dynasties.*
  Shanghai: People's Publishing House, 1988.
Xu Tianling. *Major Events of the Western Han Dynasty: The Emperors.*
  Shanghai: People's Publishing House, 1986.
Yu Guanying. *The Selected Poems of Han, Wei, and the Following Six Dy-
  nasties.* Beijing: People's Literature Publishing House, 1990.
Yuan Shu. *The Chronicles of Tong Jian.* Beijing: China Publishing House,
  1988.
Zhang Baorong. *Selected Explanations of Common Allusions.* Ulan Bator:
  Inner Mongolia People's Publishing House, 1980.

Part III

The Collapse of the Han, a Period of Disunion, and Revitalization

Power became frayed and decentralized near the end of the Han dynasty, with the responsibility for quelling provincial rebellions left to local warlords and their armies. One such warlord, Cao Cao, seized the Han central government in 196 A.D., and the last of the Han emperors was deposed in 220 A.D. by Cao Cao's son, who after the establishment of his Wei dynasty ruled most of northern China from the Wei river valley. Laws were decreed forbidding women of the royal court and eunuchs from holding strong positions of power. This period of disunion was known as the Three Kingdoms (220–265 A.D.) (as China was divided into Wei, Wu, and Shu Han Kingdoms.). In addition to the Wei dynasty to the north, a remote branch of the former Han established the Shu dynasty in the Sichuan basin through the efforts of General Guan Yu, later a legendary military hero, and Zhuge Liang. The Wei and Shu were joined by a third focal point of power in 222 A.D., when the kingdom of Wu was established around Nanjing in the lower Yangzi river valley. After 221 A.D. the period was marked by the competition among the Three Kingdoms. Despite the turmoil, the period did not lack for technological advances: gunpowder, the kite, and the wheelbarrow were invented, and coal was first used in heating.

Sanguo zhi yani (Romance of the Three Kingdoms) describes

the treacherous politics challenged by heroic feats of courage during this period. Sima Yan usurped the Wei throne in 265 A.D. and founded the Jin dynasty (Western Jin 265–317 A.D.; Eastern Jin 317–420 A.D.), which slowly disintegrated and allowed northern barbarians to cross over the Great Wall and devastate the north. The Jin fled south and established a regime at Nanjing to defend the rest of China. Four more weak dynasties followed the Jin: the Liu Song (420–479 A.D.), the Ji (479–502 A.D.), the Liang (502–557 A.D.), and the Zhen (557–559 A.D.). These dynasties seldom controlled more than the region around Nanjing. Northern China remained in the hands of barbarians, which remained divided into sixteen kingdoms, 304–439 A.D., while the south was divided among warlords. From 316 A.D. onward, successive waves of *xiongnu* and other northern and western tribes swept over the wall, and the Tibetan warrior Fu Jian unified the north in the late fourth century. His defeat at the historic battle of the Fei river at Anhui stopped all of southern China from being conquered and introduced renewed fighting in the north. In 439 A.D. Toba Tatars reunified northern China through the Northern (Later) Wei dynasty and slowly adopted Chinese traditional dress and customs; these modifications drew the two halves of the country into a whole. Indigenous Chinese turned to Buddhism in this tumultuous period, producing the cave temples at Longmen near Luoyang and Yungong near the Northern Wei capital, Dadong.

The significance of this period is the great cultural mix brought about by the barbarians who adopted Chinese culture but also introduced many elements of their own distinctive style, especially in music and the arts. Calligraphy was greatly stimulated by the need for copying Buddhist sutras (scriptures), and the Chinese language was enriched by the new ethnic vocabularies. But the breakup of the Northern Wei dynasty in 535 A.D. into western and eastern Wei allowed eventually a usurper to take the throne and once again unify all of China under the Sui dynasty.

This period of the Three Kingdoms, the Jin dynasty, the period of division of South China into numerous competing regions and the parallel period of division in North China marked by the Sixteen Kingdoms, the Northern Wei dynasty and its fragmentation, and the division of China into the Northern and Southern dynasties (420–589 A.D.) was one of incessant warfare. The by-product of this militarization of society was the emergence of powerful families holding large tracts of lands, which were paying fewer and fewer taxes to a central government. Eventually this continued the cycle of decline begun in the waning years of the Han dynasty—the independent warlords became powerful enough to challenge the central government and divide its territories. The "official" censuses did not accurately reflect the population and thereby central governments lost tax revenues. Militarism was extremely expensive and counterproductive to economic trade and agricultural productivity within these small kingdoms. At various points in the tumultuous period of the Three Kingdoms the king of Wei led forces into southern Manchuria and was able to control Korea; the king of Shu Han fought against nonethnic Chinese tribes on the frontiers in the southwestern regions of China; the king of Wu led forays into Vietnam and dominated this region. Eventually in 263 A.D. the kingdom of Wei conquered the region of Shu Han.

Beyond the twin problems of increasing militarism and lower tax bases, these small competing central governments, all desiring to reunite China and its imperial system, so glorious during the glorious days of the Han dynasty's apogee, was the problem of less effective leadership in government because the system was no longer based on merit or the examination system, but based upon family rank and status. Appointments were given to the most powerful families and their heirs. Lands were allocated on the same basis, as was the feudal peasantry to work the land.

Eventually these internal weaknesses atttracted new barbarian invasions all along the borders, Altaic and Tibetan tribes harrassing the west fringes, the *xiongnu* in the northern frontiers, and challenging revolts of conquered peoples began in the annexed territories. Just as with the Roman world in the western Mediterranean, intellectual, moral, philosophical, ethical, and economic former strength was depleted by chaos internally and threats of foreign invasion. The Han's dynastic cycle was complete and China would only be renewed by the re-invigoration of the Sui (581–618 A.D.) and Tang dynasties (618–907 A.D.), creating for China a new Golden Age. But it is to this period of warfare, disunion, and the great cultural mix following the end of the Han dynasty and before the formation of the Sui dynasty that we now turn to examine famous women who led exceedingly valuable lives in this period of upheaval.

B.B.P.

Cai Wenji (ca. 177–244 A.D.), also known as Cai Yan, was a poet who lived during the Eastern (Later) Han dynasty. She was born in Kaifeng, on the bank of the Yellow river, Chengliuyu county, Henan province, during the reign of Emperor Lindi. When her father, Cai Yong, was offered a post as court historian in the imperial library, she joined the court of the emperor at Luoyang. Cai Yong, who wrote *Xu Han shu* (Chronicles of the Han Dynasty), was an authority on Han history. Cai Wenji was tutored privately by her father and became gifted at poetry and calligraphy. She was also an expert on ancient Chinese classical music, as well as a skilled speaker, unafraid to show her wit and wisdom.

Once, when Cai Wenji was six years old, she heard her father was playing a *gu qin*, a seven-stringed musical instrument similar to a zither. One of the strings broke and she immediately identified it as the second string without looking at the instrument. Her father could not tell whether she had guessed or really knew from having an ear for music, so he deliberately broke another string, and when it popped this time, she said, correctly, "It was the fourth string." Her father knew then that her ear could judge pitch and tone quality perfectly, so he encouraged her in her own musical interests and talents.

Cai Yong, also known as Cai Bojie, supervised court officials to root out corruption. His position made him vulnerable when he accused individuals of misconduct. He had the misfortune of making an enemy out of Liu He, a high court official, who falsely accused Cai Yong of crimes. Having been found guilty, Cai Yong went to prison for a time; after his release he was sent into exile with his family when Cai Wenji was a year old. Nine months later he was granted a pardon by the emperor Han Lin and the family was able to return to Luoyang, the Eastern Han capital.

As the family prepared for its journey, Cai Yong inadvertently offended Wang Zhi, the governor of the region where they had been living in exile, and the governor reported these circumstances to the emperor. Fearing imprisonment again if he and his family returned to Luoyang, Cai Yong fled southeast to the regions of Wujun and Huji (now Jiangsu and Zhejiang provinces), where the family was to live for twelve years in exile.

The Emperor Hanlin died in 189 A.D. Later that year, under his successor, Emperor Shao, Dong Zhuo, the highest court official, recalled the Cai family from exile. Cai Yong was asked again to become a high court official, with the attendant prestige, status, and rank. Dong Zhuo, who was pulling the strings behind Emperor Shao, wished to replace the emperor with someone of his choosing and returned the capital to Chang'an. Thus the Cai family went to Chang'an, following their patron.

By then sixteen years old, Cai Wenji married Wei Zhongdao and moved with her husband to his home in Hedong. Two years later, Wei Zhongdao died, without any children. Cai Wenji returned to her home in Chengliu.

The year of Cai Wenji's marriage her father, unbeknownst to her, died in prison, after a court coup that had caused Dong Zhou to flee and landed Cai Yong in prison. Later, in 194–195 A.D., Dong Zhou returned to the court and was subsequently murdered after attempting to seize power.

Soon afterward, parts of North China were overrun by the *xiongnu* mounted horsemen from the north seeking slaves and booty. Cai Wenji was taken north as a captive and married to a *xiongnu* tribal chief named Zuoxian; they had two children, a son and a daughter, and lived in the region of the southern *xiongnu* tribes (modern-day southwestern Inner Mongolia). Cai Wenji later wrote of her feelings about having been spirited away from her Han homeland and taken captive by "barbarians" of the north, who slept in tents, migrated with their animals, ate mutton, wore skins and furs, and traveled, often on foot, in the freezing snow. Part of her poem "Agony, or Grief and Indignation," shows how much she longed for her homeland and possibly freedom from the *xiongnu*.

> *Frost and snow covered the ground all over.*
> *The wind howls even in the summer.*

With a puff it blows up my fur.
The rustling sound came to my ear.
Missing my parents, endless sighs I heave.
Hearing visitors come, great delight filled me
But none sees how disappointed I feel.
Knowing he wasn't from my home.

Fortunes at the Han court turned once again in her favor during the time of the last emperor of the Han dynasty. Cao Cao, now the highest court official, realized that the great work started by Cai Yong, the *Xu Han shu,* was not yet complete and he wanted to bring Cai Wenji back to court to finish the work. Cao Cao ransomed her back through negotiations and gifts, persuading Zuoxian that the great historical work was essential, and thus Cai Wenji returned home. But, by *xiongnu* custom, her children had to remain with their father in the north. This caused her tremendous anguish, as she wretched herself from her children, and again she described her feelings in her poem "Agony" (Grief and Indignation).

Another poem, "The Eighteen Laments," is also credited to Cai Wenji; it so perfectly cadenced that it has been set to music.

Despite her pain, she was able to channel her energies constructively both in poetry and scholarship and edited more than four hundred of her father's articles, working in the imperial library. Surely the ebb and flow of fortunes lost and recovered were the real source of energy and strength behind her vivid poetry, which reflected real-life high drama, rather than the sanguine events of harmonious court life. Having experienced bad times, she could still appreciate the good times, as reflected in her "I See My Blooming Years Again," written during the years of her historical work in the Han court. This work is very different from "The Eighteen Laments," which is said to have been written from the chants she recited at her father's tomb upon her return from the north, vividly depicting her plight as a captive of the *xiongnu.*

After the death of Zuoxian, Cai Wenji was reunited with her children. A special envoy from the southern *xiongnu* brought them to her at the capital. Cao Cao arranged a new marriage for her to Dong Si, a county magistrate. But not long afterward

Dong Si was condemned to death for breaking the law. Cai Wenji went to Cao Cao to plead for her husband's life. The execution order had already been dispatched, but she asked Cao Cao to send a swift horse and rider with a new directive before it was too late; he honored her request and later pardoned Dong Si. In gratitude, Cai Wenji wrote from memory hundreds of articles to store in the imperial library, as the originals had been destroyed in previous upheavals.

Just as Cai Wenji survived the fall of the Han dynasty, so her poetry has survived down to the present. Her life story has often been retold in plays, which show her to be a model of "lofty spirit" and passion for survival.

Barbara Bennett Peterson

Sources

Liu Naihe, "Gifted Lady Cai Wenji in Eastern Han Dynasty," *Famous Women of Ancient Times and Today* edited by *Chinese Woman Magazine*, published by the Hebei People's Publishing House, 1986; Zhu Lin, "I Played the Role of Cai Wenji," *Women of China* (February, 1979), pp. 27–28.

Madam Sun (b. ca. 189 A.D.), who lived during the end of the Eastern (Later) Han dynasty and the beginning of the Three Kingdoms period, was the wife of Liu Bei, one of the leaders of the Three Kingdoms. She was born in Fuchun, Wu county (modern-day modern Fuyang county, Zhejiang province). Her father was Sun Jian, also called Wentai, who was said to be a descendent of Sun Wu, the great militarist of the Spring and Autumn period. Her mother, Wu, was a native of Wu state. Together, they had four sons—Sun Ce, Sun Quan, Sun Yi, and Sun Kuang—and the daughter who later became Madam Sun.

The Suns had been distinguished local officials for generations. At the end of the Eastern Han dynasty, Sun Jian suppressed the Yellow Turban uprising (a rebellion in East China led by Daoist religious leaders known for wearing yellow head cloths) and was promoted to being general of Changsha prefecture. In 192 A.D. Sun Jian was killed in an ambush while fighting Liu Bei (as the two struggled to dominate China and to reunify it during the time it was divided into the Three Kingdoms—Wei, Shu Han, and Wu). Henceforth, in Jingzhou, and afterward, the family led a destitute and homeless life moving from place to place from 192 to 200 A.D.; Wu died in 202 A.D.

Sun Ce and Sun Quan had carried on their father's fight against Liu Bei. But after Liu Bei captured Jingzhou, and Sun Quan consolidated his position in the eastern areas of the Yangzi river, they were both faced by a new threat from the northern military commander Cao Cao. Sun Quan feared imminent death at the hands of Liu Bei, so he proposed a marriage alliance with his sister and a truce so that they might join forces against Cao Cao; Liu Bei accepted.

In 209 A.D. Liu Bei visited Sun Quan in Jing (modern-day Jingkou, Zhenjiang, Jiangsu province) to seal the bargain, and then Sun followed him to Gong'an. Initially the marriage was harmonious, but later, because it had been made out of political necessity, became fraught with mutual suspicion instead of love. Madam Sun and Liu Bei began to distrust each other. She built another city about 5 miles outside Chanling (modern-day Gong'an county, Hubei province) and went there to live. There was a considerable age difference between the two: Liu Bei was forty-nine and she in her early twenties. Madam Sun also had a facile imagination and was high spirited. She was proud of being Sun Quan's younger sister and sometimes appeared bold, willful, and adventuresome. Seeming amoral, she flaunted established laws. But above all, they represented different political interests and political powers, which unavoidably led to their mutual suspicion and vigilance. Madam Sun always surrounded herself with numerous soldiers and attendants, all armed with swords and spears, prepared for any contingency. Liu Bei feared for his safety within his own household.

In 215 A.D., shortly after Liu Bei captured Yizhou, a region disputed between the two rivals, without having made concessions or early overtures of appeasement to Sun Quan, it was inevitable that the alliance would fall asunder and Madam Sun would attempt to return to her brother's camp. Sun Quan sent ships to meet his sister; Madam Sun in the meanwhile had made a hostage of the crown prince—who was the son of Liu Bei and Empress Gan. Apparently Madam Sun planned to hold the prince for ransom or force other concessions from Liu Bei. Liu Bei's forces discovered what she had done and rescued the crown prince, forcing Madam Sun to leave without him, to return to her home region of Wu.

When Cao Cao died in 220 A.D., his son took the throne, proclaiming the Wei dynasty. Liu Bei proclaimed himself the emperor, naming his dynasty the Shu Han. And in 222 A.D. Sun Quan declared his own dynasty, the Wu. Thus China was divided into three warring kingdoms.

Madam Sun, acting as a politician in a strategically important political marriage, sacrificed her own personal happiness to further the interests of her family and native region. Perhaps this is why so many place names commemorate her. The Embroidery Forest Mount, 2 miles southwest of Shishou county in Hubei province, is where Liu Bei married Madam Sun. It was so named because, in Madam Sun's eyes, the forest looked as if it were made of many sheets of beautiful silk. In this place the Embroidery Forest Pavilion was built. Two miles east of Shishou county is the Watching-for-Husband Mount, where she supposedly awaited her husband's return from his military campaigns on the Golden Rock Stand. Madam Sun is said to have been buried in the river at Daoji, above which the Favored Madame Temple was built in her memory.

During the Qing dynasty she was granted the posthumous title of Madame of Moral Integrity, and a plaque was created with an inscription lauding her "intelligence and beneficence."

Liu Aiweng
Tao Danyu, trans.

Sources

The Records of the Three Kingdoms, vols. 32, 43, 36, 37, 46, and 50; *The Records of Huayang State*, volume 6, which included the life story of Emperor Liu; Actual Accounts of Jiankang; *The Records of the Prefecture of Taiping*. John K. Fairbank and Edwin Reischauer, and Albert M. Craig,

East Asia, Tradition and Transformation, revised edition. Boston: Houghton-Mifflin Company, 1989.

Xing Xianying (190–269 A.D.) was born during the Eastern (Later) Han dynasty and died at the beginning of the Western Jin dynasty, during the turmoil of the Three Kingdoms period. Her original hometown was in Longxi prefecture (now Lingtao county, Gansu province), and she later settled in Yangqu in Yingchuan prefecture (now Yuxian county in Henan province). Her father, Xing Pi, held a high-ranking position as an imperial adviser and third-grade ministerial official. In addition to Xing Xianying, Xing Pi also had a son, Xing Zhang.

When she was very young, Xianying was very clever and eager to learn, so she became quite knowledgeable and resourceful. Around 205 A.D., when Xianying was sixteen, she married Yang Dan, who was from Taishan prefecture (modern-day Tai'an county, Shandong province). His family was then illustrious and aristocratic. Later, Yang Dan attained the high-ranking position as minister of sacrificial rites.

In 217 A.D., Chao Pei and Chao Zhi, two princes of Chao Chao, king of the Wei kingdom, fought each other for the position of crown prince. Chao Pei prevailed and became besotted with success to the point of grabbing Xing Pi by the shoulder, shouting: "Mr. Xing, how happy I am!"

Xing Pi told Xianying this story and wanted to hear her opinion. Xianying sighed: "The crown prince is the person who will ascend the throne to administer state affairs; he has a heavy responsibility and should be concerned about this country and his people. How can he, on the contrary, feel so complacent? It seems that the Wei kingdom cannot remain prosperous for very long!"

Xianying's brother, Xing Zhang, later became a *canjun* (deputy official offering military advice) to General Chao Shuang. In 249 A.D., Sima Yi, the emperor's tutor (equivalent to a first-grade official) took advantage of the emperor's absence on a trip with Chao Shuang to hold a memorial ceremony for the imperial ancestors; he closed the gates of the city and launched a coup. Lu Zhi, the key assistant in charge of military affairs to Chao

Shuang, led the soldiers of the General Court to break open the gate to meet Chao Shuang outside the city. He asked Xing Zhang to go with him, but Xing Zhang was uncertain and scared, so he went to his elder sister for advice. Since the emperor was outside the city, and the emperor's tutor has closed the gates, would this not create war, he expressed his worries to her in confidence.

Xianying replied, "Not everything under heaven can be predicted, but I guess that this is something that the tutor has to do. Before Ming Huangdi, the Emperor Chao Rui of the Wei dynasty, passed away, he held the hand of the tutor to entrust him to lead after his time. Is there any imperial official, civil or military, who does not know about it?"

Both General Chao Shuang and the tutor were entrusted with the heavy task of protecting and advising the emperor. Nevertheless, Chao Shuang made arbitrary decisions and took peremptory actions, attempting to push aside the tutor. Chao Shuang was accused of being profligate. Xing Xianying advised her brother to support the tutor in replacing the emperor's chief general, whose actions were seen as being unfair to the court. "What the tutor is doing, in my opinion," confided Xing Xianying, "is trying to get rid of Chao Shuang."

Xing Zhang then asked: "Will the tutor be successful?" Xianying answered: "Why not! Chao Shuang, with limited talent, is no match for the tutor."

Again Xing Zhang asked: "If so, is it not necessary for me to leave the city?" Xianying replied: "How can you not go out of the city? It is an important principle for a man to be devoted to his post. When we see the ordinary people in trouble, we are supposed to give them our sympathy. So you can by no means betray your superior! Now that you are entrusted by others, you should fulfill your duty despite the risk to yourself. You had better follow Lu Zhi out of the city!" Xing Zhang thought what his sister had said was reasonable, so he followed Lu Zhi out of the city.

Later, Chao Shuang gave up, and Sima Yi killed him along with a few of his confederates. Xing Zhang was safe from any trouble and reflected, "If I had not followed my sister's advice, I would have been in a bad spot."

In 263 A.D., the imperial court appointed Zhong Hui as the Zhenxi general, in charge of the military affairs in the Northwest. When Xianying heard this, she asked Yang Hu, her nephew: "What's the real meaning of appointing Zhong Hui to a position in the west?" Yang Hu replied: "Perhaps he is expected to lead an army to wipe out the Shu kingdom." Xianying said: "Zhong Hui is the kind of person who considers himself no ordinary being, and he is very arrogant and willful. He is not the kind of person who will always like to be subjected to others. In my opinion, he is perhaps a careerist with illegitimate ambition." Yang Hu was disturbed by what she said and hastily stopped her from saying more.

Unexpectedly, Zhong Hui asked to have Xianying's son, Yang Xiu, become his adviser, which concerned Xianying. She said: "Earlier I worried about the imperial court when I knew that Zhong Hui was going west. I did not expect that today disaster would befall my family. But it is the great affair of state to wipe out the Shu kingdom, and for that purpose that he wants Yang Xiu. It seems that Yang Xiu has no choice but to go." Yang Xiu repeatedly pleaded with Sima Yi not to send him to the west, but without success. Xianying then advised her son to go, to fulfill his duty, but to do so cautiously and always morally.

Recalling his mother's advice, Yang Xiu cautioned Zhong Hui to give up on his ambition of wiping out the Shu kingdom and becoming king over the area. Despite having admonished the powerful leader, Yang Xiu not only returned home in good health, but was rewarded by the imperial court.

Being a noble woman, Xing Xianying also possessed the virtue of being thrifty. Once her nephew presented her with a silk quilt, which she thought was too extravagant. At the same time, she felt it improper to decline the gift, so she turned the quilt inside out when using it. Although it was a trivial thing, it was still an unusual act in the extravagant time of the Wei and Jin dynasties.

Xing Xianying, with her extraordinary wisdom, had not only saved her brother and nephew from danger, but had also taught them by her example of moral behavior. Her brother Xing Zhang became the imperial minister in charge of palace security; her eldest son, Yang Jing, was made secretary-general of Shangshu (the imperial secretariat); and her second son Yang Xiu, was the the imperial official in charge of the nomination of the military personnel. Although Yang Xiu was later criticized for his extravagance, he always tried hard to recommend even those who were more capable than he was, and his political integrity was still praiseworthy. Her nephew, Yang Hu later became a famous minister of the Western Jin dynasty and was remembered fondly by the people. Xing Xianying had taught her family significant moral values and distinguished upright behavior which made her a moral model in history and contributed to her survivial in the period of the Three Kingdoms.

Yang Debing
Zhu Zhongliang, trans.

Sources

The Biographies of the Renowned Women: the biography of "Yang Dan's Wife, Xing," the 96th vol.; *The Biography of the Relatives of the Emperors on the Mother's or Wife's Side*: The biography of "Yang Xiu," the 93rd vol. and "The Biography of Yang Hu," in the 34th vol. of *The History of the Jin Dynasty*. Beijing: Zhonghua shuju, 1974; The biography of "Xing Pi," in the 25th vol. of *The History of the Three Kingdoms* by Kim Pu-sik, 1145 A.D.

Madam Yuan (ca. 220–265 A.D.), the wife of Xu Yun, was born in Weishi, Chenliu (modern-day Weishi county, Henan province). Her father was Yuan Qi (also called Boyan), and his official rank *weiwei ging* was third grade, as a minister in charge of palace security. It is said that she had a brother Yuan Kan.

The Yuan family of Chenliu once produced great poets and philosophers such as Yuan Yuan and Yuan Ji, father and son, gaining it great fame for its cultural accomplishments. Madam Yuan an eager student, who benefited from the academic environment in which she grew up, so it was not surprising that she became very knowledgeable. Her appearance, however, did not match her intelligence, which cast a shadow over her marriage prospects. Her father nevertheless made her a good match in Xu Yun.

Xu Yun, also called Shizong, was born to a famous family in Gaoyang, Hebei Province. He was not only good looking but also clever and eager to learn.

At that time, marriage between a man and a woman was decided upon by the parents, so the married couple did not meet until their wedding day. Therefore, when Xu Yun saw his bride on the wedding night, he was hesitant to enter the bridal chamber, which naturally made the whole family very embarrassed and worried. Strangely, the bride did not seem to be worried.

The lack of intimacy between the two continued for sometime thereafter, until one day, she heard that a young guest had come to visit the family. Madam Yuan ordered a maid to find out who the guest was, and the maid reported: "It is Huan *lang*" (*lang* being a term of endearment referring to one's husband), a good friend of her husband. When Madam Xu heard this, she was very glad and said: "Since Huan *lang* is here, it will be easier to solve the problem—he will persuade Xu *lang* to come to see me." This Huan *lang* was a famous and gifted scholar—Huan Fan. Madam Yuan had heard so much about his resourcefulness and believed that he would scold her husband for his attitude. As expected, Huan Fan did admonish Xu Yun: Since the famous Yuans of Chenliu gave you this plain-looking girl in marriage, she must possess something extraordinary. How can you find out her good points when you don't spend any time with her?

Finding his words reasonable, Xu Yun steeled himself to enter the bridal chamber to meet his bride. But, once before her, he really could not tolerate the ugly face of his bride, so he started to leave the room. Madam Yuan understood that if Xu Yun left, he would not return. So she rushed up to him and grabbed his clothes, asking him to stay. Xu Yun said angrily, "The Confucian scriptures say that a perfect woman should possess 'four virtues'—how many of them do you have?" (The "four virtues" of a woman, according to the Confucian rites of the Zhou dynasty, are *fu de* [a woman's morality], *fu yan* [a woman's facial expressions], *fu rong* [a woman's appearance], and *fu gong* [a woman's needlework].)

Madam Yuan replied, "I possess every one of them, except that my appearance is little below the standard!" Then she retorted: "I was also told that a scholar should possess a hundred virtues—may I ask if you possess every one of them?'' Very proudly, Xu Yun said: ''Yes, I do!'' Madam Yuan then said, ''For a scholar, the most important thing is a noble morality. But you just attach importance to appearance, rather than morality, so how can you say that you possess every virtue?'' Her words made Xu Yun flush and ashamed, and he began to respect the bride. His esteem grew from respect to affection, and then from affection to love; together, they had two lovely sons.

By then Xu Yun had become the official of the imperial court responsible for the nomination and promotion of officials—the *Li Bu Lang*. During that period, perhaps because he had selected too many of his fellow villagers, a complaint against him was lodged with the emperor. Emperor Chao Rui (who ruled the Kingdom of Wei 227–239 A.D.) while trying to reconsolidate China's empire during the Three Kingdoms, became very angry and ordered the guards to arrest Xu Yun. When Madam Yuan heard that her husband was about to be arrested, she realized the seriousness of the situation. She rushed out without even taking the time to put on her shoes and begged her husband over and over again: ''The emperor is a wise monarch, so you can only convince him by reasoning. You should never plead with him for mercy by weeping!'' Heeding this warning, he replied with perfect assurance when the emperor questioned him. He replied: ''When people select officials, first and foremost they should know them well. Naturally, the people your subject knows well are his fellow villagers. Therefore, the way of judging whether your subject has selected the proper officials is not to see whether they are his fellow villagers, but to see whether they are qualified. So your majesty can observe whether they are qualified. If they are not, your subject then deserves severe punishment.''

An examination showed that these officials were all very qualified. The emperor relented, praised him as a pure and honest official, and then gave Xu Yun a set of new clothes upon seeing that his robe was old and tattered.

When Xu Yun was arrested, the rest of the family all thought that disaster was upon them, so they all cried, except Madam Yuan, who was perfectly calm and collected. She said calmly: ''You don't have to worry. I think the master will return home safe and sound before long. Why don't we cook some millet gruel for him to use when he returns home.''

In 239 A.D., Emperor Cao Rui died and was succeeded by his eight-year-old adopted son. The young emperor was assisted by General Chao Shuang (of the imperial clan) and Sima Yi, the prime minister (see Xing Xianying). Ten years later, the experienced and astute Sima Yi launched a coup against Chao Shuang's clique at one stroke and accumulated imperial authority in his own hands. In 251 A.D., Sima Yi died, and his first son, Sima Shi, continued practicing autocracy throughout the imperial administration. As part of his effort to usurp the throne, Sima Shi killed Xia Houxuan and Li Feng and their entire families, who had connections with the emperor's family, as Li and Xia were the ministers who did not belong to Sima's group, in the name of conspiracy.

By then Xu Yun was a high-ranking military officer, but he was also suspected by Sima Shi because he was on friendly terms with Xia Houxuan and Li Feng. Sima Shi did not act against Xu Yun at first because he lacked any basis for removing him. In the autumn of that year, the imperial court appointed Xu Yun the Northern Garrison General to command the garrison in Yichen (modern-day Lingzhang, Hebei). When Xu Yun bade farewell to the emperor, they both cried bitterly, which aroused Sima Shi's suspicions. He exiled Xu Yun to Lelang (a part of present-day Korea), accusing him of misappropriating official property. Xu Yun died on the way to Lelang.

Madam Yuan had already realized her husband's dangerous position. She understood if her husband did not throw himself on Sima Shi's mercy, his life would not be guaranteed. But she did not advise her husband to betray the emperor and the friends for his own sake. So when her husband told her that he would be appointed to be the garrison general and would have to go far from the capital, he thought he would be saved from any disaster. Madam Yuan thought otherwise: ''I'm afraid your trouble will start right there. Why do you think it will exempt you from any trouble?'' So, when she learned that her husband had died on the way, she was surprisingly calm; without any change of her facial expression, she said: ''It is just as I predicted!''

Now the important matter confronting Madam Yuan was how

to protect the children left by her husband. Some people advised her to hide the two sons, but Madam Yuan did not think it was necessary. She understood that her husband had not been charged with a crime like plotting rebellion, which would cause the extinction of the whole family; he had only been accused of misappropriating official property, which had not been proved. Therefore, his children would not be involved in any punishment. Under such a circumstance, if she hid her sons, it would not help them; on the contrary, it would raise the suspicions of Sima Shi and serve as an excuse for further persecution of the family.

After Madam Yuan buried her husband, she remained in mourning for three years, taking the children to live near the tomb of her husband, according to the existing customs. Even then she did not lower her guard because she understood that Sima Shi would not let her off easily. She spent all her energies trying to find a way to deal with the situation.

As expected, one day Sima Shi sent a representative, Zhonghui, to offer his condolences, but actually to observe the two children. If the children were found to be more intelligent than their father, they would be instantly arrested and persecuted. When the children found out about this, they were completely at a loss, and asked their mother what to do when they met Zhonghui. Madam Yuan had a well-thought out plan and said calmly: ''Although you are all clever children, you are still too young and socially inexperienced to deal with the person like Zhonghui, who is adept at scheming. But you don't have to be afraid—your mother has found three ways for you to deal with it. If you follow them, you will have no trouble. First, when you talk with Zhonghui, you should neither speak evasively nor talk in a roundabout way; just talk straight. Second, now that Zhonghui is here to mourn your father, he will naturally pretend to be sad, so you should also weep at one side; but, as soon as Zhonghui stops mourning, you should also stop weeping. You should by no means weep unceasingly. Third, don't ask anything about the imperial court.'' The sons acted accordingly, and Zhonghui reported all this to Sima Shi, who later no longer tried to persecute them. First, Madam Yuan desired to give the people the impression that the sons were not clever enough to be a threat;

second, she told people that her sons were not overly sad over the death of their father, so they would not have a strong desire for revenge; third, she convinced people that the children were very simple-minded, without ambition, and good for nothing. These false impressions designed meticulously by Madam Yuan at last hoodwinked the experienced and astute Sima Shi and extraordinarily clever Zhonghui.

In fact, both of these children not only were not inferior to their father, but each achieved a great deal. Later, the elder son, Xu Qi, became a high-ranking official in charge of offering sacrifices to the gods and the imperial ancestors under the imperial secretariat, and the younger son, Xu Meng, became the governor of Youzhou prefecture.

Madam Yuan was an extraordinary woman, who though plain of face had great intelligence and will long be remembered in the history of ancient Chinese women. Her story was included not only in histories such as those covering the Three Kingdoms, also in books on historical figures, such as the *Shi shuo xin yu* (The Tales of the World) an anthology of novels about the Han and Jin Dynasties written by Liu Yiqing.

Yang Debing
Zhu Zhongliang, trans.

Sources

The Biographies of Xia Hou and Zhu Chao with an attachment of the deeds of Xu Yun annotated by Pei Song in the 9th vol. of *The History of The Three Kingdoms* by Kim Pu-sik, 1145 A.D.; the section on Virtuous Women, book one of the second vol. of *Shi-Shuo-Xin-Yu*; ''The First Zhen'guan Year: The Noble Ministers of Kingdom Wei,'' the 76th vol. of *Tzu-Chih-Tung-Chien* (*Zhi-Zhi-Tong-Jian*).

Zuo Fen (ca. 252–300 A.D.), or Lanzhi, was a writer who lived during the period of political disunion following the collapse of the Han dynasty. She was born in Lingzhi to an aristocratic family of Confucian scholars. Because of his intelligence and abilities, her father, Zuo Yong, was promoted from petty official to imperial official in charge of the imperial archives by the Jin claimants to the throne. Her mother had died young, and her brother Zuo Si, also known as Taichong, became famous as a man of letters.

Zuo Fen studied very hard and developed an excellent memory and gained wide-ranging knowledge. A gifted and versatile scholar, she readily composed verse and enjoyed playing word games with Zuo Si. She was also talented at calligraphy as well as embroidery, and her work was praised for its "sophisticated and fine" designs. Zuo Fen was refined, yet modest, and widely admired by her friends, who sought her wise counsel.

Although not as comely as some, Zuo Fen nonetheless captivated the attention of the Emperor Wudi of the Jin dynasty, and she was summoned to the palace in 272 A.D. and later was honored with the title noble concubine. She often confined herself to her study, but the emperor sought her out, visiting her at her residence to discuss the classics with her. Her graceful and accurate words were appreciated by her attendants as well as officials of the court. Zuo Fen contributed to imperial ceremonies such as birth and wedding celebrations and funerals, in the form of odes, poems, eulogies, or special narrative prose essays praising the deceased, and she was well appreciated for her talents. Her tasks, however, were seldom easy, as expressed in her poem "Sentiments."

After Zuo Fen was summoned to the palace, she subsequently moved her family to the capital to be near her. Zuo Si, in his "Poem to Departed Sister," detailed how they had "lost mother when they were young," and by her own admission "she lived far away from father and brother." It had been two years since they parted, and Zuo Si missed his sister very much, as they were very close.

"The Wail of Departure" was Zuo Fen's reply to her brother's poem, in which she expressed her sorrow at living apart from her family and her desire to return home to write poetry and practice calligraphy. Realities kept her at court in attendance of the emperor, and she vented her bitterness in poetry. "Homesickness," composed under imperial order, which was in reality an expression of her sad experiences and sorrow over not being able to see more of her father and brother, who lived nearby but outside the palace. "I have been sad and sorrowful, I can only cry to heaven," read the emotional lines of her poem. When she had an opportunity to see her family, "the time of meeting is so short, and the departure is so long," cried Zuo Si in his poem, and "the filled cups stay untouched, tears running down our cheeks unchecked." Even the beautiful clothes she wore while visiting her family did not compensate for the pain of separation.

In 1930 "The Epitaph and the Burial Letter (Ying) for Noble Concubine Zuo Fen" was found in an excavation in Caizhuang village. The document recounted that a gifted woman scholar named Zuo Fen died in ca. 272 A.D., the first *yong-kang* year of Emperor Huidi and that she had been summoned to the palace when she was twenty and lived there for more than fifty years. She had left a valuable literary legacy, though sources disagree as to how many volumes remain. Today the only poems available are her five *fu* (prose poetry known for its irregular rhyme and meter), two of which are incomplete, two odes, thirteen eulogies, one poem of four characters per line, and one poem of five characters per line, both in the ancient style.

The first writer in Chinese history who took women and the female experience as a central artistic theme, she eulogized women describing their features, virtues, intelligence, capabilities, love, and the education and care for their children. Of her twenty-four extant works, fourteen—nearly 60 percent—depict and praise women. Some of these were composed under imperial order, such as "Ode to Empress Yang," "Eulogy for the Empress of Emperor Wudi," "Lei to Empress Yuan," and "Lei of Princess Wan'mian." These verses were flowery expressions of honor, mere reflections of her public duty. Other works of poetry, such as "Sentiments" and "Fu of Homesickness," reflected her true private feelings and attitudes at court. Even now, many centuries later, her works still have the power to move the reader with their explicit and frank language, so revealing in their time.

Liu Aiwen
Zhu Zhongliang, trans.

Sources

Empresses and Concubines—Noble Concubine Zuo, *History of the Jin Dynasty*, 31st vol.: Biography (section one). Beijing: Zhonghua shuju, 1974, pp. 957–62; Yan Kejun, ed., Concubine Zuo in *The Writings of the Three Dynasties in Ancient History, and Qin, Han, the Three Kingdoms and Six Dynasties, Complete Writings of the Jin Dynasty*, 13th vol. Beijing: China Publishing House, 1958, pp. 1533–36; Zuo Fen in *The Poems of the Former Qin, Han, Wei, Jin, the Southern and Northern Dynasties*, 7th vol., section on: The Poems of the Jin Dynasty. Beijing: China Publishing House, 1983, p. 730. This book also contains the poem by Zuo Si, *Poem to Departed Sister*, pp. 731–32. Zuo Si's poetry was examined in *History of the Jin Dynasty*, 92th vol.: Biographies, no. 62 in the: Section on Literature, China Publishing House, 1974, pp. 2375–77; *The New Text of History of Tang Dynasty*, 60th vol.: Records, no. 50: Art and Literature (section four). Beijing: China Publishing House, 1975, p. 1597. *History of the Sui Dynasty, Reviews of Epitaphs of Six Dynasties*, compiled by Wang Zhuanghong and Ma Chengming. Shanghai: Book and Picture Publishing House, 1975, p. 16, 35th vol.: Records, No. 30: Classics (Section four), Annotations, China Publishing House, 1973, p. 1070; *Reviews of Epitaphs of Six Dynasties*, compiled by Wang Zhuanghong and Ma Chengming. Shanghai: Book and Picture Publishing House, 1975, p. 16; Jiang Liangfu, *The Chronology of Tomb Inscriptions and Biographies of Historical Personages*. Beijing: China Publishing House, 1959, p. 50.

Lady Song (ca. 282–364 A.D.) was a learned scholar granted the honorary title Perpetuator of Civilization out of respect and appreciation for her preservation of the classic *Zhouli* (The Rituals of the Zhou), also called the *Zhouguan*. It deals with a reconstruction of the government system during the time of the Zhou and describes the ceremonies, rules, and central officials of the Zhou dynasty and the Warring States period.

Lady Song was born during the turbulent period of political disunion after the collapse of the Han dynasty. Her family had been scholars for generations, studying the Confucian classics. An only child, she lost her mother when she was very young and was raised by her father, who tutored her and raised her in the scholarly tradition. This was a rare opportunity for a young woman in feudal China, and she was as well educated as if she had been a son. Like her father, she became an expert in the *Zhouli*. He entreated her: ''I have no son to inherit this book. It is up to you to preserve it.'' What he meant was that she was to memorize the entire text of this work, so that if the actual book were lost and no other accounts were available, she would be able to reconstruct it perfectly. This was how scholars' families were able to preserve many of the ancient works during times of warfare, especially when the imperial university had to be closed. This was also one of the reasons education was considered so important in China—the *literati* were the preservers of civilization and China's rich history.

The Song family had handed down copies and instruction on Zhou rituals for generations, undertaking this responsibility through family education at a time when only hand-copied texts were available. She and her family lost all their property in a series of wars that raged across the countryside during the period known as the Western Jin. The only things she was able to save were a few family books, most noticeably, the *Zhou li* (Rituals of Zhou).

By the time civil war broke out, she was married and had a son. The three fled to Shandong province, where they took refuge with a magistrate, Cheng Anshou. The magistrate gave them food and shelter, and Lady Song and her family offered in exchange to assist with the chores. Lady Song, who was accustomed to the comfortable upper-class life of the scholar class, now had to earn her own way through housework, weaving, and picking up firewood. At night she taught her son, Wei Cheng, lessons in the Zhou rituals, which he gradually committed to memory.

These lessons stood Wei Cheng in good stead: He later passed the imperial examination, qualifying for a high-ranking post in government service and for the rank of *taichang,* a favored position based on merit. Lady Song never abandoned her own scholarship; when she was working, she also recited passages from the beloved *Zhou li.*

The Emperor Fujian, who belonged to the Di nationality, ascended the throne in 357 A.D. Believing that education was the vehicle for progress and stability, he wanted to revive the Confucian classics. In 362 A.D., he visited the imperial university, which had been forced to close during the wars, and decried the fact that so many books and archival materials had been lost to flames, plunder, or pillage. A scholar at the imperial university, Lu Hu, told the Emperor Fujian about Lady Song's extraordinary knowledge of the *Zhou li*. Until that point, no one had taught interpretations of this work. The emperor summoned Lady Song and asked her to begin conducting classes for other pupils and scholars on this text. She was then eighty years old, but was in good health and in possession of all her faculties. The classes on this famous preserved ancient text were held in Lady Song's home. She taught approximately a total of 120 students the basic text as well as the interpretations of the *Zhou li*, always teaching from behind a curtain, as it was considered impolite for a woman to recite or teach in full view. Lady Song, for her efforts, was honored by the court and received ten servants for her household so that she could teach full time. Thus she carried on the tradition and the faith of her father.

A review of the essential Confucian classics places the *Zhou li*, in proper context. This book was considered one of the Thirteen Classics of ancient Chinese literature. It was originally attributed to the duke of Zhou, but later interpretations questioned this origin. Nonetheless, it stands as one of the most significant ancient pieces of classical writing. The classics throughout Chinese history were associated with the entire Confucian tradition and the concept of balance, harmony, and order. The classics, together with the vast body of commentaries, which grew up about them, became the basis for the education system, the civil service examination system, and the foundations of literature in China. They also provided the entire Chinese social order with systems of ethics, rituals, philosophy, and social relationships, codified into laws. The most important of these classics fall into several categories: Five Classics, Thirteen Classics, and the Four Books. The first of the Five Classics, the *Shi jing* (Classic of Songs), consists of 305 songs (some are poems and some are hymns) dating from about the tenth to the seventh centuries B.C. Their strict rhythm, meter, and rhyme demonstrate that they are the product of a well-educated, upper-class *literati*, not simply folk songs. The *Shu jing* (Classic of Documents, also known as the Book of History) is a mixture of early Zhou documents, such as political and philosophical speeches. Later scholars "wrote in" lost portions of the text, recreating some of the destroyed original materials. This has provoked and inspired much scholarly debate as to which material is primary and which is secondary in this collection, which dates over some two thousand years. The third of the Five Classics, the *Yi jing* (Classic [or Book] of Changes, also called the Book of Divination), deals with the eight trigrams (mathematical combinations) commonly used in Chinese divination which evolved after oracle bone divination (scapulimancy) (Chinese writing on scapulae or shoulder bones of an ox asking questions to the gods.) This is a valuable book as it shows the changes throughout the Zhou dynasty, through constant additions or supplements to this text, in the views of omen lore and divination. The fourth classic, the *Chun qiu* (Spring and Autumn Annals), gave its name to the historical period it covers (722 to 481 B.C.) and deals with historical events in the state of Lu, the home province of Confucius. The *Li ji* (Book of Rites), the fifth Confucian classic, was compiled as late as the second century B.C. and elaborates on the rites and rituals from the Zhou period. These five classics are all connected with Confucius because he used the *Shi jing,* and the *Chun qiu* as sources of instruction, as shown by a close reading of the *Lunyu* (Analects) of Confucius compiled by his students. The Thirteen Classics is a reference to another popular method of classifying these same works and making several additions to create the number thirteen instead of just five classics.

The Thirteen Classics include the five mentioned above, but counts the *Chun qiu* as three separate texts and adds five other classics to the list: the *Li ji, Yi li* (Ceremonies and Rituals), *Zhou li, Lunyu, Mengzi* (Mencius), *Xiao jing* (Classic of Filial Piety), and the *Erh-ya* (Literary Exposition). The *Erh-Ya,* from the third century B.C., was a collection of glossaries to literary texts and marks the beginning of scholarly emphasis on dictionary making to keep pace with the evolution of various scripts or ways of writing classic Chinese characters as well as keeping a record of new words and knowledge.

The classification system known as the Four Books divides the *Liji* into two parts—*Da xue* (Great Learning) and *Zhong yong* (Doctrine of the Mean)—and adds two other masterpieces—the *Lunyu* and the *Mengzi*, which reflects Mencius's philosophy and teachings.

The *Zhou li*, which Lady Song had committed to memory, was long, detailed, and significant for future generations of students and scholars. Like Confucius, Lady Song was a great teacher inspired by the early texts. In the Confucian tradition admired by scholars, Lady Song is properly praised as a *junzi,* a gentlewoman of all the Confucian virtues—uprightness and inner integrity, righteousness, loyalty, and conscientiousness toward others, altruism, and above all for love of her country and displays of humanity.

Barbara Bennett Peterson

Sources

Chu Han, "Saving a Classic From Oblivion," *Women of China*, November, 1986; Wang Peifang, "Xuan Wen Jun Who Spread a Nearly Extinct Learning," (translated orally from Chinese by Fang Hong) in *Famous Women of Ancient Times and Today, Women of China.* Edited by *Chinese Woman Magazine*, published by Hebei People's Publishing House, 1986. "Lady Song," in *The Dictionary of Famous Women of Hua Shia* (China), Hua Shia Publishing House, Beijing, 1988), translated form Chinese by Lucia P. Ellis.

Xie Daoyun (b. ca. 376 A.D.), a poet who lived during the Eastern Jin dynasty, came from a distinguished, noble family. Her father, Xie Yi, was a general who belonged to one of the northern immigrant groups that entered China during the period of disunion following the collapse of the Han dynasty. The Xie family was one of the pillars of defense for the Eastern Jin dynasty.

Xie Daoyun's uncle, Xie An, was an outstanding statesman noted for his scholarly and administrative skills. Her brother, Xie Xuan, together with Xie Shi, defeated Fu Jian (the ruler of the Former Qin) and his infantry force of sixty thousand at the famous battle of Feishui in 383 A.D. with only eight thousand troops.

All of Xie Daoyun's family as well as her husband Wang's family were notable figures of the Eastern Jin period; their family names became synonyms for noble and influential house-holds in Chinese literature, especially poetry.

Xie An spent his childhood with the family of Xie Yi. After Xie Yi's death, Xie Daoyun went to live in the household of Xie An. Xie An loved nature and music and took great pleasure in educating his children, nieces, and nephews in these subjects. One day, while lecturing to them, it suddenly snowed. He com-posed one line of a poem for the children, hoping the children would compose the next line: "What does the white flying snow look like?" he asked; Xie Daoyun replied, "It is like wisps of catkin fluffs flying in the wind." Impressed with her quick wit, Xie An praised her, and others lauded her as a "talent praising catkin fluff."

A good friend of Xie An's was Wang Xizhi (321–379 A.D.), who was known as the "sage calligrapher" for his exquisite, personalized style of calligraphy. Wang's younger son, Wang Ningzhi, who also excelled in calligraphy, was well educated and so was selected as head of the prefecture. Ningzhi and Xie Daoyun married and had several sons, but their marriage was less than happy. Her husband was very superstitious; he became a devout Daoist and shut himself in a tiny room to pray for long periods. His religious fervor and his belief in ghosts and super-natural deities came to clash with his responsibility for defend-ing Kuiji county (modern-day Shaoxing county, Zhejiang prov-ince).

In 399 A.D., insurgents in Kuiji, under the leadership of Sun En, rose up in rebellion against the government. The local pop-ulation asked for government troops to protect them and put down the rebellion, but Wang Ningzhi responded merely by say-ing he had already petitioned the gods to send tens of thousands of troops to defend their region. Before long, the insurgents overran Wang Ningzhi's position, and he and his sons were killed.

Upon hearing of their deaths, Xie Daoyun let the servants flee the residence; she killed several rebels as they approached, but she was soon captured. The rebels were on the verge of killing her grandson (her daughter's son, Liu Tao), who was only a young boy, when Xie Daoyun stepped boldly forward and asked that he be spared and that she be killed in his place. "The matter concerns only Wang family members; it has nothing to do with the Liu family. If you insist on killing people, please kill me first," she said. Moved by her bravery, the rebels let her go free.

She lived a secluded life in Kuiji writing poems and essays. There were originally two volumes of her writings, but only a few poems have survived.

Liu Aiwen
Xu Kaichang, trans.

Sources

A brief biography of her appears in the *Jinshu* (History of the Jin Dynasty), vol. 96, Beijing: Zhonghua shuju, 1974; additional information can be found in *Zi zhi tong jian* (History as a Mirror), vol. 111, 3497–98, Beijing: Zhonghua shuju, 1956; Bai Shouyi, ed., *An Outline History of China*. Beijing: Foreign Languages Press, 1982.

Madam Han (b. ca. 378 A.D.), a military adviser, became famous for the defense of Xiangyang, Hubei province. The place and date of her birth, the date of her death, and her family history are all unknown. Madam Han's husband, Zhu Dao, because of his talent, was appointed as junior officer (or captain) and then prefectural governor. Their son, Zhu Shu, also known as Zilun, was a famous general during the middle period of the Eastern Jin dynasty 317–420 A.D., which ruled from Nanjing, while it attempted to recapture the North. Early in the reign of Jin Emperor Xiaoyang, he was appointed junior general in Nanzhong and prefectural governor in Liangzhou.

In February 378 A.D., three years after Zhu Shu received this appointment, Fujian of the Early Qin dynasty in an adjacent region sent an army of more than a hundred thousand men led by senior general Fu Pi and others to besiege Xiangyang in this period of chaotic rivalry to control areas of China. By April, when the Qin army fought on and pressed Mianbei (near Xiangyang), Zhu Shu still did not pay it any heed because he assumed that the Qin army had no boats to cross the Han river.

Not until the Qin general Shi Yue led five thousand cavalrymen fighting swiftly across the river did Shu gather his forces to defend the main wall of the city. After the front wall was taken, the Qin army attacked the main wall.

Madam Han was then in Xiangyang with her son. She felt strongly about preserving her city's integrity and was familiar with the military situation; but she also knew that her son was arrogant, imperious, and did not take the enemy seriously. When she heard about the arrival of the Qin army, she was disturbed about the defense measures for protecting the city. She got up on the city wall to check on its conditions, and when she got to the northwestern corner of the wall, she found problems: It was not sturdy, so it would be the easiest part for the enemy to surmount if it was not reinforced. She then led more than a hundred servant girls and able-bodied women to build a slant wall more than 66 meters (39.37" = 1 meter) long at that northwest corner.

As expected, the Qin army attacked the northwestern portion of the wall with its main forces. The Jin forces collapsed and moved to defend the new wall built by Madam Han. The Qin army launched a fresh attack on this new wall, which held up against their advances. The number of Qin troops killed or injured was high, so they were forced to retreat temporarily. Ever since then, that part of the wall has been called "Madam's Wall" by the people of Xiangyang.

Apparently, Madam Han's prudent, careful, and strict defense strategy did not have much influence on her son. In the spring of 379 A.D., Zhu Shu did strike several times and won a few battles, but when he saw the Qin troops retreat, he relaxed his vigilance. Finally Zhu Shu was captured after being betrayed by traitors who collaborated with the Qin army, who in the end conquered Xiangyang.

However, Madam Han's patriotism did influence her son deeply. While in a Qin prison, Zhu Shu tried to escape to nearby Jiankang but failed. After his release, when the Qin launched the famous battle of Feishui in an attempt to wipe out the Eastern Jin, Zhu Shu led the army to the front, and this time he was victorious. After the Feishui battle, the Qin dynasty collapsed. Having gone through so many struggles, Zhu Shu became a more mature general. It is said that the success of Zhu Shu owed itself to the influence, guidance and education of his mother, Madam Han.

Liu Aiwen

Sources

Book of Jin, Vol. 81, Lie Chuan no. 51, "Zhu Shu," The Publishing House of China, 1st edition, 1974, p. 2133; *Zi zhi tong jian*, Vol. 104, Jin Hi no. 26, *Jin Emperor Shiao-Wu, The Third and Fourth Years of Tai-Yuan*. Beijing: Zhonghua shuju, 1956, 3285, pp. 3288–89; *Illustrated Annals of Yuan-Ho County*, Shan-Nan-Dao No. 2, Shiang-Yang County, Shiang Prefecture, China Publishing House, 1st edition, 1983, p. 529.

Su Hui (ca. 380–440 A.D.) was a poet who became well known around the year 400 A.D. The daughter of a county official, she was a native of Wugong county, Shaanxi province. At the time she was born, competing powers arose in northern and southern China. Later the Early Qin regime was set up and extended firm control over the vast northern areas. A period of prosperity and economic boom followed the new regime's adoption of policies such as encouraging agriculture and allowing the growth of Confucianism. Su Hui grew up during this stable and flourishing period.

She was an elegant young woman, with a talent for writing poems. When she was sixteen, she married Dou Tao, a handsome young county official descended from a general. He was very capable in literature and martial arts and had great career prospects. It was supposed to be a very satisfactory marriage. But her husband met Zhao Yangtai, a prostitute who was adept at singing and dancing. Her husband took Zhao as his concubine, which made Su Hui jealous and caused her to beat Zhao. Dou Tao was not happy with Su's behavior.

In 379 A.D. Dou Tao was dispatched to Xiangyang, which the Qin had taken from the Eastern Jin dynasty ruling the south. Su Hui, because of her dislike for Zhao, refused to go with her husband and stayed at home. Dou Tao left for Xiangyang with his concubine. They sent no communication to Su Hui, who was now overcome with regret. She missed her husband and decided to weave a brocade and put all her longing, worry, and sadness into it. This colorful brocade, which measured about one square foot, contained about eight hundred words. It was said that there were more than two hundred poems on it, which could be read from any direction or angle; hence, the name "Xuanji tu" (Picture of Rotating Astrolabe), or "Hui wen" (Rotary Composition). Su Hui sent this brocade to her husband, and he was so moved by her gift and loyalty that he separated himself from his concubine and welcomed Su Hui to his side with grand ceremony.

Su Hui wrote many articles, totalling some five thousand words, but all her writings were lost in the wars of the Sui dynasty. But her "Xuanji tu" was still read down to the time of Empress Wu Zetian in the Tang dynasty, and young people of that time adopted the use of brocades the size of handkerchiefs as symbols of their love bonds.

Shi Molin
William Cheng, trans.

Sources

"Dou Tao Qi Sushi," in *Jin shu*, volume 96, published by Zhonghua Shuju, November, 1974; "Zhijin Huiwen Ji-Gaowuzong Huanghou," in *Quantangshu*, volume 97, published by Zhong Shuju, October, 1983.

Empress Yi (ca. 380–450 A.D.), the empress of Li Xuansheng, was born in Ji county, Tianshui prefecture (in modern-day southeastern Gan'gu county, Gansu province) during the period of the Sixteen Kingdoms 304–439 A.D. when the throne in North China was claimed by a number of competing barbarian and Chinese leaders. Yi was talented at composing *ci* (*ci* poetry is lyric verse written to popular tunes) and *liang* poetry (poetry of the Liang dynasty 502–557 A.D., one of the Six Dynasties) and had cultivated noble aspirations and educational interests since her childhood. She first was married to Ma Yuanzheng of Fufeng prefecture (in the northwestern area of modern-day Jingyang county, Shaanxi province), but he died young; she remarried, this time to Li Xuansheng, as his secondary wife. After their marriage, she was melancholy and reticent for more than three years, and she took better care of the children borne by Xin, Li Xuansheng's first wife, than her own children, which included a son and several daughters.

Li Xuansheng was born in Chengji county, Longxi (near the modern-day Gansu province) and came from a big family. History books describe him as "an eager student since childhood, steady and generous in character, tolerant in temperament, good at history and Confucian scriptures, excellent at phraseology." As a young man, he was well known for his skill in the martial arts and his ability to recite Sunzi's *Art of War*.

In 399 A.D., Duan Ye, king of the Northern Liang in Northern China, made Li Xuansheng governor of Xiaogu county (in the western part of present-day Dunhuang, Gansu province). Because Li had imperial connections, local officials appointed him governor of Dunhuang prefecture. In 400 A.D., he was made, in succession, the governor of Shazhou prefecture, the king of Liang, and again the governor of Dunhuang. Then he and his supporters, struggling to reunite China in the earlier tradition of the Han, broke away from the Northern Liang to establish the Western Liang regime. During all this turbulence of competition with other powerful throne claiments, Yi offered her husband support and became his capable assistant. Among the people there arose a saying: "Li and Yi jointly rule Dunhuang." In 417 A.D., Li Xuansheng died, and his son Li Xin by Yi succeeded him as king of Western Liang. Yi then became dowager queen.

Under Li Xuansheng's rule, attention was paid to agricultural production, culture, and education, as well as defense, leading to the cautious usage of military forces; thanks to Yi's help, the small kingdom was not only consolidated with each passing day but also developed economically. But after Li Xin ascended the throne, he made the laws rigid and punishment cruel. At the same time, he ordered the construction of an extravagant palace and refused to listen to any opinions but his own. Consequently, the people became poorer, and the kingdom was weakened. So the neighboring kingdom of the Northern Liang wanted to take advantage to wipe out the Western Liang.

In 420 A.D. Juqu Mengxun, king of the Northern Liang, claimed to be sending a punitive expedition to the Western Qin southward and lured Li Xin to join him. The ruse worked to encourage mobilization of forces, but suspecting a double cross, Li Xin decided to command the army in person, to launch a sneak attack on the capital of the Northern Liang and Juqu. When Yi found out about this, she thought it was a military risk that had no chance of succeeding, so she tried to stop it. She said to Li Xin: "Our kingdom, with its narrow territory and small population, was established not long ago, and our defense force is still deficient. How can you take such reckless action for an unrealistic plan? Juqu Mengxun is not only valiant, but also well versed in the art of war. You are far from his match. I have noticed that he has been wanting to gobble up our kingdom for years. Before your father passed away, he repeatedly urged you that one can never be too prudent in directing military operations. How can you forget all about it? For the small kingdom like ours, the most feasible plan is to try to improve domestic politics, build up strength, and then seek the chance to launch an operation. If Juqu Mengxun is extravagant and cruel, his people will naturally come over and pledge allegiance to you. If you do not rule benevolently, you will not escape being reduced to his slave. You are risking everything on a single venture, and I think you will not only suffer a defeat but ruin the whole kingdom."

But Li Xin turned a deaf ear and commanded thirty thousand infantrymen and cavalrymen to march eastward to the Northern Liang, only to be trapped by the enemy and suffer a great failure. By then his generals all advised him to withdraw the troops to their own capital, but he was too concerned about saving face and made further errors. He retorted: "Since I have not listened to what my mother said, I deserve the humiliation of failure. If I don't kill Juqu Mengxun myself, how can I dare to see mother again?" As expected, not only were his troops wiped out, but he himself was killed, and still worse, his kingdom was soon lost to the Northern Liang.

After the annihilation of the Western Liang, Yi was sent to Guzang (in modern-day Wuwei county, Gansu). Juqu Mengxun met her and offered his best wishes. Yi had a reserved manner and replied very coldly: "Since the Li family has been wiped out, I have nothing more to say!" Some people then tried to persuade her to soften her attitude, saying: "Now your life and that of your children are under their control. Why should we still be arrogant?"

Yi replied: "The prosperity or decline of a kingdom and the life or death of an individual are all predestined. How can I, the dowager queen, weep all the time like ordinary women? As an old woman, I regret that I cannot sacrifice my life for my kingdom. How can you then expect me to be afraid of being killed and beg to live as somebody's slave? If you are going to kill me, that's just what I wish, too." When Juqu Mengxun heard her say this, he gained respect for this unyielding woman. He then decided not to kill her, but to have his son Mao Qian marry one of her daughters. But Mao Qian married a second time, this time to a princess of the Northern Wei; Yi's daughter returned to her mother's side and, before long, died of melancholy. Yi did not weep, but instead kept caressing the body of her daughter, saying: "Why did you not die earlier?" To her, this marriage had not been an honor but a humiliation.

By then, Yi had been sent to live in Jiuquan, and Juqu Wuwei, who commanded the garrison of Jiuquan, repeatedly said to her: "Your children and grandchildren now all live in Yiwu [present-day northeastern Anxi county, Gansu]. Do you not want to go there?" At first, Yi did not comprehend what he meant, so she put him off by saying casually: "Now that my children and grandchildren have been sent to the wild border area, and I am thus old, I don't expect to live many more years. So how can I want to go there to be a ghost in a strange land?" But when she saw that the vigilance of the guards slackened, she secretly ran away to Yiwu.

When Juqu Wuwei discovered her flight, he sent cavalrymen to capture her. Yi said to the envoy chasing her: "It is your master who permits me to go to the north, so why then does he contradict himself and send cavalrymen to capture me? You might as well cut off my head and take it back—I will never

go back to Jiuquan alive!'' The envoy found her to be so determined that he stopped trying to force her to return. After she
arrived in Yiwu, she lived with her children and grandchildren
for the rest of her life.

Yang Debing
Zhu Zhongliang, trans.

Sources

*The Biographies of Renowned Women: The Biography of Yi, the Empress of
Li Xuansheng, the King of Wushao of Liang*, 96th vol.; *The History of the
Jin Dynasty*. Beijing: Zhonghua shuju, 1974; "The Biography of Li Xuansheng, King of Wushao of Liang and his son Shiye" the 87th vol.; *The
History of Jin Dynasty*; "The fourth Long'an Year of Emperor An of the Jin
Dynasty" (in 400 A.D.), the 111th vol., "The Thirteenth Yixi Year of Emperor An of the Jin Dynasty" (in 417 A.D.), the 118th vol., "The first year
of Yongchu of Emperor Wu of Song Dynasty (in 420 A.D.); the 119th vol.
of *Zi zhi tong jian* (History as a Mirror). Beijing: Zhonghua shuju, 1956.

Madam Meng (b. ca. 380 A.D.) was the wife of Meng Chang,
who led a rebellion against the cruel Emperor Huan Xuan. The
exact dates of her birth and death are unrecorded, but she is
believed to have been born at the end of the Eastern Jin dynasty.
It is known that her maiden name was Zhou and that her cousin
was married to Meng's younger brother, Meng Yi. She was from
a wealthy and well-positioned family and entered her marriage
with a large dowry. Meng Chang's ancestral home was in
Pingchang prefecture in the state of Qingzhou (modern-day
Shandong province). Because there had been great turbulence in
northern China at the end of the Western Jin dynasty, Meng's
family had moved south to live in Jingkou (modern-day Zhenjiang in Jiangsu province).

In 402 A.D., Huan Xuan, the warlord of Jingzhou (modern-
day Hubei province), annexed the Northern Army commanded
by Liu Laozhi, who was forced to commit suicide. Most of the
Northern Army generals were forced to choose between becoming fugitives and being killed. Made up mostly of immigrants
from the north, the Northern Army had been an army of high

combat effectiveness, which operated out of Jingkou and Guangling in the middle and late periods of the Eastern Jin dynasty.
At the end of 403 A.D., Huan Xuan had usurped the throne of
the Jin dynasty, proclaiming himself emperor. Huan Xuan's
frenzied persecution of the generals of the former Northern
Army, as well as his corrupt politics, soon aroused resentment
among the former army leaders and the masses of peasants.

Soon a rebellion against Huan Xuan centered in Jingkou and
Guangling (modern-day Yangshou, Jiangsu) was brewing, led
by Liu Yu, a former general of the Northern Army. On hearing
rumors of the impending rebellion, Emperor Huan Xuan sent
two of his younger brothers to crush any uprising.

When these events unfolded, Meng Chang was a military and
administrative chief executive in Qingzhou prefecture. Seeking
a position at court and offering his assistance, he went to the
capital, Jiankang (modern-day Nanjing), where his many talents
soon came to be appreciated by Emperor Huan Xuan. Meng
Chang was passed over for promotion by the emperor, however,
because of a malicious report delivered by Liu Mai, a fellow
villager with whom he had been on bad terms. Because his ambition had been thwarted and avenues of achievement now
seemed closed to him because of slander, Meng Chang went to
Jingkou to join Liu Yu in his rebellion.

Attempting to raise money for the rebellion, Meng Chang
intended to sell all his family property, but a large part of this
property had been the dowry of his wife, so he had to obtain
her consent before selling any of it. Relating to his wife the
plans for rebellion, he cautioned her: ''I think you had better
divorce me before it is too late, and return to your parents'
home, lest you become involved in the risky plot of rebellion,
which might end in failure. If the rebellion is a success, it will
not be too late for me to bring you back to enjoy a rich and
noble life together.''

To this Madam Meng replied: ''You should first ask your
parents' consent for a matter as serious as leading a rebellion,
since they are still alive. You do not have to ask for my consent,
as I completely support the idea. If the rebellion ends in failure,
and the entire family is reduced to slaves and maids by the
authorities, we would have to go out and work to support our

parents. How could I think of divorcing you beforehand and returning to my parents' home?'' Realizing that her remarks were intelligent and well intended, he agreed, saying nothing further about his need to sell her property.

As he rose to leave, Madam Meng, sensing his discomfort, said: "You seem to have more to say. Perhaps you are here not only to seek my consent for you to take part in the rebellion but for the property.'' Before her husband could speak, she cried out, holding their infant daughter outstretched in her arms: "I will not begrudge this sacrifice if our treasured daughter can be sold for money for the great cause such as this rebellion, not to mention my property!'' She handed all her savings, as well as her dowry, over to her husband, explaining to her friends that the money was for her husband's other legitimate purposes, without mentioning the plot of rebellion.

Meng Chang's military uniforms were all red, and as the date of the rebellion drew near, more uniforms were needed. In order to secure more red cloth, she feigned an aversion to that color, saying to her cousin, Meng Yi's wife: "Last night I had a nightmare. I am afraid it is the red things in your house that caused my fears; if we could remove those 'disgusting red objects' from your home, I might be freed of this misfortune.'' Her cousin, taken in by this ruse, presented all the red cloth in her home to Madam Meng; and seven new red uniforms were soon readied for combat.

In 304 A.D. the rebellion headed by Liu Yu and Meng Chang overthrew Emperor Huan Xuan. Meng Chang and his wife enjoyed great distinction for their roles of meritorious service. Stories of Madam Meng's generosity, wisdom, courage, and resourcefulness have been handed down through the ages, earning her a well-respected place in Chinese history.

Yang Debing
Zhu Zhongliang, trans.

Sources

The History of the Jin Dynasty. Beijing: China Publishing House, 1975, vol. 96, the section on "Biographies of Renowned Women;" *Zizhi tongjian*, the 133th vol., section titled "The First Year of Yuanxing of the Eastern Jin

Dynasty'' (in 402 A.D.), ''The Third Year of Yuanxing of the Eastern Jin Dynasty'' (in 404 A.D.).

Empress Feng (442–490 A.D.), consort of Emperor Wen Chendi, regent for two emperors, and originator of the land equalization policy, was born in Xindu (modern-day Jixian county, Hebei province). Her father, a government bureaucrat, was Ma Lang, and her mother's maiden name was Wang. As a child, she was well educated in the classical Han Chinese tradition and was considered resourceful and decisive.

Feng was selected as a noble lady of the court by the Emperor Wen Chendi of the Northern Wei dynasty and soon was selected as his empress. In 465 A.D. Emperor Wen Chendi died, to be succeeded by the crown prince who served as Emperor Xian Wendi and conferred the title of empress dowager upon Feng.

In 476 A.D. she became grand empress dowager and regent for the next two emperors as they were too young to rule in their own names. During her regency, she undertook a series of political and economic reforms that enabled the consolidation of the Northern Wei dynasty, accelerating the breakup of the former clan and slave systems associated with the Tuoba clan of the Xianbei nationality and allowing the development of feudalism. This feudalization paved the way for the reforms of Emperor Xiao Wendi.

When Emperor Xian Wendi ascended the throne, he was only twelve, and Feng was only twenty-four. Yi Hun, the prime minister, became autocratic, dismissing court officials who disagreed with his policies and attempting to reduce the emperor to a mere puppet. Feng secretly took the initiative and had Yi Hun executed; having accomplished this act, she held power in her own hands for a year. After a year of stabilization, she transferred power to Emperor Xian Wendi, who administered through Feng as regent. Four years later, the young emperor, finding politics distasteful, desired to hand over power to his uncle, Wang Zhitui. This idea met strong opposition from both military and civilian officials at court, and the plan was put aside.

Emperor Xian Wendi had his differences with Grand Empress Dowager Feng. For example, they often disagreed over personnel and appointments at court. Feng was especially fond of Li Yi, an imperial minister, but the emperor disliked and distrusted him, and, taking matters temporarily into his own hands, had him executed. Feng was outraged. On another occasion, General Xue Huzhi was demoted to a mere gate guard by the empress dowager, but Emperor Xian Wendi elevated him to a post as garrison general. By 476 A.D. the differences in their political views had become so great that, in the sixth year of his rule, the eighteen-year-old Emperor Xian Wendi passed power to his four-year-old son, the crown prince who would rule as Emperor Xiao Wendi. Feng afterward poisoned former Emperor Xian Wendi to death.

Emperor Xiao Wendi was very pliable, and once again Feng easily dominated imperial politics. Learning from her past mistake of handing over power too early, this time she did not hand over power to the emperor until twenty years after she came to power, at her death in 490 A.D. During this twenty-year period, she accomplished two major goals: the land equalization system and the *Hanization* of the Northern Wei dynasty, through which more Han Chinese dominated positions of power than leaders with connection to the outside "barbarians."

While Feng lived, Xiao Wendi was an emperor in name only; everything, large and small, was decided by the grand empress dowager alone. The land equalization system was put into effect in 485 A.D., when the emperor was still a minor. The lands were divided and given to the peasants as individual farmland, so as to guarantee an increased tax base for the survival of the Northern Wei dynasty. This system tied the peasants to their land and enabled the imperial court to levy taxes according to the value of the property, thus guaranteeing the stability of the empire.

To complement the land equalization system, the system of the three chiefs was put into place as part of the administrative reform of 496 A.D., upon the recommendation of Li Chong, a large landowner of Han nationality. The system of the three chiefs established a system for land ownership registration so that peasants could not escape taxation or the obligations of labor on imperial projects. A chief of a *ling* was appointed for every five households, and a chief of a *li* was appointed for every five *lings*; and a chief of *dang* was appointed to oversee five *lis*. The function of these chiefs (who oversaw the administrative units called ling, li, and dang as officials) was to check the household registration, supervise the production of agriculture, levy and collect farm taxes, and recruit laborers for the corvée (labor on imperial projects) and soldiers for the army. Feng realized that the Xianbei people who dominated the Northern Wei dynasty were culturally backward in comparison with the Han Chinese, and she endeavored to change their customs, forcing them to adopt Han Chinese manners and customs of refinement. In 483 A.D., under a edict from Feng, a mandate went forth banning intermarriage between people of the same surname, a custom that had been practiced by the Xianbei inhabitants. Anyone who failed to obey the new edict would be punished severely. Thus the *Hanization* of minority nationalities (making them more like Han Chinese) in China progressed. Emperor Xiao Wendi, growing up under Grand Empress Dowager Feng's tutelage, continued these policies.

Feng left a legacy of stabilization, having put into positions of great power able ministers such as Li Chong and You Min'geng, who would carry on her wise decrees in their capacity as outstanding administrators of the Northern Wei dynasty. She possessed extraordinary political talent and knew her subordinates well enough to match positions and abilities. Through her elegance, refinement, taste, and astuteness, she contributed greatly to the grandeur of her era. Like many other female rulers, Feng used her power as regent to full advantage sometimes cruelly, manipulating the youthful emperors to do her bidding; but her actions were, she believed, in the best interests of the people, and the land equalization system will always be remembered as one of the great liberal accomplishments in Chinese history.

Feng lived simply, hating extravagance. She ordered her funeral to be as simple as possible, charging that her tomb could not be bigger than 30 square feet and that no funerary objects were to be buried with her.

Wang Caizhong and Shu Aixiang
Zhu Zhongliang, trans.

Sources

Bei Shi, History of the Northern Wei Through the Sui Dynasty. Beijing: China Publishing House, 1982; *The History of the Wei Dynasty.* Beijing: China Publishing House, 1982; He Ciquan, *Collection of Reviews on History.* Shanghai: People's Publishing House, 1982; Han Guopan, *An Outline of the History of the Wei, Jin, Northern and Southern Dynasties.* Shanghai: People's Publishing House, 1982; Zhu Shaohou, *Chinese Ancient History.*

Madam Liu (ca. 450–500 A.D.) was born in Pengcheng (modern-day Xuzhou, Jiangsu province) and later moved to Jingkou (modern-day Zhenjing, Jiangsu). The exact dates of her birth date are not available, but it is inferred that she lived between the years of the mid- to late Eastern Jin dynasty. Madam Liu was born to a general whose family was famous for bravery through numerous generations. Her great grandfather Liu Yi, governor of Bianjun prefecture, was a good horseman as well as a crack shot. Her father, Liu Jian, excelled at martial arts and held official title as general of punitive expeditions. Her brother, Liu Laozhi, who was brave and skillful in battle, was first the vanguard general of the Northern Army, a combat-ready army composed of immigrants from the north, and later its commander-in-chief.

As a child, she developed a strong character and high and noble aspirations. When she grew up, she married a man named He, although the date of their marriage and the given name of her husband are not known. From the few available facts about him, it can be inferred that her husband's hometown was in Tan county of Donghai prefecture (modern-day Tancheng county, Shandong province) and, like the Liu family, he moved to Jingkou to settle. All indications show that He probably joined the Northern Army and that the He family's status was similar to that of Liu family. Madam Liu had a son, He Wuji, who was ambitious from childhood, as well as loyal, brave, and generous.

In 402 A.D., Huan Xuan, the warlord of Jingzhou (modern-day Hubei province), annexed the Northern Army, and Laozhi was forced to hang himself. His generals also encountered persecution. The next year, Huan Xuan usurped the throne and proclaimed himself emperor.

He Wuji was friendly with Liu Yu, a general in the Northern Army, so the two began to make plans to overthrow Huan Xuan. Madam Liu had hated Huan Xuan for killing her elder brother and was eager for a chance to avenge him. When she saw her son frequently talking secretively with Liu Yu, Madam Liu guessed what they were planning and inwardly rejoiced but feigned ignorance of their plot.

One night, when He Wuji was writing behind a screen, Madam Liu, covering the candle light with some object, stood on a stool and then sneaked a look over the screen. When she saw that her son was writing an official denunciation of Huan Xuan, she could no longer conceal her excitement. She rushed to her son, choking with sobs: "I am really no match for Madam Lu of Donghai (see Madam Lu), who led a rebellion against Wang Mang. To avenge her family member, and oppose tyranny, she dared to act without hesitation. But I worried too much and delayed putting my ideas into action for so long. Now that you are taking action, my deep hatred can be mobilized for revenge!" Then she began to ask who else was part of the plot and was pleased to hear that Liu Yu was the chief plotter because he had learned from Liu Laozhi, who displayed outstanding military talents. When she began to analyze the situation in detail, she determined that Huan Xuan would surely be defeated and the rebellion would succeed, so she encouraged her son to act boldly. Because Madam Liu was a well-read, intelligent, and capable person, the result afterward was precisely as she had predicted.

Yang Debing
Zhu Zhongliang, trans.

Sources

Bei Shi, History of the Northern Wei Through the Sui Dynasty. Beijing: China Publishing House, 1982; *The History of the Wei Dynasty*. Beijing: China Publishing House, 1982; He Ciquan, *Collection of Reviews on History*.

Shanghai: People's Publishing House, 1982; Han Guopan, *An Outline of the History of the Wei, Jin, Northern and Southern Dynasties.* Beijing: People's Publishing House, 1983; Zhu Shaohou, *Chinese Ancient History.*

Madam Xian (ca. 515–610 A.D.) was a general and military strategist famed for keeping the Li nationality in the south of China loyal to a succession of rulers during three different dynasties the Liang, the Chen, and the Sui. Her family belonged to the Li nationality, and she later became the recognized political and military leader of the southern Yue people, who lived in the geographical area of Lingnan (now part of Sichuan, Guizhou, and Yunnan provinces, all located in the south), then ruled by a variety of tribal kingdoms. As the leader of the southern Yue people, she controlled and protected about ten thousand families, who were all Li.

Madam Xian lived during the chaotic period following the collapse of the great Han dynasty. During this period barbarians invaded from the north, causing many of the Han Chinese to flee southward and attempt to establish a succession of governments in the south. The entire period from the fall of the Later Han to the rise of the Sui is called the period of the Six Dynasties and includes the smaller time period of the Northern and Southern dynasties.

Originally, the Li lived in stone caves, but when Han Chinese culture spread southward, they began to build houses. Earlier, the Li had been governed by a matriarchy, and in Madam Xian's time some matriarchal aspects remained, despite the prevalence of Han feudal customs, so she enjoyed a great deal of freedom, power, and authority. When she was growing up in Gaoliang (west of the present-day Yinjiong in Guangdong province), her dream was to have the many different tribal groups in her area live harmoniously together, and she often quelled the martial spirit in her brother, who was prone to attacking other groups. She is well remembered in Chinese history for maintaining friendly relations between the Li and the Han Chinese during periods of dynastic upheaval. Madam Xian accomplished this by supporting the central government of each dynasty in power, yet knowing when to change sides and support a new dynasty. Thus she protected her geographic region from devastation and her people from plunder and worked for national unity.

As was often the case in Han Chinese history, good relations were believed to be cemented by marriage alliances. Hence, Feng Rong, the magistrate-governor of Luozhou, asked Madam Xian to marry his son, Feng Bao, who was governor of Gao-liang. After the presentation of numerous generous gifts commensurate with her station, Madam Xian accepted the marriage proposal. It was common tradition among the Li people, in keeping with the ancient matriarchy, that she keep her own name after marriage. Her presence in Gaoliang guaranteed the loyalty of the Li to her husband as the governor, and she assisted him in ensuring the Li chieftains' support of the central government.

The capital most often used in this tumultuous period was Jiankang (now called Nanjing). In 502 A.D. one of the relatives of the founder of the Southern Chi dynasty rebelled and formed the Liang dynasty 502–557 A.D. This Liang founder, known as Liangwu, was a great patron of Buddhism and his reign was one of the longest in this period of instability. In the last years of his life, Emperor Liangwu was challenged by Hou Jing, a rebel leader, and many provincial magistrates supported the open rebellion. Hou Jing had captured Jiankang, and the emperor had called forth his supporters to rescue him, but many, such as Li Qianshi, refused to answer the emperor's summons.

Li Qianshi now plotted rebellion himself, but he needed Madam Xian's support. In 550 A.D., he attempted to lure Feng Bao to Gaozhou in Guangdong province, but she suspected a trap and persuaded Feng Bao not to go. Li Qianshi had planned to force Madam Xian to support him by kidnapping Feng Bao, but this ruse had not worked. Several days later, Li Qianshi openly rebelled against the emperor, attempting to seize power. Madam Xian was angry, as now the rebellion spread to her own region, where she governed. She decided to retaliate against Li Qianshi. Disguising her troops as porters, she ventured forth into Li's city Gaozhou with gifts, saying she wished to placate him because her husband had declined his earlier invitation. Once inside the city, her troops revealed themselves, staged an armed attack from within, and captured the city, forcing Li Qianshi to flee.

Subsequently, Madam Xian cooperated with the forces of Chen Baxian to put down the rebellion of Hou Jing, and in 557 A.D. she supported Cheng Baxian's rise to power as emperor of the new Chen dynasty. Soon afterward, her husband died.

Shortly thereafter another rebellion broke out in Lingnan against the new Chen government. Immediately Madam Xian sent her son, Feng Pu, to quell the rebels, and she arranged for a meeting between Emperor Chen Baxian and the tribal rebel chieftains in Danyang. This second rebellion was suppressed with Madam Xian's help, and the emperor rewarded Feng Pu by naming him magistrate of Yangchun.

In 567 A.D., Ouyang He, a Guangzhou magistrate, rebelled against the Chen. Madam Xian was the rebel commanders' greatest obstacle. Ouyang He captured Feng Pu and held him hostage, hoping to force her to support him. She had to choose between challenging Ouyang He, thus risking her son's life, and supporting the rebellion by inaction. Once more putting her sense of patriotism and idealism for a unified nation ahead of her personal desires, she committed herself to opposing Ouyang He and threw her support behind the central government of the Chen dynasty. Madam Xian garrisoned the borderlands of her region and prepared to be attacked. Her forces won the subsequent battle, defeating Ouyang He and forcing her son's release from prison. She had effectively kept the Li forces united and in support of the Chen dynasty amid open rebellion. The court now honored her for her military achievements.

In 589 A.D. the Sui dynasty came to power after thirty-two years of Chen rule. The Sui would once more reunite most areas of China, ending the Northern and Southern dynasties period. The rise of the Sui marked the end of the Six Dynasties period, which had aimed at restoring the unity of the Han. The Sui dynasty, like the Tang that followed it, was revitalized by the mixture of so many barbarians from the north and the great cultural mix they had produced.

Madam Xian, by now over seventy, was viewed as "the mother sage" of the region inhabited by the Li. When the new

Sui commanders came to review her troops, she joined them on horseback in a suit of armor for a full dress parade review of her forces. Sui officials sent Wei Guang into the region of Lingnan later to survey the area and to measure its loyalty. Several tribal chieftains resisted his actions, either seeking independence or desiring to show support for the former Chen rulers. The Sui court then asked the deposed former Chen emperor to write a letter to Madam Xian, asking for her full support and asking that she collaborate with the Sui in putting down armed resistance in her region. Madam Xian agreed, and sent her grandson, Feng Hun, to welcome Wei Guang. Her friendship, diplomacy, tact, and valor assisted the Sui in consolidating its control over Lingnan.

Gradually, as the Sui government began to levy new taxes for its many projects, reducing the profits of large landowners in the Lingnan region, many tribal chieftains again took up rebellion. Wang Zhongxuan, a tribal chieftain, opposed these harsh economic measures, and many other tribal leaders pledged to support him in rebellion. Madam Xian again supported the central government of the Sui, pursuing her ideal of national unity. She sent another grandson, Feng Xuan, to put down the rebels in her area; he balked, out of friendship with one of the tribal chiefs, and she disciplined him by putting him in prison. Madam Xian then sent yet another grandson, Feng Weng, to assist the Sui in putting down the rebel forces in Lingnan, and he was successful. After this uprising, Madam Xian negotiated with the tribal chieftains and used diplomacy to keep them in line and loyal to the Sui. As a reward, Emperor Wendi constructed a mansion named for her, gave her a status similar to that of an imperial general, and granted her a special seal, which authorized her to mobilize her own forces to protect the interests of the Sui in her region. People called her a ''rare gentleman lady general.''

During her last years there was a harsh magistrate, Zhang Na, who taxed the minority nationalities very heavily, affecting her region. She drafted a letter to the Sui court, complaining of his misuse of authority and greed. The emperor investigated the charge, found Zhang Na guilty of many crimes, and ordered him executed.

By the time the Sui dynasty fell in 618 A.D., Feng Weng was the governor of Lingnan. Many people of his region tried to force him to break with the new dynasty, the Tang; like his grandmother, however, he remained loyal to the central powers when they ruled justly. Like Madam Xian, he envisioned a region in which all nationalities would live together harmoniously. After Madam Xian died, temples were erected in Guangxi and Guangdong provinces to memorialize her.

Madam Xian was not only a great general but also a visionary protecting the identity and rights of minority nationalities that desired to coexist peacefully with their Han Chinese neighbors.

Barbara Bennett Peterson

Sources

Bei Shi, History of the Northern Wei Through the Sui Dynasty. Beijing: China Publishing House, 1982; *The History of the Wei Dynasty.* Beijing: China Publishing House, 1982; He Ciquan, *Collection of Reviews On History.* Shanghai: People's Publishing House, 1982; Han Guopan, *An Outline of the History of the Wei, Jin, Northern and Southern Dynasties.* Beijing: People's Publishing House, 1983; Zhu Shaohou, *Chinese Ancient History.*

Sources for Part III

Actual Accounts of Jiankang; The Records of the Prefecture of Taiping.

Ayscough, F. *Chinese Women: Yesterday and Today.* New York: Da Capo, 1975.

Bai Shouyi, ed. *An Outline History of China.* Beijing: Foreign Languages Press, 1982.

Bei Shi, History of the Northern Wei Through the Sui Dynasty. Beijing: China Publishing House, 1982.

Chen, Zhi. *Hanshu Xinzheng* (Biographies of Relatives on the Empress's Side during the Han Dynasty). Tianjin: Renmin chubanshe, 1980.

Cheng, L.; Furth, C.; and Bon-ming, Yip. *Women in China.* Berkeley: Institute of East Asian Studies, 1984.

Chu Han. "Saving a Classic from Oblivion." *Women of China* (November 1986).

Dictionary of Famous Women of China. Beijing: Zhonghua shuju, 1988.

Fairbank, John K., Edwin Reischauer, and Albert M. Craig. *East Asia: Tradition and Transformation*, rev. ed. Boston: Houghton-Mifflin Company, 1989.

Famous Women of Ancient Times and Today. Women of China, ed. Beijing: Hebei People's Publishing House, 1986.

Han Guopan. *An Outline of the History of the Wei, Jin, Northern and Southern Dynasties*. Beijing: People's Publishing House, 1983.

He Ciquan. *Collection of Reviews on History*. Shanghai: People's Publishing House, 1982.

He Jiexian. "Madame Xian Upheld the Unity of Nationalities and the Whole Country." *Learned Journal of Heibei Normal School,* no. 1 (1987).

History of the Wei Dynasty. Beijing: China Publishing House, 1982.

Illustrated Annals of Yuan-Ho County. Beijing: China Publishing House, 1983.

Jiang Liangfu. *The Chronology of Tomb Inscriptions and Biographies of Historical Personages*. Beijing: China Publishing House, 1959.

Kim Pu-sik. *History of the Three Kingdoms* (Samguk sagi), 1145 A.D.

Jinshu (History of the Jin Dynasty). Beijing: Zhonghua shuju, 1974.

New Text of History of Tang Dynasty. Beijing: China Publishing House, 1975.

O'Hara, A.H. *The Position of Women in Early China*. Taiwan: Mei Ya Publications, 1971.

Quantangshu. Beijing: Zhonghua shuju, 1983.

Reischauer, Edwin O., and John K. Fairbank. *East Asia, The Great Tradition*. Boston: Houghton-Mifflin, 1960.

Wan Nan. "Woman Leader Who Worked of National Unity." *Women of China* (January 1982): 35–36.

Wan Shengnan. *Madame Xian*. Beijing: Zhonghua Books Bureau, 1980.

Wang Zhuanghong and Ma Chengming, comp. *Reviews of Epitaphs of Six Dynasties*. Shanghai: Book and Picture Publishing House, 1975.

Wei, K.T. *Women in China*. Westport, CT: Greenwood Press, 1984.

Yan Kejun, ed. *The Writings of the Three Dynasties in Ancient History, and Qin, Han, the Three Kingdoms and Six Dynasties, Complete Writings of the Jin Dynasty*. Beijing: China Publishing House, 1958.

Zhu Lin. "I Played the Role of Cai Wenji." *Women of China* (February 1979): 27–28.

Zhu Shaohou. *Chinese Ancient History*.

Zi zhi tong jian (History as a Mirror). Beijing: Zhonghua shuju, 1956.

Zuo Fen. *The Poems of the Former Qin, Han, Wei, Jin, the Southern and Northern Dynasties*. Beijing: China Publishing House, 1983.

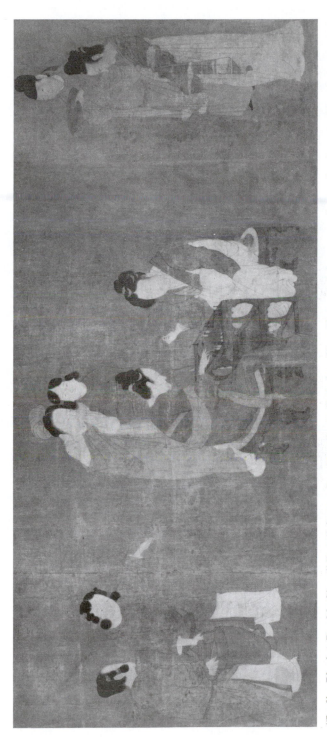

"Ladies Playing Double Sixes." Detail from a handscroll, attributed to Chou Fang, eighth century. Ink and colors on silk. *(Courtesy of the Freer Gallery of Art, Smithsonian Institution, Washington, D.C.)*

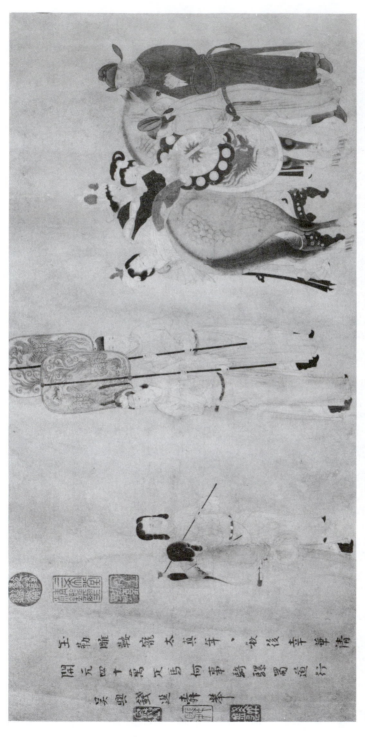

"Yang Guifei Mounting a Horse." From a section of a handscroll by Ch'ien Hsuan (c. 1235–1301) probably a copy after Han Kan (eighth century). Ink and colors on paper. *(Courtesy of the Freer Gallery of Art, Smithsonian Institution, Washington, D.C.)*

Palace Concert. By anonymous, Tang dynasty. *(From the Collection of the National Palace Museum, Taiwan, Republic of China. Used with permission.)*

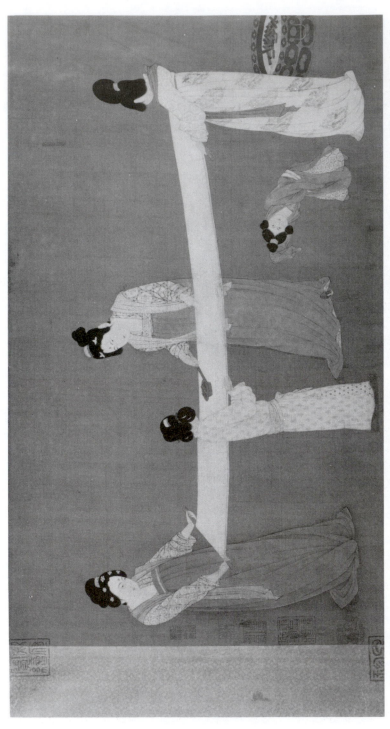

"Court Ladies Preparing Newly Woven Silk, early twelfth century. Attributed to the Emperor Hui-zong, 1082–1135. Chinese, Northern Song dynasty. Handscroll, ink, colors and gold on silk. (Chinese and Japanese Special Fund. Courtesy of Museum of Fine Arts, Boston. Used with permission.)

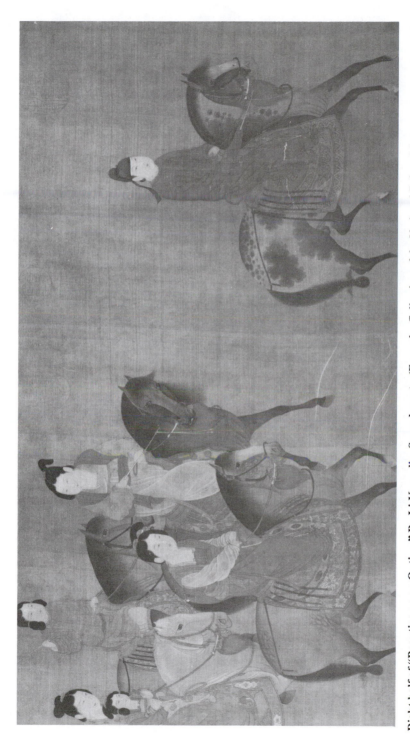

Right half of "Beauties on an Outing." By Li Kung-lin, Song dynasty *(From the Collection of the National Palace Museum, Taiwan, Republic of China. Used with permission.)*

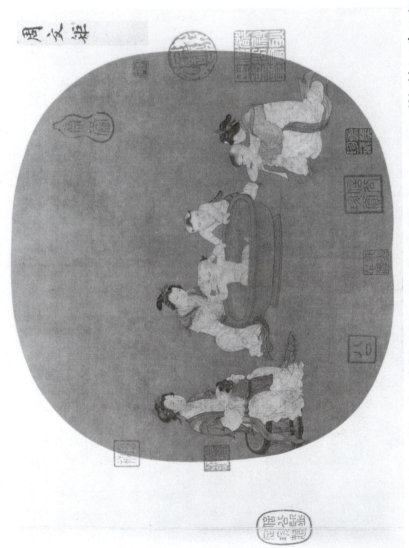

"Palace Ladies Bathing and Dressing Children." One side of a fan, full color on paper, twelfth–thirteenth century. *(Courtesy of the Freer Gallery of Art, Smithsonian Institution, Washington, D.C.)*

"Spring Morning in the Palace of Han." By Chiu Yang, Ming dynasty. *(From the Collection of the National Palace Museum, Taiwan, Republic of China. Used with permission.)*

Empress Ci Xi *(Reproduced from the collections of the Library of Congress.)*

Part IV

The Sui Dynasty and China's Golden Age, the Tang Dynasty

The golden age ushered into China with the Tang dynasty was preceded by the short-lived Sui dynasty, founded by Yang Jian. After the period of political disunion that followed the collapse of the Han dynasty, Yang reunified China, establishing his capital at Chang'an. He rebuilt parts of the Great Wall that had collapsed and began the construction of the Grand Canal linking the waterways of the Yellow, Huai, and Yangzi rivers. This canal allowed the rich, food-producing areas in South China to export grain to feed North China. The economic prosperity generated by the canal laid the foundation for the Tang dynasty. Despite its ambitions the Sui dynasty was short-lived for several reasons. Its rulers attempted too much too quickly and became mired in an ill-fated military campaign in Korea, and resources were overextended in military wars in Vietnam and Taiwan, money was depleted by vast construction projects of palaces, walls and canals, and the frontiers were threatened in the North by the Eastern Turks.

The military losses inspired rebellions that eventually led to the overthrow of the Sui by Li Yuan and his son Li Shimin. They founded the Tang dynasty, which also had its capital at Chang'an; this dynasty would serve as a model for the high cultures that emerged in Korea, Japan, and Vietnam. Militarily the Tang armies were very strong and beat back the barbarians at the frontier north of the Great Wall. In 630 A.D. these armies defeated the Turks and took control of the Tarim Basin, greatly extending Tang authority and power north of the Great Wall into Central Asia. In that region, the Tang rulers made alliances and agreements with the Mongols and other peoples, gradually reopening the old Silk Route and allowing for the prosperity of the Tang dynasty. The Silk Route was extended from Chang'an across the steppes of Central Asia and into the Middle East, terminating at Antioch in Syria, Constantinople, the capital of the Byzantine empire, Jerusalem, and Cairo. These East-West connections greatly invigorated the cultural life of Tang society. Paintings from the period show Tang court ladies on horseback playing polo; they even played at night by candlelight because of the gentry's enthusiasm for the sport imported from Persia. Across this Silk Route was also a delicate food exchange of such delicacies as fruits and nuts, in addition to the normal volumes of silks and porcelains traded for Middle Eastern wares such as handmade rugs and copper plates.

The Tang rulers brought back the Confucian examination system to prepare and train the civil service. These examinations, which were basically open and based on merit, strengthened loyalties to the Tang emperors, who at first ruled wisely through a well-educated staff of civil bureaucrats throughout the far-flung empire. China's borders reached their greatest extent during this period. Civil servants were also instrumental in reinvigorating and carrying forth the field equalization system developed earlier which was a land democratization innovation that broke up the large estates, granting land to the peasants so that each household had roughly a equal parcel on which the family could raise commodities and be taxed by the government above what they needed for their own sustenance.

The cultural and artistic life of the Tang dynasty soared with the poetry of Li Bo (701–762 A.D.) and Du Fu (712–770 A.D.). Li Bo was the poet of the common man, while Du Fu was held in greater respect by the scholars. Du Fu's ''cottage'' (actually a spacious home) in Chengdu is today an honored historical monument often visited by tourists. These two most famous

Tang poets were good friends and occasionally twitted each other's works. In the following verse, for example, Du Fu poked fun at Li Bo's love of wine:

> As for Li Bo, give him a jugful of wine,
> And he will write a hundred poems.

And the playful, bohemian-spirited Li Bo riposted:

> Here! Is this you on the top of Fan'ge mountain,
> Wearing a huge hat in the noonday sun?
> How thin, how wretchedly thin, you have grown!
> You must have been suffering from poetry again.

The art of crafting Chinese poetry was a well-respected form of expression throughout Chinese history as the Classic of Songs *Shijing* (Shih Ching) offered early examples during Zhou times of its early forms, shi (*shih*) or songs, *yueh-fu* (folks songs), *fu* (rhymeprose), *tsan* (hymns) and *sung* (odes). The shi (*shih*) was the early standard for poetry and for poetical self-expression. This form was conservative and related to Confucian thought. During the late Tang, a new form, the *ci*, which were verses written to popular tunes, became popular and by the Song dynasty, this was the preferred form, although the *shi* never completely died out.[1] The writing of poetry was related to being a cultivated individual, scholarly and well rounded. Poems were written to commemorate great state occasions, special events, celebrations, as well as for artistic individual expression. The earliest poetry may be related to shamanistic incantations during special rites and later developed into the form of poetry that became associated in China with scholarship and the examination system for the civil service.

The Tang dynasty was also famous for having witnessed the invention of printing, a process that began with wood blocks upon which entire pages were carved. Printing was necessary to meet the demand for Buddhists' scriptures (sutras), which were increasing in popularity. The Daoists also wanted mass-produced charms and amulets and prayers. In addition to the religious motivations behind the innovation in printing, the secular business world wanted all types of books, reproduced for commercial and scholarly purposes. Almanacs, dictionaries, and other basic reference works began to be printed on a large scale. Paper had been invented in China much earlier, in the first century A.D., and by the fifth century, Chinese officials were stamping their documents with ink stamps. These techniques gradually improved and extended into woodblock printing. The earliest woodblock printing was done in China in about 600 A.D., but the oldest preserved text is a scroll called the "Diamond Sutra," printed in 868 A.D. and discovered in a cave in northwestern China. There is also evidence that by the eleventh century the Chinese had invented movable type, which revolutionized education and made books, most certainly purchased by parents to educate their sons, more available to daughters as well. It became easier for a talented young woman to share in these growing benefits of scholarship as books became available and were passed around among family and friends. A woman certainly enjoyed greater freedom during the Tang than she did subsequently, during the Song dynasty, when elite young women were forced to bind their feet.

But the initial splendor of the early Tang dynasty did not last because of corruption at court and contracting imperial boundaries, which generated a smaller tax base. In 755 A.D. a revolt broke out under the leadership of a military governor, An Lushan, and Tang Emperor Xuanzong had to flee for his life. The emperor's favorite, Lady Yang, was forced to commit suicide. The emperor abdicated in favor of his son, and the rebellion was finally suppressed. But the full power of the emperors and the full glories of the imperial court were never fully restored. State revenues declined, Buddhist temples were sacked for spoils to support diminished government revenues, trade diminished, and gradually upheavals and peasant unrest culminated in the collapse of the dynasty.

Yet another rebellion was led by Huang Chao, who proclaimed himself emperor, sacked Guangzhou, devastated the countryside, and in 906 A.D. directed one of his subordinates to assassinate the Tang emperor. Chaos followed, in a period known as the Five Dynasties period, when no one single ruler or province held control over all of China. Not until the Song dynasty would China once again be unified.

B.B.P.

Notes

1. Alex Preminger, ed. *Princeton Encyclopedia of Poetry and Poetics.* Princeton, New Jersey, 1974 ed., pp. 117–124.

Princess Pingyang (ca. 600–623 A.D.), a general, was the daughter of the first Tang emperor Li Yuan. Princess Pingyang was instrumental in bringing her father to power through efforts to overthrow the Sui dynasty. The organizer of the "Woman's Army," which led the Tang forces to victory, she assisted in laying the foundation for China's golden age, the Tang dynasty. Her brother Li Shimin, who also aided in the overthrow of the Sui, would become the second Tang emperor. Princess Pingyang died while very young, and her father granted her the title *zhao*—which meant someone who was very wise, cultivated, and virtuous, and made many contributions—as well as the title "princess."

The period of the Sui dynasty corresponded to the earlier period of the Qin eight centuries earlier; as the Sui would lay the foundation for the greater Tang dynasty, so the Qin had laid the foundation for the Han dynasty. The founder of the Sui dynasty, Yang Jian (known as Sui Wendi, the "cultured emperor") had reunited China in 589 A.D., subduing the last of the Southern dynasties. The Sui to its credit reunified China after almost four centuries of political division, which encompassed the period of the Six dynasties, stretching from the collapse of the feudal Han to the rise of the Sui. The age of the Northern and Southern dynasties was the last part of the age of the Six dynasties. But, like the Qin predecessors, the Sui leaders were overly ambitious, expanded too rapidly, demanded too much of the populace in the form of taxation for expensive projects—such as constructing the Grand Canal, rebuilding the Great Wall, and launching overseas expeditions into Korea—and therefore did not last very long. The second (and last) Sui emperor, Yangdi, known as the "emblazoned emperor," probably succeeded his father in 604 A.D. by murdering him. Even thought the Sui were responsible for restoring a stable and unified government to China, Yangdi was seen as one of the great Chinese villains, who lost the mandate of heaven. The downfall of the Sui perhaps began with the Sui Wendi's overexpansion into what is now northern Vietnam; this was followed by Yangdi's foray into southern Vietnam in 605 A.D., after he ascended to the throne. Yangdi also sent expeditions into Taiwan as well as Sumatra (now in Indonesia) and demanded the payment of tribute. At the same time, the Sui forces moved to recapture lands in northern China and repossessed important parts of Central Asia. Some of the tribes of the Eastern and Western Turks acknowledged the authority of the Sui. In 609 A.D. the Sui conquered a mixture of Tibetan and Mongolian peoples who had threatened the Silk Route across Central Asia to the western Mediterranean. Overburdened and exhausted, the Chinese people deeply resented Yangdi's final expedition in 612 A.D. against the Korean Kingdom of Koguryo in what is now North Korea and southern Manchuria. Internal revolts broke out in 613 A.D. and 614 A.D. that forced him to terminate his expansionistic forays and return home. Gradually the peasant uprisings were joined by the nobles and their armies, ensuring the dynasty's overthrow. Yangdi tried to quell the peasant outbursts and to purge his government of those nobles who raised his suspicions.

Li Yuan, the father of the future Princess Pingyang, was a military commander in Taiyuan. He led a large army and held several key military positions, so he was viewed as influential and, at the same time, threatening. The Sui Emperor Yangdi ordered that Li Yuan be imprisoned to neutralize his forces, but when the capital came under siege in 617 A.D., the emperor rescinded the order. Li Yuan now realized that if he did not rebel publicly he would soon become a target. He secretly sent his messengers to Hedong, summoned his son Li Shimin to his side, and sent emissaries to Chang'an to recall Cai Shao, Pingyang's husband, who was living at the Sui court as the leader of the palace guards protecting the crown prince. Cai Shao informed his wife of his plans, worrying that she would be in danger and persecuted once his abandonment of the Sui court became known. She counseled him that she could take care of herself and escape. Cai Shao then left to join Li Yuan's rebel forces in Taiyuan.

Several days later, Pingyang also left the court and found her way to her family's estate in Hu county. The surrounding countryside was experiencing a severe drought, causing widespread starvation. Pingyang generously opened the estates' food stores to the people in the area. She thus made these peasants her allies, and from the most able-bodied among them she formed her Woman's Army to support the forces of her father and brother, then in open rebellion against the Sui.

Pingyang also made allies of other rebel forces contending in the region for leadership. News spread from Taiyuan of her father's successes, and this aided her efforts to persuade other rebels to join with her forces in a united front against the Sui. Many rebel groups were in the region, but Pingyang cleverly received support from the most able groups. One of the factions was led by Shi Wanbao, a martial arts expert committed to liberating the peasants. His rebellion had been joined by a cousin of Li Yuan, and after Pingyang heard this news, she persuaded her father's cousin to convince Shi Wanbao to join her Woman's Army. She was successful in this endeavor, thereby expanding her forces greatly. It is a credit to her negotiations, resources, and abilities that a man such as Shi Wanbao would chose a place his fate and future of his troops in the hands of a female general. From this point on, the two forces now fought as one against the Sui.

Pingyang also persuaded the commander, He Panren, who commanded more than ten thousand troops in his personal army (and had convinced the Sui prime minister to join him as well), to join her Woman's Army and cast his fate with hers. He promised to coordinate his plans and strategy with hers and fight as one unit against the Sui. Another commander, Li Zhongweng, relinquished his military force to join the Woman's Army. Together, Pingyang, Shi Wanbao, He Panren, and Li Zhongweng, fighting under the banner of the Woman's Army led by Pingyang, took the capital of Hu county.

The rural people saw Pingyang's forces as liberators rather than conquerors, offering them food and drink upon arrival. Many new forces were now eager to fight under her banner, and the ranks of the Woman's Army swelled. Pingyang was a strict leader: She forbade looting, rape and pillage, since their commission by army ranks would discredit her aims and limit her success.

After its victories, the army distributed food, winning over the populace in the captured territories. When the Woman's Army grew to some seventy thousand troops, the Sui forces began to take it seriously and launched an attack on Pingyang's position, but were routed.

Li Yuan and Li Shimin made great gains in other regions. Since Pingyang had the Sui forces on the run in Hu county, Li Yuan's forces defeated the bulk of the Sui army, a blow from which the Sui never recovered. In the final defeat of the Sui forces, Cai Shao had joined his calvary forces to Pingyang's. Emperor Yangdi fled southward during this uprising, and he was assassinated in 618 A.D.

Li Yuan then established the Tang dynasty, with himself as its first emperor; he gave Pingyang the rank of marshal, allowing her to have her own military aides and staff, just as a prince would be entitled to. But the struggle to gain the throne for her father had exhausted Princess Pingyang and she died not long afterward, at the age of twenty-three.

In honor of Pingyang's having once guarded a strategic pass in Pingding county, the pass was renamed "the Young Lady's Pass" after her death. Her father, grief-stricken at her death, ordered an elaborate funeral, complete with military honor guard. In explaining his reasons to the court for this extravagant display, he said: "As you know, the princess mustered an army that helped us overthrow the Sui dynasty. She participated in many battles, and her help was decisive in founding the Tang dynasty. . . . She was no ordinary woman."

The Li family had been ennobled during the Northern Zhou dynasty and had intermarried with the barbarian allies and families of the north. Hence when the Tang dynasty was established, it soon made vast inroads into Central Asia, reclaiming the Tarim Basin and making alliances to protect the Silk Route with many tribes to which they held personal links. Li Yuan took the reign title Gaozu, or "High Progenitor." He reigned for only a short while and then in 626 A.D. abdicated the throne in favor of his ambitious son, Li Shimin. Li Shimin after his death was called Taizong or "Grand Ancestor." His reign was viewed as the high point of the Tang dynasty.

Although it was her father and then her brother who reigned as emperors, it should not be forgotten that Princess Pingyang was also a guiding military factor in the Tang's rise to power. She would have been pleased to witness the grandeur of her country's Golden Age, an age that well represented her sense of beauty, nobility, honor, and valor.

Barbara Bennett Peterson

Sources

Cao Wenzhu, "From Insurgent to Princess," in *Women of China*, August, 1986: Cao Wenzhu, "The Central Commander of the Woman's Army Supporting Her Father and Brother's Uprising," (orally translated by Fang Hong from Chinese) in *Famous Women of Ancient Times and Today*, edited by *Chinese Woman Magazine*. Beijing: Hebei People's Publishing House, 1986. For the general background of the Sui and Tang periods, see Edwin O. Reischauer and John K. Fairbank, *East Asia, the Great Tradition*. Boston: Houghton-Mifflin Company, 1960. Other sources are Bo Yang, *Genealogical Tables of Chinese Emperors, Empresses, Princes and Princesses*. Beijing: China Friendship Publishing House, 1986; Zhu Zhuocun, *Biographies of Famous Chinese People in Each Dynasty*. Beijing: Zhonghua shuju, 1988.

Empress Shunxian (605–641 A.D.), consort of Emperor Taizong of the Tang dynasty, was born in Chang'an. Her ancestors were of Xianbei nationality, and their original surname was Tuoba, later changed to Zhangsun. Her ancestors had been imperial officials for several generations. and her father, Zhangsun Hao, served as a general commanding the right wing of the cavalry for Commander You Xiaowei during the Sui dynasty. Her mother was a daughter of Gao Jingde, the governor of Yangzhou during the Sui dynasty. Her brothers were Zhangsun Xinghu, Zhangsun Heng'an, and Zhangsun Wuji, and her half-brother was Zhangsun Anye. Her father died when she was nine years old, and she and her brother Zhangsun Wuji were forced by their half-brother to live in the home of Gao Shilian, an uncle. She was given to Li Shiming, the crown prince, as a concubine when she was thirteen years old, and in 627 A.D., when he succeeded his father as emperor, she was elevated as his empress.

The empress was a capable assistant to Emperor Taizong, as well as a shrewd politician and virtuous woman. Contemporary accounts record that she "was filial to the ancestors, showed respect for concubines and palace maids, and tried hard to be a capable assistant of the emperor."

Tang shu (The History of the Tang Dynasty) recounts: "When the imperial concubines or even the low-ranking palace maids were sick, she would go and visit them with medicine and food; everyone in the palace loved her." This harmonious relationship within the palace was an essential precondition to Taizong's successful reign.

The empress treated the interests of the Tang regime first and foremost, never desiring to form her own political faction or party. She thought poorly of the earlier empresses in China's past who had brought members of their own family to court to enrich themselves and gain power. In an article she criticized Empress Ming of the Eastern Han dynasty, describing the downfall of the Han dynasty as rooted in the earlier empress's inability to "control and limit the employment of her relatives." A power struggle between the relatives of the emperor and empress had, in her view, torn the Eastern Han dynasty asunder. Therefore, she always prevented members of the Zhangsun family from becoming prime minister. Zhangsun Wuji was already a man of great distinction, and Emperor Taizong wanted to appoint him to an imperial post. She had attempted to block his appointment, but the emperor turned a deaf ear to her pleas. The emperor appointed Zhangsun Wuji as senior general of the left wing of the military forces and as the chief minister of the imperial personnel department of the imperial secretariat. The empress then secretly tried to persuade her brother to decline the appointments. Her entreaties to the emperor not to elevate her relatives to such a high station convinced the emperor to appoint Wuji to a lower-ranking post. Throughout her entire life, she implored the emperor not to "confer the important and powerful posts" on members of her family. She did this to protect them from attacks, believing this would reduce court intrigue and maintain the integrity of the powerful Tang dynasty. In addition, she placed the guardianship of the princes and princesses under the protection of the Tang imperial regime. The wet nurse of the crown prince, Madame Sui'an, once complained that "the utensils are inadequate in the eastern palace; I humbly request that you supply us with more." The empress rejected the idea, replying: "For the crown prince, what counts is his morality and his good name. There is no need to worry about insufficient utensils." Thus she placed virtue and ethics ahead of indulgence and luxury, again to maintain the integrity of the court.

When her daughter, Princess Changle, was about to be married, several members of the court, attempting to secure the favor of the emperor, wished to present her with extravagant dowry gifts. Wei Zhen, minister of state, cautioned against this, saying it would be inappropriate to give twice as many gifts to Princess Changle as, earlier, to Princess Chang, the daughter of Emperor Gaozu. Empress Shunxian agreed with Wei Zhen and rewarded his good judgment with silver and silks, praising his righteousness and virtue.

As Empress Shunxian, she was both adviser and supervisor to Emperor Taizong and enjoyed reading as well as talking about history with her husband. They enjoyed exchanging views, and both benefited. Emperor Taizong praised her openly, saying that the "empress offers excellent advice; I benefit greatly." Open dialogue and public praise illustrated to others how respectful Emperor Taizong was of his empress. She also cautioned him against harsh discipline and anger within the palace, tactfully persuading him to employ sound judgment. One day, when the emperor lost his temper, "venting his anger on the palace maids for no good reason," she cautioned him: "I am also angry, but it is my fault. I did not give them correct orders. Your majesty should not be angry with them. I will explain everything to you later. Inside the palace, punishment cannot be employed at will." Her admonishment of Emperor Taizong was respected.

On another occasion, when Emperor Taizong was about to kill a horsemen whose horse had died suddenly, the empress managed to halt the execution. She told him the story of An Zhi, who persuaded Duke Lei not to kill a horseman under similar circumstances. He accepted her remonstrance, realizing his cruel behavior. She once told the emperor, "Honest words often do not please one's ears, but every ruler of the state and every head of a family should understand their importance. If one can act justly, then he can control society; if good advice is not heeded, politics will be chaotic. If your majesty understands this lesson well, it will benefit all people of our society." She often stood up for Wei Zhen, once saving him from being condemned because she believed he upheld the best interests of the emperor. She also argued for another imperial minister, Fang Xuanling, whom the emperor had banished from the court, returning him to his native region after a disagreement. As she lay dying, she spoke well of Fang Xuanling, encouraging the emperor not to forget him or his service at court.

Empress Shunxian advocated frugal living and did not behave like an aristocrat. In 640 A.D., she fell ill, and there was no effective treatment available. When the crown prince recommended the "pardon of criminals and heretics if the illness could be treated," she criticized the idea, saying "to pardon the criminals is a matter for the state, so we must not do it recklessly." She believed "heretics erode a nation and weaken the people. The emperor does not tolerate the heretics. So we cannot let him do what displeases him just for my case." She desired to die rather than circumvent the state's authority, continuing to cling to virtue and despise favoritism, believing it weakened the state.

Nonetheless, the crown prince, with the aid of Fang Xuanling, presented the emperor with a request to pardon criminals and heretics if the empress's life could be saved. Agreeing to this idea, the Emperor Taizong was about to issue a general pardon when he was stopped by his wife herself. Again her virtue could not be so dishonored, she pleaded that the construction of her tomb be built on a hill of a mountain and only plain pottery and wood be used. She desired a humble burial that would not overburden the people whose taxes would be used to pay for it. At her request, the pardon of criminals and heretics was not issued. She died at the age of thirty-six and was buried on Jiuzong mountain in a tomb dug out of the hillside known later as Zhaoling mausoleum.

After her death, it was revealed that Empress Shunxian had written a ten-volume book on the virtuous deeds of ancient Chinese women, titled *The Principles of Women*. She had confided earlier to an intimate that she compiled the book to establish norms for her own behavior, but had not told the emperor about her work. When it was brought to the emperor's attention, he read the work and suggested that it be published, believing the book to be good enough to be passed down to later generations. Later, one of her poems was considered so lovely that it was included in *The Poems of the Tang Dynasty*.

The emperor grieved over the loss of Empress Shunxian. Several imperial ministers, attempting to console him, remarked that he should not be overly mournful. But the emperor replied that he had lost a fine assistant. He appreciated her words of remonstration in the palace, and that was why he could not forget her. She had provided the Emperor Taizong with a valuable mirror in which he could honestly view himself, and strengthened China by her wise counsel. Realizing this fact, historians later referred to her as "the fine assistant of the Emperor Taizong of the Tang dynasty." Her honest criticism given out of love made her a virtuous role model remembered by generations.

Song Ruizhi
Ma Li

Sources

The Old Text of the History of the Tang Dynasty, vol. 51, the Biographies (Book One) section: The Empresses (section one), "Empress Wende (Shunxian) of Emperor Taizong," pp. 2164–67 and the Biographies (Book Fifteen) section: "Zhangsun Wuji," p. 2446, published by China Publishing House, 1975; *The History of the Sui Dynasty*, vol. 51, the Biographies (Book Sixteen): "Zhangsun Hao," pp. 1329–33, published by China Publishing House, 1973; *The History of the Tang Dynasty* (section ten): The Sixth and Tenth Zhenguan Year of Emperor Taizong, p. 6096, pp. 6120–23 in the 194th vol. of *Zizhi tong jian* (History as a Mirror). Beijing: Zhonghua shuju, 1956; "Justice," (section sixteen), vol. 5, pp. 166–167, and "The Acceptance of Remonstrance," (section five), p. 58, vol. 3, in The Major Events of the Zhen'guan Years," published by Shanghai Ancient Books Publishing House, 1978; Huang Hezhou, "Basic Research on the Origin of Empress Zhangsun,'' *Renwen zazhi* (Magazine of Human Studies), Shaanxi Province, issue no. 2, 1986.

Princess Wencheng (ca. 620–680 A.D.) was a Tang dynasty princess married to the founding king of Tibet, Songzan Ganbu (or Songtsen Gampo). She was instrumental in popularizing Buddhism and making it the national religion of Tibet through founding the Jokhang temple in Lhasa. Through her marriage, an alliance was created between the Han Chinese people of the Tang dynasty and the Tibetans. Princess Wencheng was a daughter of a member of the emperor's family and was adopted and raised by Tang Emperor Taizong and Empress Shunxian (see Empress Shunxian). She was given a Confucian classical education and grew up in the luxurious court of Chang'an during the early days of the Tang dynasty. Bestowed with the title princess as an honor, she enjoyed the educational advantages of Chang'an, which at that time was one of the most cosmopolitan capitals of the world.

Many leaders from areas bordering China asked the Tang emperor to grant them a Han Chinese bride. Past emperors had made peace and military alliances through marriages arranged between princesses and the chiefs of the outlying minority tribes in the north and the west, thus maintaining the state's security and keeping the Silk Route open. Through these arranged marriages, friendship as well as culture passed into vast areas on the periphery of China, as cultivated Chinese women carried religion, writing, knowledge of sericulture, and agriculture to the less-developed tribal kingdoms, formerly loose nomadic tribes. The Tang dynasty also followed this practice.

In 607 A.D., Songzan Ganbu unified Tibet, with Lhasa as the capital. He was eager to attract Tang technology to his country and desired to bring Han culture, art, and living standard to Tibet. Hence, in 634 A.D. he asked the Tang court for a Han bride. His first request was refused, as Tibet was remote and as yet somewhat unknown. In frustration he declared war against the Tang for this insult, but was defeated. But in his second attempt to secure a Han bride, he was successful. In 640 A.D. Songzan Ganbu sent his prime minister, Ge'erdongzan, to

Chang'an to ask for a marriage alliance as a symbol of friend-ship and as a signal that he wished to develop trade relations and cultural exchange. As a gift to the Tang court, Ge'erdongzan's retinue carried some 5,000 *liang* of gold (1 lb = 9.07 *liang*, or about 8,800 oz. of gold). Emperor Taizong was impressed and consented to give the lovely, cultured Princess Wencheng in marriage to Songzan Ganbu.

This marriage alliance was one of the most important in Chi-nese history because it marked the beginning of a political link between China and Tibet and became the basis of China's future claim to this region. Princess Wencheng understood that she was being asked to play an important role in Tang politics, as rep-resentative of the new bond of friendship between the two coun-tries. Anticipating that she would miss the court advantages she would leave behind, Emperor Taizong gave her a large personal dowry of silk clothing, fine furniture, expensive jewelry, books (many of which would find their way into the Tibetan libraries), and gifts such as farming implements, seed-grains, technical manuals, and musical instruments that she could share with her new people. Thus, the borders of Emperor Taizong's empire were made secure. Newly formed Tibet now also bordered on a friendly ally.

One of the most important items Princess Wencheng brought to Tibet was a gilded statue of the Sakyamuni Buddha made of bronze. Later, this sacred object was housed in the Jokhang tem-ple, built under the care and supervision of Princess Wencheng. Located in the oldest part of the city, the Jokhang temple became one of Tibet's holiest places, but only the great hall and the first two stories still stand from the original structure. Above the entrance are two enormous copper *dagobas* (structures holding sacred Buddhist relics) covered with gold leaf. Between them is a gilded prayer wheel held by two gilded goat statues. Inside is the original Buddha statue brought by Princess Wencheng, cer-emoniously sitting on a gold throne surrounded by two pillars of solid silver. The temple also holds statues of the princess, her husband, and his other wife, a Nepalese he married through an-other friendship alliance.

Escorting Wencheng to Tibet, where she was married, was a large convoy of retainers and her escort, Li Daocheng. On the

Qinzang plateau, the Tibetans warmly welcomed her with gifts of horses, cattle, boats, and yaks. She was given food and drink for her retinue, and they sang her a song of welcome:

> *Don't be afraid of crossing the prairie*
> *A hundred horses are waiting for you.*
> *Don't be afraid to climb over the snow*
> *A hundred docile yaks are waiting for you.*
> *Don't be afraid to ford the deep river*
> *A hundred horse head boats are waiting for you.*

It took Princess Wencheng a month to travel from Chang'an to Lhasa. Songzan Ganbu met her near Lake Zalin and accompanied her party into the capital, where a musical greeting was offered. He respected her cultivated tastes and adorned himself in the rich silk clothes she had brought him. Their nuptial chamber was in the grand Potala (Buddha's Mountain) palace built by Songzan Ganbu on the sacred mountain Putuo Hill. Only a part of the original palace survives. The oldest remaining section is the Guanyin temple, located in the Red Palace, wherein Princess Wencheng assumed her wedded life with her new husband.

Although Buddhism had been known in Tibet before the arrival of Princess Wencheng, it was her faith and the construction of her Jokhang temple for worship that helped spread and popularize the faith in Tibet, later laying the foundations for the emergence of the Dalai Lamas and the administration of Tibet as a theocracy. Perhaps it is appropriate that the statue of the Buddha Princess Wencheng brought was the historical or Sakyamuni Buddha, who always appears crossed-legged on a lotus flower as in meditation. Before Buddhism became prevalent in Tibet, the common local religion was Bon, a faith filled with demons and magic.

Songzan Ganbu married not only Princess Wencheng and the Nepalese Princess Tritson but also three Tibetan women, whose children founded Tibet's Tubo dynasty. Together they all lived in the grand Potala palace, filled with thousands of rooms; later it would be the home of the Dalai Lama and house thousands of monks. The enormous structure faces south, high on the side of the mountain overlooking Lhasa.

According to legend, she and her husband, to symbolize the friendship between Tang China and Tibet, knelt before the Jokhang temple after its completion and planted saplings of willow trees that she had brought from Chang'an. It is said that the old willow tree trunk in front of the temple-monastery today was one of those trees. Princess Wencheng had also brought with her artisans and craftsmen who introduced science and technology. The arts of paper-making and new techniques in metallurgy, in weaving of textiles, and in architectural design were introduced, as were the principles of grinding wheat, making pottery, constructing field tools, brewing wine, and making ink stock. The Tibetans mastered Han techniques of agriculture and adopted the Chinese system of planting. Many gave up their animal-skin tents, reminders of their nomadic days, and constructed Chinese-style houses. The upper class eventually adopted silk clothes and cultivated the art of embroidery. Princess Wencheng introduced the lunar calendar into Tibet, and the planting cycles adopted from China based on this calendar improved agriculture, as did the introduction of her seed-grains. She had also brought a musical band with her, and this enlivened music at court and influenced Tibetan music with the introduction of stringed instruments. Some of the original musical instruments she had brought as gifts can be seen each year on February 13, according to the Tibetan calendar, and are well preserved.

Her husband had sent an emissary to India named Sambhota to learn a system of writing; afterward, he created an alphabet for Tibetan based on Sanskrit. This new system of Tibetan writing was adopted within twenty years and was widely used to write down laws, records, and Buddhist scriptures. The new language stimulated trade and economic exchange as well between Tibet and China.

Tibet prospered, and when Emperor Taizong died, Songzan Ganbu sent fifteen different types of elaborate Tibetan jewelry as sacrificial offerings to honor him. When the new Tang emperor ascended the throne, the king of Tibet also presented a letter assuring the new ruler of his military loyalty and in return was made magistrate of Xihai. As further evidence of good relations, when Songzan Ganbu died in 650 A.D., the Tang emperor sent a high court official to attend the funeral and pay his respects to Princess Wencheng.

During the lifetime of Princess Wencheng, Tibet adopted more and more Chinese culture, for example, the Chinese system of carrying the postal mail with horsemen carrying mail satchels a hundred miles and then changing horses to ensure swift delivery. This system improved the lines of communication with Chang'an. The system of alliance through marriage continued after Wencheng's death: the Tang princess Jincheng married the Tibetan king Chidai Zhudan, which allowed Chinese culture to continue to flow into Tibet.

Princess Wencheng lived in Tibet for forty years. When she died, the Tibetans held a great funeral for her; heretofore, the funerals of women in positions such as Wencheng's were not recorded. The date of her death is commemorated in Tibet with the recitation of her good deeds for Tibetans, who wear paper hats and hold bamboo poles. Other holidays commemorate the day of her arrival and her birthday. On these festive occasions plays are staged that retell her life story: a goodwill ambassador who married for diplomacy's sake, but became much more than a goodwill envoy, as she spread the Buddhist faith, thus influencing irreversibly the fortunes and future of her adopted people.

By the tenth century, the religious movement of Buddhism in Tibet, began to assert political leadership as well as spiritual. The monasteries were fortified, their wealth, influence, and estates grew, and the lamas began to assert authority over their flock of faithful Buddhists. In 1572 A.D. the first Dalai Lama was proclaimed, a titled conferred by the Mongols whose chief was Altan Khan, with Dalai meaning ''ocean'' and Lama meaning ''man of profound wisdom.'' Hence Dalai Lama means one whose knowledge is as deep as the ocean. The Dalai Lama in turn appointed the Panchen Lama who ruled from Xigaze, two hundred and twenty-seven miles from Lhasa. The thirteenth Dalai Lama proclaimed Tibet independent from China in 1913. When the Communists came to power in 1949, they reasserted control over Tibet and established Tibet as an Autonomous Region in 1965. Many temples and monasteries in Tibet were destroyed during the Cultural Revolution in China, but fortunately the Jokhang Temple founded by Princess Wencheng remains, a

Empress Wang, who hoped to make Wu Zetian her ally to counter the affections of the emperor for another concubine, Xiao. Wu Zetian fended off the enemies of the emperor, who fell in love with her and married her. Soon she subdued all rivals. At court, treachery was a high art form that Wu Zetian practiced with finesse, as shown by one story of how she replaced the empress. The empress enjoyed visiting the palace nursery alone to see Wu Zetian's new infant daughter. After one of her visits, Wu Zetian hid in the nursery to await the uproar that would ensue when her infant would be found dead, *supposedly* killed by the empress. Gaozong discovered the atrocity, and in the palace investigation, all the palace maids supported the circumstantial evidence implicating the empress, and the empress was thus unfairly accused and defamed and dethroned.

Because she was of low birth, however, Wu Zetian faced strong opposition to being elevated. One faction at court led by Changsun Wuji and Prime Minister Chu Suiliang opposed her becoming empress, while Li Yifu and Xu Lingzong supported her, urging her selection, and eventually convinced the emperor that the choice was his alone. Gaozong made Wu Zetian his empress, in 655 A.D., a couple of months after deposing Wang, dismissing the concubine Xiao, and reducing them both to commoners. Wu Zetian, already exerting her power and influence, rewarded her supporters, banished her enemies, and had the former empress and concubine whipped a hundred times each and ordered them to be thrown into wine jars after having their hands and feet cut off. Her revenge complete, she turned to seek new sources of power.

One source of power was the examination system, which allowed promotion to government service by merit rather than by noble birth. Thus, eventually Wu Zetian was increasingly able to outflank the aristocracy at court and subjugate them. Other sources of power were her three sons by Emperor Gaozong, whom she used to camouflage her thrusts for individual power. Yet another source of her power was the confidence she shared with her husband and her ability to take control of many affairs of state with his blessing when he fell ill. A final source of her power drew from a loyal civil service and army, successful graduates of the examination system, and her personal selections at court. People whom she had selected and chosen to promote remained fiercely loyal to her. This power base lasted half a century, during which time she consolidated and enlarged the gains of the brilliant Taizong.

In 660 A.D., when her husband became ill, Wu Zetian assumed administrative powers. Gradually the emperor, feeling duped, attempted to recover his power, but failed; having thwarted this attempt to unseat her, Wu Zetian had Shangguan Yi, a palace official, executed for his role in the aborted plot. In a direct challenge to the emperor, Wu Zetian had bested him, a fact that did not go unnoticed. She was known now as the "second sage" and ruled with uncontested power. Humiliated, Gaozong, possibly at the behest of Wu Zetian, abdicated in favor of their son, Crown Prince Li Hong. Wu Zetian seized this opportunity to grab the throne in competition with her own son.

Wu Zetian was a great patron of Buddhism in China, a faith encouraged by the prosperity and peace of the Tang and the communications and flow of pilgrims along the Silk Route. Taizong's reign had allowed Buddhist temples and monasteries to proliferate and thrive as never before. Buddhism found its greatest patronage later, around 700 A.D., under Wu Zetian, when Buddhists condoned and encouraged her assumption of power. As remolded in China, Buddhism became a religion that buttressed the state and served the monarchy and society. The monasteries were centers of learning that provided Wu Zetian with ministers at court who gained their positions through the examination system. Buddhism counterbalanced Confucianism—traditionally the ideology of the titled aristocracy and landed nobility—binding the common people to the state, serving as the state's spiritual guardian, and legitimizing her rule by providing religious functions and ceremonies for Wu Zetian's imperial lines. Thus Buddhism was supported as a spiritual branch of the administration, and Buddhists returned the favor in kind.

The most popular sect given state support during the eighth and ninth centuries was the Tiantai sect (in Japanese, Tendai), named for Mount Tiantai, a great Buddhist center in Zhejiang. Fitting neatly with Wu Zetian's policies, this sect was very eclectic, promoted compromise, stressed the Mahayana (Greater

Vehicle) concept of relative truths and organized conflicting doctrines into different levels of validity.

Buddhism as a philosophy also aided in blending the many different kinds of people over which Wu Zetian held suzerainty. The capital Chang'an (now Xi'an), and later Luoyang, often welcomed foreigners from all over Asia to trade, and Buddhism coexisted peacefully with Middle Eastern religions such as Zoroastrianism, Nestorian Christianity, and Manichaeanism, as well as Confucianism.

Wu Zetian had successfully used the examination system to create a true meritocracy drawn from the whole country, and for the first time in China's history this group was seriously challenging the aristocracy for leadership in government. In addition to relying on this civil service bureaucracy, Wu Zetian often handpicked the provincial military leaders from ranks outside the nobility, and they could be counted on to defend her interests.

Crown Prince Li Hong died under mysterious circumstances. He had outraged his mother by asking Emperor Gaozong to allow the forty-year-old daughters of concubine Xiao to leave the court and pursue their own lives. Shortly thereafter he was found poisoned, and his mother was suspected though nothing was ever proved. His successor as crown prince was Li Xian, Wu Zetian's second son, and she granted him some powers at court possibly to prepare him for the succession. But in 680 A.D. she accused him of plotting rebellion and conspiring against her and demoted him to commoner status, naming Li Xian, her third son, crown prince.

Emperor Gaozong died in 683 A.D., and Li Xian ascended the throne, known as Emperor Zhongzong. His performance, or perhaps deference, was judged wanting by Wu Zetian, so she dethroned him and renamed him Prince of Luling, Fangzhou, Hubei province. She then named Li Dan, her fourth son, Emperor Ruizong; afterward she then stripped her grandson Li Zhongzhao, son of Li Xian, of his royal status and forced Li Xian to commit suicide. Her youngest son, seeing intrigue and family confusion around him, remained carefully in Wu Zetian's good graces, doing her bidding. For all practical purposes, Wu Zetian ruled with an iron hand, deciding all matters of state as supreme ruler.

While legitimizing her rule through her male heirs, she nonetheless aroused opposition from factions of officials. Duke Xu Jingye organized a plot to depose her in 684 A.D., but vindictiveness and acquisitive self-serving intentions among the conspiracy's organizers derailed the plot and the rebel leaders were killed by Wu Zetian's forces. Four years later this sequence was repeated, with Wu Zetian once more victorious.

Wu Zetian was a superb propagandist on her own behalf. She began a public education policy directed toward gaining the throne in her own name and own right. In April 688 A.D., she had her nephew employ a carver to engrave a large stone with eight characters reading "The sage mother has come down to earth." This stone, Wu Zetian's supporters claimed, was a sign from heaven giving her the mandate to rule. Buddhists collaborated in spreading and legitimizing her claims to full power. Fa Ming, a Buddhist monk, wrote four volumes publicizing Wu Zetian as an incarnation of the Maitreya Buddha and promising that she would supplant the Tang dynasty with her own. This suggestion and announcement became a self-fulfilling prophecy. Other followers began to clamor for her ascension, and she claimed the title *huangdi* in 690 A.D. Emperor Ruizong, having no choice, acquiesced, even petitioning the empress to take the surname Wu. Wu Zetian's rise to power was complete.

Wu Zetian also used a cultivated system of informers and spies who loyally aided her efforts against political enemies, many of whom were members of the nobility. In 686 A.D. she began to grant favors and promote those who informed on opponents. When given a horse to get to court, informants, mostly commoners, gave Wu Zetian knowledge of any possible uprising or coup attempt, sustaining her in power; this resulted in the death of many members of noble families. Wu Zetian cleverly divided the rich from the poor for her own gain. She was especially adapt at ferreting out opposition to her rule in Shanxi province, the origin of the Tang dynasty's power. She had earlier moved her capital from Chang'an to Luoyang to free herself from the grip of aristocrats at court and to carry out her democratizing reforms, such as the meritocracy in administrative leadership created by the operation of the examination system, more smoothly.

The imperial examination system centralized state power and broke down inherited power. Wu Zetian doubled the number of candidates who passed the examination, called *jinshi*. She often gave the examinations at her court and congratulated the successful *jinshi*, winning their loyalty. After she assumed full imperial powers, she began a similar civil service examination for military officers and bound them to her reign in like fashion. Most were chosen from the ranks of the common people.

At various times in her career, Wu Zetian was called "a scorpion, wolf, and a jackal," but whatever opponents called her, she was praised for providing strong leadership and spawning prosperity. By the time she abdicated in 705 A.D., the population had nearly doubled from what it had been a half century earlier, largely because of her statecraft, which democratized China to some extent. The rise in population is probably due to a program she instituted reclaiming vast agricultural lands. Stressing the development of agriculture, she revised the official agriculture (the official book on agriculture during her reign)—*Zhaoren*. This book's policy statement stated that counties and prefectures that reclaimed land and produced surplus grain would be rewarded, whereas those areas where there was population exodus because of tyrannical overlords would be punished. Her political life was connected to landlords who held small or medium-sized properties, not the aristocracy. Thus she encouraged a careful husbanding of China's productive resources including land and laborers.

Wu Zetian, using the Uighur tribes as allies, recaptured the Tarim Basin and re-established China's boundaries enjoyed during Emperor Taizong's time. She was also very supportive of China's minority groups and retained their friendship. She maintained a system of envoys who traveled to foreign capitals and received many foreign emissaries. The Silk Route flourished under her direction, creating wealth, prosperity, peace and stability. A great patron of education and the arts, she gave lavishly to scholars, who wrote 442 volumes in 20 categories at her behest.

Artists carved Buddhist images in grand style at the Longmen Grottoes in Luoyang, Henan province, where it is said one of the Buddhist statues bears her likeness.

In 705 A.D., when in her eighties, she was deposed in a palace coup that set her aside and restored Emperor Zhongzong to the throne. He named his mother the great sage and then restored the name of the dynasty. Later that year, Wu Zetian died. She was buried with her husband at the Qianling tombs in Qian county. As she requested, a blank tablet was mounted at the entrance to her tomb. She believed posterity could write its judgment of her, speaking of her qualities as a competent ruler, who chose officials based on merit rather than social position. One of her biographers, C.P. Fitzgerald, wrote: "The transformation of Chinese society in the Tang period from one dominated by a military and political aristocracy to one governed by a scholarly bureaucracy drawn from the gentry was promoted by her policy. . . . She stabilized the dynasty and ushered in one of the most fruitful ages of Chinese civilization."

The approach to the tomb of Wu Zetian is a long avenue lined with sixty-one statues that show the length and breadth of the grandeur of the Tang dynasty, including officials and representatives from Turkestan, Mongolia, and other parts of Central Asia. The figures are the symbols of loyalty and tribute to Wu Zetian's China, in its golden age, much as the friezes at Persepolis suggested the enormity of the Persian empire at its height. Her lovely tomb is a fitting reminder of China's only daughter of heaven.

He Hongfei

Sources

C.P. Fitzgerald, *The Empress Wu*, 2nd ed., 1968; (his biography used original Chinese sources in the New and Old T'ang histories); R.W.L. Guisse, *Wu Tse-t'ien and the Politics of Legitimation in T'ang China*, 1978; Nghiem Toan and Louis Ricaud, *Une traduction juxtalineaire commentee de la biographie officialle de l'Imperatrice wou-t'ien*, 1959, is an annotated French translation of the official biography of Empress Wu included in *The New T'ang History (Hsin T'ang Shu)*. Chinese sources includes: Xiong Deji, *On Wu Zetain*, translated by Wei Lun Jie, 2 vols.; Bo Yang, *Genealogical*

Tables of Chinese Emperors and Empresses, Princes, and Princesses. Beijing: China Friendship Publishing House, 1986; *Records of Chinese Figures*, compiled by the Knowledge of Literature and History editorial department. Beijing: Zhonghua shuju, 1985; Edwin O. Reischauer and John K. Fairbank, *East Asia, the Great Tradition.* Boston: Houghton-Mifflin, 1960; C.P. Fitzgerald, *Son of Heaven: A Biography of Li Shih-min*, 1933. L. Perry and B. Smith, ed., *Essays on T'ang Society*, 1976. Danielle Elisséeff, *La Femme au Temps des Emperers de Chine.* Paris: Stock/L. Pernound, 1988. Chu Nan, "History's only Daughter of Heaven," *Women of China*, April and May, 1986. Chen Guocan, "Empress Wu's Tomb (Xi'an) and Its 61 Mystery Figures," *China Reconstructs* (August, 1983).

Shangguan Wan'er (664–710 A.D.), a Tang dynasty poet and court official, was one of the most talented and colorful women in China's history. Smart and ambitious, she was involved in powerful struggles in the court of the Tang dynasty. She was a native of Shaanzhou (now Sanmengxia, Henan province), but lived in the Tang capital, Chang'an (now Xi'an). Her grandfather Shangguan Yi was a high-ranking official in the court, and so was her father, Shangguan Zhi. Her mother came from the Zhen family, but little about her is known. Her mother's younger brother, Zhen Xiuyuan, was also a noble and a high-ranking official.

In late 664 A.D., both Shangguan Yi and Shangguan Zhi were killed upon orders from Wu Zeitian (see Wu Zetian) because they had led a faction of dissatisfied palace officials who petitioned Emperor Gaozong to dethrone Wu Zetian as empress. Wu Zetian was victorious in this power struggle, and she held sway over the empire. So after these executions, Shangguan Wan'er, then an infant, and her mother were kept at the palace to work as slaves.

Shangguan Wan'er grew into a pretty and lively girl noted for her intelligence and scholarship. One day, Wu Zetian summoned Shangguan Wan'er for a test, ordering this slave girl to write an essay in her presence. Without hesitation the fourteen-year-old girl wrote a splendid article. Wu Zetian was pleased and henceforth kept the girl by her side as her trusted aide.

The Tang dynasty was the golden age of Chinese poetry, and, as times were prosperous during Wu Zetian's rule, there developed a custom both inside and outside the palace of writing or reciting poems at banquets. The empress and her princesses often asked Wan'er to write poems for them because she could write poems in different styles for different people at once, and her poems were usually the best. People admired her quick wit, and her poems became widely read and recited throughout the imperial capital.

Favored and supported by Wu Zetian, Wan'er organized poetry competitions at court and served as a judge. The winners were presented with a gold cup. The greatest poets and court scholars of the time all accepted or obeyed her comments on their writings, which was unusual in the male-dominated society of the period.

Shangguan Yi had been a great poet in the early Tang. He wrote in an ornate, flowery style that came to be named for him: "Shangguan style." The *Collected Poems of the Tang Dynasty* contained twenty poems by Shangguan Yi and thirty-two poems by Wan'er. These represent only a small number of the poems they wrote in their lifetime, but most of the others have been lost.

Shangguan Wan'er contributed greatly to the promotion and development of Tang poetry and academic studies. As she was trusted by Wu Zetian, she was sometimes also placed in charge of drafting edicts and decrees. She made proposals to enlarge the imperial library, bring more scholars to the court, and recruit more scholars for the imperial examinations. This was why there were so many outstanding Tang poets, such as Wang Bo (650–693 A.D.), all of whom were her contemporaries. Within twenty years, the Tang court had gathered the best scholars in China.

But it proved dangerous to work under a ruthless empress. Once Wan'er offended Wu Zetian and was about to be put to death. But Wu Zetian needed her talent and decided to have Shangguan Wan'er disfigured instead, by having one Chinese character cut or burned onto her face. Afterward, Wan'er was more careful, but more ambitious. Increasingly she became involved in the power struggle in the court between Wu Zetian and her detractors. But then Wan'er had a love affair with Wu Sansi, Wu Zetian's nephew, and switched allegiance to side with the Wu faction.

Emperor Gaozong died in 683 A.D., and Wu Zetian ruled the empire unchallenged. In 690 A.D. she proclaimed herself the first emperor of the Zhou dynasty. She no longer hid her power behind the male heirs, her sons. After 696 A.D., the thirty-two-year-old Shangguan Wan'er took full charge of imperial decrees.

In 705 A.D., Wu Zetian was deposed, Emperor Zhongzong was reinstated, and then Wu Zetian died. As a measure of his trust in her, the emperor bestowed on Shangguan Wan'er the title *zhaoyi*, the highest title for a female court official, and exonerated Shangguan Yi and Shangguan Zhi, conferring official titles on them posthumously. Emperor Zhongzong was under the sway of his wife, Empress Wei (see Empress Wei), who hoped to assume as much power as had Wu Zetian. So Shangguan Wan'er, as a mistress of Wu Sansi, was in a dangerous position. She thus aligned herself with Empress Wei, who in turn needed Shangguan Wan'er's talent.

All this angered the emperor's Li family. One day in mid-707 A.D., Prince Jiming (Li Zhongjun) staged a palace coup and killed about twenty members of the Wu clan, including Wu Sansi. Prince Jiming demanded that the emperor hand over Shangguan Wan'er. To win the emperor's support, she said: "Now they want to kill me, then it will be your turn to die." Emperor Zhongzong offered her help and protection. Later Prince Jiming, stripped of his royal title, was defeated and killed.

In 710 A.D., the emperor was poisoned by Empress Wei. Subsequently the young and capable Prince Linzhi (Li Longji, the son of Li Dan, who later reigned as Emperor Xuanzong) marched his troops into the capital and killed Empress Wei and her entire clan. Shangguan Wan'er was arrested; she pleaded innocent, but was found guilty and executed. She was a victim of factionalism at court.

Emperor Xuanzong did not pardon her, but he did greatly admire her talent. In 720 A.D. he ordered the collection of Shangguan Wan'er's poems and writings, which were then edited into twenty volumes. Many of her poems were well written, though some were written on ceremonies and festivals without much depth of feeling. Nevertheless, Shangguan Wan'er is well remembered as one of the Tang dynasty's greatest poets.

Shi Muling
Xu Kaichang, trans.

Sources

Xin Tang shu (New History of the Tang Dynasty). Beijing: Zhonghua shuju, 1975; *Jiu Tang shu* (Old History of the Tang Dynasty). Beijing: Zhonghua shuju, 1975; *Quang Tang shi* (Complete Poems of the Tang Dynasty), vol. 5, 60. Beijing: Zhonghua shuju, 1960.

Empress Wei (d. 710 A.D.) was the ruthlessly ambitious wife of Emperor Zhongzong in the Tang dynasty. Her grandfather, Wei Hongbiao, was a military official; her father, Wei Xunzheng, was sent into exile by Empress Wu Zetian; her mother was Madam Cui; and her four brothers were all killed by Ning Chengji and his brothers, who were leaders of the minority population in Qinzhou.

In 680 A.D., Li Xian (the third son of Empress Wu Zetian and Emperor Gaozong) became crown prince and shortly thereafter made Wei his concubine. In late 683 A.D. Emperor Gaozong died; Li Xian succeeded him, with the reign title Emperor Zhongzong. The following year Wei became empress. But her husband was soon deposed by Wu Zetian, who elevated her fourth son, Li Dan, as emperor. Wei followed her husband, who had been demoted to being prince of Luling, Fangzhou, Hubei province.

In 705 A.D. a palace coup deposed Wu Zetian and returned Li Xian to the throne. Empress Wei gave birth to four daughters and a son named Prince Yide.

After his resumption of power, Emperor Zhongzong tried every means to revive the Tang dynasty. He reduced the number of temples to lighten tax burdens; he exempted the population from one year's taxation and the people in Fangzhou from three years of military service; he released three thousand maids from service in the imperial palace; he clarified the laws and punishments; he encouraged new government proposals and criticism; and he rehabilitated and settled numerous historical judicial cases. These efforts were quite successful.

But the people became disillusioned when Empress Wei began to interfere in state affairs. The emperor and empress had gone through terrible hardships in their exile and had developed a very close relationship. The emperor actually was a timid and weak-willed person, and at one point during their exile he had become frightened, wanting to commit suicide when he heard there was an envoy sent from the capital to Fangzhou. When this happened, his wife stopped him, saying: "It is very common for us to have fortune or misfortune; it won't be worth anything if you die for it." His death would solve nothing she had counseled; it would be better to be an active reformer. Regaining his courage, he placed his trust in his wife and swore that if he ever regained the throne he would not hinder her ambitions. After the emperor's restoration, Empress Wei, taking advantage of her husband's previous promises, formed her own clique to assist her in her later seizure of power. Even after Wu Zetian's death, Wu's clique, though reduced, was still very powerful; it included people like Shangguan Wan'er (see Shangguan Wan'er) and Wu Zetian's nephew Wu Sansi, who were still at court. Empress Wei realized that she had to include them in her own clique if she wanted to amass her own power. Empress Wei placed Shangguan Wan'er in the administrative office in the imperial palace and persuaded the emperor to make her an official empowered to initiate documents for him.

The imperial court thereafter was riddled with intrigue. General Zhou Rengui, who had aided Empress Wei in avenging her parents' death, was granted a noble rank, grand general and envoy to supervise five governors. Wu Sansi and Huzeng Huifang, a Buddhist monk who could do nothing but curry favor with the nobility, were granted important titles in the court. Empress Wei had control over Prime Minister Cui Shi, Defense Minister Zong Chuke, and others. A new powerful clique combining Empress Wei's forces and Wu Zetian's remaining forces wielded power over the whole court, making Emperor Zhongzong a mere puppet.

Next, Empress Wei set out to remove and kill all her political enemies. Five honest and upright officials who had battled Wu Zetian in order to restore Emperor Zhongzong were angry at the arrogant and domineering Empress Wei. The empress hated these officials and framed them with stories of slander in front of the emperor to dishonor them. The emperor listened to his wife and dismissed them. Empress Wei eventually convinced the emperor to drive them out of the capital and exile them to remote areas as minor officials. Later she had them and their relatives executed based on fabricated charges.

Some just and brave individuals tried to persuade the emperor to stop her, but they all fell prey to her plots. In mid-706 A.D., a court officer Wei Yuejiang sent a report to the emperor charging that Empress Wei had conspired with Wu Sansi in planning a rebellion. The emperor did not believe the story and wanted to have the officer executed. Later, heeding the warnings of some ministers, the emperor punished him with a severe beating instead of execution and exiled him to Lingnan. Although in exile, the unfortunate officer was still killed by General Zhou Rengui under instructions from Empress Wei.

In mid-710 A.D., Lang Ji from Dingzhou wrote the emperor about Empress Wei and Defense Minister Zong, who were conspiring to rebel. When Empress Wei received this news, she made a tearful scene in front of the emperor, who was hesitating over accepting the information. She kept imploring the emperor until the emperor gave the order to execute Lang Ji. Shortly thereafter, General Yan Qinrong from Xuzhou wrote to the emperor: "Our society has been seriously damaged both by the empress, who is interrupting state affairs and is loose in morals, and by her clique, including her daughter Princess Anle. If we do not stop them, it might be dangerous in the future." Empress Wei and her supporters were frightened about the report, and they immediately sent their own people with their fabricated imperial edict to Xuzhou and killed General Yan. The emperor finally realized what was going on and became angry about the fabricated edict. Now, there was nothing for Empress Wei to do but kill her husband.

The following month, Empress Wei ordered the poisoning of the emperor's favorite food, steamed cakes. He ate the cakes, brought in by a maid, and after a while he felt pains in his stomach. Soon he could not control himself and began to thrash around in bed. When the hypocritical empress rushed into the palace, the emperor could not speak but opened his eyes wide, glaring at the empress in horror. His death came soon after.

The sudden death of the emperor fueled rumors and tension among the public. Empress Wei did not announce the funeral at once. Instead, she dominated the imperial court and pressed her ambitions. One of her sons was to be crowned as emperor. She took measures to control the situation, such as deploying troops to guard the capital and put them under the leadership of her family or her followers; she sent troops to Junzhou, Hubei province, to take precautions against General Li Chongfu there; she appointed her trusted followers as ministers and let them stay in the eastern capital; and she forged a will purported to be the emperor's. Then, Empress Wei made her sixteen-year-old son Li Chongmao, first, crown prince and, then, emperor. As the Emperor Yangdi, he legally permitted Wei's domination over the court. With all this done, she announced the funeral and the ascension of her son as emperor and herself as empress regent.

But empress regent was not her desired title. Her further steps were to put members of her family in all the important positions in the imperial palace and the capital garrison force. They awaited only the removal or assassination of the young new emperor and other opponents before they could openly seize power.

At this critical moment, Li Longji (the son of Li Dan, who later became the Emperor Xuanzong) staged a coup and retook the throne in 710 A.D. Li benefited from the aid of military leaders and garrison soldiers who opposed Empress Wei and support from his aunt, Princess Taiping (a daughter of Wu Zetian) and numerous military officials. He gained powerful assistance from the garrison troops, who killed several of Empress Wei's generals. When Li led his people into the palace where the empress regent was staying, her own guards joined him in rebellion. Frightened, Wei rushed out of her door in only her underwear. With the help from Yang Jun and Ma Qinke, she ran to a camp to get a horse. The soldiers there hated her wrongdoing so much that they killed Yang and Ma at once. Trembling with fear, Wei begged the soldiers to spare her life, but it was no use: The soldiers cut her body in two and sent her head to Li Longji. Then, Wei's daughter and all the members of Wei's faction were arrested and executed.

Wei's evil misdeeds caught up with her. After her restoration as an empress, she had led a dissipated life. Wei committed adultery with several people, one of them her groom. She diverted funds to build Buddhist temples, with the bigger ones usually costing small fortunes and wasting money and man-power. The empress especially favored Princess Anle, her youngest daughter, who was born during their exile in Fang-zhou. With the connivance of her mother, Princess Anle was extravagant, spending large sums of state money to build her own palace.

At her funeral Wei was given the courtesy of a first-rank official, but later she was reduced in rank and re-recorded as a civilian commoner.

Song Ruizhi

Sources

"Houfeishang, Liezhuan Diyi," in *Xintang shu*, vol. 76; "Houfeishang, Liez-huan Diyi," in *Jiutang shu*, vol. 51.

Princess Taiping (d. 713 A.D.) was the youngest daughter of Emperor Gaozong of the Tang dynasty and Empress Wu Zetian (see Wu Zetian). How she came to be named Taiping, which means peace, is an interesting story. Before the princess's first marriage, the king of Tibet sought a marriage alliance with the Tang dynasty, but Emperor Gaozong and Empress Wu did not agree. Instead, to show that she was needed at home, they built a temple called Taiping and made the princess its head, thus she was called Princess Taiping.

Tall and plump with a chubby face—regarded as typical of richness and honor in ancient China—Princess Taiping was bright, courageous, and resolute. Although Wu Zetain had four sons, she was fond of none of them. She thought that Princess Taiping took after her, so she was the favorite. Wu often asked her to take part in discussing state affairs, and this prepared Princess Taiping for a future career in palace politics.

In 681 A.D., Princess Taiping married Xue Shao, the son of her aunt, Princess Chengyang, and had two boys and two girls. In 688 A.D., Li Chong, the king of Longya, led his army against Wu Zetian. Xue Shao was reported to have had poor relations with Li Chong that were not in the Tang emperor's best interest and was sent to prison, and died there. After Xue Shao's death,

Wu Zetian murdered her nephew Wu Muji's wife and asked Princess Taiping to marry Wu Muji. She agreed and, with Wu Muji, had two boys and a girl.

Princess Taiping became deeply involved in the political rivalry between Wu Zetian and Empress Wei. Late in the career of Wu Zetian, her court favorites, Zhang Yizi and Zhang Zongchang, played power politics, framed innocent ministers, lived a life of luxury and extravagance, and thus made the government corrupt from within. The other five ministers wanted secretly to eliminate the two Zhangs. Princess Taiping not only supported their plan but joined them herself in order to restore morality at court. So the five ministers staged a palace coup early in 705 A.D. and killed the two Zhangs. They forced Wu Zetian, who was seriously ill, to abdicate in favor of her son, Li Xian, who had earlier reigned as Emperor Zhongzong. Princess Taiping's special position and her support played a very important role in the coup, which restored not just the emperor but capable officials to administer the empire. After Emperor Zhongzong regained the throne, he granted her the honorary title Princess Zhenguo Taiping and gave her more territory.

But the Emperor Zhongzong proved a fatuous coward. The throne was really controlled by Empress Wei (see Empress Wei) and Wu Zetian's nephew Wu Sansi, who murdered innocent people, took bribes, and bent laws. In 707 A.D. Crown Prince Li Zhong and General Li Daolu staged a coup d'état and killed Wu Sansi, but ultimately failed in their efforts to take power and subdue Empress Wei. According to the old edition of the *Tang shu* (History of the Tang Dynasty), the coup was supported by Princess Taiping and Prime Minister Xian Lidang. After this, Empress Wei wanted to take over from the emperor, so she and her daughter, Princess Anle, poisoned the emperor in 710 A.D. and made Li Chongmao, then sixteen years old, the crown prince and then emperor. Real power was held by Empress Wei. In order to clear the road to the highest position, Empress Wei also wanted to murder Princess Taiping. At the critical juncture, Li Longji (the son of Li Dan, who later became the Emperor Xuanzong) and Princess Taiping planned to stage another coup. With the help of her son, Shu Zhongjian, the coup was successful. Empress Wei, her daughter, and her followers were killed, and their clique was completely eliminated. Because the new emperor was a little boy, the officials wanted Li Dan, then prime minister, to become the emperor. No one dared to speak out, however, until Princess Taiping was bold enough to tell the little boy: "Everybody turns to the prime minister, little boy; this is not your seat." With these words, she pulled the boy from the emperor's throne. She and others then supported Li Dan's ascension as emperor.

Princess Taiping rendered outstanding service and gained greater prestige. Her power became ever more illustrious, and her territory became ever larger. Her palace, like the emperor's palace, was guarded by soldiers. Her three sons were made princes, and her relatives and friends were put in important positions. She could always talk directly with the emperor for hours at a time, and her suggestions were always adopted. Individuals she recommended would be favored and promoted by the emperor; five of seven prime ministers in succession rose with her recommendation. Many worthy officials who had lost their posts were able to be restored with her support. She discussed and helped decide all military and state affairs. If she did not go to the palace, the prime minister would go to ask for her opinions. Her prestige and property exceeded the emperor's.

She annexed territory unscrupulously. Her land spread past the outskirts of the capital, and she owned hundreds of slaves and had many female attendants. She now lived a luxurious life and had an illicit affair with a monk named Hui Fan, and she asked the emperor to promote him to be a sainted abbot. With the princess as his backer, the monk violated laws unscrupulously and robbed common people of their property, but no official dared to punish him. For example, Top Censor Xui Qianguan recommended that the emperor impeach the monk, but the censor himself was framed and reduced in station because of the intrigues of Princess Taiping.

Princess Taiping's desire for power made Li Longji angry with her; at the same time she regarded him as a political rival. When Li Longji was made crown prince, she spread rumors that he was not the eldest son of Li Dan, the Emperor Ruizong, and should not be made heir to the throne. Princess Taiping sent her followers to watch him and even placed her trusted people around him. She participated in plans for another coup. In 711 A.D., the princess suggested that the prime ministers depose the crown prince, but this suggestion was refused. Meanwhile, Li Longji received aid from trustworthy older ministers such as Yao Zong, Su Jin, and Zhang Shui. The situation favored the prince. In 712 A.D., Emperor Ruizong abdicated the throne in favor of his son and called himself an overlord, though he retained real power. But Princess Taiping's influence was still firmly entrenched and potentially great. So the struggle between them became even more intense. In mid-713 A.D. the struggle reached its peak. Princess Taiping decided that the time had come to stage a coup. She conspired with her followers to dethrone Emperor Xuanzong and have him poisoned. But the emperor learned of the plot; some of her followers were caught and killed, others managed to escape. Princess Taiping ran away to a temple in the mountains and hid there for three days. After she returned, she was killed at her home. Her sons and remaining followers were also killed. As further punishment, her husband's grave was destroyed.

Princess Taiping joined and supported two coups that contributed to reform and improvements of the Tang dynasty and the development of society. But later in life she became more interested in amassing her own power. In the end, the survival of the Tang dynasty was furthered by her death.

Liu Aiwen
Yin Jun, trans.

Sources

"Book of the Ancient Tang Dynasty" published by the Chinese Publishing House in 1975. *Zi zhi tong jian* (History as a mirror). Beijing: Chinese Publishing House in 1956.

Madam Gong Sun (ca. 700–756 A.D.) was a prominent fencing-dancer in the Tang dynasty. Her life span corresponded to the reign of the Emperor Xuanzong, and during her lifetime China was a mighty country with great economic prosperity. Music and dancing came into vogue soon after she was born. Emperor Xuanzong enjoyed singing and dancing very much and in 714 A.D., he set up a large training center in Penglai palace to raise and train excellent performers. The large number of girls were sent to this training facility later became excellent artists, called *Liyuan dizi* (Performers of the Li Garden). Madam Gong Sun was the most outstanding among them.

Madam Gong Sun was beautiful in appearance and elegant in style. Her special contributions in the art of dancing made her a celebrity at that time. She was often invited to perform for the emperor. Du Fu, one of the greatest poets in the Tang dynasty, once wrote about her:

> *Among thousands of imperial maids,*
> *Gong Sun ranks as supreme fencer.*

When dancing, she always put on martial attire and held a shining sword, creating a unique charm. She even became a idol for a number of aristocratic young girls who adored her just because she dared to wear a man's military attire.

Apart from performing in the imperial palace, Gong Sun went out on tour, giving shows across the country. She had several special programs such as: "Linli qu" (Melody of Neighbors), "Pei jiangjun" (General Pei), "Mantang shi" (All-around Hall), and "Xihe jianqi huntou" (Fencing Dance in Xihe). By mixing fencing and Huntou dancing together, she pioneered a new style of dance that incorporated swaying, buoyancy, and graceful postures. In 717 A.D. she gave a performance, regarded as her finest, in Yancheng, Hunan province. At the time of her performance, people from different regions all gathered in Yancheng to see and appreciate this famous lady. Gong Sun, in her martial attire, danced by waving two swords in her hands. The two shining swords were moving like shooting stars across the sky. The audience was dazzled by her. The great poet Du Fu himself was there and he described the performance on the spot:

> *Pretty woman Gong Sun,*
> *Fencing dance stirring;*

Crowd of people marveled,
Bright sky fainted.

Gong Sun's dancing was so well known that it was appreciated and attended by many social celebrities. Many young dancers and other artists learned and benefited from her dancing skills and artistic displays. Even the outstanding calligrapher Zhang Xu was inspired to perfect his writing style after he watched Gong Sun's performance. Zhang originally had specialized in *caoshu* ("grass writing," a kind of script), and he improved his style by adopting the galloping and flowing postures in Gong Sun's dancing. Fencing is something totally different from writing, but as soon as it becomes an art form with a distinctive style, it influences many other arts. Zhang Xu later became known as the king of cursive writing.

Gong Sun trained several students. Her best pupil was known as Madam Li Shi'er. Unfortunately, the dancing arts of Gong Sun were eventually lost because all the performers of the Li Garden palace school were scattered after the revolt of An Lu-shan in 755 A.D., which greatly weakened the Tang dynasty. In spite of this, Gong Sun should not be forgotten in Chinese dancing history and was often remembered for her vibrant and passionate display of sword dancing.

Zhang Yu

Sources

Zheng Chuhai, *Mingxing Zail* (yiwen) in the Tang dynasty; *Taiping Yulan*, vol. 574; *Guoshi Bu* vol. one, by Lizhao; Deng Kiying and Nie Shi-jiao, *Du Fu Xuanji*.

Jiang Chaipin (ca. 720–755 A.D.) was a concubine of the Tang dynasty Emperor Xuanzong. She was born in Putian (now in Fujian province). Her father, Jiang Zhongxun, was a doctor. At the age of five, Jiang Chaipin could recite many difficult poems and loved poetry. From 713 to 741 A.D., the eunuch Li Shi was sent on a diplomatic mission to Minyu. Here he found Jiang

Chaipin, whom he considered extremely beautiful, and he took her to the palace. At that time, there were forty thousand concubines in the palaces of the emperor, including the palace at the western capital Chang'an (now called Xi'an), where she was to reside, and in the palace in Luoyang, the eastern capital of Tang dynasty. Emperor Xuanzong liked her very much, and after he had married her, he regarded his former concubines as lightly as dust.

She enjoyed plum blossoms very much, so her dwelling was named "the plum pavilion," after the many plum trees planted around her residence. When the plum blossoms were in flower during the winter, she gazed upon the beauty of the plum blossoms deep into the night. So Emperor Xuanzong called her "concubine Mei" or Plum Fairy. Jiang Chaipin danced, it was said, as trippingly as a wild goose and played a flute made of jade. Her dance attracted all the people at court, who would watch her dance and shout: "Bravo!"

Later, when a rival concubine, Yang Yuhuan, a beautiful but a jealous girl, entered the imperial palace, Emperor Xuanzong was captivated by her and became gradually estranged from Jiang Chaipin. Soon afterward, because Yang was jealous of her, Jiang Chaipin was forced to transfer to the Luoyang palace and the emperor visited her no more. But soon, even while lying in Yang's warm arms, Emperor Xuanzong thought of Jiang Chaipin. He tried to meet once more with Jiang Chaipin, but Yang, having discovered this love tryst, quarreled with the emperor. After that, he did not dare to meet with Jiang Chaipin again.

Alone at the eastern palace, Jiang Chaipin felt lonely and wrote a poem called "Eastern Flower," describing her depression and loneliness when she confronted the broad sky of stars and cool moonlight after nightfall. Her sadness and complaints were expressed clearly. It has been said that when Jiang Chaipin was neglected, Emperor Xuanzong secretly bestowed one *hu* (string) of pearls upon Jiang Chaipin, but she refused to accept it and in return wrote a poem, "Thanks for Bestowing the Pearls":

> *The Willow-leaf eyebrow was not drawn,*
> *The remaining makeup and tears wetted the red silk.*

> Since then, I have not washed or dressed,
> Why grant pearls to console me?

After reading this poem, the emperor felt saddened and ordered the court musician to compose a musical score to the poem called "One Hu of Pearls."

During the rebellion of An Shi in 755 A.D., Jiang Chaipin died. The emperor was not aware of this and had officials look for her everywhere. Later, Li Shi presented a picture of Jiang Chaipin to Emperor Xuanzong, who thereupon wrote a poem on the picture in mourning. Of all the poems of Jiang Chaipin, only "Thanks for Bestowing Pearls" and "Eastern Flower" survive. Her other poems—such as "Bamboo Flute," "Orchid," "Pearl Garden," "Plum Blossom," "Phoenix Flute," "Glass Circle," "Scissors," and "Leaning Against Window"—all have been lost.

Pen Chi
Bi Qiyu, trans.

Source

Tang Shu, *History of the Tang Dynasty.*

Li Ye (ca. 720–784 A.D.), also called Ji Lan, was a poet during the Tang dynasty. She was the youngest child in her family; her parents' names are unknown. According one of her poems:

> *I have lived in the remote Wu mountain since my childhood*
> *and I seemed in a dream land while listening to that musical spring*
> * water.*

It is largely because of this poem that *Tang caizi zhuan* (Gifted Scholars in the Tang Dynasty) referred to her home as being in Xiazhong, but does not tell the exact county. But *Quan Tang shi* (Complete Collection of Tang Dynasty Poetry) states her home was in Wuxing because she spent most of her life in and around Wuyue (now Jiangsu and Zhejiang provinces), an area mentioned prominently in her poems.

Li was clever and talented at a premature age. When she was six, her father once held her up to enjoy their beautiful garden, and she improvised a poem, "Ode to the Rose," which went, in part:

> *How could the flower defend its young and sweet heart*
> *if the flower is in full blossom but still not well cultivated?*

Her father could not help frowning and sighed: "Although she is talented, I am not sure about her future behavior, which might go beyond the typical feminine nature and values."

Li later became a Daoist priest, but the reason and timing for this was unknown. In this age, those who became Daoist priests were not all driven by poverty. On the contrary, they were highly respected by the people because of their virtues and leadership roles. Li Ye, with her brilliant talents in poetry and music, attracted more attention than other priests because she was gifted, easy-going, and cheerful. As her father had earlier feared, however, she did not take pains to cultivate a "women's four virtues"—proper speech, modest manner, good appearance, and diligent work.

With her long hair stretching to her shoulders, her gown fluttering in the wind, and her musical instrument carried in her hand, she traveled across green mountains and blue rivers in the Jiangsu-Zhejiang region to recite poems and play music with her friends.

Truly, she was a Daoist free spirit. This active priest became well acquainted with many writers and poets, among whom were the famous poets Liu Changqing, Lu Yu, and Jiao Ran (a monk). These men sometimes gathered in temples in the mountains, and sometimes strolled along lake shores, enjoying themselves, as if they were supernatural beings. And they often asked Li Ye to join in their merriment and poetry writing sessions. Their cheerful voices and melodious music enhanced the beauty of the quiet lakes and mountains. On these occasions, there would be bright and romantic feelings in Li Ye's poems. Liu Changqing called her "the most talented poet among women." But when the friends separated, or when she was sick and stayed alone aboard a boat, there would be sentimentality in her poems, as in her poem "Xiangsi yuan" (Yearning and Resentment):

> *The ocean water is as deep as something beyond our knowledge,*
> *but it is just as half—deep as our yearning;*
> *the ocean water could meet its shores,*
> *but I never know the end of my yearning."*

This kind of sentimental poetry made up the largest part of her writings. Her lifestyle was something her father was worried about in her earlier years, and she was often criticized for frivolity, but she loved her lifestyle, and many others envied her freedom and talent. Li followed her own path and freely enjoyed herself among friends and the natural beauties through decades. Her prestige grew with her age, and although she was not as famous as the historian Ban Zhao, who had lived during the Han dynasty, according to contemporary scholars, she was the brightest female of her era.

The time of Li Ye's greatest popularity was in the mid-Tang dynasty, just after the rebellion of General An Lushan and Shi Siming in 755 A.D.. Although in North China there were rebellions and warlords fighting, South China was enjoying a cultured flowering. Most poets stayed in southern cities for comfort and quiet, and their poetry basically reflected their social life and romance. The eighteen poems by Li Ye in the *Quan Tang shi* were primarily writings full of social commentary and sentimentality, but there are subtle differences between the artistic conceptions of poets who lived at court or in the cities and Li Ye, who spent most of her life in the woods and along the rivers as a single Daoist priest.

She retained her grace and charm until her later years. In 779 A.D., in the time of the Emperor Daizong, Li Ye, then in her fifties or sixties, had an audience with the emperor. The poem she wrote before she went to the capital for the special audience showed that her age and ill health would prevent her from staying in the capital for long; her mind and heart were attached to the evergreen natural surroundings. It was said that she stayed in the imperial palace just over a month and was granted many rewards from the emperor in appreciation of her talented poetry skills.

Then in 783 A.D., during the reign of Emperor Dezong, Chang'an was occupied by a rebellious official named Zhu Ci, who later proclaimed himself Emperor Qin. Emperor Dezong fled the capital, but Li Ye was captured and, under duress and threats, was made to write a poem praising Zhu Ci (the poem has not survived). Zhu Ci was defeated the following year, and Emperor Dezong returned in midyear. The emperor punished Li Ye for giving in and writing the flattering poem for the rebel, even though she was elderly and weak. Li Ye died as a result of this cruel torture. Her poetry, however, has survived in various collections of Tang poetry, and her lifestyle and love of solitude in nature were well praised for generations.

Shi Molin

Sources

"Li Ji-Lan" in *Tang caizi zhuan xiaojian*. Beijing: Zhonghua shuju, 1987; "Li Ye" in *Quan Tang shi*, vol. 805. Beijing: Zhonghua shuju, 1960, "Li Ye," vol. 888.

Madam Yang (ca. 740–783 A.D.) was a great military warrior in the struggle against rebellious governors at the end of the Tang dynasty. The *Lienu zhuan* (Biographies of Famous Women) and the *Xin Tang shu* (New Tang History) relate that in 755 A.D. the Tang dynasty began to decline following a rebellion led by An Lushan and Shi Siming. Even though the Tang emperor's line was restored to the throne, his power was constantly threatened by feudal warlords in the provinces. This feudal separation and fighting became sharper from north to south, and several independent kingdoms sprang up that openly opposed the Tang court. Those who suffered the most from these wars were the civilians, who usually supported the Tang court to fight the rebellions. Some women became very prominent in that period. One was Madam Yang.

In 783 A.D., General Li Xilie of Jianxing, who controlled the western bank of the Huai river, was supposed to suppress a northern rebellion, but he betrayed the Tang dynasty by declaring himself king of the region and attacking and looting provincial cities. The incapable emperor escaped from the capital and General Li became more threatening after he took over Bianzhou, an important city in Henan province. When General Li came near the city of Xiangcheng, its magistrate, Li Kan, was frightened and ready to desert the city. But his wife, Madam Yang, told him to fight by every means with the enemy, to die for the emperor or your people in the fighting, and receive thereby honor. If he ran away, as the city's top leader, he would be disgraced. Her husband asked sadly how he could fight with limited troops and supplies. Madam Yang retorted, that if he deserted the city and escaped that meant he gave the city together with its people and wealth to the rebelling army. That would only further support the rebellion, and ruin the nation, and he would die dishonored. When she saw her husband was thinking about her idea, she added that he should apply all the money in the city to encourage the citizens, to raise their morale, and organize a willing-to-die corps in defense of their homes and property. Li Kan felt inspired by his wife's ideas, even confident, and he immediately called his troops and people to the city-government courtyard and declared that they should defend their homes and city. Even though he would be assigned to another place in a year, the local people had family property to protect as well as the ancestral tombs. Now, everybody present at the meeting was indignant, with tears in their eyes, and showed their desire for fighting. Li Kan promised he would be with them to protect the city. All those who would fight the enemy with stones would be awarded a thousand dollars he promised; all those who can fight the enemy with knives will be awarded ten thousand dollars. Several hundred people responded to him and followed him to the city wall. Madam Yang led a group of women to cook for the forces. When the rebel army arrived, the people of Xiangcheng had everything ready.

Magistrate Li was wounded during the fighting and returned home to recover. But Madam Yang followed her husband home and immediately castigated him: "If you leave the battlefield, who else will risk his life? I've prepared wine for your victory celebration, but now we are faced with defeat because of your personal retreat; as a man, you should not care too much about your personal safety, or your little wound.'' Li admired her ardor and returned to the city wall, though still in pain, to conduct his soldiers. The people of Xiangcheng were so united and brave that the enemy lost confidence and had to withdraw when their commander, Li Xilie's son-in-law, was killed.

Xiangcheng was saved, and Li Kan was rewarded by the emperor. But Madam Yang was the person to whom the people knew they owed the victory because of her military inspirational leadership. The *Xin Tang shu* recorded her only as Madam Yang, the wife of the magistrate Li Kan. But in 806 A.D. Li Xiang, a philosopher and writer, rewrote her into history, praising her as a noble woman for her bravery, courage, wisdom, valor, and spirit. He believed that she embodied the virtues set down by Confucius when he said: ''A just-minded person is always fearless,'' and gave Madam Yang her proper place in history for defending Xiangcheng.

Shi Molin

Sources

"Yang Liefu" in the book *Xin Tang shu* (New History of the Tang Dynasty). Beijing: Zhonghua shuju, 1975, vol. 205, biography 130; "Woman Warrior: Madame Yang Defends Xiang City," by Chu Nan, in *Women of China* (November 1985): 32–33.

Yang Guifei (or Yang Yuhuan) (716–756 A.D.) was the favorite concubine of the Tang Emperor Xuanzong (685–726 A.D.). Her title Guifei means the highest ranking imperial concubine. Her real name was Yuhuan, meaning jade ring and her Daoist name was Taizhen. She was born in Yongle, Puzhou, roughly the present-day Ruicheng in Shanxi province. As her father died at an early age, she was left in the care of her father's younger brother Yang Xuangui. Clever and beautiful, she fully understood the temperament of the Emperor, and she entertained him with singing and dancing. A story widely circulated that

Yang Guifei herself taught the operatic musicians and actors in the Pear Garden, which was then the imperial theatre, to sing the tune called "Nishang Yuyi" and to dance to its tune. Both this tune and her dancing became all the rage at that time.

Originally Yuhuan was a concubine of Prince Shou, one of the sons of Emperor Xuanzong. The Emperor's favorite at the time was Wu Guifei, but when she died, the Emperor became very depressed. There were many other beautiful women in his palace, but the Emperor was attracted to none of them. But then the Emperor asked that a search be made, both inside and outside of the palace, to seek a new concubine to take her place. Later on Yuhuan was recommended to him and he fell in love with her at first sight, taking her from his son. At the time, he was already sixty and Yuhuan was in her twenties. To deceive the public, Emperor Xuanzong arranged for Yuhuan to become a Daoist priestess and granted her a Daoist name Taizhen, as she was then living in the Daoist temple, Taizhen. Shortly afterwards this so-called "Daoist priestess" was brought to Xuanzong's imperial palace by stealth. In 745 A.D., Yuhuan was granted the title Guifei.

Because Yang Guifei was in such good graces with the Emperor Xuanzong, her three sisters were conferred the titles of Lady of Guo, Lady of Qin, and Lady of Han. Yang Guozhong, her cousin, was also promoted to prime minister from a trivial local official's position. With Yang Guifei at the center of the clique known as the Yang family, they lived a life of extreme luxury and extravagance. For example, there were 700 hundred silk weavers and embroidery workers who specially served Yang Guifei, making her garments. Every time she rode a horse, the most powerful eunuch in the palace, Gao, would hold the bridle for her himself. Yang Guifei loved to eat fresh lichis, and the Emperor sent imperial edicts to officials in Lingnan and Chuandong, two famous areas of production, both several hundred miles away from the capital city Chang'an, to deliever lichis by rapid horses. In order to guarantee the freshness of the color and flavor of the lichis, the officials who were in charge became rapidly fatigued along the way.

At that time, many officials tried to fawn on Yang Guifei by presenting her with rare curios in order to win her support in securing higher paying positions. An Lushan, a general of mixed stock and military governor on the frontier districts, was among them. This was a period when politically there was growing tension and rivalry between the imperial court and the regional military commanders. An Lushan recommended himself to be an adopted son of Yang Guifei, thus winning more trust from the Emperor. She complied with his request, as seemingly, An Lushan was good company and harmless enough. Both Emperor Xuanzong and Yang Guifei were amused by this stout, amiable, and robust character. But in fact, An Lushan was ambitious and had sinister intentions. An Lushan began recruiting men to enlarge his army secretly and wanted to claim the imperial throne. Dangerous weaknesses had begun to appear internally with the central finances and increasingly the empire was dependent upon foreign mercenaries who were "foreign allies."

The corruption and extravagance of the ruling class greatly intensified the class contradictions and aggravated the social crisis. Following the series of natural disasters, in the winter of 755 A.D., An Lushan launched an armed rebellion against the Tang Dynasty with the intent of "riding the court of evil ministers." His rebel army captured Loyang and then the capital city Chang'an the following summer, and An Lushan proclaimed himself the new emperor. Xuanzong, Yang Guifei, and Yang Guozhong, and an assortment of palace personnel fled in panic in the direction of Sichuan. When they arrived at Maweiyi, the escorting soldiers mutinied and refused to proceed. The troops killed Yang Guozhong, then they demanded the execution of Yang Guifei. The intimidated Emperor, fearing for his life, was forced in humiliation and despair to consent to her being strangled. Lady Yang bade farewell to Emperor Xuanzong sadly and hung herself with a silken cord she had received from a Buddhist temple. She was barely forty, during these troubled times caused by revolution and upheaval. Her body was wrapped with cotton-padded mattresses and buried at the side of the post road hastily and carelessly. In July of the same year, Emperor Xuanzong abdicated in favor of one of his sons. Lady Yang had become a victim of the court intrigues and political turmoil. After the rebellion of An Lushan was put down, Yang Guifei was bestowed the title of Empress posthumously in 757 A.D. Lady

Yang's body was reburied in Chang'an. The new Tang Emperor asked the artisan-painters to draw a portrait of Yang Guifei and hung it in his palace. He would view the portrait every day, reminiscing about the past. The greatness of the early Tang dynasty was never fully reclaimed and slowly the empire decayed until it fell in 907 A.D.

The romantic misery of the Emperor Xuanzong and Yang Guifei has been a favorite subject for Chinese painters and poets ever since. In the poem "The Song of Everlasting Sorrows" written by Bai Jiuyi, one of the famous poets of Chinese history, the two lovers have been poetically depicted as two one-winged birds flying together in heaven, neither of them could fly alone. They are also depicted as two branches of one tree growing together on earth, neither of them could grow alone. Unserving love and unbroken sorrow inspired the poet and the immortal masterpiece brought a love story far and wide.

Jing Jian
Yunchuan Luo

Sources

Edwin O. Reischauer and John K. Fairbank, *East Asia, the Great Tradition,* Boston: Houghton-Mifflin Company, 1960, 1988; L. Cheng; C. Furth; Yip Bon-Ming, *Women in China,* Berkeley: Institute of East Asian Studies, 1984; K.T. Wei, *Women in China,* Westport, CT: Greenwood Press, 1984; G.B. Winsatt, *The Bright Concubine and Lesser Luminaries: Tales of the Fair and Famous Ladies of China,* Boston: J.W. Luce, 1928.

Bao Junwei (ca. 750–800s A.D.) was a poet who lived during the Tang dynasty; the dates of her birth and death are not known, nor is her ancestral origin. The only available information about her is a sketchy biography that appeared in the appendix of *Quan Tang shi* (Complete Collection of Tang Dynasty Poetry) and in *The Complete Prose of the Tang Dynasty,* which included an essay of hers entitled "The Letter Begging to Return Home," her report to the emperor asking for permission to return home. From these pieces, a general outline of her life can be gleaned.

Junwei, also known as Wenji, lived from the late eighth century to the beginning of the ninth century. Her father, Bao Zhenjun, was a scholar who gave Junwei a good education at home beginning in her childhood. There is no record of when she married, but it is recorded that her husband died, leaving her a young widow. Having no brothers, the filial Junwei then returned to her mother's home to live because her mother was lonely after the death of Junwei's father, when her family's financial situation declined.

From childhood and throughout her life, Junwei had a talent for composing poems. She was so accomplished as a poet that she became as famous in Chinese history as the five Song sisters (see Song Sisters).

Li Shi, who reigned as Emperor Dezong, summoned Junwei to the palace because of her fame in writing poetry and appointed her to the job of singing and composing poems during special palace activities such as banquets, tea parties, and imperial outings. She often received awards from the emperor for her excellent poems. Still, she was not happy living at the palace and missed her mother, as they had become emotionally dependent on each other.

After no more than a hundred days in the palace, she could no longer tolerate the lifestyle, so she summoned her courage to write a petition to the emperor, asking his permission to return her home. In this short piece, she first expressed her gratitude at having her poetry appreciated by the emperor. Then she wrote about the weakening situation of her family, the difficult situation of her elderly mother living alone and her feeling of deep anxiety about her mother at every moment. Finally she beseeched the emperor to "grant her the greatest favor" to let her return home and look after her mother, "so that the old mother can enjoy your majesty's graciousness in every single day your majesty grants her." The wording of the prose was simple, but every word was passionate. Even today people are moved by the piece. But, because of the deficiency of the historical records, it is not known whether the emperor granted her request, or how she lived the latter half of her life.

There should have been many poems composed by Junwei passed down, but today only five poems survive, included in

The Collection of Youxuan, The Chronicle of Tang Poems, and *Quan Tang shi*. Her poems were all about the scenes in the palace. Her mental state was very tranquil, for she did not seek fame or wealth. Because she had high and noble interests, her works were not contaminated by the frivolous and vulgar tendencies at the palace. Her poems were graceful, fresh, and pure and therefore characteristic, it is said, of her own life, as she composed poems out of her true feelings.

Zhu Zhongliang

Source

Fu Xuanzong. *Collected Biographies of the Gifted Scholars of Tang Dynasty*. Beijing: China Publishing House, 1987, vol. 2, Book One, 334.

Song Sisters of the Tang dynasty refer to Song Ruoxin (d. 820 A.D.), Song Ruozhao (d. 825 A.D.), Song Ruolun (dates unknown), Song Ruoxie (d. 835 A.D.) and Song Ruoxun (dates unknown). They were descendents of Song Zhiwen, a famous poet who won first prize in a court poetry competition organized by Shangguan Wan'er during the reign of Wu Zetian (624–705 A.D.) (see Shangguan Wan'er).

These five sisters were born in Qingyang county, Beizhou (now Qinghe, near Beijing) to Song Tingfen, who taught them at home. In addition to five daughters, he also had a son. The sisters were all intelligent, while the only son was of mediocre intelligence.

Song Ruoxin wrote *Woman's Analects* in imitation of the *Analects* of Confucius. Her book was a dialogue between a Lady Song and her pupils, such as Ban Zhao, the first female historian in Chinese history. She used this dialogue as a textbook for her younger sisters to teach them how to behave. This is why, it was said, these five Song sisters were all decent, chaste, and obedient. None of them wanted to think of marriage, as they wanted to make their family known first and foremost for learning.

As soon as the provincial governor, Li Baozhen, came to know the charming and intelligent Song sisters, he recommended them to the emperor's court in Chang'an (now Xi'an). In 788 A.D., the Emperor Dezong summoned them to test their knowledge of the classics. They were also ordered to write a composition. They all did well, even distinguishing themselves. Well satisfied with their display, the emperor had the five sisters come to the palace and gave their father an official position.

Emperor Dezong was learned in poetry himself. He often asked the five sisters to write poems at banquets and other special events. Young as they were, the sisters received respected positions as titled scholars at court. Unexpectedly, the youngest of the five sisters died at the palace shortly thereafter. But the eldest sister, Ruoxin, worked as a librarian in the imperial library for almost thirty years, from 791 to 820 A.D. Although she remained at the court for so long, little information has been discovered about her life there.

Ruozhao was social and amiable and was popular. In 821 A.D., she took the imperial library position left vacant by her sister's death and was formally appointed the official in charge of the accounts, literature, seals, and keys of the palaces. Ruozhao worked as a tutor for the ladies-in-waiting, the princesses, and their husbands. After living at the court for thirty-seven years, she died in 825 A.D., having won the title "Lady Liang Kuo." She was given a grandiose burial.

Then in 827 A.D. Ruoxie took over the librarian position, after she had been living in the palace for forty years. Emperor Wenzong greatly respected this elderly lady. She took part in political affairs, but in those years the palace eunuchs came to hold sway at court and courtiers formed coteries. Ruoxie fell victim to court intrigue. In mid-835 A.D., she was falsely accused of bribery and ordered by the emperor to commit suicide. The surviving members of the Song family—the son, together with his wife, his daughter, and others, a total of thirteen people—were exiled to remote areas of Guangdong or Fujian province. Thus ended the Song sisters' influence at court.

When, in their youth, the five Song sisters were originally summoned to the capital, the townspeople were proud of them and congratulated them. Later, as the sisters one after another died in the palace, and the remaining members of the Song family went into exile, the townspeople built up the Songs' old residence, establishing it as a memorial to the Song family and their service at court.

Quan Tang shi (Complete Collection of Tang Dynasty Poetry) contains three poems written by the Song sisters: one each by Song Ruoxin, Song Ruozhao, and Song Ruoxie. The five sisters became role models for Chinese scholars in later dynasties and have remained examples of strong, independent scholars down to the present day.

Shi Mulin
Xu Kaichang, trans.

Sources

Quan Tang shi (Complete Poems of the Tang Dynasty). Beijing: Zhonghua shuju, 1960, 67–68; *Xin Tang shu* (New History of the Tang Dynasty). Beijing: Zhonghua shuju, 1975, 3508–09; *Jiu Tang shu* (Old History of the Tang Dynasty). Beijing: Zhonghua shuju, 1975, 2198–99.

Xue Tao (ca. 768–832 A.D.), a noted poet of the Tang dynasty whose works appear in the *Quan Tang shi* (Complete Collection of Tang Dynasty Poetry), is praised in Chinese history for composing nearly five thousand poems and songs. Eighty-nine of her poems are in the *Quan Tang shi,* commissioned by the Qing Emperor Kangxi. Xue Tao was born in Chang'an (now Xi'an), the capital of the Tang dynasty, but when she was a small child moved with her family to Chengdu, Sichuan province, where her father was an official. Her family called her by other affectionate names, such as *Hongdu* (great breadth), inferring that she had great breadth of knowledge and learning as a result of her father's teaching, especially in the art of writing poetry. On one occasion, her father composed the first two lines of a poem:

> *In the courtyard stands an ancient wutong tree,*
> *The towering trunk pierces the clouds.*

Xue Tao continued her father's poem, exhibiting her skill:

Its branches welcoming birds from south and north,
Its leaves buffeted by the changing winds.

Her father was disturbed by the ominous words of the last line. He died when she was seventeen or eighteen, and she had to support her widowed mother. Her reputation as beautiful and talented spread widely, and in 785 A.D. she accepted a position in the household of the governor of Sichuan, Wei Nie, who ordered her to recite poetry as he drank wine to relax or to recite at banquets to entertain his guests. But at the same time he reduced her to a singsong girl, or official courtesan.

Yet her poetry and profound learning were admired by eleven successive Sichuan governors and many famous officials and scholars. Famous poets such as Yuan Zhen, Bai Juyi, Liu Yuxi, and Du Fu were all her admirers. The poet Wang Jian even offered a petition to the court recommending that she be appointed to a high official position, but Wang's recommendation was not taken. Yet, from that time forward, she was addressed as a "secretary" in the Sichuan governor's bureaucracy. Wang Jian also wrote a poem in admiration of Xue Tao:

Near the Wanli Bridge lives a woman secretary,
Leading a secluded life among loquat blossoms.
Although there are many gifted women,
None can compare with her in poetic grace.

Later, some Chinese writers, mirroring this poem's imagery, referred to singsong girls as "secretaries" and their abodes as "loquat blossom lane."

Although loved by the governor of Sichuan, Xue Tao once offended him, and as a result she was banished to a frontier town. Her poem "To Wei After Being Banished to a Town on the Borderland" expressed her emotions:

I heard that life in the border city was hard,
Only now do I begin to understand,
I would feel ashamed to sing those banquet songs
To people guarding the frontiers.

And her poem "To Wu After Being Exiled to the Borderland" expresses her regret at having to leave the governor's court:

> Drawing reins on a ridge in the freezing weather,
> Bitter winds and sleet chill my bones.
> If they would show mercy and let me go back home,
> Never again will I enjoy landscapes and painted screens.

Her poems reflect the cold and barrenness of Sichuan frontier towns in the Tang dynasty. Yet her poems also convey the poet's self-chastisement for she had been living lavishly in Chengdu amid painted golden screens, silks, and paintings of landscapes and longed to return to her former opulence. Xue Tao was soon recalled to the Sichuan court.

Secretly unhappy with her life as a courtesan, Xue Tao expressed her longing for a conventional domestic life of marriage and children in the following poem:

> A pair of mandarin ducks nestle in the pond,
> Inseparable from dawn until dusk.
> And when they have a fledgling to care for,
> With one heart nurture it amid lotus leaves.

But since she was a singsong girl in the Sichuan governor's court, it was most difficult for her to marry. She was reputed to have had a love affair with the poet Yuan Zhen (779–831 A.D.), who had been briefly the governor of Sichuan. Xue Tao had been ordered to attend Yuan Zhen, and after their separation, they exchanged many poems and letters. Yuan Zhen's longing for Xe Tao can be seen in this poem:

> Delicate is the Brocade river, elegant is Emei mountain,
> Both nurtured the poets Zhuo Wenjun and Xue Tao.
> Your ready tongue is as eloquent as a parakeet's,
> Your poetry as dazzling as the phoenix's plumage.
> Poets all pause in their writing,
> Each lord dreams of an adroit writing brush.
> Separated by mist and water, I yearn for you,
> The clematis will be blooming, the rosy clouds aloft.

Yuan Zhen praised Xue Tao in a poem:

> The velvet waters of Jinjiang, the
> delicate beauty of Mine,
> In the mind's eye they are
> Wenjun and Xue Tao.

After Yuan Zhen left Chengdu, Xue Tao moved to Bijifang (Green Cockerel Lane), where she had a special pavilion built that she named "Yinshilou" (House for Reciting Poetry). She began wearing a Daoist gown and immersed herself in writing memorable poetry. About ten years later, in 823 A.D., Yuan Zhen was sent to work in Zhejiang province. He was on the verge of sending for Xue Tao, but suddenly became attracted to another poet and singsong girl there named Liu.

In 830 A.D., Li Deyu came to Chengdu to take up his post a governor of Sichuan, and he ordered a new building be erected to guard the outskirts of the city. The purpose of the new building, called Choubianlou (Border Command Tower), was to guard against the minorities that threatened China's frontier in the southwest. Xue Tao wrote "Choubianlou" to commemorate the construction:

> You lived among the birds and clouds
> as eight summers ran their course;
> The forty zhou of west Sichuan
> you ruled with an iron hand.
> O Generals, I beseech you,
> covet not the Qiangman's horse,
> But stand upon the highest ground
> to guard the borderland.

She was warning the soldiers who took up their posts in Choubianlou not to become greedy and think of crossing the border of the frontier to capture the barbarians' horses; they should properly look to merely defending the border, which was their only duty. She remembered the hardships of life on the cold frontier. Her verses were noted for their clarity and beauty of language, restraint and visual vividness. In spite of her lowly position as a courtesan, she developed a spiritual elevation and was strong, even in times of solitude. She took pleasure in the simple things of life and used her poetry to express her innermost thoughts as her poem "Longing for Spring" illustrates:

> *When flowers bloom, none share my gladness;*
> *When flowers fade, none share my woe.*
> *When comes the lonely lover's sadness?*
> *'Tis when the flowers come and go.*
> *I know the grass that I befriended,*
> *To leave unto a lover true.*
>
> *The sorrow of spring has barely ended,*
> *When wails of birds are heard anew.*
> *Happy times are remote as ever,*
> *But scenes of youth are aging fast;*
> *The one I love comes to me never,*
> *in vain I hold this tender grass.*
>
> *The bough that blossoms forth in glory,*
> *May veil a lonely lover's woe;*
> *The tear-stained glass will tell my story,*
> *But will the spring wind ever know?*

Xue Tao endured many trials and challenges and went on to achieve great fame and prestige. She was a first-rate calligrapher as well as a gifted poet. A later Song dynasty writing manual, *The Calligraphy Manual of the Xuan He Period* (1119–1125 A.D.), commented: Xue Tao's "cursive script especially seems influenced by the style of the famous Jin dynasty calligrapher Wang Xizhi (321–379 A.D.)." Even more unusual for a woman in this period, Xue Tao also made good-quality writing paper, which consisted of small sheets of red paper and water from a well in Wangjiang park in Chengdu, which is named after her. In a pavilion nearby is her portrait, along with poetic inscriptions left by famous people to honor her memory. When she died, Duan Wenchang, then governor of Sichuan, wrote an epitaph on her tomb, honoring her life and artistic poetry.

Liu Aiwen
Xu Kaichang, trans.

Sources

Quan Tang shi (Complete Poems of the Teng Dynasty). Beijing: Zhonghua shuju, 1960; Zhang Peng-zho, *Xue Tao Writing Paper*, People's Literature Publishing House, 1983 (in Chinese); Liu Zhiji, *The Relationship Between Yuan Zhen and Xue Tao.*

Lu Meiniang (ca. 791 A.D.) was a craftswoman born in Nanhai (now Guangzhou) during the Tang dynasty. She was presented to the royal court as tribute when she was fourteen (about 805 A.D.). A descendant of one of Lu brothers who taught the emperor of the Bei dynasty, Meiniang was said to have been born beautiful, with thin and long eyebrows. Even when she was quite young, Meiniang was very clever and her craftsmanship was incomparable. Once on a small handkerchief, she embroidered seven volumes of *Fu hua jing* (Buddhist sutras). No character was any larger than half grain of rice, and all the strokes as thin as hair. Not a word was missing. Meiniang was especially good at making parasol (umbrella) covers and designs—*Fei xiang gai* (Flying Immortal Covers). It was made by, first, dividing a strand of silk into three, then dyeing them in five colors and knitting them into five layers of forming an umbrella cover. On the cover there would be designs of the continent and three islands, god and goddess, a unicorn and phoenix. Moreover, the figures on it could not have numbered less than a thousand. The cover of the umbrella had a diameter of more than 3 meters, but weighed only 3 liang (50 grams). Meiniang also put a paste on it that made it twist like a small dragon, but was very hard to break.

The rulers were also surprised at her technical embroidery. Emperor Shuzong not only praised her but honored her as a goddess and invited her to live in the palace. She was given a precious ring, a sign of high honor in Chinese feudalism. Although Meiniang had consummate skill, she did not want to become rich as a result of her talent, but preferred a free and peaceful life. Though she resided at the palace, her lifestyle was very simple and plain. Despite receiving favors from the emperor, she did not want to live in the palace, so she left to become a Daoist and live as an ascetic in a temple. When she returned to Hainan, Meiniang was given the name Xiaoyao (free and unfettered).

After she died, it was said, her room filled with a beautiful fragrance. When they began to bury her, her followers found her coffin very light. Surprised at this, they opened the cover of the coffin and found only a pair of shoes. From then on, people who went to Hainan often claimed to see her as she floated on the sea or in colored clouds. She became a mythical creature rather like a fairy.

Li Xiangxian, a contemporary of Meiniang, wrote the *Biography of Lu Xiaoyao* in appreciation of her skill and will. But he was not very famous, so the biography has not survived and Lu Meiniang's achievements are little known.

Zhang Yu
Yin Jun, trans.

Sources

The Miscellaneous of Du Yang, the middle vol.; *The Notes of Tai Pin*, vol. 66.

Niu Yingzhen (ca. 806–830 A.D.) was a writer who lived during the Tang dynasty under Emperor Xianzong. Her husband, Yang Tangyuan, was a son of the Yang family in Xiannong (now Lingbao county in Henan province). Her father, Niu Su, the author of *Jiwen* (Documentary History), was very knowledgeable and paid great attention to Yingzhen's education. Yingzhen showed her gifts in her early years: She had a good memory and could repeat almost everything she heard. When she was thirteen, she could recite nearly two hundred volumes of the Buddhist scriptures and more than a hundred volumes of the Confucian classics and history, which amazed all her family and relatives.

Once, her father was ready to teach her the *Zuo zhuan* (Zuo Biography), but on the very night they were to begin the topic, she suddenly started reciting chapters in the thirty-volume *Chun qiu* (Spring and Autumn Annals), without missing a single word. The most astonishing thing was that she seemed to do it as if in a trance and seemed to have a dialogue with an unseen, controlling person. She was called several times by her astounded father, but did not answer. After waking up she could not even explain what had happened. When she was given the Confucian *Analects*, she already knew every word.

Although her life was short, Niu Yingzhen showed her brilliant talents in literature by writing more than a hundred essays and by exhibiting her all-embracing knowledge in all schools of religion and philosophy. Preoccupied with scholarship, she was usually engaged in dialogue or debate with famous literary figures such as Wang Bi, Zheng Xuan, Wang Yan, or Lu Ji. In those talks, she was always clear in her thinking and sharp in her viewpoint. The girl who discussed knowledge in her sleep, as she came to be known, sometimes dreamed about "eating" books; her writings became even more beautiful after she had several such dreams and "had eaten" several dozens of volumes. Her peers were astonished at her voracity for learning and her accomplishments.

The extant writings of Niu Yingzhen, completed during her trance-like state, appear in *Wangliang wen ying fu* (Demons and Monsters Talk with Their Shadow). In this book, she told a story about demons and monsters and blamed their shadows for her trances. In *Zhuangzi-qiwulun*, she blamed their shadows for being unable to free the body from disease, to radiate enthusiasm, to enjoy sunshine, and suggested the shadow was responsible for the unhealthy body. By this analogy, she professed her determination to wait and endure the bitter, dark, and tortuous trancelike periods and expressed hope that her body would regain its strength. This book reflected her profound knowledge by employing all kinds of classical idioms and linguistic delicacy.

In her lifetime she was looked upon as a child prodigy and was a strong role model for women who desired an education because she was revered and admired in spite of her afflictions.

Zhang Yu

Sources

The article "Niu Yingzheng Zhuan" in *Tangdai congshu*, vol. 9; the article "Caifu Zhuan—Niu Su Nu" in *Taiping guangji*, vol. 271.

Guan Panpan (b. ca. 810 A.D.) was the wife of Zhang Yin, governor of Xuzhou (in Jiangsu province) during the Tang dynasty. There is little information available regarding the place and date of her birth.

Originally a prostitute in Xuzhou, Guan Panpan was famous for her beauty and her talents in dancing, music, and poetry. Zhang Yin came to love her and admitted her to his home first as his concubine and then as his wife. He built her a special mansion called *Yanzi lou* (Swallow Mansion), and he arranged magnificent banquets to show his respect for her when she first arrived. Later, Zhang Yin bought her an even more magnificent mansion, but died shortly thereafter and left the young Guan Panpan alone.

With deep sorrow at losing her beloved husband, she decided not to remarry and returned to Swallow Mansion to live by herself. For ten years afterward, she replied to all the letters she received in the form of poems. She produced three hundred poems, which were collected as *Poems in the Swallow Mansion.* These delicate poems were well regarded by poets of the time, except Bai Juyi, one of the greatest writers of the Tang dynasty, because he could not understand Guan Panpan's loyalty to her dead husband. He mocked her in a poem, asking if she wanted to remain chaste, why not follow her husband in death?

> *Lots of gold he bestowed on you,*
> *All he got was not your heart;*
> *Having benefited from his love and care,*
> *Why don't you repay your debt by following the dead?*

While reading the mocking poem by Bai Juyi, she cried. "It is not because I couldn't show my loyalty by dying with him, but because I was afraid of ruining his reputation by that way of dying, as people might think that he wanted me to be buried alive with him.'' Suffering from his disrespect, Guan Panpan tearfully replied with ''He Baigong shi'' (Reply to Bai Juyi's Poem), one of only four surviving poems:

> *Only a sallow face as a widow,*
> *Like a withered peony post-spring;*
> *Why wrong me for my chastity,*
> *Why blame me for not following the dead?*

These were her last words. Ten days later she died from depression and fasting. As she was dying, she wrote:

> *Like kids unaware of complication,*
> *spoil black on my snowlike chastity.*

The other three surviving poems, published in *Quan Tang shi* (Complete Collection of Tang Dynasty Poetry), all reflect her lonely life in Swallow Mansion and yearning for her husband:

> *The lonely lights shining with morning frost,*
> *Up from the double bed where I slept alone;*
> *Long yearnings full of my night dream,*
> *Even further than the ends of earth.*

> *Dim clouds over the mountains pine trees,*
> *Gloomily I sat in Swallow Mansion;*
> *No more dancing since your death,*
> *Costumes abandoned with ten-years' dust.*

> *Seeing the geese returning from the north,*
> *Swallows back to their nests;*
> *No interest in my harp, flute,*
> *who cares for the dust, cobwebs on them.*

From the moral perspective of feudal Tang society, Guan Panpan's chastity was praiseworthy, especially as her husband was highly respected for his honesty and achievements. But in modern times she was praised for her contributions to ancient Chinese literature, particularly women's literature. Even her tragic story inspired many excellent writings, such as Wang Zhong-mou, *Yanzi lou zhuan* (The Story of Swallow Mansion), written in the Yuan dynasty; Hou Kezhong, *Guan Panpan chuanfeng Yanzi lou* (Guan Panpan and the Spring Swallow Mansion); Bai Juyi's opera "Yanzi lou (the Swallow Mansion)"; and Su Dongpo's, *Yong yu le* (tonal patterns and rhyme schemes of the ancient *ci* poetry) written while the author was climbing the stairs through Swallow Mansion.

As a model of female virtue for her chastity after the death of her husband, she is well remembered in Chinese literature. In modern times she has been praised for her clear, carefully crafted poetry.

Zhang Yu

Sources

Bai Juyi shiji, vol. 15; *Quan Tang shi*, vol. 802; *Jingshi Lielue*, and *Qing-zheng Lie*, by Feng Men-long in the Ming Dynasty History (in Chinese); *Tangshi Jiwen*, vol. 78, by Ji You-gong in the *Song Dynasty History*.

Empress Liu (ca. 890–926 A.D.), whose birthplace was Chenan in Wei (now Chenan county, Hebei province), was the wife of Li Cunxu, who reigned as Emperor Zhuangzong, during the Tang dynasty. The name she was given at birth was Liu Jin'gui. Her father, Liu Kui, was also named Liu Shanren (meaning "mountain people") because he made his living by selling me-dicinal herbs gathered in the mountains. Liu Jin'gui's mother was killed in a battle, and Liu had no brothers or sisters.

When she was six, Jin'gui was abducted and taken to the palace by Yuan Jianfeng, the first leader of the cavalry's "Black Riding Troop" of the imperial guard. The young girl waited on Madam Cao, who was the second concubine of Ke Yong, the Emperor Jin.

Emperor Jin had six sons, the eldest of whom was Li Cunxu, born to Madam Cao. The emperor had a deep affection for Li Cunxu, who often accompanied his father into battle. In 908 A.D., Emperor Jin died, and Li Cunxu succeeded him. After he ascended the throne, one of his first acts was to capture and execute his uncle, Li Kelin, and his adopted brother, Li Ciyun, who wanted to plot a rebellion. His authority thus established, Emperor Zhuangzong then chose strong and able administrators to assist him in governing the empire and strengthened the army to bolster his reserve power.

Emperor Zhuangzong showed filial obedience to his mother, paying her a visit after every battle. She knew that he enjoyed singing, dancing, and drama, so she usually gave a banquet for him and gathered the singers to please him and to alleviate his fatigue from fighting. On one occasion, after he sang a song resonantly, it was Jin'gui's turn. She was then nineteen years old and very beautiful. Her voice filled with passion, in order to attract the emperor's attention and affection, she sang:

> *How shining the sun in the sky is!*
> *How despotic the men on battlefield are!*
> *The enemy army was beaten back into the hills, terrified.*
> *What high prestige the troops deserve!*
> *The hero of the world is the emperor.*

The song was vivid, exciting, and bold. The emperor, feeling flattered, recognized the song's true purpose and meaning. He could not help clapping his hands and awarding her with some wine. The emperor could not hide his admiration for both Jin'gui's talent and her pleasant appearance from his mother. When the feast was over, Madam Cao asked Jin'gui to remain and wait on her son while he slept. Several days later, the emperor bade her remain with him and gave her a palace in which to live.

After Liu Jin'gui came to live at the palace, she had rivals for his affections in the imperial concubines Lady Han and Lady Yun. Although they were both born to noble families, Han and Yun had no children. In 910 A.D. Jin'gui bore the emperor a son, named Jiji. Because the child resembled him and was his eldest, the emperor loved Jiji very much. Jin'gui now came to be known as Madam Liu.

To further bind the emperor to her, Jin'gui trained a group of singers and compiled songs and dramas extolling his bravery.

To honor the emperor's mother, Jin'gui prepared a succession of musical programs, for which the emperor praised her. Jin'gui seized this opportunity to make a request that she and Jiji accompany the theatrical troupe to Yecheng, to raise the morale of the troops stationed there. The emperor agreed, admiring Jin'gui's patriotism.

Later, her shows were carried to many cities for morale purposes. In 916 A.D. the empress beat back an invading army's attack. A grand musical performance to congratulate her husband was planned. Emperor Zhuanzong emerged with a new inspiration and transmitted an order to teach the songs to the soldiers themselves, which they greatly enjoyed. Jin'gui gained the emperor special affection by her ability and scheming, and her status gradually rose above that of the other ladies of the court.

From 912 to 913 A.D., Emperor Zhuangzong, to avenge his father, defeated enemy Qie Dan at Yi county and killed the traitor Li Rengong. He had completed things that were handed down as unfinished problems from his father's reign. Another uncompleted problem was the abolition of the Liang army. Meanwhile Madam Liu cherished the hope of becoming empress because she was so loved by the emperor and she had a son; the problem was that her family background was so humble, so she concealed it. Once her father happened to see that the emperor took Madam Liu to hunt north of Yecheng. He confirmed that Madam Liu was the daughter who had been taken from him when she was young, and he entertained high hopes of visiting her. When the emperor heard of this news, he ordered that Liu Shanren be interrogated. Liu told the story of his daughter's abduction by imperial forces and said his family name. The emperor, hearing the report, allowed Madam Liu to hear about this discourse. Madam Liu was so astonished and upset to think that her confession of her humble background would prevent her from becoming empress that she steeled her heart against her father. She lied to the emperor, telling him that her father had died long before and that she had personally witnessed his death. She lied about the old man and ordered the gate keepers to beat the visitor with a stick. The old man turned out to be Liu Shanren, who thereupon left the palace in tears.

In late 923 A.D., the emperor defeated King Bianjing of Liang, and the Liang kingdom was subjugated by the Tang dynasty. This completed the tasks left unfinished by the emperor's father. The emperor was so proud that he began to seek enjoyment. First, he moved the capital to Luoyang to show that he was the master of Central China. Then, he decided to choose an empress. The upright concubine Han, who was from a noble family, should have become empress in the ordinary course of events, but the emperor removed all objections to making Madam Liu empress, leaving Madam Han and Madam Yun concubines.

Her powers now well extended and entrenched, Empress Liu now interfered in national affairs, drawing her trusted followers to her side and eliminating dissidents. This caused political turmoil and crisis. She gave her favorite court singers positions of power, and they were willing to do her bidding. For example, singers Jin Jing and Shi Yanqiong became high-ranking administrators. Only one official, Guo Chongdao, dared to warn against her practices directly. In 925 A.D. the emperor ordered a punitive expedition in Sichuan province to put down rebels. His son, the now-fifteen-year-old Jiji, was made commander, and Guo Chongdao asked to be his vice-commander in order to strengthen his position by doing a meritorious deed. The quelling of the rebellion took seventy-five days. Then, Guo asked Jiji to rid the court of eunuchs and officials who had been members of Empress Liu's singing troupe, saying: "The singing officials and eunuchs in the court are holding power now, and this is not in our national interest. Now you have performed meritorious service to put down the rebellion. You will be established as crown prince after returning. I hope you will kill all the evildoers then." Soon, these words were heard by Emperor Zhuangzong's respected official Li Chongxi, who did not get along with Guo; Li hated him for giving such advice to Jiji. At the same time, Emperor Zhuangzong sent a eunuch, Xiang Yanci, to bring gifts to the army, and Guo treated him coldly. Li Chongxi fomented discord. When he returned to the capital, Xiang Yanci told the emperor that Guo acted arbitrarily, forced Jiji to do his bidding, reported less combat success than Jiji had achieved and hinted at embezzlement of property. The emperor was upset by this report. Xiang also incited ill will with Empress Liu, saying there was much gold and silver captured in Sichuan. Empress Liu was angry with Guo's behavior and encouraged Emperor Zhuang-zong to punish him. Just at that time when the emperor remained undecided, Guo asked to stay at Sichuan to execute Wang Yan's enemy officers and men who gathered as rebels in the mountain forest. Emperor Zhuangzong doubted him at once and sent a eunuch called Ma Yan'gui to make an on-the-spot investigation.

Knowing that the emperor had not given him any orders to deal with Guo, Empress Liu wrote an imperial edict behind her husband's back. It ordered Jiji to kill Guo, and she let the eunuch tell him: "Make a prompt decision and do not hesitate or bungle matters." Jiji did not obey the order at first, but, forced by Ma Yan'gui, Jiji finally killed Guo Chongdao and his three sons. Then, Empress Liu ordered the death of other members of his family who lived in Luoyang. When news of this incident spread, Guo's old subordinates, who heard that they would be killed sooner or later, felt uneasy. So a friend of Guo's, Zhao Zaili, and others now started a mutiny, forming an army to attack Yecheng, Weicheng, and Bocheng. The garrison force defending Luoyang became alienated from the emperor because it was not pleased with Emperor Zhuangzong's special love and trust of Empress Liu and the eunuchs and his harsh attitude toward his officers and men.

Empress Liu, who was keen on gathering property and trea-sure, was greedy. She sent court officials to gather property and tribute from all parts of the country for her middle palace. In 925 A.D., Li Ciyun, Emperor Zhuangzong's adopted brother, led an armed rebellion. He marched toward Luoyang, claiming that he would seek the traitors out. Because he could not pay the army to defend the capital, Emperor Zhuangzong wanted to reward the army with food and drink purchased with the court's gold and silver, and he asked Empress Liu to handle this matter. But Empress Liu hoarded the imperial wealth, unwilling to share it with the soldiers. Emperor Zhuangzong had no choice but to lie to the officers and men that he would distribute the five hundred thousand *liang* of gold and silver coins to them as soon as they reached the cap-ital from Sichuan. But the army was unwilling to trust the em-peror, saying: "The empress loves property. She is not willing to bring out the court property and jewelry.'' In 926 A.D. as the emperor led mounted troops to suppress a rebellion started by Guo Men'gao, he was hit in the chest with two arrows and tumbled down the porch of Jiangliao palace. Bleeding and thirsty, he asked his empress to come to his aid. But the empress refused because she was busy packing her valuables and court treasury for her flight from the capital.

After Emperor Zhuangzong died, Empress Liu fled Luoyang with Li Cunwu, her husband's younger brother, taking the most expensive gold and silver jewelry with them as they sped away on horseback. Empress Liu and Li Cunwu went to Jinyang and along the way became involved romantically.

Li Ciyun ascended the throne, reigning as Emperor Mingzong. Hearing about a rebellion in the capital, Jiji led his army back. The officers and men fled throughout the journey. Knowing he would soon be killed, Jiji decided to hang himself. Empress Liu became a Buddhist nun. Emperor Mingzong sighed: ''The previous emperor was brave and wise, but unfortunately he was poisoned and bewitched by the evil woman with the family broken and decimated.''

The emperor sent his men to Jinyang to force Empress Liu to hang herself. By this time, Empress Liu, coming to see the error of her ways, blamed herself: ''I gave up my father and departed from my husband. I should answer for my evil. I have wiped out the Li's imperial power, and I have wiped out my own.'' She was thirty-six years old when she died.

Song Ruizhi
Zhou Yaolin, trans.

Sources For Part IV

Bai Juyi shiji.

Bo Yang. *Genealogical Tables of Chinese Emperors, Empresses, Princes, and Princesses.* Beijing: China Friendship Publishing House, 1986.

Booz, Elisabeth B. *Tibet.* Lincolnwood, IL: Passport Books, 1986.

Cao Wenzhu. ''From Insurgent to Princess.'' *Women of China* (August 1986).

Chen Guocan. "Empress Wu's Tomb (Xi'an) and Its 61 Mystery Figures." *China Reconstructs* (August 1983).

Chu Nan. "History's Only Daughter of Heaven." *Women of China* (April and May 1986).

Chu Nan. "Woman Warrior: Madame Yang Defends Xiang City." *Women of China* (November 1985): 32–33.

Collected Poems of the Tang Dynasty.

Deng Kiying and Nie Shijiao. *Du Fu xuanji.*

Dictionary of Famous Women of China, Beijing: Huaxia, 1988.

Elisséeff, Danielle. *La Femme au Temps des Empereurs de Chine*. Paris: Stock/ L. Pernoud 1988.

Famous Women of Ancient Times and Today, ed. *Women of China.* Beijing: Hebei People's Publishing House, 1986.

Fitzgerald, C.P. *The Empress Wu*, 1968.

Fitzgerald, C.P. *Son of Heaven: A Biography of Li Shih-min.* 1933.

Fu Xuanzong. *Collected Biographies of the Gifted Scholars of Tang Dynasty.* Beijing: China Publishing House, 1987.

Guisse, R.W.L. *Wu Tse-t'ien and the Politics of Legitimation in T'ang China*, 1978.

Guoshi Bu vol. one, by Lizhao.

History of the Sui Dynasty, China Publishing House, 1973.

History of the Tang Dynasty.

Huang Hezhou. "Basic Research on the Origin of Empress Zhangsun." *Renwen zazhi* (Magazine of Human Studies), no. 2 (1986).

Ji Zhong. "Princess Wencheng, A Chinese Dance Drama." *Women of China* (April 1980): 20–21.

Jingshi Lielue.

Jiu Tang shu (Old History of the Tang Dynasty). Beijing: Zhonghua shuju, 1975.

Liu Zhiji. *The Relationship Between Yuan Zhen and Xue Tao.*

Major Events of the Zhen'guan Years, Shanghai: Guji, 1978.

Nghiem Toan and Louis Ricaud, *Une traduction juxtalineaire commentee de la biographie officielle de l'Imperatrice Wou-t'ien*, 1959 is an annotated French translation of the official biography of Empress Wu included in *The New Tang History (Hsin Tang Shu).*

Perry, L., and B. Smith, ed. *Essays on T'ang Society.* 1976.

Quan Tang shi (Complete Poems of the Tang Dynasty). Beijing: Zhonghua shuju, 1960.

Records of Chinese Figures, comp. Knowledge of Literature and History editorial department. Beijing: Zhonghua shuju, 1985.

Reischauer, Edwin O., and John K. Fairbank. *East Asia: The Great Tradition.* Boston: Houghton-Mifflin Co., 1960.

Shu Fen, *History of the Liao Dynasty.*

Song Dynasty History.

Taiping guangji.

Taiping Yulan, vol 574.

Tang caizi zhuan xiaojian. Beijing: Zhonghua shuju, 1987.

Tangdai congshu.

Tuo Tuo, *History of the Liao Dynasty.*

Wan Shengnan. *Princess Wencheng.* Beijing: Zhonghua shuju, 1988.

Xin Anting. *Chinese Historical Figures.* Beijing: Gansu People's Publishing House, 1983.

Xin Tang shu (New History of the Tang Dynasty). Beijing: Zhonghua shuju, 1975.

Xiong Deji. *On Wu Zetain*, translated by Wei Lunjie, 2 vols.

Zhang Pengzhou. *Xue Tao Writing Paper.* People's Literature Publishing House, 1983.

Zheng Chuhai. *Mingxing Zail,* (yiwen).

Zhu Shaohou. *The Chinese Ancient History.*

Zhu Zhuocun. *Biographies of Famous Chinese People in Each Dynasty.* Beijing: Zhonghua shuju, 1988.

Zi zhi tong jian (History as a Mirror). Beijing: Zhonghua shuju, 1956.

Part V

The Song and Yuan Dynasties Revitalize China

During the Song dynasty (960–1279 A.D.), emperors and women of the imperial court revitalized China initially under the leadership of General Kuangyin, who became the dynasty's first emperor and established his capital at Kaifeng. This dynasty reunified China after the period of the Ten Kingdoms which dominated South China and the Five Dynasties, which had dominated the North following the fall of the Tang dynasty. The emperors readopted the policy of paying annual tribute to the Khitan Tatars in Liao of 100,000 ounces of silver and 200,000 pieces of silk. The Khitans established the Liao dynasty in areas of northern China between 947 and 1125 A.D. The fall of the Tang dynasty had left China vulnerable to these external disorders during the so-called Five Dynasties period, in which warlords competed. But Kuangyin had restricted the power of his commanders and relied upon civil officials. The Song had subdued the secessionist states of the south, but they continually had problems in the north, hence the payment of the annual tribute and the appeasement of the Khitans and the Liao dynasty's rulers. All Song military forces were placed under the command of the Emperor's court, limiting warlordism.

The central government had regained power and during the Song dynasty there were advances in medicine such as inoculation against diseases including smallpox and the invention of the magnetic compass. During this period the Chinese developed accurate maps of the world, excelling in cartography and relief maps.

The Song dynasty unfortunately also saw the introduction of female foot binding, which relegated women to an ornamental status in a wealthy economy. This cruel custom molded the foot into a lily shape by binding the toes backward with cloth strips. Women of the upper classes, appearing dainty-footed, adopted this style for themselves and their daughters; in addition to being painful, this custom severely limited their freedom of movement outside the house and kept them in a subordinate status. But, thus "handicapped," these women did not have to work, illustrating their membership in the elegant, refined, upper classes.

Daoists preserved knowledge by describing and investigating the order of nature related to minerals, plant and animal life, and pharmaceuticals. Neo-Confucians succeeded in restoring Confucianism to its former place of pre-eminence in Chinese thought, a place it was to hold until the middle of the twentieth century. Buddhism, which emphasized personal, individual contemplative habits, became the religion of the masses. Intellectuals wrote books, especially on chemistry, zoology, and botany and utilized algebra in their calculations, which had been invented by the Arabs. Improved printing techniques allowed wider circulation of knowledge.

By the end of the fifteenth century, East Asian society was more inventive than its Western counterpart, just emerging from the late Middle Ages, in applying useful knowledge for human purposes. Confucianism was an influence here, with its emphasis on the development of social order and the application of reason and logic.

The Song central government was greatly strengthened by the utilization of the Board of Academicians as an advisory council to the Emperor, as was the Bureau of Military Affairs. Also the Emperor surrounded himself with six ministries, a Department of State, a Board of Censors, and a Finance Commission. Thus, the new rulers took secure control over tax collections and governmental spending and the military forces to defend the empire. Because the Song Emperors took direct control of the census and the collection of taxes in a much more efficient manner than earlier periods, the state revenues were three times as large as during the Tang dynasty. The capital Kaifeng had been selected for its location near the junction of the Yellow river and the Grand Canal, and through improved communications and internal trade, especially the movement of rice from the lush Southern regions to the North, the Emperor ruled more securely, and the population of China began to rise rapidly, creating a time of unparalleled prosperity. At the local levels, China was administered through a system of prefectures, districts, and provinces with all officials responsible to the Emperor. This lower level bureacracy was strengthened by the examination system which attracted new talent to civil service. The most sought after degree was the *chin-shih* in letters, which was received through the examination involving original, creative, and analytical thinking. Thus the former control by the old families of power on the civil service was destroyed and new minds and ideas entered governmental service from the lower ranks of society. The powers of the eunuchs at court were curtailed; the empresses, concubines, and their relatives were prohibited from accepting positions of influence within the court. Thus, through governmental centralization, the Song rulers created a long period of stability that allowed culture and the arts to flourish once again, and economic prosperity and overseas trade once again offered China a prominent place in Asia. "Commerce" became a respected enterprise, large commercial cities sprang up, small shops lined prominent streets, and international goods entered China in great volumes. Trade guilds or *hongs* developed as westerners called them (in Chinese *hang*) as trade developed in specialty areas along certain streets (*hangs*). Large scale operations developed. Money widely circulated.

Around 1069 A.D., the Chinese economist Wang Anshi (1021–1086 A.D.) reorganized land holdings and government finances. He believed that the ruler was responsible for providing his subjects with the necessities of life. He expressed his social philosophy as follows: "The state should take care of the entire management of commerce, industry, and agriculture into its own hands, with a view to succoring the working classes and preventing them from being ground into the dust by the rich." His philosophy was widely adapted and contributed to the mindset that accepted communism in the twentieth century.

Wang initiated an agricultural loan program to relieve farming peasants of the intolerable burden of high interest from unscrupulous moneylenders. He initiated a system of fixed commodity prices and appointed boards to regulate wages and planned pensions for the aged and unemployed. This system looks remarkably like the New Deal policies adopted in the United States in the 1930s. Wang also revamped the existing state examination system so that emphasis was placed less on literary style and memorization of the classics than on practical knowledge. A generation after Wang's reform, reforming zeal and efficiency broke down, which led to the rescinding of Wang's new programs. During the Northern Song, China's population was estimated at more than 100 million; it continued to rise with marked improvements in production and the expansion of internal and external trade. Improvements were made in Chinese navigation and shipbuilding. The magnetic compass was used as early as 1119 A.D. Oceanic travel oriented China outward, into the world.

But China's attention outward put its Northern frontier at risk. Eventually China north of the Yangzi river was captured by the barbarians from Manchuria, the Jurchens, who established the (Jin) dynasty in the north. During the time of Song Emperor Hui Tsung (1100–1125 A.D.), the Jurchens in northeastern Manchuria revolted against the Khitan Tartars who ruled the Liao dynasty comprising the sixteen northern prefectures of China and proclaimed their own Jin dynasty. Viewing this as an opportunity to retake these regions dominated by the Liao, the Song Emperor now declared himself to be an ally of the Jurchens. In battle, the Song forces did poorly; the Jurchens however conquered the Khitans and destroyed their Liao dynasty in 1125 A.D.; the way was now open for the Jurchens to sweep into all of Northern China and they captured Kaifeng in 1126 A.D. forcing Song armies to flee south, where they re-established a government in 1127 A.D. These events mark the boundary between the Northern and Southern Song. The capital of the Southern Song was Nanjing, where the court settled in 1127 A.D.; after that date it held no control over northern China. The Southern

Song established a vast overseas maritime empire based upon vast trade across the waters of Asia and the Pacific. The Song dynasty developed an efficient monetary system using copper coins, which circulated widely to Japan and other countries in Southeast Asia. Paper money printed and backed by the government also began to circulate widely. Many foreigners—Arabs and Persians—lived in the Southern Song's port cities, such as Guangzhou, where shops and trade bazaars developed.

China's commercial revolution took place before the great commercial revolution of the Renaissance in Europe but produced similar results—urbanization, the rise of a gentry class made from trade, a more egalitarian society with more opportunities for individuals of talent, a new exhuberance in the arts and literature, with ironically a romantic view of nature and the past just at the time that commercial cities were on the rise. Song paintings of misty mountain scenes especially reflected this romanticization of the beauties of nature. Art became more secular and less devoted to religious themes. Leisure-time amusement sections of the emerging cities boasted tea and confections shops and specialized restaurants. Houses where female entertainers performed were well frequented; puppet shows and theatres became pastimes supported by the new urban classes and their growing commercial wealth. The system of concubinage spread as a result of the rising standards of living. Multi-storied buildings sprang up as building techniques improved and the typical Song styled roof top with the edges turned upward became fashionable. Additional incomes supported new homes, commissioned paintings, and collections of Chinese antiques.

With the rise of a gentry or merchant middle class came the popularity of *ci* poetry during the Song, as opposed to the older, formal, stylized *shi* (or shih) poetry style that had been popular during the Tang dynasty. The *ci* poetry appeared first as lyrics or verses of popular songs and used the venacular or common language. Also prose writing during the Song became less formal and conservative and more free, expressive, and direct. Great encyclopedias were compiled to preserve knowledge utilizing the new methods of printings such as *The Mirror as History* (Zizhi tongjian) by Sima Guang (1018–1086 A.D.). The ideal of a cultivated individual during the Song was one who was a professional scholar who was also a painter, poet and writer and philosopher. That is why so many women in this period are both painter and poet or writer and poet. Neo-Confucian ideology permeated the artistic expressions of the Song, much more so than either Buddhism or Daoism. The philosopher Zhu Xi (Chu Hsi) (1130–1200 A.D.) interpreted the Classics and became famous for his commentaries and teachings which were widely accepted by Neo-Confucianists.

Weaknesses began to re-appear internally, however, as large wealthy families began to emerge to challenge the Emperor and more financial drains were placed on the court. The area controlled by the Southern Song dynasty eventually was captured by the Mongols, who established the Yuan dynasty 1271–1368 A.D. in all of China, north and south. Until the middle of the twelfth century, the Mongol peoples had no national organization or identity but lived as isolated tribes, moving with their grazing animals over vast expanses of territory. The animals provided all that they needed—skins for their tents, food for their table, and *kumiss* (fermented mare's milk) for their pleasure. The Mongols traded with the Chinese for implements they could not make themselves, such as iron pots, some grains, and luxury items. They had migrated as nomads for centuries until they were banded together by Genghis Khan, born about 1162 A.D. At birth, as the story goes, he had held a blood clot in his hand, symbolizing future military greatness. Originally called Temujin, meaning man of iron, he would avenge his father's early death and in 1206 A.D., because of his achievements in battle, was renamed Genghis Khan, or universal ruler, at a *kirlti* (general Mongol meeting). He became one of the greatest organizing geniuses of all time and banded together more than a million Mongols, who fought together as a synchronized war machine using cavalry techniques and firing bows and arrows as they rode. Mongol warriors slept in the saddle, traveling night and day on campaigns, and lived on dehydrated milk and the blood of their horses. Genghis captured Beijing, the capital of the northern Jin empire, in 1215 A.D., and his son completed the conquest of the Southern Song. China was henceforth incorporated into a world empire that extended through Russia with the khanate of the Golden Horde and into the Middle East. At the height of its power, the Mongol empire stretched from the Danube to the Pacific Ocean.

After the death of Genghis Khan, the empire was administered by his sons and grandsons under the general leadership of a single great khan. The conquest established a Pax Tatarica, which reopened the Silk Route. Kubilai Khan, Genghis's grandson (1215–1294 A.D.), moved the Mongol capital from Karakoram to Beijing after accepting the post of Great Khan in 1260 A.D.; he would remain in this post until 1294 A.D. Kubilai fought a war with his own brother, who challenged Kubilai's move to the east because he feared the Mongols would be culturally absorbed by the Chinese. His brother's fears were well justified: The Mongols adopted Chinese customs and brought back the examination system for public office and the Tang administrative system that had worked so well.

Because Mongol leaders distrusted the local Chinese, the Mongol administration employed many foreigners. Marco Polo visited (ca. 1275–1292 A.D.) and worked in the court of Kubilai Khan and later wrote his *Tales of Marco Polo*, which fascinated West Europeans about the lifestyle in China. Polo remarked on the Yuan efficiency: "upon every great high road, at a distance of twenty-five or thirty miles . . . there are stations, with houses of accommodation for travelers. . . . At each station there are four hundred good horses kept in constant readiness, in order that all messengers going and coming upon the business of the Grand Khan, and all ambassadors, may have relays . . . and be supplied with fresh horses. . . . It is so wonderful a system, and so effective in its operation, as it is scarcely possible to describe." The arts flourished during this "barbarian" dynasty, which witnessed the integration of music and culture from the Middle East. Central Asian dance became especially significant. At the same time, the Mongol Yuan dynasty became special patrons of Beijing Opera.

Cultural exchange was considerable during these medieval times. Gunpowder was exported across the Silk Route to the West, as well as the Chinese arts of papermaking, woodblock printing, and the magnetic compass. Sorghum was introduced in China from India, and the Byzantine cloisonné technique from Persia.

But the Yuan dynasty overextended itself with Kubilai Khan's attempts to invade Japan. Because of these foreign adventures, domestic taxes were increased, sparking unrest. Interclan and fratricidal rivalry amongst the dynasty's rulers hastened its overthrow. Natural disasters such as floods in the North China plain and widespread famines undermined imperial strength. This culminated in the overthrow of the Yuan dynasty in 1368 A.D. and the rise of the Ming dynasty.

B.B.P

Xulu Ping (879–936 A.D.) was the wife of Ye Liaboger, the first emperor of the Khitan tribes (later called Liao) dynasty who proclaimed himself emperor of the Khitan tribes in 907 A.D., to found the dynasty. This was a loose confederation of Khitan tribal groups that gradually expanded Southward to take control of the sixteen prefectures in North China by 947 A.D. In that year the Chinese dynastic name (Liao dynasty) was taken. Her family's name was Xulu, and she had given names in both Chinese—Ping—and Khitanese—Rollidor. Her ancestors were of Uighur nationality. Her father, Po Gu (also Ke Wo), was a patriarch of the Yaonian clan; and her mother was the daughter of Yongdesh, king of the Khitan kingdom. After Xulu Ping married Ye Liaboger, who reigned as Emperor Taizu, she became an important assistant to him in conquering and ruling the country as she was bold, decisive, and clever. After his empire was established, Ye Liaboger declared himself "Heavenly Emperor" and his empress "the Earthly Empress Responding to Heaven."

In 916 A.D., Emperor Taizu led troops to conquer the west and thus left his base insufficiently protected. Availing itself of the opportunity, the antagonistic Shi Wei tribe came forward to attack. The empress immediately had the army ready and defeated the invading enemy in the battles; because of this, she earned a respected name among the northwestern tribes. The empress was noted for her deep political insight and her ability in assigning people to positions that were best suited to their talents. At that time, Liu Shouguang, governor of Youzhou (present-day Beijing and neighboring areas) in the Boltai kingdom was in a difficult situation and he sent Han Yanhui, one of his ministers, to the Khitan kingdom to ask for aid.

Han Yanhui, however, made the emperor angry because he would not kneel down to him when they met at the court. In his anger, Emperor Taizhi defamed Han and then punished him by sending him to the countryside to look after horses. The empress, however, saw that Han was an able man and said so to her husband: "Han Yanhui was loyal to his own Han Chinese emperor and refused to do anything improper for one in his position. These facts show that he is both loyal and able. Instead of putting him to shame, you should honor him and give him an important position." Emperor Taizu listened to his wife and summoned Han Yanhui for a discussion in which he discovered Han's unsurpassed talents and wisdom. He was very pleased and so he appointed Han Yanhui to be a staff officer. Han proved a great help in reforming old traditions, conquering other tribes, making new laws, building the new capital, and developing agriculture. His efforts greatly helped to advance the feudalization of the Liao dynasty.

Empress Xulu also worked positively to eventually annex Youzhou, conquering the Boltai kingdom, and had a series of other military and diplomatic achievements. Throughout she had cautioned patience and perseverance as this story recounted. Once Li Sheng, the king of Wu, presented Emperor Taizu with some special oil, which burned more ferociously when water was poured over it. The emperor was overjoyed; he immediately selected thirty-thousand cavalry and contemplated leading them to attack Youzhou with the burning oil. Empress Xulu disagreed, saying, "Has a city ever been attacked with burning oil?" Pointing to the young tree in front of their tent, she asked, "Can the tree remain alive with its bark removed?" The emperor answered, "Of course not." Then she stated, "Youzhou has its land and its people, so it is just like a tree. A tree has to rely on its bark and branches, and a city has to rely on its people and the land. What we need to do is to send no more than thirty thousand cavalry to pester the people there and to interfere with the production constantly. Thus the city will fall within three years. Why take unnecessarily cruel military action? If we fail to take the city using the burning oil, the Han will laugh at us and our Liao empire could collapse." Emperor Taizu was thus persuaded against using burning oil. The Liao kingdom, north of China proper, was becoming stronger but could ill afford to take unnecessary chances.

Emperor Taizu died in 926 A.D. Empress Xulu demanded

many times that she be buried with him, but she was dissuaded by the pleading of her children and the earnest persuasion of her relatives and court ministers. However, to show her love and sincerity, she cut off one of her hands and put it in the emperor's coffin, so that it could be buried with him. Afterward she was called "Empress Dowager with a Missing Hand."

After her husband's death, Empress Xulu acted as a regent to Ye Libei, their eldest son who had been crown prince for three years. It was said that his father, Emperor Taizu, did not believe that Ye Libei was the one to bring stability and prosperity to the empire. Instead, the late emperor had pinned his hopes on their second son, Ye Ludeguang. Therefore the empress proposed that Ye Lubei offer Ye Ludeguang the crown, and he consented. In the winter of 927 A.D., Ye Ludeguang ascended the throne, reigning as Emperor Taizong.

Empress Xulu was now named empress dowager, and in 938 A.D. she was given a more elevated name, "Empress Dowager of Supreme Charity, Supreme Humanity, and Simplicity Responding to Heaven."

As an empress dowager, she did not withdraw from politics. Making use of her long years of administrative experience, she exerted great influence on state administration and was greatly worried about the fact that the emperor occupied himself wholeheartedly in warring against the Later Jin dynasty, ruled by the Han. The Liao dynasty lost large numbers of people and animals in the fighting, which was greatly opposed by the people both in the Liao empire and in the Later Jin. Empress Dowager Xulu asked her son whether he would consider letting the Han rule over them. "Absolutely not," he replied. "Then why do you want to rule them?" she retorted. "Moreover, even if you can take Han lands, you will not be able to remain there long. If some disasters happen during the continuous war, you might lose, and then what can you do?" Then she went on to suggest making peace with the Han, so that the two sides could coexist.

Among her sons, the one she best liked was her youngest son, Li Hu. The otherwise smart and liberal-minded dowager empress was both stubborn and blinded concerning him. Though courageous, Li Hu was extremely cruel. He was apt to torture people either by carving words on their face, or drowning them, or burning them to death. But she never disciplined her son for his behavior and even attempted to put him on the throne.

In 947 A.D., Emperor Taizong died on his way to the south. Empress Dowager Xulu pronounced Li Hu the new emperor. At the same time, the imperial ministers elevated Ye Luruan, the eldest son of Ye Libei, to rule as Emperor Shizong. Hearing the news, the dowager empress became furious and led an army with Li Hu to prevent Ye Luruan from returning to the palace, in the north. Li Hu's army was defeated at Tai Dequan, and then the two opposing sides were stalemated, each occupying one bank of the Yellow river. The dowager empress was not willing to yield, but she was persuaded to change her mind by Ye Lu-wuzhi, one of the ministers. Li Hu reacted angrily to his mother's actions: "Since I am the emperor, how can you accept Ye Luruan as the emperor"? Ye Luwuzhi responded, "Ye Lu-ruan had been accepted as our emperor and the overall situation is therefore decided, so it is better to agree." So the dowager empress made up her mind to make peace with Emperor Shi-zong. She said sadly to Li Hu: "Your father and I have loved you more than we have loved your brothers, but, as the proverb says: 'A spoiled child will not continue his father's cause; an extraordinarily beautiful woman will not bless the family.' It is not that I do not intend you to be the emperor, but that you have proved unfit."

The civil war for the crown now ended, Empress Dowager Xulu was banished from the court and exiled to Zuzhou (south-west of present-day Balingzur in Inner Mongolia), placed under house arrest for the rest of her life.

Luo Yunhuang
Zhu Binzhong, trans.

Sources

Tuo Tuo, *History of the Liao Dynasty*, vol. 71; *Notable Women in History*, vol. 1, pp. 180–183.

Madam Huarui (b. ca. 935 A.D.), a native of Qingchen, Sichuan province, was one of the most charming and beautiful girls in

Chinese history. In order to ingratiate himself with Emperor Mengchang of the later Shu dynasty, her father, Xu Kuang-zhang, offered her as a concubine. (Following the collapse of the Tang Dyasty in 907 A.D. this dynasty competed during the period of the "Ten Kingdoms" to rule over parts of China under their command. Central and South China suffered turmoil in this period of the "Ten Kingdoms," there, while the various Northern parts of China were ruled as "Five Dynasties" from 907–960 A.D.) Because the emperor admired her beauty and charm, he admitted her as a royal concubine with the title Madam Huarui. By naming her Huarui, which means pistil, the emperor hinted that her charm and tenderness were comparable to the pistils of flowers.

The emperor loved her deeply and later promoted her to a higher rank. One summer night, the emperor took her to a summer resort in Mokechi. In admiration of his charming wife and the pleasant weather, the emperor composed a short poem describing her beauty.

> White, smooth, sweatless your skin,
> Its fragrance sweeping the hall with wind.

When this poem was published, it was on everyone's lips. Writings on her superb beauty widely circulated at that time, and Madam Huarui became a symbol of beauty for many centuries to come. Once, when she accompanied the emperor to the city wall, as she often did, she lost her white fan, which was then picked up by someone. Soon, people everywhere started making fans like hers and calling them *xiangxueshan* (snow and fragrant fan).

During the turbulent days at the end of the Tang dynasty which collapsed in 907 A.D., many refugees had come to Sichuan from Central China. One effect of this migration was that the refugees contributed to the cultural advances in Sichuan. Many scholars and *literati* from the North moved South to various courts and patrons, seeking positions where they could. Emperor Mengchang encouraged literature and displayed his own great literary talent. Under his influence, Madam Huarui began to compose poetry, a skill she continued to cultivate for the rest of her life. On her way to Kaifeng, for instance, she wrote a poem on a hotel wall:

> Leaving the conquered homeland,
> I with broken heart and agony;
> Long and painful the spring,
> Sad cuckoo on my riding way.

In 965 A.D. the later Shu dynasty was overthrown by the leaders of the new powerful Song dynasty which would reunite China, led by Emperor Taizu. The victorious emperor longed to meet the beautiful Madam Huarui, and he sent his officials to bring her to the capital, Kaifeng. Now established as a distinguished concubine in the Song emperor's palace, she grew downhearted because she missed her former lover, now deceased. She had loved Emperor Mengchang both because of his affection for her and because of his talents and brilliance. Huarui thought daily about him, but had to conceal her feelings. She later made a picture of the former emperor and used it to memorialize him, telling people that the figure was the god of fertility. When the emperor asked her about the picture, she replied: "Those who pray to this god will have more children." Unaware of her real feelings, the emperor merely thought she wanted to bear him children.

Continuing to write poetry, she expressed her indignation at the fall of the later Shu dynasty in "Shu guowang shi" (Words on My Country's Fall):

> Your white flag flying on the city wall,
> Hoodwinking me inside the palace;
> Swords deserted from a million soldiers,
> Why no hero in the battle?

This emotional poem marked her as a patriot and a poet. Together with her other poems, which numbered around a hundred, it was published in the Quan Tang shi (Complete Collection of Tang Dynasty Poetry).

After living in the Song palace for more than ten years,

Madam Huarui died. Though richly endowed with beauty, she was also very intelligent and talented. Her importance in Chinese history is signaled by the inclusion of a biography of her in *Shiguo chunqiu* (The Spring and Autumn Annals of Ten Countries).

Zhang Yu

Sources

"Qingshi Lielue, Qingchou Lie" by Feng Meng-long in the Ming Dynasty History; "Shiguo Chunqiu, Houshu two, Houzhufei Zhangshi, Huifei Xushi Liezhuan"; *Quan Tang shi* (Complete Collection of Tang Dynasty Poetry). Trans. by Soame Jenyns, *T'ang Dynasty Poems*. London: J. Murray, 1940.

Empress Dowager Xiao (953–1009? A.D.) was the wife of Emperor Jingzong of the Liao dynasty 947–1125 A.D. Named Chuo, she was from the Guojiu branch of the Khitan tribe. Her father, Xiao Shiwen, was a prime minister in the northern Khitan government, which had received tribute from the Song government as reward for its aid against the Tungusic people of Pohai in the east. Later he served in the Liao dynasty, proclaimed by the Khitans in 946 A.D., when this tribute was discontinued. The Liao empire of the Khitan tribes ruled over areas of the northeast corner of China, southern Manchuria, and Mongolia.

When Xiao Chuo was very young, she began to show her intelligence. She excelled in many things both domestic and artistic. Her father often said happily: "This daughter will become a high-minded girl." This prophecy proved true as his daughter became a ruler of the Liao dynasty, ruling parts of northern China.

In 969 A.D., when Emperor Jingzong ascended the Liao throne, Xiao Chuo was chosen to be a mid-ranking concubine. Soon afterward she was given the title of empress and bore a son, Ye Lilongxu. When her husband was very young, a coup d'état had taken place in the court in which his father, Emperor Shizong, and his mother, Xiaolie, were both killed. Although Emperor Jingzong survived, he was physically injured and mentally affected. After he took the throne, he could not manage the complicated political affairs of the court, so all state affairs fell on the shoulders of Empress Xiao.

In 983 A.D., Emperor Jingzong died and was succeed by Ye Lilongxu, who reigned as Emperor Shenzong. Xiao Chuo was named empress dowager. As the emperor was only eleven years old, his mother again had to act as head of state. The empress dowager shouldered the heavy load of ruling the Liao empire, which bordered and controlled parts of northern China. In 983 A.D., she was granted the title "Chen Tian Empress Dowager."

During her capable reign, she undertook a series of political and economic reforms. First, she attached importance to and depended upon the ministers of Han Chinese nationality and recruited many Han Chinese intellectuals from the landlord class to participate in government and political affairs. Han Chinese began to hold posts that in the past had only been held by Khitan aristocrats. A Han Chinese named Han Derang was especially respected by Empress Dowager Xiao, who gave him the position of minister of *guming* (regent). Once a Khitan aristocrat contradicted Han Derang and Han's father. Han Derang's family was so angry that they killed the aristocrat, but the empress dowager did not punish Han Derang. Moreover, as Han Derang often won victories over the Northern Song armies, he was promoted frequently and viewed as a hero. Finally, he came to hold great military and political power within the Liao empire.

Many other Han nobles also distinguished themselves working for Empress Xiao, such as Han Deran, Han Dewei, Han Dechen and Han Deni, who were all put into important civil service positions. The political and economic measures suggested by these advisers were beneficial for the feudal system to develop smoothly in those border regions in Northern China dominated by the Liao dynasty.

Empress Dowager Xiao tried to reduce the number of captured slaves gradually and attempted to improve their situation. During the wars against the Northern Song, the number of slaves captured by the Liao dynasty did not exceed seven hundred, much less than that during the reigns of Emperor Taizu and Emperor Taizong. She also lifted a ban on masters releasing their slaves without permission. Every person who was forced to be a slave could be freed from slavery and registered as a subject of the prefecture and county. Those slaves who were in debt could free themselves from slavery by working as herdsmen, peasants, workers, or craftsmen protected by Liao feudalism.

Moreover, in every region dominated by the Liao dynasty, she carried out the "Law of Two Taxes" of the Tang dynasty and implemented the feudal system of uniform taxation. Above all, she set about revising the law and gradually worked out the laws of the Tang dynasty among the Khitan, changing the Khitan aristocrats' policy of discrimination against the Han Chinese. Because of the empress dowager's intelligent strategy and tactics and her successful control of the ministers, they were able to manage state affairs with acumen. All this sped up the process of feudalism within the Liao dynasty and strengthened this area against Northern Song forces.

The empress dowager was skilled not only in politics but also in military affairs. She mounted a series of military campaigns against neighboring states. The Liao dynasty was the closest neighbor of the Northern Song, and the two shared a tense political relationship. During Empress Dowager Xiao's regency, she first defeated the Northern Song military attempt to recapture Yanyun. In 986 A.D. the Song Emperor Taizong (Zhao Kuangyi) wanted to recapture the regions of Yanyun earlier ceded to the Liao. However, his army suffered disastrous defeats at Qigongguan (near present-day Zhuo county, Hebei). During the war, Empress Dowager Xiao either commanded troops in person or sent troops to fight against the Northern Song. The great victory made the Northern Song see the Liao as a major threat and also consolidated the strength of the Liao dynasty. Empress Dowager Xiao and her son led two hundred thousand soldiers southward to fight with the Northern Song. As Liao troops took advantage of a weak point in the Northern Song defense, they entered Tanzhou (modern-day Puyang county, Hebei) and were approaching the capital city, Dongjing. Song Emperor Zhenzong was at a loss. Prime Minister Kou Zhun proposed that the emperor direct the battle, and Emperor Zhenzong took his advice. Though assuming command, he still planned to make peace. After Empress Dowager Xiao weighed the pros and cons, she agreed to accept a truce with the Northern Song, which stipulated that the Northern Song deliver an annual tribute of 100,000 taels of silver and 200,000 bolts of silk to the Liao. Further, Song Emperor Zhenzong as a sign of respect had to call Empress Dowager Xiao "his aunt" and consider Emperor Shenzong "his brother"—an event later known as "A Peace Pact at Tanzhou."

With this pact, the Liao and the Northern Song reached parity in power. For about a hundred years afterward, the two dynasties lived at peace with each other, which made for a stable environment for both sides. As a result, the Han Chinese strengthened their ties with the Khitan and other "barbarian" nationalities on China's borders. This period strengthened the Liao feudal government which in no way viewed themselves as "barbarians" or inferior to the Han Chinese and consolidated their holdings in northern China.

Empress Dowager Xiao was also instrumental in establishing friendly relations with the western Xia and Korea. The rulers in the western Xia were basically obedient to the Liao. Because Korea did not have close relations with the Liao, it was suspicious of the Liao court and was not obedient to the Liao. In late 992 A.D., Empress Dowager Xiao attacked Korea and made a military incursion. In early 993 A.D., she concluded a peace treaty with Korea, stipulating that about a hundred miles east of the Yalu river be ceded (from Song control) to Korea. This relationship between the Liao and Korea was maintained for nearly twenty years. Korea sent ten young students to Liao to study the Khitan language. In return, the daughter of the Liao emperor married the king of Korea.

Good relations between the Liao and the western Xia people as well as the rulers of Korea made the Song avoid attacking the Liao; more important, it created a relatively peaceful environment allowing political, social, economic, and cultural communication and development among the northern nationalities.

Empress Dowager Xiao's civil and military contributions to the Liao dynasty played a great role in the development of the Liao government's system of governance. During Emperor Shenzong's reign, the Liao dynasty experienced its golden age.

In late 1009 A.D., Empress Dowager Xiao died. In 1052 A.D., she was aptly renamed the "Intelligent Empress," for her no-

table political and social reforms during the rise of the Liao
dynasty.

Song Ruizhi
Ma Li, trans.

Sources

Shu Fen, *History of the Liao Dynasty*, vol. 1; Zhu Shao Hou, *The Chinese
Ancient History*.

Li Qingzhao (1083–1151 A.D.), China's greatest female poet,
specialized in *ci* poetry—lyric verse written to popular tunes.
Considered a genius, she is described by historian Hu Binqing
as an "epoch-making poet on an equal footing with her (male)
contemporaries in prosody, rhetoric, and creation." Li is praised
for the originality of poetic imagery, emotional language, and
the harmony of verses. She also wrote (shi) *shih* poetry, or poetry in regular verse, but few poems of this style have survived.

Li Qingzhao was born in Shandong province, during the reign
of Emperor Shenzong. She grew up in Jinan, which is called
"the city of fountains." The home in which she grew up is now
a historical site where some of her poetry is displayed. Both
sides of her family comprised scholars and well-known officials.
Her father was Li Kefei, a scholar at the Imperial Academy in
Kaifeng who later served the Song court as minister of rites. Her
mother was a granddaughter of Wang Gongchen (1012–1085
A.D.), a poet and essayist.

Li Qingzhao was educated at home by her parents, who were
highly cultured and appreciated classical learning; thus she received an education, unlike most girls of her era. She was more
interested in becoming a scholar than were her brother, Li Mang,
and her sisters. Early on, possibly with the encouragement of
her mother, who was also a poet, she developed a talent for
writing *ci* poetry.

Li Qingzhao became a well-known figure in her hometown
for her poetry, literary talent, and exquisite diction. She estab-

lished herself as a competitive poet when she wrote two *shi* poems to rhyme with a poem by a friend of her father's, Zhang Lei (Zhang Wenqian), written after the discovery of an eighth-century monument celebrating the restoration of royal authority after the uprising of An Lushan during the Tang dynasty. Openly critical of his shallowness and lack of understanding of the events commemorated on the monument, she was praised by her father and the *literati* circle. This encouraged her to develop her potential as a poet in a society that traditionally did not accord women with great respect. With her family applauding her triumphant bettering of the friend's poem, her boldness and confidence were given free reign.

When she was eighteen, she married Zhao Mingcheng, then a student at the Imperial Academy who became well known for his explanations of ancient inscriptions found on bronzes and stone monuments. His father, Zhao Tingzhi, who served as minister of the interior and later as prime minister, also encouraged her poetry.

One of her early poems speaks of her relationship with her husband, who graduated from the Imperial Academy two years after their marriage:

> I bought a spray of Spring in bloom
> From a flower carrying pole.
> It is covered with tiny teardrops
> That still reflect the pink clouds of dawn
> And traces of morning dew.
> Lest my lover should think
> The flowers are lovelier than my face
> I pin it slanting in my thick black hair
> And ask him to compare us.

(From Li Ch'ing-chao, translated by Kenneth Rexroth and Ling Chung, *Complete Poems.* Copyright 1979 by Kenneth Rexroth and Ling Chung. Reprinted by permission of New Directions Publishing Corp.)

One of her most famous poems was written while her husband was away at the Imperial Academy: Longing for his return, she wrote him a poem on a silk handkerchief, "Sorrow of Departure" to the tune of "Cutting a Flowering Plum Branch":

Red lotus incense fades on
The jeweled curtain. Autumn
Comes again. Gently I open
My silk dress and float alone
On the orchid boat. Who can
Take a letter beyond the clouds?
Only the wild geese come back
And write their ideograms
On the sky under the full
Moon that floods the Western Chamber.
Flowers, after their kind, flutter
And scatter. Water, after
Its nature, when spilt, at last
Gathers again in one place.
Creatures of the same species
Long for each other. But we
Are far apart and I have
Grown learned in sorrow.
Nothing can make it dissolve
And go away. One moment,
It is on my eyebrows.
The next, it weighs on my heart.

(Translated by Kenneth Rexroth and Ling Chung in *Li Ch'ing Chao Complete Poems*, a New Directions Book, New York 1979, 27. Reprinted by permission.)

Their literary interests made Li Qingzhao and her husband extremely compatible, and she continued to entertain the *literati* socially in their home. Upon graduation, he was employed as a court functionary. Together the couple saved their money and collected bronzes, calligraphy, paintings, jade, stone inscriptions, and antiques of all kinds. They wrote poems to each other expressing their love and enjoyed discovering their historical treasures together and researching their history, recording every detail carefully. The two often entertained themselves by reading books together at night, asking questions based on their reading. Li Qingzhao often accompanied her husband on his official business and to social gatherings. When he went alone, she would send him poems to keep him company. For imagery, she used the chrysanthemum, Chinese flowering crabapple, wine, wind, moon and moonlight, birds, cold rain, and leaves. Her poetry was in a graceful and restrained style that came to be called the *yi'an* style.

But their lives were shaped by the power struggles at court between rival factions—struggles that weakened the Song to the point of its collapse in the north by 1126 A.D. For the first seven years of their marriage, Li Qingzhao and her husband lived in Kaifeng. These years were filled with tension, as in 1102 A.D. Li Kefei was exiled from the court. Li Qingzhao wrote poems to her powerful father-in-law, then the deputy prime minister and one of the rivals of her own father's faction, imploring him to reinstate her father. "Your fingers are burned," she wrote in one poem, "while your heart grows cold." In 1103 A.D. it was decreed that no further marriages could take place between members of the rival factions, placing Li Qingzhao in a precarious position. But in 1105 A.D. amnesty was granted for her father, who then returned to court. Her powerful father-in-law became the prime minister, but in 1107 A.D. lost favor and was dismissed, and died soon thereafter.

Lacking their former influence and protection, the Zhao family was persecuted, and the couple left the capital for the south. They journeyed to Qingzhou and remained in exile for at least ten years. Zhao Mingcheng served as magistrate first in Laizhou and then in Qingzhou. They passed the time with their hobbies of deciphering stone tablets, and bronze inscriptions, collecting antiques, paintings, and precious jade carvings. Together they collaborated on *Jin shi lu* (The Study of Bronzes and Stone Inscriptions), viewed as an important work because ancient inscriptions recorded history and recounted the great accomplishments of Chinese leaders. They entertained themselves by reading from the classics, asking each other questions, and rewarding correct answers with sips of tea.

Li Qingzhao wrote of her feelings at the moment in her poetry. On her thirty-first birthday, she had her portrait painted, and her husband wrote the following poem in the top corner of the painting:

To Poetess I-an on the Occasion of Her
Thirty-first Birthday Anniversary:

Her poetry is pure and elegant,
Her person modest and dignified,
A real companion for me
In my retirement.

Some of her poetry is blatantly erotic:

Tired of swinging
indolent
I rise
with a slender hand
put right
my hair
the dew thick
on frail blossoms
sweat seeping through
my thin robe
and seeing
my friend come
stockings torn
gold hairpins askew
I walk over
blushing
lean against the door
turn my head
grasp the dark green plums
and smell them.

(Translated by James Cryer in *Plum Blossom, Poems of Li Ch'ing-chao.* Carolina Wren Press, Chapel Hill, NC, 1984. Reprinted by permission from Carolina Wren Press.)

A similar eroticism is found in the following:

Come with evening
ranks of wind and rain
was away
the fires of sunset
I finish tuning the pipes
face the floral mirror
thinly dressed
crimson silken shift

translucent
over icelike flesh
lustrous
in snowpale cream
glistening scented oils
and laugh
to my sweet friend
tonight
you are within
my silken curtains
your pillow, your mat
will grow cold.

(Translated by James Cryer in *Plum Blossom, Poems of Li Ch'ing-chao.* Carolina Wren Press, Chapel Hill, NC, 1984. Reprinted by permission from Carolina Wren Press.)

Soon after Li Qingzhao and her husband went into exile, there was an invasion from the north led by the Jurchens, from the Tungusic branch of the Altaic peoples. They had overthrown the Khitan Tatars who had earlier established the Liao dynasty in Manchuria and parts of northern China. The Jurchens invading the northern regions of China established the Jin dynasty and pushed slowly toward the Yangzi river. Appointed magistrate of Zichuan in Shandong by Emperor Qinzong in 1126 A.D., her husband was apprehensive about accepting the post as the capital of the Song fell under siege to the Jurchens. The Northern Song fell in 1126 A.D., and a boundary was established along the Huai river dividing the area still controlled by the newly reconstituted government of the Southern Song from that under the Jurchens. During this turmoil, Li Qingzhao and her husband remained on the move until 1128 A.D., when they settled in Jianning (modern-day Nanjing). Because of the invasions, they had fled, leaving most of their collected bronzes, antiques, and paintings behind. As the Jurchen invasion spread southward into the middle of China, Li Qingzhao satirized the Song emperor for acting cowardly and criticized the nobles and troops who crossed the Yangzi in flight southward:

Alive we need heroes among the living
Who when dead will be heroes among the ghosts.

I cannot tell how much we miss Xiang Yu,
Who preferred death to crossing to the east of the river.

In 1128 A.D., during the reign of Emperor Gaozong, Zhao Mingcheng resumed official office in Jianning as a magistrate. Then he was appointed to Huzhou in Zhejiang province and made plans to establish his family in Jiangxi. In 1129 A.D., at the age of forty-eight, her husband died while en route to a new post in Jiankang. As the Jurchen invaders attacked Jiankang, Li Qingzhao fled alone southward, arriving in Hangzhou in 1132 A.D. In the following she expressed her feelings as a bereaved widow:

Search. Search. Seek. Seek.
Cold. Cold. Clear. Clear.
Sorrow. Sorrow. Pain. Pain.
Hot flashes. Sudden chills.
Stabbing pains. Slow agonies.
I can find no peace.
I drink two cups, then three bowls
Of clear wine until I can't
Stand up against a gust of wind.
Wild geese fly overhead.
They wrench my heart.
They were our friends in the old days.
Gold chrysanthemums litter
The ground, pile up, faded, dead.
This season I could not bear
To pick them. All alone,
Motionless at my window,
I watch the gathering shadows.
Fine rain sifts through the wu-t'ung trees.
And drips, drop by drop, through the dusk.
What can I ever do now?
How can I drive off this word—
Hopelessness?

(From Li Ch'ing-chao, translated by Kenneth Rexroth and Ling Chung, *Complete Poems*. Copyright 1979 by Kenneth Rexroth and Ling Chung. Reprinted by permission of New Directions Publishing Corp.)

She fled to Yongzhai, Shaoxing, and Chuxian, returning in 1131 A.D. to Shaoxing and in 1132 A.D. to Hangzhou. She took up residence in Hangzhou with her brother. In 1132 A.D. she married Zhang Ruzhou. In contrast to her earlier marriage, this marriage was unhappy because he mistreated her. (Some scholars, for example, Kenneth Rexroth and Ling Chung, dispute whether a second marriage took place, but the majority cite the second marriage as having taken place.) She divorced him, after only a hundred days.

Once again alone, she remained a scholar, completing the manuscript of the ''Collection of Inscriptions on Ancient Bones and Stone Tablets,'' which she started with her first husband. Her poetry now took on a melancholy air of gloom and nostalgia, partly because the invaders had succeeded and weakened the Song dynasty. There are only a few sublime and heroic poems. According to the *Song shu* (History of the Song dynasty), she wrote six volumes of poetry and seven volumes of essays, but most of these writings were lost during the Jurchen invasion and occupation of northern China.

Later she wrote one of her most important poems, which speaks of the solitude of old age:

> *The gentle breeze has died down.*
> *The perfumed dust has settled.*
> *It is the end of the time*
> *Of flowers. Evening falls*
> *And all day I have been too*
> *Lazy to comb my hair.*
>
> *Our furniture is just the same.*
> *He no longer exists.*
> *All effort would be wasted.*
> *Before I can speak,*
> *My tears choke me.*
> *I hear that Spring at Two Rivers*
> *Is still beautiful.*
> *I had hoped to take a boat there,*
> *But I know so fragile a vessel*
> *Won't bear such a weight of sorrow*

Today her poems are read partly as a commentary on the society of the Song dynasty and partly because of their eternal beauty of composition, as "her delicate sensibility, her keen observation, her profound love of nature, her clear and simple language, her original imagery and expression and above all her rich experience in life made her worthy of the honors bestowed upon her memory." The most outstanding qualities of a poet are sensibility, ideals, and creative power, wrote Hu Binqing: "It is universally accepted that Li Qingzhao is China's greatest poet." At a time when women traditionally did not have the opportunity to secure a good education or a place of honor, she was fortunate to have put her education to good use crafting *ci* poems that elevated her stature, immortalizing her name.

Powerful and visionary, the poetry of Li Qingzhao portrays a woman confident in her craft and ambitious enough to seek literary greatness in a society that traditionally ascribed to women, as Hu Pin-ching (Hu Binqing) wrote, "no freedom of thought, no freedom of action, no freedom of love, and no freedom of expression."

Barbara Bennett Peterson

Sources

James Cryer, *Plum Blossom, Poems of Li Ch'ing-Chao.* Chapel Hill, NC: Carolina Wren Press, 1984; Hu Pin-ching, *Li Ch'ing-chao.* New York: Twayne Publishers, Inc., 1966; Kenneth Rexroth and Ling Chung, *Li Ch'ing Chao Collected Poems.* New York: New Directions Books, 1979; John A. Turner, *A Golden Treasury of Chinese Poems.* Seattle and London: The Chinese University of Hong Kong and distributed by the University of Washington Press, 1976; Cheng Jun-song et al., *The Seventy-Two Great Figures of China's Nations.* Beijing: Shanxi People's Publishing House, 1985; Xu Gongchi, et al., *The Heroes Before Our Time.* Beijing: Zhanghua shuju, 1986; Xu Peijin, *Li.* Shanghai: Guji, 1981; Department of History Nanking University, *A Dictionary of the Famous Figures in Chinese History.* Nanjing: Jiangxi People's Publishing House, 1982. Adapted and reprinted with permission from Deborah Klezmer, ed., *Women in World History* (Waterford, CT: Yorkin Publications)

Liang Hongyu (ca. 1100–1135 A.D.), a general and a Chinese national heroine, lived during the transitional period from the Northern to the Southern Song dynasties.

Liang Hongyu was born in Chuzhou, Jiangsu province. Her father was a military commander garrisoned in the north protecting China's frontiers from the barbarian *xiongnu*, so she grew up with a knowledge of military tactics, weapons, and strategy. When she was very young, her father taught her the importance of tactical planning and how to use certain weapons with dexterity. Liang Hongyu, like her father, was fiercely loyal to the Song central government, and, when he was killed in battle, she dreamed of someday taking his place. After her father's death, she returned to Central China.

At the same time, the Nuzhen tribe was growing rapidly and becoming more powerful north of the Great Wall. The Nuzhen formed a confederation known as the Jin kingdom. Eventually, they felt powerful enough to challenge the Song dynasty below the Great Wall, and their invasion met little resistance because the central Song government was rife with corruption, intrigue, and cowardly rulers. The corrupt Song leaders fled southward as large areas of the northern reaches of China came under Jin control. The Southern Song, as it came to be known after 1127 A.D., continued to rule part of China in the south. This was a period of accommodation and appeasement.

This was the backdrop for Liang Hongyu's desire to make her country strong in the face of the invading Jin forces. Her military tradition extended back through the ages, but she found herself in an age of transition where military values were no longer viewed as important. She resented the weakness of the Southern Song rulers who had abandoned the northern territories to the invaders.

Her aspiration of actually becoming a warrior or military officer herself would be difficult to realize, given the feudal traditions limiting the role of women. In 1121 A.D. she married Han Shizhong, then a low-ranking military officer, who became one of China's most outstanding generals. He trained her in the arts of war, and her fortunes followed his. Together they made their life in the various military camps where they were both assigned and had at least two sons. She fought all over northern and central China, from west to east and north to south during the Jin invasions. Han Shizhong always fought at the head of his troops, rather than merely directing from a place of safety. For this he was greatly admired, and their fortunes and high military appointments increased with each victory. Ultimately Han was given the position of a general in command of some of the Song forces battling the Jin. All along the way, Liang Hongyu's quick mind, versatile tactics, and calmness in danger complemented his success.

When Han Shizhong was elevated to marshal, she acted as his close military assistant. In one of the battles with the invading Jin forces, the Song garrison commander of Luanzhou in Shanxi province was killed defending the city. Han Shizhong was defending a pass nearby known as Lianglang Pass, and upon hearing of the city's capture, he rushed, with his eldest son, to recapture Luanzhou. His hasty advance turned out badly, and he and his forces found themselves encircled. Alerted to their danger, Liang Hongyu mustered her forces and rushed out to liberate her husband and his troops. Just before leaving on this mission, she told her younger son's wet-nurse: "Should anything happen to me, please bring him up for me and treat him as if he were your own son. Tell him about his parents' aspirations and encourage him to fight for his country when he grows up."

Upon approaching the captured city, Liang Hongyu was approached by Wu Zhu, the commander of the Jin army, who wished to discuss with her the release of her husband rather than fight her, since he feared her reputation as a valiant warrior-strategist. He promised he would free her husband, son, and their troops if she would lay down her arms; he also promised to give them all Jin titles of nobility. Liang Hongyu was not taken in by this ruse. Unbeknownst to her, her husband had already broken out of the encirclement with his troops, so Wu Zhu really had nothing to offer her. Nonetheless, she refused to betray the Song for whom she fought and attacked the city, eventually losing the battle, but maintaining her honor. Her forces had been outnumbered, and she believed at the time that she was fighting to save her husband, son, and country. Even in defeat she was wildly acclaimed for her bravery and patriotism.

The Jin forces captured the Song capital located at Bianjing (now Kaifeng in Henan province) in 1127 A.D. Two Song emperors were captured, and, after a brief power struggle for control of the Southern Song's region, Prince Zhaoguo made himself emperor of the Song, re-establishing the Song capital at

Linan (now Hangzhou). He did not negotiate for the release or return of the two captured emperors for fear of losing his own self-proclaimed power.

The military forces of the Southern Song were never strong enough to capture the lost territories in the north. In spite of these losses and hardships, the Southern Song era introduced some motifs that remained until the end of the dynastic system in 1911 A.D. Whereas Buddhism had been strengthened during the grandeur of the Tang dynasty, neo-Confucianism became the philosophy in the Song era and would dominate politics through the last emperor. The Southern Song also saw rapid growth of commerce and a much more highly developed money economy. The dynasty focused much of its energies southward, developing trade through maritime commerce with Southeast Asia and West Asia as far as India and the Persian Gulf. The tax base was shifted from a head tax on individual peasants to more generalized taxes on land and commercial property. The gentry class, which ruled southern China, represented an amalgam of the old landed aristocracy and the new commercial merchants. Moreover, the center of culture had shifted to the cities from the rural areas, and this produced an enlightenment period in the arts and scholarly works of the Song.

Further, the intellectual Zhu Xi, a scholar of the Confucian classics, developed a moral theory, the *Lixue*, that allowed women in Chinese society to be restrained. Zhu Xi suggested that a woman in China was to be dominated first by her father, then by her husband, and then by her son. This philosophy would become even more pronounced in the Ming dynasty. Confucian ideology looked down upon women, and Zhu Xi's teaching was a real factor in the decline of female status. In the preceding dynasties, there had been many emperors who belonged to minority nationalities, but in the Song and Ming, there were none. The society of these minority nationalities had retained some of the values of matriarchal society and tended to be more generous to women. In the absence of this tradition at court during the Song, women disappeared as famed scholars and warriors, although a few poets remained.

The life of Liang Hongyu is even more remarkable when one considers that the Song dynasty was a period in which that status of Chinese women was on the decline, as shown, for example, by the introduction of foot binding. This is precisely why Liang Hongyu was viewed as so outstanding and so different from the typical woman. She had escaped foot binding as well as the institution of concubinage. The Southern Song's maritime commercial economy spawned brothels and teahouses, which further degraded women. That Liang Hongyu could emerge as a strong general in this period is testimony to her greatness and valor.

From the beginning, the invading Jin had been conscious of themselves as a race separate from the Han Chinese. To maintain control over their conquered regions of North China, troops were garrisoned at scattered points throughout the region and were expected to rise up upon a call to defend their gains. In the early days of the Jin dynasty in northern China (while the Southern Song held the south), Jin armies were only made up of Nuzhen and excluded the local Chinese. Thus power was held through technological superiority, as the northern Chinese peasants were deprived of weapons. Slowly, intermarriage between these two people erased their differences.

The Southern Song had suffered military reverses because many leaders at court had desired capitulation rather than devastation. They retreated through negotiation after losses in the field. In Linan, the new emperor, Zhaoguo, soon reversed this policy of appeasement and made plans to regain lost territories. He removed the capitulators from the court, brought in new leaders willing to follow his policies. This vitality was short-lived, as one of his military commanders, Miao Fu, staged a coup d'état, forcing the emperor to flee. Miao Fu now demanded that the son of Emperor Zhaoguo be made emperor with the empress dowager as regent. Secretly desiring to seize the throne himself, Miao Fu hoped to use the empress dowager as a front of legality until the time was right for his own grab for power.

When the news of Miao Fu's coup attempt to take the throne of Emperor Zhaoguo reached Liang Hongyu and her husband, they were dismayed, knowing that intrigues within the court would lead to the further collapse of Song spirit and defensive capabilities. Han Shizhong and Liang Hongyu decided to return to the new capital and crushed the insurgent rebellion, maintaining a united front against the enemy. Knowing this, Miao

Fu captured Liang Hongyu and her younger son and held them hostage to nullify the forces and power of Han Shizhong in Xiuzhou (now Jiaxing) near Linan. Meanwhile, Miao Fu tried to persuade Liang Hongyu to throw her support to the rebellion.

At first she pretended to agree, upon condition that she be given an audience with the dowager empress, the regent. Her wish granted, Liang Hongyu seized the opportunity to tell the dowager empress privately about the conspiracy to topple her and her young son from power. Liang Hongyu again had shown that her first allegiance was to her country and Song authority. Deeply moved by her selfless spirit, the dowager empress said: "The state is in danger. Please go and ask General Han to end the rebellion." Twenty-four hours later, after an exhausting horseback ride, Liang Hongyu arrived in Xiuzhou and convinced her husband to march to the capital and end the rebellion. She and her husband were successful. In appreciation and recognition of her part in ending the attempted coup, Hongyu was granted the title "Madame Huguo," an honorific title of praise meaning a woman who defends her country. She also was placed on salary by the state as a military general, the first time a woman had been so honored in China.

The borders between the Southern Song and the Jin dynasty established in North China were never stable, and Jin forces frequently made forays deep into Song territory to threaten the capital. On one such foray, Jin troops captured the city of Hangzhou in 1130 A.D. and looted the environs. The Jin forces had come only for booty this time and retreated northward. Near Jinshan they were intercepted by the forces of Han Shizhong aboard ships in the Yangzi river. Maneuvering her own flagship into visual position of the retreating Jin ships, Liang Hongyu signaled to Han Shizhong's ships with flags, indicating the path of the enemy's retreat. Beating a drum loudly to bolster its own forces' morale, the Song ships were victorious. Liang Hongyu's part in this famous ordeal was known as "beating the drums in the Battle of Jinshan."

A large Jin army was bottled up by the ships of Han Shizhong and was marooned at Lake Huangtiandang for forty-eight days, their escape blocked by Song forces. The army of Han Shizhong numbered 8,000, while the Jin army bottled up on the island comprised 100,000. The marooned Jin commander was Liang Hongyu's old nemesis Wu Zhu, who had beaten her at Luanzhou. She longed for revenge and vindication. Wu Zhu sued for peace, offering to return the booty he had gathered in his plunder, but Han Shizhong refused. While the Song forces awaited backup troops, the wily Wu Zhu escaped after cutting a channel to reach an unprotected part of the river and escaped.

The retreating Jin forces fought their way northward until they crossed the Yangzi river about 1135 A.D.. Liang Hongyu and her husband volunteered to cross the river to Chuzhou and provide for its rebuilding and defense. The two turned their military forces into a large work force to rebuild houses, replant fields, and secure oxen. Chuzhou once again became a prosperous city and a line of defense for the Southern Song.

Six months after returning to Chuzhou, Liang Hongyu became ill from overwork and died. Beloved by her countrymen in her native region, she was buried at the base of Linyan Hill in Suzhou. The Song emperor showed his honor and respect for her by giving her family 500 taels of silver and 500 bolts of cloth, a large sum at that time. History, legend, plays, and songs still recall the valiant warrior Liang Hongyu, who not only beat the drums but marched with her own forces fighting in the field to victory.

Barbara Bennett Peterson

Sources

Yi Mian, "A Military Commander Fighting Against the Jin," (translated from Chinese by Fang Hong, Wuhan University), in *Famous Women of Ancient Times and Today*, edited by *Chinese Woman Magazine*. Shijia zhuang: Hebei People's Publishing House, 1986; Chu Nan, "A National Heroine from the Past," in *Women of China*, January, 1981; "Liang Hongyu," in *The Dictionary of Famous Women of Huaxia* (*China*). Beijing: Huaxia, 1988 (translated from Chinese by Lucia P. Ellis). Consultation with Wu Jianrong and Zhu-lei, history department, Wuhan University.

Sun Daoxuan (ca. 1100–1150 A.D.), also called Chongxu Jushi, was a famous poet of the Song dynasty. She was born in Jian'an (modern-day Jian'ou), Fujian. Daoxuan was exceptionally clever as a child and had an extraordinary memory; she could fluently recite whatever she had read just once, from the classics to history. When she grew up, she married a man named Huang, and they had a son, Huang Zhu.

When Sun Daoxuan was thirty years old, her husband died. She swore she would never remarry, but instead would live independently with her son and make her own way. Daoxuan also undertook to teach her son to read and write. At the same time, she composed poetry in her spare time, writing numerous *ci* poems and some prose.

As an adult, Huang Zhu was talented at composing poems, but he refused to hold any public position. He led a reclusive life and left to later generations *The Collection of Guchen,* a compendium of poetry filled with beautiful language and deep feeling.

Although Sun Daoxuan wrote a vast number of pieces, she destroyed many of her works in later years. After her death, Huang Zhu showed his appreciation for his mother's wholehearted care and cultivation by trying to collect them, aided by the fact that some had been passed down verbally.

Zhang Si'nan collected six of her poems as part of *Notes of a Traveling Official;* Huang Sheng included her most famous five pieces in *Selected Ci by Women Poets of the Tang and Song Dynasties.*

Sun Daoxuan collected her most noted eight pieces in *The Ci.* Her works shared one common characteristic: they were all fresh, graceful, mild and implicit with a lingering taste. Her "Zui si xian" (tonal patterns and rhyme schemes) are examples of this:

> Sunset clouds are red.
> Evening haze surrounds the mountain,
> fog separated pine trees.
> Wind brings my sleeves waving,
> flying like a frightened swan goose.
> My heart is heavy like a rock,
> my hair is white like a cloud.
> My light image moves only in moonlight.

Sorrow and regret, year after year,
the age changes my appearance.
Past experiences melted into the heaven,
a decade elapsed without notice.
Recalling the dream in Yunxuan Pavilion,
but the spring is over.
The colorful phoenix is far away,
the xiao* tunes were gloomy;
the night is tranquil,
but the regrets are plentiful.
The jade has long been buried in earth,
the east wind makes my heart broken.

(*The *xiao* is a verticle bamboo flute.)

The misty scenery, the tranquility, and the profound meditation in her poetry leave a lingering image. Later generations came to compare Sun Daoxuan to Li Qingzhao for her *ci* poetry.

Song Ruizhi
Zhu Zhongliang, trans.

Sources

The Notes of a Traveling Official, eighth vol., by Zhang Si'nan (Song dynasty); Huang Sheng. *Selected Ci by Women Poets of the Tang and Song Dynasties*, tenth vol. Beijing: Zhonghua shuju, 1980.

Tang Wan (ca. 1130–1155 A.D.), a poet, was the first wife of Lu You (1125–1210 A.D.), who became famous for his patriotic poetry. Her finest poetry was inspired by her sorrow at being parted from her first husband because of feudal traditions.

Tang Wan was born in Yuezhou, Shanyin county (now Shaoxing, Zhejiang province), during the Southern Song dynasty. Lu You's family was also from Shanyin. Tang Wan's father was Tang Hong, a maternal uncle of Lu You; hence Tang Wan and Lu You were cousins. Tang Hong had been a minor government official for several years, but was removed from office when he differed with the central bureaucracy over the issue of fighting the invading Nuzhen tribe, then overrunning the northern regions of China.

Lu You's circumstances were similar, as his father, from a scholarly family, had lost his position at court owing to unrest caused by the Nuzhen invasion and various court intrigues. Lu You's father had taken his family back to Shanyin. Both the father of Lu You and the father of Tang Wan had been displaced, and both determined to study and write poetry rather than enter public life again. Certainly this devotion to poetry influenced both Lu You and Tang Wan, as they had played together as children while their fathers discussed politics, composed poetry, and wrote essays. Both fathers had taught their respective children to write and recite poetry.

Tang Wan enjoyed the urban and cultivated milieu in which she found herself as a young woman. Lu You was a youth of great taste and literary skill. By the time he was twelve he was writing poems, and, by the age of eighteen, he had established a reputation as a poet. Both Tang Wan and Lu You wrote a style of poetry called *shi* (or *shih*), which placed great emphasis on achieving naturalness in syntax and on vocabulary that reflected the vernacular language. The style originally appeared in the late Han. Lu You wrote a total of twenty thousand poems, of which 9,200 have survived. Tang Wan was a sensitive and sentimental young woman, who was equally adept at crafting fine *shi* (or *shih*) poetry. While they were courting, the two often entertained each other with the delights of poetry. Their childhood friendship turned to love and affection, and eventually their respective parents also encouraged their marriage, as the families were very close friends. They were married and settled down in wedded bliss.

The *shi* poetry in which Tang Wan and Lu You excelled consisted of a lyric with a five-syllable meter. Reflecting the disruption of the times, this lyric poetry was typically Daoistic, lamenting the corruption of the world and asserting with vehemence the point of view of the individual in conflict with society. For all its Daoistic individualism, however, even this lyric poetry showed a preoccupation with form and a considerable degree of rigidity. During the Tang dynasty, the seven-syllable line was developed to parallel the more standard five-syllable meter. In the Song period, the *shi* poetry form became more rigid and gave way to a new form, the *ci*. The *ci* had originated in the lyrics for popular songs sung in the city teahouses and brothels. The *shi* were also chanted, but the only tune to these chants was provided by their own strict pattern of word tones. The *ci* were now sung to popular tunes and thus had freer tonal patterns and were naturally quite irregular in meter. *Shi* poetry was highly literary; the *ci* was more colloquial. The *ci* were at first looked down upon by the literary *shi* poets, but, during the later Song, it was fashionable for poets to write both *shi* and *ci*.

Tang Wan and Lu You shared deep feelings because they had known each other since their childhood. Their emotions were perfectly in tune, and together they created and recited poetry. Perhaps out of envy, or perhaps because Tang Wan did not observe closely enough the feudal rites and rituals expected of a new wife living in her husband's parents' home, her mother-in-law began to ridicule her for inattention and became critical of her behavior, saying Tang Wan did not show her the proper obedience. Such a traditional role may have felt unnatural for Tang Wan because she had known her mother-in-law all her life, had so often visited her household, and was already a member of the family because she was a cousin long before she was a wife. Tang Wan loved to engage in conversations about poetry with Lu You and passed the time in this scholarly way, without dutiful performance of obligations to his mother. She realized her error too late or perhaps perceived her mother-in-law's attitude too late. For the mother-in-law's part, she had expected Tang Wan to be obliging, obedient, and amiable, but to her surprise Tang Wan was independent within her household. She felt Tang Wan did not show her mother-in-law the proper respect for her place in the family; the mother-in-law also was critical of her lack of conversation with others in the extended family and social community, since she spent all her time with her husband. For newlyweds, this was perhaps natural; but for a critical mother-in-law, this was disrespectful and insulting. Tang Wan also refused to be overly dramatic about showing emotion, unlike others in the household, who would cry several times a day to show their concern over Lu You's father, who was sick and dying. She loved her father-in-law, but could not falsely conjure tears at will, thus angering her mother-in-law even more. Tang Wan's mother-in-law began to look around for another, more traditionally dutiful wife for Lu You.

As tensions mounted, Lu You's mother saw the daughter of Madam Wang, who was extremely docile, reserved, and obedient. Lu You, who loved Tang Wan very much for her energy, intelligence, wit, and charm, did not find Wang attractive. Nevertheless, Lu You's mother asked her son to divorce Tang Wan on two grounds: (1) Tang Wan did not serve her in-laws well, and (2) their discussions of poetry forced Lu You to neglect his studies. The heartbroken Lu You, compelled to do his mother's bidding out of respect for feudal tradition, sent Tang Wan, much against his true feelings, back to her family. Even though Lu You had pleaded with his mother to relent, she was unmoved. Lu You dared not go against his mother's will, yet he still attempted to lessen the impact. He rented a house near his family's compound and installed Tang Wan there, so that he could meet with her. He hoped his mother's anger would recede, and she would come to her senses and not force his beloved Tang Wan to be sent away. He pleaded again and again for her to forgive Tang Wan. Unfortunately, a servant reported all his comings and goings to his mother. She proceeded to the house in which Lu You had installed Tang Wan, not knowing that the couple had just rushed out in fear of her arrival, and she raged at the empty house, now more determined than ever to separate the couple using her rights under feudal tradition. No sooner had Lu You divorced Tang Wan than his mother forced him to marry the docile daughter of Madam Wang. But Lu You never forgot his first love, Tang Wan. Tang Wan subsequently also remarried.

Some years later, when Lu You was thirty years old, he had an opportunity to visit Sheng's garden, which belonged to a family friend. There he unexpectedly ran into Tang Wan and her second husband. She glanced at him from afar, feeling great anguish and sorrow, while he too experienced great torment and grief. Tang Wan's husband, suspecting their feelings, graciously sent some wine and fruit to that part of the garden where Lu You was standing, as he and Tang Wan walked away. Drinking the wine quickly, Lu You expiated his grief by writing a famous *ci* poem on the wall surrounding Sheng's garden:

From a warm and tender hand:
This cup to huangteng *brew;*
As spring returns to this land,
The willow blooms anew.
But cruel is the wind that blows,
And frail our bonds of bliss;
I taste years of parting years of woe,
In this cup of bitterness
How wrong! Wrong! Wrong!
Spring's unchanged from long ago,
But we are thin and pale;
Rose-tinted tears on thy kerchief flow,
'tis all of no avail.
Pond, pavilion are idle here,
Our vows are staunch and true, but where
Shall I send my love today?
'Tis through! Through! Through!

Shortly afterward, after Lu You had left the garden, Tang Wan, unaware that Lu You had written a poem, walked with her husband through that part of the garden where Lu You had stood. She gazed at his poem, which spoke of his lost love and commemorated their former happiness. Reading the verse brought tears to her eyes, as she remembered the cruel separation forced by her former mother-in-law. Returning home, she became ill and composed this *ci* poem from her bed.

Cruel is the human heart,
And frail are worldly ties;
In teeming rain the day departs,
Too soon the flower dies.
The evening wind is cold and dry,
Flicking a tear or two;
By the balustrade along I sigh,
I would send my thoughts to you,
'Tis hard! Hard! Hard!

Things are changed from yesterday,
And we must live apart;
Love lost is like a swing they say
Swaying deep in the heart.

The lonely bugle sounds the morrow,
Night is passing away;
Lest others know about my sorrow,
I must feign a smile by day.
Feign! Feign! Feign!

Tang Wan's *ci* poem, in response to Lu You's, reflects her poignant sorrow at a love lost and happiness ripped away. Tang Wan died soon after composing these lines, and Lu You came to know about her poem soon thereafter. He was filled with remorse for having written the words on the garden wall that had rekindled her sorrow. She inspired his famed poetry for the rest of his life, as a poem written when he was eighty-four reveals:

The flowers of Sheng
Garden are fair as
brocade,

Many knew me in
times long past,

They knew too, that
Beauty in the dust in laid:
Why must our dreams
vanish so fast?

His poems to Tang Wan not only marked their undying love for each other but also served as a critique of the feudal traditions.

After her death, Lu You turned his attention to his poetry career, committing himself and his skill to patriotically preserving and strengthening the Southern Song. He studied for and passed the civil service examination. He was appointed as an official and fought with the Southern Song forces attempting to repel a Nuzhen invasion that had begun in 1125 A.D., the year of his birth. He was critical of the Song forces for not driving out the invaders in order to regain control over the northern territories. Lu You eventually lost his official appointment because of his hawkish views when the peace faction came to increasingly dominate the Song court. For the same reason, he failed to advance as an imperial official; thus he followed the cycle experienced by his father and Tang Wan's father. In fact, he was demoted four times for speaking out against court policies and finally resigned his post and went into retirement. He continued to write patriotic poems and also wrote in celebration of the simple rural life and contentment of the peasantry. Lu You, like Tang Wan, was a master of poetic expression and used both direct description and highly personalized and emotional symbolism. Poetry, considered the highest form of literary expression in Song China, had evolved from the magical spells or the ritual incantations and the highly formalized forms of oral storytelling of ancient times before the evolution of writing. These "songs" or "poems" were highly rhythmical so that they could be committed easily to memory for the ages.

The love poems written by Lu You and Tang Wan to each other, reflecting their eternal love and shared happiness, are among the most famous poems in Chinese history. After he retired, Lu You went frequently to Sheng's garden, where he had last seen Tang Wan, writing again and again poems of his love for her.

Barbara Bennett Peterson

Sources

Dong Naiqiang, "A Tragic Love Story of Feudal China," in *Women of China*, June, 1982; Dong Naiqiang, "First Wife of Lu You Who Died Because of Feudal Rules," in *Famous Women of Ancient Times and Today*, (orally translated from Chinese by Fang Hong), edited by *Chinese Woman Magazine*. Shijiazhuang: Hebei People Publishing House, 1986; "Tang Wan" (translated from Chinese by Lucia P. Ellis) in *The Dictionary of Famous Women of Huaxia*. Beijing: Huaxia, 1988. Books on Lu You which contain insights into the life and times of his wife Tang Wan are: Cao Jimin, *Lu You*. Beijing: Jiangsu People's Publishing House, 1982; Qi Zhipin, *Lu You*. Beijing: Zhonghua shuju, 1961; Qi Zhipin, *Lu You*. Shanghai: Guji, 1978, 1979; Yu Chaogang, *Lu You*. Beijing: Heilongjiang People's Publishing House, 1982.

Sources to Part V

Cao Jimin. *Lu You*. Beijing: Jiangsu People's Publishing House, 1982.
Cheng Junsong et al. *The Seventy-Two Great Figures of China's Nations*. Beijing: Shanxi People's Publishing House, 1985.

Chu Nan. "A National Heroine from the Past." *Women of China* (January 1981).

Clement, Egerton, trans. *The Golden Lotus*. London: G. Routledge, 4 vols., 1939.

Cryer, James. *Plum Blossom, Poems of Li Ch'ing-Chao*. Chapel Hill, NC: Carolina Wren Press, 1984.

Department of History, Nanking University. *A Dictionary of Famous Figures in Chinese History*. Nanjing: Jiangxi People's Publishing House, 1982.

Dong Naiqiang. "A Tragic Love Story of Feudal China." *Women of China* (June 1982).

Dictionary of Famous Women of Huxia. Beijing: Huaxia, 1988.

Famous Women of Ancient Times and Today, ed. *Women of China*. Shijia-zhuang: Hebei People's Publishing House, 1986.

Hu Pin-ching. *Li Ch'ing-chao*. New York: Twayne, 1966.

Huang Sheng. *Selected Ci by Women Poets of the Tang and Song Dynasties* Beijing: Zhonghua shuju, 1980.

Hung, William, *Tu Fu* (Du Fu), *China's Greatest Poet*. Cambridge: Harvard University Press, 1952.

Lee Yao, E.S., *Chinese Women: Past and Present*. Mesquite, TX: Ide House, 1983.

Qi Zhipin. *Lu You*. Beijing: Zhonghua shuju, 1961; Shanghai: Guji, 1978, 1979.

Quan Tang shi (Complete Collection of Tang Dynasty Poetry). Trans. by Soame Jenyns, *T'ang Dynasty Poems*. London: J. Murray, 1940.

Rexroth, Kenneth, and Ling Chung. *Li Ch'ing Chao Complete Poems*. New York: New Directions Books, 1979.

Turner, John A. *A Golden Treasury of Chinese Poems*. Seattle and London: Chinese University of Hong Kong and University of Washington Press, 1976.

Waley, Arthur, *Chinese Poems*. London: G. Allen and Unwin, 1946.

Waley, Arthur, *Translations From the Chinese*. New York: Alfred A. Knopf, 1941.

Wang Chi-chen, Trans. *Dream of the Red Chamber*. New York: Twayne, rev. ed. 1958.

Winsett, G.B., *The Bright Concubine and Lesser Luminaries: Tales of Fair and Famous Ladies of China*. Boston: J.W. Luce, 1928.

Xu Peijin. *Li Qingzhao*. Shanghai: Guji, 1981.

Xu Gongchi et al. *The Heroes Before Our Time*. Beijing: Zhanghua shuju, 1986.

Yu Chaogang. *Lu You*. Beijing: Heilongjiang People's Publishing House, 1982.

Part VI

The Ming and Qing Dynasties and the Coming of the Opium Wars

The Ming dynasty (1368–1644 A.D.) was established by Zhu Yuanzhang (Chu Yuan-chang, reign title Hongwu [Hung-wu]; 1328–1398 A.D.), a military adventurer who had not been a member of the gentry class but had worked his way up through the Chinese political world. His efforts to exert firm control were harsh, and he often saw conspiracies against him. Floggings became institutionalized at his court in Nanjing. Executed officials were stuffed and hung in their successor's office. After his death, a power struggle erupted among his four sons; the victor was the fourth son of Hongwu, who had administered the district of Beijing for his father. He reigned as the Yongle Emperor (Yunglo; r. 1403–1424 A.D.), made Beijing the capital, and built the Forbidden City, which became his palace and administrative center. Beijing's city walls extended 14 miles in circumference and 40 feet in height. The Forbidden City was 5 miles in circumference and housed the throne halls with gold-tiled roofs. This imperial compound was the center of Chinese culture.

The Yongle Emperor's policies rebuilt the Chinese economy, which led to an increase in the population. New methods were employed in rice production with the introduction of drought-resistant champa rice, which could yield two crops a year. New irrigation methods were also developed, oxygenating the water of the rice paddies with fish and special paddle-pedaled pumps. Initially taxes were reduced, which made him popular with commoners. He also distributed lands to the peasants to increase the tax base and to expand his hold over the peasantry. The emperor encouraged the military and made positions in both the military and the civil service hereditary. The court made full use of eunuchs, who were employed at the highest levels because they were trusted to enter the private chambers of the women (the back palace) at court.

The Ming dynasty in the beginning was a time of opulent splendor, during which the wealthy enjoyed rosewood furniture, heavily embroidered silk clothing, lovely blue and white porcelain, elaborately carved ornamental and decorative jade, lacquerware in reds and blacks, cloisonné vases and jewelry, and magnificent homes for extended family members. Often the production of these wares was directed in state-owned factories; their quality was regulated by craft guilds. Delicacies such as shrimp, water chestnuts, fine wine, roast duck, fresh fruit, noodle and vegetable specialties, and other elaborate fare, balanced for health and nutrition, graced the dining tables of both homes and restaurants. The commercial prosperity generated during the Song dynasty was sustained during the Ming, and money continued to circulate widely until 1450 A.D., when paper money became worthless and China resorted to payment in copper and silver only. Urbanization and commercialization continued at a rapid pace. In 1397 A.D. Ming criminal and civil laws were codified and promulgated.

The state examination system was heavily relied on for the recruitment of government bureaucrats. Examinations were held at the county and then the prefectural levels that qualified an applicant for the equivalent of a bachelor's degree (*xiucai*, or flowering talent) and entry into the *literati* or gentry class. A further set of examinations was held at the provincial level that would award the successful applicant with the *zhuren* (recommended man) degree and allow him to go on to try for the *jinshi* (presented scholar) degree in the capital.[1]

The good life was supported during the early Ming by a strong central bureaucracy, which organized China's population of 120 million at a time when all the states in Europe combined were home to fewer people. Ming China was the strongest and most sophisticated central government in the world during the fifteenth, sixteenth, and seventeenth centuries. The central administration, based on the Six Ministries and other imperial organs, extended to a parallel structure for the military, and both were balanced by the censors. The country was divided into 15 provinces, 159 prefectures, 234 departments, and 1,171 counties (*xian*). To ensure impartiality, magistrates were forbidden to oversee their home provinces. The military was organized into units of 5,600 men. The army was professionally trained and salaried. Although there was an ongoing effort to restore the ancient tradition of citizen-soldiers, the Ming continued to rely on trained professional armies. In part to help support these professional troops, households were required to pay various taxes, such as the Ming Summer Tax on special crops grown between spring and summer and the Autumn Tax on crops harvested in the fall. General taxes were based on the Double Tax of the eighth century and households for purposes of collecting labor services due the state, organized under the *lijia* (village-section) system.[2] During the later Ming, the government raised further funds by selling civil-service positions, which bypassed the examination system and diluted the prestige of the degrees.

The imperial court supported the publication of new knowledge in compendiums such as the *Encyclopedia of the Yongle Period*, published in 1407 A.D. in more than eleven thousand volumes. The great encyclopedia planned in France during the Enlightenment may have been based on this tradition in Ming China. Other great compilations include those by the scholar Li Shizhen in 1578 A.D. on medicinal drugs, which described the principle of inoculation against smallpox long before it was known in the West.

Ming China's scholars were interested in everything from medicine to technology, from poetry to ethics. Their writings indicate growing attention to a wider audience of educated women. Although the imperial system banned women from taking the civil service examinations, women were educated in ever-increasing numbers at home, especially in wealthy families. Courtesans were often expertly trained in poetry and song to entertain their well-educated male companions.

The *literati* of this period, as in centuries earlier, during the Zhou dynasty and Confucian times, believed that the individual was essentially good and saw the need for the moral leadership of the emperor, as the son of heaven, to lead China's people. Many magistrates and scholars performed volunteer public services without payment, believing that it was their moral duty to serve the court and the country. Traditions established earlier— filial piety, ancestor worship, the use of characters in a writing system, divination, Confucianism and its concept of the five basic human relationships to govern good conduct, the extended family, and an appreciation and love of the arts—all continued to evolve during the Ming on a large and grand scale.

In foreign relations, all states that wanted to trade with China paid it tribute and came as vassal states willing to perform the kowtow, prostration, and gift giving and to submit to having that trade regulated—ideas developed by the Yongle Emperor. He also portrayed China as the Middle Kingdom (*Zhongguo*), which led ethnocentrism to flourish during this period. No one could trade with China without the emperor's permission, and the court attempted to control piracy in coastal waters.

Fearing a possible coup by one of his brothers who had fled the country, the Yongle Emperor launched a series of overseas expeditions in part to hunt down any possible rival and to expand his own power and prestige. The Ming dynasty under this emperor is most famous for the seven voyages led by Zheng He between 1405 and 1433 A.D. At the time, China's fleet was enormous: It had vessels measuring 370 × 150 feet that could carry horses. These treasure ships, or junks, were built in Nanjing; the flotillas of them gathered at Fujian, from which the ships sailed to Java, Sumatra, Ceylon, Calicut (on the Indian coast), and the Middle East, such as the coast of Hormuz, and from there to the Swahili ports of the East African coast, such as Malindi.

China's imperial trade extended as far as the western coast of Africa and the island of Zanzibar. Large-scale trade developed with Southeast Asia. The Ming emperors gained considerable prestige from their overseas empires. Large Chinese overseas settlements grew up in these areas of overseas trade and continued to thrive until the arrival of the Portuguese and Spanish during the era of European expansion in the late fifteenth and early sixteenth centuries.

In addition, the Yongle Emperor rebuilt the Grand Canal, which extended from Beijing southward to the Yangzi Basin, connecting the Yellow, the Huai, and the Yangzi rivers. This canal was of crucial importance because the southern regions helped feed the colder, northern regions.

The Mongols threatened northern China continually, yet the Yongle Emperor's administration was able to hold them at bay. He ended the Ming voyages in part because of the renewed threat from the Mongols. But subsequent rulers were weaker and had less success in holding off the Mongol invaders. After he died, the Mongols captured his successor, the Yingzong Emperor, holding him for ransom.

Under the Yongle Emperor's successors, revolts began to flare up in some of the tribute states, including Vietnam, and Japanese pirates (Wako) began raids along the coast of China. In Japan, the Kamakura shogunate had repelled the Mongols from their territory in the thirteenth century, but after it collapsed it was replaced by the Ashikaga shogunate, which never effectively held control over all of Japan. China was able to exploit these events and force Japan to submit to tribute payments if Japan wanted to enter the lucrative China trade.

Despite the splendors of the early Ming dynasty, internal and external threats began to mar its progress. Natural disasters such as floods and famines created hardships among the peasantry, caused production to decline, and thereby eroded the tax base. Homeless bands roamed the countryside, some turning to banditry. Because of shrinking tax revenues, state-owned irrigation and flood control projects were left in disrepair or abandoned. The judicial system fragmented over land contracts and rental agreements. In the cities and the countryside, economic dislocation was widespread, as evinced by the strikes of silk weavers complaining of heavy taxes and low wages in Suzhou in the early 1600s. The growing lack of control over the lower reaches of society spread upward to the court during the reign of the Wanli Emperor (r. 1572–1620 A.D.), as the court relied too heavily on eunuchs and corruption became commonplace. The Wanli

Emperor became disillusioned, stopped attending to imperial duties, and allowed vacant positions at court to remain unfilled. Intellectuals began to criticize the general breakdown in morality and in 1611 A.D. formed the Donglin Society, a philosophical society seeking reform that later became politicized.[3]

Externally, the court had difficulty maintaining the tribute system established to regulate overseas trade. Technically, Japan was a vassal tributary state, but Japanese pirates trawled the trade routes between Japan and China in the 1500s. Japan invaded Korea, a major ally of China, in the 1590s, and Chinese imperial forces waged a war to defend Korea, but at great cost. Because of its own internal problems, Japan pulled its military forces out of Korea in 1598 A.D., but its growing military power remained a threat to China. During this turmoil, China had allowed Portugal, which had taken hold in Macao, to take over administration of the trade between Japan and China, an activity that would provide an opening wedge for Western traders to expand their opportunities. Large quantities of silver, first from Japan and then from the West, began to circulate in China as a result of this trade, causing widespread inflation and exacerbating economic dislocation and imbalances between rich and poor.

Economic dislocations were the harbingers of serious peasant uprisings led by Li Zicheng in Shaanxi province. In 1644 A.D. he attacked the environs of Beijing, sacking the Ming tombs and thus forcing the Chongzhen Emperor to go into mourning and then, amid plague and siege and capture of the capital by Li's rebel forces, to commit suicide by hanging himself on the hill of the imperial garden outside the Forbidden City. Internal revolt had brought down the last Ming ruler and opened the way to foreign conquest of China.

Li Zicheng's control of Beijing was challenged by a loyalist Ming general, Wu Sangui. Li marched out of the city to subdue General Wu, but the latter joined forces with the Jurchen (see Chen Yuanyuan) and the Jin dynasty, established in the north by Nurhaci in 1616 A.D. The Jin forces were formerly led by Huang Taiji (Huang T'ai-chi), who in 1636 A.D. changed the name of the dynasty from Jin to Qing. He died in 1643 A.D., leaving his ninth son as his heir and his brother Dorgon as regent. In 1644 A.D., Dorgon joined forces with General Wu, battled against Li Zicheng, and defeated him. The Jurchen and their Qing dynasty leadership then claimed power in Beijing, installing Huang Taiji's heir as the Shunzhi Emperor (Shun-chih; r. 1644–1661 A.D.). Thus ended the Ming dynasty and began the Qing.

The Jurchen, now calling themselves Manchus, established a firm grip on the imperial apparatus of rule. The traditional Six Ministries of the Ming were combined with the Manchu eight-banner military system (wherein fighting units were organized into groups under identifiable flags or banners). Former Chinese military men were forced to style their hair in a braid, or queue; Manchu style of dress became mandatory; and the Chinese tradition of footbinding was prohibited for Manchu women and phased out entirely among non-Manchu women. The Manchus controlled the land and its allocation, oversaw tax collection, restarted irrigation and flood control projects, established a social ranking system based on ethnicity, maintained the examination system and the restrictions on foreign trade, and consolidated power throughout the provinces. The Shunzhi Emperor's son, who reigned as the Kangxi Emperor (K'ang-hsi; r. 1661–1722 A.D.), put down the Revolt of the Three Feudatories (1673–1681 A.D.), integrated Taiwan into China (1683), negotiated China's border with Russia in the Treaty of Nerchinsk (1689 A.D.), subdued the Zunghar tribes in western China (1670s), installed a Dalai Lama in Tibet loyal to the Qing (1720 A.D.), maintained Confucian traditions, expanded the civil service examinations to allow more opportunities for Han Chinese, and published vast historical compendiums to justify and glorify his reign. The Kangxi Emperor also came to depend on Western scholars, in particular the Jesuits, because of their great learning and his eagerness to tap Western science and technology.[4] Through exposure to foreign influences, China slowly began to open itself up to the world. Westerners would use this opening to demand ever-increasing trade privileges, which resulted in the so-called unequal treaties forced on China in the early 1800s.

The Coming of the Opium Wars

Western domination of China began during the Opium Wars. The Portuguese has opened trade with Japan and China, first opening the port of Macao and developing it as a colony in the sixteenth century. The Dutch traded with the Spice Islands and Borneo and Sumatra in Indonesia, developing a trading entrepôt on Formosa in the seventeenth century. The Dutch were followed by the British, who opened trade on the Chinese mainland through Guangzhou during the late seventeenth and early eighteenth centuries. Russians traded through Siberia with northern China, and many settled along the border areas.

The British East India Company held a crown monopoly to trade in the East until 1833 A.D., when the monopoly was lost and the government allowed "private English trade" with numerous contenders. This important shift from monopoly by one crown-chartered company to many free English traders greatly expanded competition, creating additional burdens on the Chinese system of vassalage. These traders greatly expanded the illegal trade in opium.

The Chinese system of vassalage developed during the Ming dynasty was still in force. Foreign traders legally traded thought Chinese government-sanctioned cohong merchants who were responsible to the *hoppo* of Guangzhou. Direct British contact with Beijing was unattainable. Opium had been used for centuries, but in 1729 A.D. its use, except as medicine, was made illegal and in 1796 A.D. its importation was made illegal as well. But the illegal trade in opium, which was grown in British India, carried by ship to China and smuggled in, had increased between 1800 and 1821 A.D., with the average number of chests totaling 4,500 a year, each one containing about 133 pounds of opium. This influx of the drug greatly expanded the illegal smoking of it. The smuggling was handled by small vessels called scrambling dragons, which took small consignments of opium from much larger foreign ships anchored off shore. By 1838 A.D. there were 40,000 chests of opium imported a year, and the next year opium smuggling became punishable by death. This trade had grown to such heights largely because the British East India Company had lost its monopoly, and more illegal traders entered the opium market competition.

Diplomatic missions to establish trade treaties and regulate opium traffic were undertaken by various individuals, most notably Lord Napier in 1834 A.D., but they were unsuccessful. The British demand for extraterritoriality also proved problematic, as did the British demands for diplomatic representation, the abolition of the cohong merchants, and the right to free trade.

These problems led to the outbreak of the first Opium War (1840–1842 A.D.) after the Chinese destroyed an illegal cargo of opium in Guangzhou and the British sought restitution. The Treaty of Nanjing, signed in 1842 A.D., opened five treaty ports to foreign trade—Shanghai, Fuzhou, Xiamen, Ningbo, and Guangzhou. It also ceded Hong Kong island to the British until 1997 A.D. China was forced to pay an indemnity of $21 million, thus aggravating the silver drain that had plagued China for centuries. American traders received the same terms as the British did after they negotiated the Treaty of Wang Hiya (Wanghia) in 1844 A.D. Hence the entire European continent, as well as the United States, became directly involved in the interior of China—trading, developing concessions, and establishing residences and foreign structures in the concessions.

In part as a response to foreign intrusion, the Taiping rebellion sought to topple the Qing dynasty and establish the Heavenly Kingdom of Great Peace. This rebellious upheaval caused further isolation of the treaty ports and strengthened foreign encroachments as well as excuses for additional demands on China.

These circumstances led to a second Opium War from 1852 to 1856 A.D., sparked by the killing of a French missionary in the interior and the running of guns to aid the rebels. The British secured the Treaty of Tianjin, ending the war and thus allowing the free navigation of the Yangzi river, trade in the interior of China, legalization of the opium trade, and the establishment of diplomatic residences in Beijing. Hence most of the foreign demands were met by the Chinese, and the British went on to expand their interests in China in maritime and postal affairs. Foreign control of parts of China continued in 1863 A.D. with the formation of the Shanghai International Settlement, which created its own government in the concession area, its own roads, police force, taxes, and recreational facilities. Portugal took formal control of Macao in order to police the area and control smugglers. The British colonial office set up a branch office in Kowloon to encourage "cooperative policies" and built residences there to establish a toehold in the area.

China was also beset by problems from without, such as the Sino-Japanese war of 1894–1895 A.D., which China lost. Russia exploited this opportunity to secure the right to build the Chinese Eastern Railway from Manchuria to Vladivostok, and the Germans took control of concessions on the Shandong peninsula. These events led directly to Chinese demands for political reform, a self-strengthening movement and the Boxer Rebellion, which attempted to take over the foreign legations in Beijing in 1900 A.D. The Society of the Harmonious Fists, or Boxers, attempted to overthrow the Qing dynasty and loosen the foreign grip on China. The signing of the Open Door notes temporarily stopped the cutting up of the country and other states agreed to protect China's territorial and economic integrity.

Thus the Opium Wars and the aftermath of European intrusion weakened China, setting the stage for the rebellion led by Sun Yat-sen. The empress dowager Cixi died in 1908 A.D., leaving the throne to her grandnephew Puyi, who became the last emperor of China.

Sun Yat-sen had issued his *Three Principles of the People*, explaining his plan for governing China through "nationalism, democracy, and people's livelihood." He received aid from abroad as well as within China to overthrow the Manchu rulers and establish a republic. This came to pass on October 10, 1911 A.D., later known as Double Ten Day; on this day Sun established a provisional government, later to proclaim a republic the following January.

Sun Yat-sen and his wife, Soong Qing-ling, greatly assisted China's intellectual development and visionary direction for the future. She and her two sisters, Meiling (who married Chiang Kai-shek) and Ailing (who married Kong Xiangxi, later the president of the Bank of China) set new trends for the modern Chinese woman. They were greatly admired and dedicated to the advancement and betterment of the Republic and its people.

B. B. P.

Notes

1. John K. Fairbank, Edwin O. Reischauer, and Albert M. Craig, *East Asia: Tradition and Transformation* (Boston: Houghton-Mifflin, 1998), pp. 188–89.

2. Ibid., pp. 185–87; Albert Feuerwerker, *China's Early Industrialization: Sheng Hsuen-hua and Mandarin Enterprise* (Cambridge: Harvard University Press, 1958); Ssu-yu Teng and John K. Fairbank, *China's Response to the West: A Documentary Survey* (Cambridge: Harvard University Press, 1954); Ping-ti Ho, *The Ladder of Success in Imperial China: Aspects of Social Mobility, 1368–1911* (New York: Columbia University Press, 1962); Etienne Balazs, *Chinese Civilization and Bureaucracy: Variations on a Theme* (New Haven: Yale University Press, 1964).

3. Jonathan Spence, *The Search for Modern China* (New York: W.W. Norton, 1999), pp. 7–26; Sybille van der Sprenkel, *Legal Institutions in Manchu China: A Sociological Analysis* (London: Athlone Press, 1962); O. Edmund Clubb, *Twentieth-Century China* (New York: Columbia University Press, 1964).

4. John K. Fairbank, Edwin O. Reischauer, and Albert M. Craig, *East Asia: The Modern Transformation* (Boston: Houghton-Mifflin, 1965), vol. 2, pp. 15–64; Spence, *Search for Modern China*, pp. 27–71; Arthur W. Hummel, ed., *Eminent Chinese of the Ch'ing Period (1644–1912)* (Washington: U.S. Government Printing Office, 1943), pp. 295–300; Wang Daocheng, "Cixi taihou," in *Qingdai renwu zhuangao*, ed. Qingshi bianweihui, ser. 2, vol. 8 (Beijing: Zhonghau shuju, 1993), pp. 1–19.

Huang E (1498–1569 A.D.) was a famous writer during the Ming dynasty. Born in Suining, Sichuan, she was also known as Xiumei, but most people called her Madam Huang. She was the second wife of Yang Shen, who was also a writer. Although her life was full of frustration, grief and indignation, she made great achievements in literature by writing many outstanding works.

Huang E was the second daughter of Huang Ke, the imperial minister of works in charge of irrigation, transportation, and engineering. Her mother was also from an aristocratic family and well educated. Thanks to this scholarly background, Huang E received a good education at home. She read extensively and became skilled at composing various styles of poetry. Well versed in classics and history, she became an expert of *sanqu* (a type of verse with tonal patterns modeled after folk tunes).

Yang Shen, also known as Sheng'an, was born in Xingdu, Sichuan, the son of Yang Tinghe, a famous scholar. As a child, Yang Shen was clever and resourceful. At the age of eleven, he began to display his talent at poetry and prose. In 1511 A.D., he came in first in the imperial examination and was appointed as an imperial official in charge of writing and editing archives. As an official, he was honest, upright, and unyielding and opposed the excessive extravagance of the ruling court.

In 1517 A.D., Yang Shen submitted a petition to Emperor Wuzong, trying to halt the emperor's merry-making trip to the area of Juyong Pass, lest the local people be disturbed and their farmlands spoiled by the activities of the large entourage. But Emperor Wuzong refused his petition, so Yang Shen returned home, on the pretext of being ill.

In 1518 A.D. his wife, Madam Wang, passed away; the next year, he married the twenty-two-year-old Huang E. They found each other congenial, and he had a great deal in common with her since both of them were accomplished in literary works.

The newlyweds lived in the Pomegranate Pavilion on Gui lake, near Xingdu, which was a scenic spot with blue ripples on the lake, shadowy trees, singing birds, fragrant flowers, and a pleasant climate. The scenic spot provided them with exceptional opportunities for enjoying the beauty of nature, which inspired them to compose poetry, eulogizing the sweetness and happiness of their married life. Very often they would stroll along the bank of the lake and in the woods of osmanthus trees to reply to each other in poems, fully expressing their feelings. At that time, Huang E composed "Courtyard Pomegranate":

> *Planting the seedling from the west,*
> *In the flower-flying season;*
> *I do not expect to eat its fruit,*
> *But hope it to be in full blossom.*
> *I will see no flowers of peach or plum,*
> *But wait for the intelligent branches to wake.*
> *Crimson buds catch my sight,*
> *Making me happier at night.*

Huang E expressed her intoxicated feelings of their affectionate and leisurely life in letters, as well as her sincere respect and love for Yang Shen, who also deeply loved Huang E. On one golden autumn day, they went together to enjoy the osmanthus flowers. Yang Shen picked a branch of the fragrant flower and pinned it on Huang E's hair. Looking at his flowerlike and beloved wife, he could not help chanting:

> *In the treasured woods there is a jade,*
> *To be surrounded again by yellow osmanthus;*
> *The golden flowers weigh down the branches,*
> *Decorating black hair full of fragrance.*

From this we can see that the newly wedded pair who were both scholarly and affectionate, led a poetic love life, full of happiness and joy. Nevertheless, Huang E was not content to lead this life of leisurely seclusion. Two years after their marriage, she encouraged her husband to engage in politics again in the capital and encouraged him to give full play to his talent.

At that time, the Ming dynasty was becoming more and more corrupt. The emperor did not care about the imperial administration but, rather, indulged himself in merrymaking, which brought politics to a low ebb. Yang Shen, however, resolutely went to the capital to be given a new post. His motto ''Getting benefits before no one and behaving righteously after no one'' encouraged him to repeatedly submit petitions to the emperor concerning the state of affairs, despite the risk of being flogged and put into jail. He maintained his highly moral and upright unyielding style.

In 1524 A.D., because of his involvement in the affair known as ''the argument of grand rites,'' which refers to the emperor's idea of conferring a posthumous title on his parents for their contribution in raising an emperor and securing an empress for him, Yang Shen was sent into exile in Yongchang (modern-day Baoshan county), Yunnan. Wanting to share the hardship with her husband, Huang E went south with him. On the way, she gave meticulous care to her unfortunate husband. At the same time, they tried to find comfort in exile in the scenic spots and historical sites that they enjoyed. Huang E found out that her father-in-law's political opponents were seeking a chance to assassinate her husband on the journey. But they did not succeed in their conspiracy because of Huang E's alertness in foiling the plot.

Huang E was determined to accompany her husband to Yunnan, but Yang Shen did not want his wife to suffer and repeatedly tried to stop her. When they reached Jiangling, Hubei, the couple, who could not bear to part, had to bid each other farewell in tears. Huang E returned to Xingdu to look after her father and other relatives of his generation, to raise her nephews and attend to family responsibilities. But she missed her husband, who was suffering in a remote area, and longed to hear from him. Not until two years after Yang Shen was sent into exile did the first letter from her husband reach her. When she read the letter, she was very sad and could not help crying for her worried and frustrated husband, who had tried to improve court moral life and instead was ruined for his efforts. So, this couple, who were deeply attached to each other, could not but talk to each other through letters.

In 1526 A.D., Yang Shen was granted permission to return
and briefly visit his father, who was seriously ill. After that,
Huang E followed her husband to Yunnan, where she took good
care of him and shared the hardships with him. In 1529 A.D.,
when Yang Tinghe passed away, she and her husband went to
Sichuan to attend the funeral, and then Yang Shen returned to
Yunnan alone, while Huang E was left to take care of the household.

Once again, Huang E lived alone in Pomegranate Pavilion,
which made her miss her husband even more. Her hard life, the
unfair fortunes of the world, and the endless worries and regrets
of living apart from her husband kindled her strong desire for
literary creation. She expressed all her feelings of missing her
husband, her sorrow, and her regrets into her poetry, prose, and
sanqu. One representative poem was the moving "A Poem for
the Man Far Away":

> *A wild goose would not fly to Hengyang,*
> *Why should I send a letter to Yongchang?*
> *Misfortune brings me sufferings,*
> *Edict sends my broken-hearted man away.*
> *It elapses one year after another,*
> *Rainy season appears, no sunshine.*
> *Letters are empty appointments,*
> *When come your words of coming?*

Between the lines, one can read her deep affection for her frustrated husband and her heartrending feelings of longing for him,
as well as her anger toward the imperial court responsible for
their separation. But in 1559 A.D., the seventy-one-year-old
Yang Shen died at the barracks in the harsh border area where
he had been exiled. The grieving Huang E had to go to the far-
off Huzhou, Yunnan, to escort the remains of her husband back
home for burial beside his father in a tomb outside Xingdu. The
death of her husband was a great blow to Huang E, and she fell
ill out of excessive gloom. In 1569 A.D., she died.

Huang E composed many poems, in both *ci* and *sanqu* styles,
that portrayed her frustrating life experience and her constant
and bitter longing for her husband. Because she did not want

the people of later generations to see her manuscripts full of sorrow and regret, she did not keep them. Few of her works have survived. Writers of later generations praised her works highly for both their content and style. Xu Wei, a famous writer, calligrapher, and painter of the Ming dynasty, thought her poetry had "a graceful taste with an elegant style and a natural application of rhymes in composing *ci*." Her contemporaries thought that Madam Huang, who was both affectionate and talented, could be mentioned in the same breath with Li Qingzhao and Zhu Shuzhen, famous composers of *ci* of the Southern Song dynasty.

No wonder admirers of later generations said: "It is rare in this world that the couple were both Ci composers." Their fame was on a par, their works and styles were hardly differentiated. This was because both of them were talented and affectionate, sharing the twists and turns of life's experience. When their *sanqu* are put together, later writers could hardly tell whose was whose, so identical in style and feeling were their poems. Most of their works had a style of gracefulness, sincerity, and smoothness with restrained touch and profoundness.

In his days of banishment for as long as thirty-plus years, Yang Shen was not overcome by the adversity, he rather made use of his ample time to read whatever available and applied himself to writing with great concentration. In the Ming dynasty, he was the number one scholar in terms of "his extensiveness of reading, the memory of the knowledge and the abundance of his works." To the later generations, he left a rich cultural legacy of books in more than four hundred categories—poetry, calligraphy, painting, astronomy, geography, musical instruments, medicine, and biology. He was a man with extensive knowledge and profound scholarship. Huang E's achievements in literature—no less than her husband—also won the respect of her contemporaries. Her well-known piece "Oriole" was the proof:

> *Lingering rain cools down the earth,*
> *Making flowers withered.*
> *Looking through misty window:*
> *Is river in sight?*
> *Only to be disappointed to see nothing.*

Letters are not guaranteed!
The unloved wild goose,
Reaches no southern Yunnan!

The artistic conception of this piece was very simple, natural, deep, and dignified. In her sorrow and anger was contained a strong consciousness of fighting. Moreover, the wording of the piece was graceful and fluent, seemingly composed at one sitting. After Yang Shen read the piece on the meditation in the rain, he was very moved and immediately picked up his pen and composed three pieces in reply so as to comfort his beloved wife. When Wang Shizheng, a Ming dynasty writer, read the pieces, he commented that Yang Shen's reply was not as good as Huang E's original *ci*.

Huang E's works were collected by later generations into *Selected Poems of the Wife of Zhangyuan Yang* (Zhuangyuan means number one scholar in the imperial examination), *Afterthought of Madame Yang's Silk Songs and Ballads*, *Yuefu of Madam Huang* (*Yuefu* are folk songs and ballads in Han style), *Letters Between Husband and Wife,* and *Sanqu of Yang Shen and His Wife.*

It is true that Huang E's poetry did not directly reflect major social events. But she did express her experience of the inconstancy of human relationship, her expectations of the peaceful and happy life, and her anger at the corrupt and inhumane society.

Huang E had been admired by later generations for her virtues and talents. In 1983 A.D., a Huang E Memorial Hall was built at Gui lake in Xingdu, in which some of her objects left behind are exhibited.

Zhang Wei
Zhu Zhongliang, trans.

Sources

Qian Qianyi, *Biographies of the Poets Attached to Their Selected Poems in History—The Supplementary Section of the History of the Qing Dynasty*, 730;

Hu Wenkai, *Textual Research of the Works by Women Writers in History*. Beijing: Commercial Publishers, 1957, pp. 142–144; *The Biographies of Women Scholars in Chinese History*, pp. 261–264; *The New Textual Research of Novels, Dramas, Songs, and Ballads*, World Publishing House, pp. 247–264; *History of the Ming Dynasty*, 192th vol.: "The Biography of Yang Shen." Beijing: Zhonghua shuja, 1974, pp. 5081–83.

Zheng Guifei (d. 1630 A.D.), an imperial concubine whose actions at court weakened the Ming dynasty, was a native of Daxing county near Beijing. *Guifei* was a title for an imperial concubine, and her surname was Zheng. She was the favorite concubine of Zhu Yijun, who reigned as Emperor Shenzong of the Ming dynasty. In 1587 A.D., after she bore him a son, Prince Zhu Changxun, she became a concubine of the highest rank.

Zheng Guifei became crafty, wicked, and merciless, as Emperor Shenzong led his dissipated life, neglecting administration of the empire for almost thirty of his forty years at the helm. She became powerful by taking advantage of this fatuous emperor and being involved in the three famous court cases in the later Ming dynasty, hastening its collapse. These three cases, which marked the decline of Ming power, were the "Tingzhang an" (the case about a stick), "Hongwan an" (the case about some medicine), and "Yigong an" (the case about changing the palace).

Because the emperor showed favoritism toward Zheng Guifei, some ministers in charge of taxes tried to advise her, encouraging her to expand her power and ambition. After Zheng gave birth to Zhu Changxun (her first child), other ministers realized that, using her growing power, she might rush to crown her own son; others urged the emperor to crown the first of his three sons, Prince Zhu Changlu (by another woman), but the emperor, influenced by Guifei, refused their request. Later ministers, including Jiang Yinling, Li Xianke, and Meng Yanghao were either demoted or dismissed by Zheng Guifei for challenging her.

In January 1598 A.D., Emperor Shenzong ordered that his three sons (by different women) be appointed kings at the same time. But the objections aroused within the entire imperial court persuaded the emperor to change course and make the firstborn son, Prince Zhu Changluo, his successor (the crown prince) and the third prince, Zhu Changxun, the king of Fuwang.

With the urging of Zheng Guifei, Zhu Changxun spent ten times as much money as was budgeted on building his palace and on his wedding. Zheng Guifei noticed that no one objected, which encouraged her to wield even more power.

In May 1616 A.D., an unknown man burst through the imperial palace gate carrying a stick and wounding the guard. He was arrested by the soldiers when he came close to the crown prince's bedroom. The emperor learned this from the crown prince and demanded an investigation. Liu, the official in charge of the city's security, tried the case and sent a report to the emperor, which declared: "The criminal was Zhang Chai, a native of Suzhou. It appears that the man is mentally distressed, but he looks rather cunning. Suggestion: send him to the criminal court for further trial." The criminal court produced the same result: a declaration of the criminal's insanity. According to the law at that time, this criminal was to be executed. But before this decision was submitted to the emperor, a prison officer, Wang, secured from the criminal a very different confession, which showed that Zheng Chai had been admitted to the palace with the assistance of Zheng Guifei's servants. Wang immediately reported this new confession to the emperor, but he was not happy to hear this. He tabled the report even though there was a public outcry to punish both the criminal and his suspected co-conspirator, Zheng Guifei. Some ministers encouraged the criminal court department to made further inquiries in the criminal's home province and interrogated two of Zheng Guifei's close servants, Pang Bao and Liu Cheng.

Later, it was discovered that these two servants and Zheng Guifei's brother, Zheng Guotai, were indeed involved in the incident. Now the target of public attacks, Zheng Guifei was embarrassed; she wept before the emperor for mercy, denying the charges. Encouraged by the emperor, she turned to the crown prince for support by weeping, kneeling, and begging. The crown prince was convinced of Zheng Guifei's good faith and pleaded her innocence with the emperor.

After all these underhanded dealings done, the emperor called his ministers and generals together, and let the crown prince himself declare that Zheng Guifei did not have any intention to assassinate the crown prince. Zhang Chai was declared mentally deficient and was to be put to death at once. All the court officials realized that they had to accept this outcome. Then, Zhang Chai, Pang Bao, and Liu Cheng were executed—but Zheng Guifei remained free. This was the "Tianzhan an," which first upset the court and caused friction among various imperial factions.

Afterward came the "Hongwan an" and the "Yigong an" one after the other, continuing the strife. In 1620 A.D., Zhu Changluo ascended the throne. He was debilitated because of his indulgence in debauchery and drinking. Once when he became seriously ill, his condition deteriorated after he took the medicine prescribed by the eunuch Zui Wensheng. Then, the doctor Li Kezhuo contributed his "Hongwan," the "miraculous medicine," which killed the emperor as soon as he took it. Many people came to suspect that the two had been bribed by Zheng Guifei.

Zhu Youxiao succeeded Zhu Changluo as emperor. His close friend, Wei Zhongxian, and nursemaid, Li Xunci, who had reared the emperor from childhood, attempted to control politics by living together with the young emperor in the Qianqing palace for his own protection. But ministers Yang Lian and Zuo Guangdo objected to this idea and forced Li to move to another palace. This incident became known as "Yigong an"; the events aroused suspicion that Zheng Guifei may have directed Li's dismissal to pave the way for her to place her own son on the throne.

The importance of the three incidents in which Zheng Guifei was involved did not lie in the cases themselves but, rather, in their function as a trigger for the political struggles in the late Ming dynasty. The suspicions and rumors about these three cases resulted in endless bickering, plots, and revenge. The main struggles were between a eunuch-led clique headed by Wei Zhongxian and the challengers led by members of the Donglin party led by disenchanted scholars, most of whom were ex-officials. Power struggles threatened imprisonment and cruel slaughter for the losers. Beginning in that period, the Ming dynasty lapsed into uncontrolled turmoil as more and more suspicion fed upon itself and weakened the rulers. Chinese historians have blamed Guifei for inciting this weakness among the Ming leadership because of her own ambitions. Factionalism was always a reality among the women in the back palace, but in this period the competitiveness reached new levels of cruelty. She died in 1630 A.D. and was buried in the Yinquan mountains in Beijing. The Ming dynasty ended fourteen years later, its "brightness" extinguished, some say, by the actions of Zheng Guifei.

Wang Caizhong and Shu Aixiang

Sources

Meng Sen, *Ming Qing shi jian yi*. Beijing: Zhonghua shuju, 1981; Fang Wenlan, *Zhong Go Tong Shi*.

Qin Liangyu (1574–1648 A.D.) was a noted general who fought the Qing invaders at the end of the Ming dynasty. She was born at Mingyuxi, Zhongzhou, Sichuan. Her father, Qin Kui, an intellectual chosen by the local government as an official, excelled at both classical Chinese and military strategy. Following his family's tradition, he educated his children at home. During the turbulent period at the end of Ming dynasty, he encouraged his children to learn the classical Chinese literary works so as to have the ability to serve both in civil and military services. He inspired his children to have ambitious goals, especially in safeguarding the countryside and their hometown.

When quite young, Qin Liangyu was deemed intelligent and clever and was a favorite of her father. Her father was ahead of his time and believed in the equality of the sexes. Therefore, he treated Qin Liangyu the same as his sons. Together with her brothers, Qin Bangping, Qing Banghan, and Qin Minping, she learned the Chinese classics, read history books, and practiced gongfu under her father's guidance. Also she modeled herself after the outstanding patriotic generals in the history books and practiced the martial arts more than her brothers. Qin Liangyu became proficient in the art of war, distinguishing herself in both horseback riding and archery. Her father praised her for her out-standing military talent.

Qin Liangyu was not only brave, intelligent, and skilled at riding and archery, but also talented at composing poetry. In addition, she was elegant and physically attractive. Thus many youths courted her, yet her father was very careful when choosing her husband.

Ma Qiancheng, the military commander of Shizhu district, was descended from a general's family, and he was both brave and intelligent. Approved by her father, he married Qin Liangyu when she was twenty-four. They loved and respected each other deeply. Ma Qianchen sought his wife's opinion in everything, even in how to discipline the army. Shizhu district lay at the border of Sichuan and Guizhou and was not an important military fort. Qin Liangyu reminded her husband of the danger even in peacetime, and she inspired her husband to achieve his ambition to make contributions to his country. In order to have a powerful army, to safeguard the borders and protect the people, she helped her husband to form the "White Stick Troop," which used spikes made of white wood for weapons.

In 1599 A.D., Yang Yinglong, the military commander in Bozhou, revolted against the central government. Ma Qiancheng took orders from the imperial court and led three thousand soldiers to suppress the rebellion, supported by Qin Liangyu, who led five hundred soldiers more. In the battle, they fought side by side, conquered seven villages, and directly occupied the Shangmu Pass. They suppressed the rebellion quickly and became prominent among all the armies coming from Sichuan. Thus the White Stick Troop was well known and celebrated for its victories.

In 1613 A.D., Ma Qiancheng offended the court eunuch Qiu Chengyuan; he was arrested and then died at the Yunyang prison, uncleared of a false charge. The government ordered Qin Liangyu to take her husband's former military office, and she thus became the military commander of Shizhu district.

In September 1621 A.D., She Congming, the military commander of Yongning, led twenty-thousand soldiers in rebellion against the government, which was headquartered in Chongqing.

He declared himself the king of Daliang, and his forces began to threaten Chengdu. Qin Liangyu led her army westward as reinforcements under the order of the imperial court. She Congming was afraid of the White Stick Troop and sent an envoy with gold and cloth as gifts for Qin Liangyu in an attempt to bribe her into not attacking. Suspecting his true purpose, Qin Liangyu killed the envoy in anger and distributed the gold and cloth among her officers and soldiers. Then she herself led six thousand crack troops and sent her brother Qin Minping and her nephews Qin Yiming and Qin Congming to lead four thousand soldiers, ordering them to move westward in two directions. Thus they liberated Chengdu. Furthermore, she led the army southward and regained Chongqing without difficulty. In 1622 A.D., the entire revolt was finally suppressed. This success in battle revealed her leadership and fighting ability, especially to the imperial court, even though it was the first time she had led the army by herself.

When Qin Liangyu took office, the Wuzhen minority nationality living in the northeast was becoming strong and threatening the Ming dynasty's rule. Wuzhen aristocrats continually launched raids into Liaodong and Central China. They looted and harassed the people, wrecking the local economy. To show her loyalty to the Ming dynasty, Qin Liangyu voluntarily plunged into fighting against the invaders.

In 1620 A.D., Qin Liangyu sent her brothers Qin Bangping and Qin Minping to lead three thousand soldiers of the White Stick Troop into the Liaodong battlefield. The next year, when they were on the way to aid the soldiers in Shenyang, they encountered the Qing (Manchu) invaders and fought bitterly. Unfortunately, they were surrounded by the Qing invaders, and Qin Bangping and his more than one thousand soldiers were killed. However, this was the first bloody battle the Ming forces fought with the Qing invaders; they killed more than several thousand enemy soldiers, dealing the Qing soldiers a hard blow.

Qin Liangyu sold her family's property for military supplies, including fifteen hundred winter coats, and sent her envoy with these coats to the capital. The coats were distributed among her generals and soldiers and raised their morale. She was thereafter able to reorganize her army. Then, she led 3,000 White Stick soldiers to the frontier against the Qing invaders and stationed her troops at the Yu Pass (Shanhai Pass), the only pass the Qing soldiers had to traverse to get to Central China. Qin Liangyu commanded the local inhabitants and soldiers to make full preparation for self-defense. Therefore the Yu Pass was fortified to prevent the Qing soldiers from invading.

At the end of 1629 A.D., Qing soldiers rushed into Chongyuan district by way of Xifeng Pass, conquered Zunha, and marched on towards Beijing. The situation was so dangerous that Emperor Congzheng issued orders to his generals to protect him. More than two hundred thousand soldiers were recruited and maneuvered into Beijing. However, most of the generals and soldiers were afraid of losing their lives and did not dare fight.

At that time, Qin Liangyu, who was training soldiers at Sichuan, heard this news and raised money for her troops again by selling her own property. Sharing a common fate with the country, she fearlessly led her soldiers in marching northward day and night to resist the invaders. On arriving at the suburbs of the capital, Qin Liangyu commanded her army to fight bravely against enemies and recovered Yongping, Zunhua, Luanzhou and Qianan. Thus she reduced the danger to Beijing.

Emperor Congzheng was profoundly impressed by the heroine who had saved his life. He bestowed upon her a military suit for a first-class official and gifts of colorful cloth, sheep, and wine. In addition, the emperor wrote four poems on her accomplishments, of which the second reads:

> *Cutting Shu silk into a military uniform,*
> *You requested to fight with a red-tasseled spear soon.*
> *Many as in this world are outstanding men,*
> *Who is ready to fight on the battlefield far far away?*

Her patriotism was greatly praised in the poem. Seldom in the long history of China was an emperor so deeply moved by a woman. Qin Liangyu trained her soldiers well, and the White Stick Troop was well disciplined. None of the soldiers molested, looted, or pillaged the population after their victories. When the soldiers of the White Stick Troop were marching to the capital, the citizens all gathered to look at them and the horses were blocked by the crowds. The people had heard a great deal about Qin Liangyu, and all crowded around to get a glimpse of her.

In the last years of the Ming dynasty, successive peasants uprisings spread across the country, threatening the rule of the imperial family. Qin Liangyu, who wished to serve the imperial court devotedly, gave her all to help suppress the peasant uprisings.

In 1633 A.D., Qin Liangyu was ordered to return to Sichuan to fight the peasants uprisings there. Early the next year, the peasant army of Zhang Xianzhong occupied Kuizhou (now Fengjie county), which was an important strategic town in eastern Sichuan province. Qin Liangyu attacked the peasants army in cooperation with General Zhang Lingfu, in Sichuan, and defeated the peasant army, which then retreated from the town. Early in 1640 A.D., when Luo Rucai's peasant army was marching westward, it was ambushed by Qin Liangyu in the Wu mountains. Later, the armies of Luo and Zhang joined forces and entered Sichuan; they tried to take Kuizhou from the Ming army three times. Qin Liangyu commanded her army to reinforce the imperial official army, but she was beaten in one battle after another, and her army was almost all lost. In the spring of 1644 A.D., once again Qin led her army to reinforce Kuizhou, but, because of a great disparity in strength between her forces and those she was fighting, her army was defeated and she retreated to Shizhu. Despite her great victories over the Qing army, she was continuously defeated by the peasant armies.

In 1644 A.D., the Qing army fought its way through the Shanhai Pass and occupied Beijing and this year marks the traditional date for the fall of the Ming dynasty. The barbarous violence of the Qing troops in the process of marching westward and southward created resistance throughout the country. The remaining peasant troops joined with the Southern Ming regime (which had fled Beijing) in battling the Qing invaders. Hence, for a time there appeared to be confrontation between North (Qing) and South (imperial Ming forces and the peasants). Qin Liangyu once again joined the line of anti-Qing troops. But a turning point had been reached, and the Ming dynasty could stand no more.

In late 1646, Emperor Longwu of the southern Ming regime granted Qin Liangyu a royal title as the "loyal marquis" and the copper seal of "the crown prince's teacher and general defense minister." By then she was past seventy, but still received orders to resist the Qing army. That battle, however, was not joined because Emperor Longwu's regime was soon overthrown. Nevertheless, Qin Liangyu maintained her firm resistance to the Qing regime. The Qing troops had invaded Sichuan, and left no land untouched, for thousands of miles; the earth was ravaged, leaving the people no way of making a living. The region of Shizhu controlled by Qin Liangyu, however, was comparatively stable since she had adopted a policy of cultivating the land and growing food for the hungry. The surrounding countryside flocked to her. She helped more than a hundred thousand refugees settle down properly. Even at the time of her death in 1648 A.D. there were still large stores of food for the troops in Wanshoushan, east of the town.

Qin Liangyu lived at the end of Ming dynasty and the beginning of Qing dynasty, when wars were frequently waged. She played multiple roles in Chinese history. As a court-appointed official, she supported the rule of the Ming government, thus joining in the government's suppression of the peasant army in Sichuan to protect the interests of the landed gentry. She mercilessly suppressed the local separatist powers, promoting the security of the society and the steadiness of the central government. But after the fall of the Ming, Qin Liangyu promoted food production and placated the people in her domain, making them more secure in the face of the new Qing rulers.

As a sign of their respect for her, some people from Sichuan living in Beijing later built the Sichuan guildhall where Qin Liangyu had stationed her troops. In the guildhall hung a portrait of Qin Liangyu in uniform. Even now, names of places near Xuanwu Gate commemorate Qin Liangyu, the outstanding military heroine who tried valiantly to save the Ming dynasty from falling to the Manchus.

Zhang Wei
Lei Wanzhong, trans.

Sources

"Biography of Qin Liangyu," in *History of the Ming Dynasty*, vol. 270. Beijing: Zhonghua shuju, 1974; Guo Moruo, "Matters about Qin Liangyu," *Sichuan ribao*, August 26, 1962; He Riyu, "Anecdotes of General Qin Liangyu of the Ming Dynasty," in *Collections of Cun Chengzhai*; Cheng Shisong, "On Qin Liangyu," *Sichuan University Journal* (February, 1987), pp. 69–75.

Fang Weiyi (1585–1668 A.D.) was an outstanding writer during the late Ming and early Qing dynasties. Her given name was Zhongxian; Weiyi was her pen name. Her father, Fang Dazheng, was a Ming dynasty official who attached great importance to the education of his children. Born in Tongchen, Anhui, Fang Weiyi began to study the composition of poems and paintings when she was still young, and she often discussed the techniques with her elder sister, Fang Mengshi, and younger brother, Fang Kongzhao. The three of them were all very talented. Fang Weiyi had great ambition when she was still a teenager. Nevertheless, the limitations placed on women by the feudal society in which she lived prevented her from having her own career, and she wished she were a man.

At the age of seventeen, she married Yao Songyi, who was very knowledgeable about the classics and Chinese history. He was very creative, and they shared similar interests, often exchanging views on the composition of poems and prose.

Not long after their marriage, however, her husband fell ill and was confined to his sick bed. Although Fang Weiyi took care of him and sent all the best doctors available to see him, he did not improve. He died after lingering for three months. The next year, Fang Weiyi had their daughter, whom she cared for with doubled affection. Unfortunately this daughter died when she less than a year old.

The loss of these two family members in so short a time dealt her a heavy blow, and she was filled with sorrow. She could not reside with her in-laws because her father-in-law had an official position elsewhere. So she returned to her family and lived alone in Qingfeng Pavilion.

Despite her misfortune, Fang Weiyi constrained her sorrow and began to study the classics and history. She also composed poetry and prose and engaged in calligraphy and painting, from which she gained much comfort.

Fang Weiyi's achievements lay in literature, mainly poetry and *ci* (poetry written to popular tunes). The style and form of her poems were very fashionable. Her writing used contemporary styles, with little influence of the ancient styles. Fang Weiyi excelled at writing poetry in all forms, for which she was praised by scholars. Her works were graceful, filled with sincere and profound feelings, and depicted the vicissitudes of her life, for example, "An Eternal Farewell," "Lament," "The Statement of a Living Person," and "Writing a Will."

The value of Fang Weiyi's literary works was also that they reflected the turbulent history of the transitional period between the Ming and Qing dynasties. Faced with the threats to the Ming order, Fang Weiyi did not just lament her sad life but, rather, expressed through poetry her concern for the fate of the country and the hardships of her countrymen. Poems such as "Go Beyond the Great Wall," "Return to Former Residence Without Companion," "Information on the Invasion During the Autumn Journey," and "Meditation of Autumn" satirized the darkness and corruption of the imperial regime of the late Ming dynasty and described the misery into which the people had been plunged by the turmoil—demonstrating deep social consciousness and awareness of the era's politics. *The Review of Ming Poems* called her poetry similar to that of Du Fu, the saint of Tang poetry; his works, like hers, were about society and its concerns; it considered her poetry vastly superior to that of most female scholars of her time.

Fang Weiyi also studied the ancient history of Chinese women and their literature, writing *The History of Palace and Boudoir Poetry* and *The History of Palace and Boudoir Literature*. She divided works by ancient Chinese women writers into two categories: the righteous (written in a sincere and graceful style) and the heretical (in a snobbish and hypocritical style). She had many original ideas about the themes, merits, and shortcomings of the works written by early women scholars in history, explained in *Criticism of Palace and Boudoir Poetry*, *Seven Questions of Ni Principles*, and *Exclamations*. These offered rare critiques of female writers by a woman and comprised an important literary criticism of Chinese ancient history. Her work of criticism and annotation was also a valuable attempt to understand and interpret women's intelligence and talent on their own merits.

Although Fang Weiyi was exceptionally intelligent, knowledgeable, and talented, she did not easily show other people her work, especially her ''poems of departure, worries, and sorrows,'' most of which were burned. Her *Songs of the Chu River* and eight-volume *Collection of Qingfeng Pavilion*, both of which survive, include only a small fraction of her writings. Sadly, few of her works survive.

Fang Weiyi was also accomplished as a calligrapher and painter. She shared the style of Madam Wei of the Eastern Jin dynasty, the first female calligrapher in Chinese history, and her paintings of landscapes with trees and birds were unsurpassed. Her sketches, especially of the Buddhist Guanyin, or Goddess of Mercy, were also very fine. Art historians Feng Jinbo and Wu Jing, in *The Painting of the State*, concluded: ''In three hundred years, there have been no more than three master painters who can be compared with her.'' Being very modest she did not easily give her calligraphy or painting to other people, so her works were rarely seen. But, once in a while, she would do a little painting on bamboo fans, which would be regarded as a treasure by the people who received these fans from her.

Fang Weiyi continued her artistic creation until she was past seventy. Her outstanding artistic achievements were a crystallization of her lifelong hard work to care for her family and her insistence on perfection.

When she lived at Qingfeng Pavilion, she gained the respect of her brother, his wife, and their children. Her sister-in-law, Wu Lingyi, was talented at writing poems, and the two women would very often discuss literature and history, as well as composing verses to each other. Unfortunately, Wu Lingyi died an early death at the age of thirty. Fang Weiyi collected Wu Lingyi's works into *The Posthumous Manuscripts of Wu Lingyi*, which enabled her works to be preserved. Fang Weiyi shouldered the additional responsibility of rearing as well as educating her nieces and nephews. Her niece, Fang Ziyao, distinguished herself in calligraphy and painting and produced works similar to her mother's. Ziyao's brother, Fang Yizhi, under his aunt's direction, could recite quite a few of the classics by the age of fifteen. He later conducted extensive studies of astronomy, rites, music, mathematics, literature, calligraphy, painting, and medicine, becoming a great scholar. Fang Yizhi's fame was on a par with the outstanding scholars and thinkers of the late Ming dynasty and the early Qing dynasty, such as Gu Yanwu, Wang Fuzhi, and Huang Zongxi. His achievements owed a great deal to his aunt's firm, persistent, and down-to-earth temperament as well as her great learning and versatility.

Fang Weiyi died at Qingfeng Pavilion in 1668 A.D., when she was eighty-three, having earned a place in the history of literature and arts of the Ming and Qing dynasties.

Zhu Zhongliang

Sources

Qiah Qianyi, *Biographies of the Poets Attached to Their Poems in History—The Supplementary Section of the History of the Qing Dynasty*, p. 736; Hu Wenkai, *Textual Research into Works by Women Writers of History*. Beijing: Commercial Printing House, 1957, pp. 66–69; *The Biographies of Women Scholars in Chinese History*, pp. 269–272.

Huang Yuanjie (ca. 1600–1670 A.D.), also known as Jieling, was a writer in the transitional period between the Ming and Qing dynasties and a master of *ci* poetry (written to popular tunes). Born in Xiushui (modern-day Jiaxing, Zhejiang province), she had a brother Kaiping, and a sister Yuanzhen, who called herself Jiede. Yuanzhen was also quite famous for her poems, collected in *The Collection of Poems in Cloud Study*. Yuanjie was also talented at calligraphy and painting.

Early on, Yuanjie had been engaged to Yang Shigong, from her village. But, because of their poor economic straits, the Yang family could not afford the betrothal gifts, and Yang Shigong left the village. Yuanjie's father and brother repeatedly asked her to marry someone else, but she would not listen to them. She even declined marriage proposals from some rich and noble families' sons, who would pay a high bride-price if she agreed to become a concubine. It was said that Zhang Pu (1601–1640 A.D.), a gifted scholar from Taichang, went to Yuanjie's home to propose marriage because he admired her as a gifted scholar. She agreed to an appointment with him, but only to look at him from behind a screen. After seeing him she said: "Zhang is a famous scholar, so I just wanted to have a look at him. Now I have seen him and understand that he has but a short time yet to live [given his age]. What a pity!" From this, her family inferred that she did not really intend to consider him as a husband, only to have a look at the famous scholar. (Quite by chance, Zhang Pu died one year later after that appointment.) Yang Shigong then returned to his native village and married Yuanjie.

Their marriage was described in *The Silent Poems* as "quiet and plain," since the two had scanty means and were indifferent to their humble situation. After the downfall of the Ming dynasty, their hometown fell into chaos. She had to trudge over the long distance between Wu (Suzhou) and Yue (Shaoxing) to make a living by selling her articles and paintings. They lived variously in Suzhou, Jinling (Nanjing), Jinsha, and Hangzhou because of the turmoil following the Ming's collapse. When she was in Jinsha, she lived in the Qiangdong garden of the Zhang family and received assistance from the owner of the garden, Wufang, and his wife, Yu. At the same time, Yuanjie made frequent trips back and forth between Jinsha and Yushan to exchange views on the working and technique of poem composition with Liu Rushi, a gifted female scholar with whom she had developed a close friendship, in her Crimson Cloud Pavilion. In the preface to her *Ode to Seclusion*, she expressed her true state of mind:

> I was born to a plain family, and I am classified as an ordinary person. My brother and I are fond of literature and calligraphy. The turbulence and chaos of war made us move to Wumen, Baixia [modern-day Nanjing], Jinsha, and finally I confined myself in Qiangdong garden. Although I live by selling my paintings and calligraphy, I have not left the garden and sold them in person. In the past, I have

secluded myself from the imperial court, from urban life, and lived by fishing on a lake or by burning charcoal deep in mountains to gather food. I will continue my life by secluding myself from society. But, I am to visit my mother, so I compose this long ode entitled "Ode to Seclusion," which I will present to my brother at home. In this ode, although perhaps I do not have as much knowledge as others did in history, I hope to be able to make up a little of the shortcomings of hermits when they secluded themselves.

She built herself a small pavilion to live in at one end of Xiling Guan bridge on the West Lake in Hangzhou, for which she gained the financial assistance of a local person named Wang Ranming. Then she moved again to Meishi (modern-day Changshu) to visit the famous female poet Shang Jinglan and her daughter-in-law.

During her later years, Huang Yuanjie was invited to be a tutor for a daughter of an imperial official in the capital. But, on the way to the capital by boat, her son Deling drowned in Tianjin, and the following year, one of her daughters, Benshan, also died an early death.

Huang Yuanjie and another famous female scholar, Wu Meichun (1601–1671 A.D.), were friends who replied to each other's letters in verse. Wu Meichun appreciated Yuanjie's talent in poetry composition. In a poem in reply to Wu Meichun, Yuanjie wrote:

> At the foot of mountain stands an empty hut to be enlivened by a
>   zither;
> I enjoy the leisure and teach my humble son to walk in bamboos
>   around,
> I am surprised to see the elderly return along;
> Wild vines mend the leaking roof,
> beautiful prose pleases me, too;
> Why don't people appreciate seclusion,
> In the primitive house stores treasured old books.

She also had literary contact with another giant of poetry, Wang Shizhen (1634–1711 A.D.). Once when she was passing through

Suzhou and Nanjing, Wang Shizhen asked for a painting from her in a poem. She painted Wang a landscape and composed a poem in reply.

> *Laziness stops me to view high mountain green,*
> *Gaining no knowledge in years brings me shame;*
> *Light ink only depicts dim images in the distance,*
> *Reality and illusion makes the peak in between.*

After her marriage, Huang Yuanjie had led a poor and unstable life and kept wandering for a long time since she lacked a permanent home. Therefore, it was natural for her to express her vexed feelings at her embarrassing condition. In her poem "Qing Ming," she wrote:

> *Leaning against the house full of anxiety,*
> *Bewildered to see others residing in a red pavilion.*
> *Dropping rain from roof brings sad feelings,*
> *Who can stop flying flowers and tears.*
> *Seedling grows to be a big willow,*
> *But the palace turned out to be in ruins.*
> *Only while cloud is visiting the hut,*
> *My heart is made heavy with thoughts.*

In "Golden Chrysanthemum Versus Lotus Flower," she wrote:

> *Stars and frosts are renowned for five times, residence had changed*
>   *twice, longing for you makes me crazy;*
> *Swallows are flying back and forth, but we only meet in dreams;*
> *The war makes our meeting impossible, time elapses for nothing.*
> *Visiting native home once, coming from a place not far, I felt from*
>   *other shore of ocean.*
> *Your visit moved me.*
> *I admired your beautiful ornaments, and your youthful appearance.*
> *Regretfully, I failed to join hands with you, and to express our true*
>   *feelings in letters.*
> *I appreciate the plum and bamboo at your home, and am looking*
>   *forward to seeing them again.*
> *The spring is not over, and flowers are in blossom. But I miss you in*
>   *vain.*

In *The Silent Poems*, scholar Wu Shen Shi Shi said of her poems: "Most of her poems are the expressions of her vexed feelings of her wandering life and loneliness. They are, nevertheless, still mild and sincere. For her misfortune, she was resentful, but not overly outraged." This was said at the time to have been a very appropriate comment.

Huang Yuanjie's works include *The Collection of Ancient Style Poems of Hua'nan Guan, The Weeds Over the Lake, The Weeds on the Lake, The Weeds of Rushi Pavilion,* and *Poems of Seclusion,* but most of these works have not survived. Her six *fu* (descriptive prose interspersed with verse) are included in the *Collection of Raizhi,* compiled by Wang Shiru, and have survived to the present. These are titled "The Fu of Wuhuai," "The Fu of Meditation," "The Fu of Autumn," "The Fu of Bamboo," "The Fu of Orchid," and "The Fu of Zither."

Many of her contemporaries praised her literary achievements. Wang Shizhen called her poems and *fu* sophisticated and disciplined, comparing her style to those of the Wei and Jin dynasties. Scholar Yu Jing Yang Qiu commented: "Her poems bear the styles of many famous poets of the Tang dynasty, and she has composed many excellent pieces both of ancient style and modern style. She could have been a giant of poetry if the themes of her works had been deeper."

There is little information available about the children of Huang Yuanjie. But *Yutai shu shi* (The History of Yutai Literature) mentions her younger daughter, described as "a lovely girl who sang poetry and copied models of calligraphy." Scholar-writer-poet Zhu Zhongmei once composed a poem praising the daughter's calligraphy. So it can also be inferred that Yuanjie's younger daughter was also worthy of being called a gifted young artist.

After a short time in the capital, Huang Yuanjie returned to the south. On the way back, she was invited to live and recuperate in Pi garden of Madam Tong in Ning'ren. She died six months later, but continued to be revered as a scholar-poet.

Zhang Jianming
Zhu Zhongliang, trans.

Sources

Ruan Yuan, *Lianzhe youxuan lu* (Chronicles of Travels in Zhejiang), 40th vol.; Tan Zhengbi, *Stories of Chinese Women Poets*; Wang Xiuqing and Hu Wenkai, *A Concise Collection of Literary Works by Famous Women in History*; Hu Wenkai, *Textual Research into Works by Women Writers in History*, 16th vol.; Liang Yizheng, *Qingdai funu wenxueshi* (History of Women's Literature in the Qing Dynasty). Taibei: Zhonghua shuju, 1958; Cai Guanluo, *Qingdai gibai mingren zhuan* (Biographies of 700 Notable Personages of the Qing Dynasty). Beijing: Zhonghua shuju, 1988; Jiang Mingfang and Wang Ruifang, *Brief Biographies of Gifted Women Scholars in China.*

Wang Ruishu (ca. 1600–ca. 1660 A.D.), a famous writer and poet in the beginning of Qing dynasty, lived during the transitional period of the late Ming and early Qing dynasties. Born in Shanying (modern-day Shaoxing, Zhejiang province), she called herself Yuxia, with the alternate names Yangraizhi or Qing Wuzhi. Ruishu was the second daughter of Wang Jizhong, an official in charge of religious ceremonies. Her sister, Jingshu, was also a writer, producing *The Collection of Purity* and *The Collection of Green Vine Study.*

Wang Ruishu not only composed poetry and *fu* (descriptive prose interspersed with verse) but often wrote prose in ancient styles as well. She read extensively from classics, history, anecdotes, and tales of witchcraft. She also enjoyed the books of Laozi and Zhuangzi in the palace library. Her father once patted her on the head and said: ''Although I have eight sons, no one is better than you!'' He was very proud of his daughter.

In the late Ming dynasty, Ruishu married Ding Ruishen (also known as Shenzhao), a candidate in the imperial examination for an official position in Qiantang (modern-day Hangzhou), who understood Ruishu's complete devotion to her artistic creations. They were not just husband and wife but good friends, supporting one another's endeavors. After they married, they had eight happy years in Beijing.

But, in 1644 A.D., when the Qing troops entered the inside palace at Shanhaiguan, they fled to Shanying in the south. For a time, they lived a reclusive and tranquil life in the ''Green Vine Study,'' the former residence of Xu Wei, a famous Ming dynasty calligrapher and painter. Then they moved to Wushan in Hangzhou for several years. During these years, she composed poems and prose, often describing the unhealthy social atmosphere and mismanagement of the last Ming leaders, including Wei Zhongxian, a treacherous court official of the late Ming dynasty. These poems expressed her deep concern over state affairs. In this period she composed more artistic works than before.

Gifted with extraordinary talent and noble ideals, Ruishu could compose poems and prose of various styles. Under the rule of Qing Emperor Shunzhi (reigned 1644–1661 A.D.) the imperial court heard of her fame and planned to invite her to tutor the concubines of various ranks and princesses in the palace, as the Western Han dynasty had done earlier in inviting Ban Zhao (see Ban Zhao), a talented and knowledgeable historian to lecture on the classics of Confucianism. Nevertheless, Ruishu did not want to become an imperial tutor and tactfully declined the appointment.

She devoted all her energy and talent to creating her artistic works. In her thirty-volume *Yinghong Collection*, she included three hundred examples of her poetry, *ci,* and prose *fu,* chronicles, biographies, epigraphs, memorials to the throne, obituaries, and epitaphs. Her other works included *Collection of Prose, The Collection of Yuyang Hall,* and *Siyu.* She also collected the poems and prose by female writers in the late Ming dynasty into the *The Collection of Prose by Women* and the thirty-volume *Collection of Poems by Famous Women.* In addition, she also compiled *The Textual Research of Empresses and Imperial Concubines in History.*

Few of her works have survived: *The Yinghong Collection,* in a rare handwritten copy, and three of her *fu,* "Fu of Cicada," "Fu of Lotus," and "Fu of Chrysanthemum"—the latter thanks to the publication of *Collection of Ranzhi,* by Wang Shiru, a Qing dynasty scholar. Of the three *fu* that have survived, "Fu of Cicada" was the most highly praised.

Wang Ruishu's contributions to researching and preserving women's contributions in history were widely admired and have often been commented upon in later histories, apart from her primary fame and contributions to poetry and prose.

Barbara Bennett Peterson

Sources

Hu Wenkai, *Textual Research into Works by Women Writers in History*, seventh vol. Beijing: Commercial Publishers, 1957; Yuan Mei, *Notes on Poetry of Siyuan*, the second vol. Xu Kuichen, *Collection of Poems of Women Writers in History*, the sixth vol. Beijing: Commercial Publishers, 1969; Liang Shaoren, *Jottings of Autumn Rain Hut*, third vol.; Liang Yizhen, *Qingdai funu wenxueshi* (History of Women's Literature in the Qing Dynasty), chpt. one of part two. Taibei: Zhonghua shuju, 1958.

Li Yin (ca. 1611–ca. 1685 A.D.), also called Jinsheng, was an outstanding poet and painter at the end of the Ming dynasty. Born in Qiantang (now Hangzhou, Zhejiang Province), an intellectual center highly developed in culture and the arts, Li Yin received a good education and was seen as extremely intelligent from her childhood. She regarded reading, especially poetry, as the most important activity in her life, disdaining too much makeup as disgraceful.

Her family suffered a decline in its economic fortunes. However, she never stopped learning: with sand on the ground as her paper and fireflies as her light in the summer, she persisted in writing and reading. Because of her strong willpower, she grew into a successful poet, painter, and intellectual.

When she was twenty, one of her poems was read by a prominent scholar, Ge Zhengqi. One sentence of this poem, "Ode to the Plum," was often quoted: "One spray spared for later spring blossoming."

Ge Zhengqi, surprised at her talent, came to admire her and soon married her despite her family's declining fortunes. After passing the imperial examination in 1628 A.D., he worked as an official in southern China. Talented at painting and composing poetry, Ge Zhengqi produced a poetry collection called *Wuyuan shiji* (Poems from the Wuyuan Garden). After their marriage, Li Yin and Ge Zhengqi lived a harmonious and happy life. Li Yin followed her husband on his frequent business trips for fifteen years, until his death. In those fifteen years, they traveled together throughout the southern and central provinces in China. Her traveling experiences in the Yellow river valley, in the Yangzi river valley, with all their local cultural and traditional differences, enlightened and inspired her to paint and write more. While traveling, while by boat or by horseback, Li Yin still never ceased painting and writing. Her surviving 260 poems were mostly done during her trips.

Li Yin specialized in painting flowers, birds, and landscapes. Following the Song dynasty artists Mi Fu and his son, Mi Youren, whose paintings used water colors to depict misty mountains, Li Yin painted misty woods and rocks, then unique among female painters. During her lifetime her drawings of flowers and birds attracted even more attention than her poetry. According to the historic records in her husband's hometown of Haining, Li Yin greatly admired the Ming dynasty painter Chen Zhen, considered the master of flower and bird paintings, and she decided to model her style after his.

Wang Shizhen, a famous painter in the early Qing dynasty, praised her paintings, calling her work excellent, especially her drawings of pine trees and eagles, bamboo and feathers. It was said in *Guo chao shihuaji bilu* (Records of Great Painters and Calligraphers in Chinese History): "Her skill is superb, very energetic. . . . She enjoyed the highest prestige among women at that time."

Ge Zhengqi praised her, saying: "In landscape painting, she is not as good as I am; but in flower and bird paintings, I am really not as good as she is." People loved her paintings, and a large number of collectors wanted to buy her works. Huang Zongxi, a well-known intellectual in the early Qing dynasty, noted that some inferior artists even forged her works, and in the Tongyi area alone there were more than forty forgers.

Although she was renowned as a painter, Li Yin was also a poet. She preferred to compare herself with the outstanding Tang poet Wang Wei, who preferred "pictures inside poems; poems inside pictures." Her poetry was clear and graceful, like morning dew on a young tree, a thin cloud, or a gentle drizzle. Even some senior poets had to admit her perfection in poems. The 260 poems that survive were collected in *Zhuxiao xuan yincao* (Poems from Zhuxiaoxuan Pavilion), and *Xu Zhuxiao xuan yincao* (More Poems from Zhuxiaoxuan Pavilion).

Her poetry expressed her indignation about the corruption of the later Ming dynasty and the death of numerous patriots. She wrote with sorrow:

> *Honest people are dying,*
> *Turbulence fills the country;*
> *Who is aware of disasters,*
> *Crazy is the whole court;*
> *Rulers enjoy only deer-hunting,*
> *Seeing tragedy will be too late;*
> *What's the use of my tearing,*
> *Only a barren memory or an ancient hero.*

The hero she refers to is Sheng Baojie, a nobleman of Chu. When his region was under attack Sheng went to the rulers of Qin for aid. Like Sheng, Li Yin wanted to do something to help her country and hoped the Ming emperor would ask for assistance against the invading Manchu forces, which later toppled the Ming in 1644 A.D. She felt more remorse when she saw the blooming *yulan* magnolia in the spring, as she wrote:

> *Eternal regret of our subjugation,*
> *Tasting it now from my wine*

She also described the misery brought by the Qing army's Southern Expedition:

> *The intruding cavalry at midnight,*
> *Mournful shouting soaring all around;*
> *Fire burning on the mountains,*
> *Empty bird nests for hundreds of miles.*

She even regretted that she was a woman:

> *A patriot without martial art,*
> *Knitting my brows facing invaders.*

Li Yin was only thirty-five when her husband died in 1645 A.D. She lived alone for forty more years in near-poverty, continuing to write poetry. She stayed at Zhuxiao Pavilion and cultivated plants. Lacking financial support, she made her living by weaving and painting. In spite of her situation, she continued to compose poetry to express her sorrow and loneliness. At the end of her life Li Yin reached her poetic heights by employing more profound themes, making solemn and passionate creations reflecting her patriotism for the fallen Ming grandeur. She wrote in "Qiumu shuhuai" (Autumn Emotion):

> *Shamed by cheap tricks,*
> *and adoring me as an old lady;*
> *Fearful of the unknown life,*
> *Sighing for my remaining days.*

Li Yin, a brilliant poet, died alone in about 1685 A.D., but was well remembered for her poetry and paintings depicting the beauties of nature while on her early travels and later for her cogent and analytical verses reflecting the turmoil of transition between the Ming and Qing dynasties.

Wang Xuehua

Sources

Ge Zhengqi, Preface to *Zhuxiaoxuan yincao* (Poems from Zhuxiaoxuan Pavilion); Ruan Yuan, *Lianzhe youxuan lu* (Chronicles of Travels in Zhejiang); Wang Shizhen, *Chibei ou tan*, vols. 12 and 18; Xu Naochen, *Guochao gixou xiangheji*, vol. 1; Li Huan, *Guochao Qixianleizheng Chugao*, vol. 5.

Empress Xiao Zhuang Wen (1613–1668 A.D.), born Bembutai, was the imperial consort of Huang Taiji, who was an outstanding statesman of the early Qing (1644–1911 A.D.) dynasty. The daughter of Prince Jaisan, she was born into a Mongolian noble family in the Korcin tribe of the Borjigit clan. Her family's noble background made it possible for her to be highly esteemed by the Chinese when she was a child. Considered very clever and diligent, she was wise and became well versed in political strategy. Her wisdom and ability matched her beauty.

On March 10, 1628 A.D., she was accompanied by her brother Uksan to Postzing, where she was married to Huang Taiji (the eighth son of Nurhaci d. 1626 A.D.). At that time, she was only fifteen years old, while he was in his twenties. She had three daughters through this union: Princess Cui Lun Yong Mu

Cheng, Princess Cui Lun Shu Hui Cheng, and Princess Cui Lun Shu Zhe Cheng. In 1628 A.D. Huang Taiji ascended the throne of Hurhachi's Jin Dynasty and Xiao Zhuang Wen was granted the title of imperial consort. He became emperor of his newly proclaimed dynasty the Qing in 1636 A.D. On March 15, 1638, A.D., Xiao Zhuang Wen gave birth to Fulin, the ninth son of the emperor. In 1643 A.D., the emperor suddenly died, appointing no successor, and, after a period of instability, the young Fulin ascended the throne, reigning as the Emperor Shunzhi (1648–1661 A.D.). Empress Xiao Zhuang Wen thereafter became the empress dowager.

Empress Xiao Zhuang Wen witnessed the great political changes during the early Qing dynasty. She played an active part in the establishment of the Qing dynasty and helped unify the country following the wars between the Ming and the Qing.

Empress Xiao Zhuang Wen greatly aided the early Qing dynasty's rulers in their efforts to win power and then assisted them in holding on to their newly won power. Empress Dowager Xiao Zhuang Wen worked closely with the emperor to establish internal domestic policies, guiding and advising him. It was said that the last important minister of the Ming dynasty, Hong Chenchou, was persuaded to surrender by Xiao Zhuang Wen. Her steady hand on the tiller of political strategy during the early Qing established an excellent reputation for her and her heirs in Qing influential circles. Huang Taiji had employed many Chinese in his six ministries, re-established a competitive exam system for civil service, reformed the Jurchen language, and renamed his people from Jurchens to "Manchus." He had conquered Korea in 1638 A.D.

When the emperor Huang Taiji died after a sudden illness, Xiao Zhuang Wen was heartbroken and initially wanted to be buried with him. But she was dissuaded from doing so by all the ministers, who believed her children needed her.

Because Huang Taiji had not designated an heir, a power struggle ensued among the ministers. At that time, the strongest claimants were the younger brother of the emperor, Dorgon, and the emperor's eldest son. Empress Xiao Zhuang Wen used her political acumen in balancing the divided ministers and the claimant each faction supported. But soon Dorgon, seeing that his claim was weaker, put forward the idea of making the young Fulin the emperor and won the assent of the other factions. Dorgon was appointed regent for Fulin who ruled as Emperor Shunzhi. Dorgon and Jingalang helped the boy-emperor govern, a strategy planned by Empress Xiao Zhuang Wen, who thereby made the government of the Qing dynasty stable and unified.

But a short while after Fulin became emperor, Dorgon's ambitions resurfaced and grew, with the trappings and resources of his power as a trusted adviser at court. In 1644 A.D., Dorgon commanded Qing troops in an invasion of Beijing. In September of the same year with Beijing now firmly in the hands of the Qing military forces, Empress Xiao Zhuang Wen went to Beijing, followed by the boy emperor Shunzhi. She saw, however, that Dorgon had now formed a military clique and pursued selfish interests, even striking the people who disagreed with him. Dorgon had taken all power into his own hands, making the whole city bow to his will, but she succeeded in preventing Dorgon from stealing the throne from Shunzhi. In 1650 A.D. Dorgon died, without accomplishing his goal of becoming emperor. Empress Xiao Zhuang Wen then carefully placated the aristocracy and endeared the generals to her to retain their loyalty.

She also brought daughters of the nobility into the imperial palace so that they might become well educated and serve her. She even carefully arranged marriages to build family alliances with her own. For example, Empress Xiao Zhuang Wen arranged for the fourteenth daughter of Huang Taiji to marry Wu Yinxiong, in order to placate a barbarian nationality on the northern frontier.

The long struggle during the early Qing dynasty had devastated the production of food crops, so she argued that the people in the country should be given lower taxes. In addition, the empress used the state silver to help people in famine-stricken areas: In 1656 A.D., she knew that the people in Jifu district had a poor harvest, and she granted them 30,000 liang of silver. Such deeds gradually allowed the society to regain its strength and stability.

In 1661 A.D., Fulin the Emperor Shunzhi died. The grandson of Empress Xiao Zhuang Wen, Xuanye, then only eight years old, ascended the throne, reigning as Emperor Kangxi. She supported Emperor Kangxi in matters of state and in relations with the ministers, sharing her experience, knowledge, prestige, and accomplishments. Empress Xiao Zhuang Wen enjoyed high prestige, speaking openly as a respected administrator and dowager empress.

When Emperor Kangxi was ten years old, his mother, the imperial consort Chi He, died. From then on, Emperor Kangxi was brought up by his grandmother. Empress Xiao Zhuang Wen taught him important lessons and formed his ability to deal with state affairs, helping Emperor Kangxi become the most famous emperor in Chinese history.

Empress Xiao Zhuang Wen played an important role in eliminating ministers who were conservative and backward, disrespectful and contemptuous, and surrounded herself and the court with ministers willing to do her bidding. In 1673 A.D., after a rebellion known as The War of the Three Feudatories (1673–81) broke out, Empress Xiao Zhuang Wen exhorted the emperor to fight against the rebellious armies calmly and carefully. She sent messages and called for help, observed enemy troops, and advised the emperor to send General Dao Xueshi to command the troops battling the rebellious armies. As a result, the rebels were defeated badly and the rebellion was gradually suppressed.

In September 1687 A.D., Empress Xiao Zhuang Wen fell ill and took to her bed. Emperor Kangxi took care of her and did not leave her side. On January 27, 1688, A.D., Empress Xiao Zhuang Wen died. Before her death, she had asked Emperor Kangxi to allow her to be buried near the mausoleum where Huang Taiji was laid to rest. Acceding to her wishes, the emperor had his grandmother buried at the Eastern mausoleum of the Qing dynasty in Heibei province.

Li Benyi

Sources

"Queen Xiao Zhuang Wen," in *The Dictionary of Famous Women of Hua Hsia (China)* translated from Chinese by Lucia P. Ellis, Hua Hsia Publishing

House, Beijing, 1988. For an early history of the Qing Dynasty see Edwin R. Reischaer and John K. Fairbank, *East Asia, The Modern Transformation*, Boston: Houghton-Mifflin Company, 1965.

Yi Xiaoluan (1616–1632 A.D.) was a poet during the late Ming dynasty who died on the eve of her marriage at the age of sixteen. Yi Xiaoluan came from a scholarly family in Wujiang (near Suzhou, Jiangsu province). Her father, Yi Shaoyuan (1589–1648 A.D.), was a *jinshi,* or scholar who had passed the imperial examination; he became an imperial official, but retired early. Yi Xiaoluan's mother, Shen Yishou (1590–1635 A.D.), was also a writer. This couple had five sons and three daughters, all of whom were well educated; all three daughters composed poetry.

Xiaoluan, the youngest of the three, was brought up by a cousin on her mother's side who had lost all of her own children when they were in their infancy. Zhang Qianqian was also a learned woman, and she devoted herself to the education of Yi Xiaoluan, who could, at four years old, recite Chu Yuan's hymns and eulogies and, at ten, could compose poetry. Early in her teens, Xiaoluan returned to live with her parents.

Yi Xiaoluan's mother was proud of her youngest daughter, often comparing her to the poet Xie Daoyun of the Eastern Jin dynasty (see Xie Daoyun). Xiaoluan, who was skilled at calligraphy, and her two elder sisters all worked diligently on their scholarship, writing poems and essays and learning to paint. The sisters also played chess and the guitar together.

In 1632 A.D., Yi Xiaoluan was about to be married to Zhang Liping, a rising young scholar of promise but she fell ill and died before the wedding. Her eldest sister, Yi Wanwan, mourned her death so much that she herself died of grief two months later. Two years later, they lost the second of their five sons. Grief stricken, Shen Yishou died in 1635 A.D., having written numerous lovely poems and eulogies in memory of her deceased daughters. The remaining daughter, Yi Xiaowan, wrote "Dream of Mandarin Ducks" about the three girls in her family.

After the Ming dynasty fell in 1644 A.D., Yi Shaoyuan left home to become a monk. He died broken-hearted in 1648. Before his death, he compiled *Complete Works of the Household Noon Dream Hall*, which contains all the writings of his wife and three daughters and has survived down to the present.

The writings of this uniquely talented family have been appreciated by many writers, who listed their names among the noted writers they most admire. Even Japanese scholars often quoted from them. The Japanese sinologist Yagisawa Gen, in his 1959 A.D. book *A Study of Ming Dynasty Dramatists*, devoted an entire chapter to the Yi family. The story of Yi Xiaoluan was often repeated as a romantically tragic story of a life cut short just as it was about to flower.

Zhang Wei
Zhu Kaichang, trans.

Sources

Yi Shaoyuan, *Complete Works of the Household of Noon Dream Hall*; Qian Qianyi, *Biographies of the Poets Attached to Their Selected Poems in History—The Supplementary Section of the History of the Qing Dynasty*; Jiang Mingfang and Wang Ruifang, *Brief Biographies of Gifted Women Scholars in China*.

Chen Yuanyuan (1623–1681 A.D.) was a noted prostitute-singer (courtesan) who later became the lover of Wu Sangui, a Ningyuan general in the Ming dynasty and governor of Pingxi at the beginning of the Qing dynasty. Wanfen was her pen name; her formal name was Yuan, and in her childhood she was known as Yuanyuan.

She was born into a peasant family in Suzhou. Her father's family name was Xing. Since her family was too poor to support her, she was sold to a person whose name was Chen Huolang. Her foster family was led by a peddler who loved singing. He sold all his wares in order to attract good singers. There were always a dozen entertainers at his home singing day and night. Chen was greatly influenced by them and became an excellent singer and dancer. But her foster family too was becoming poorer and poorer. Soon, she was forced to roam the streets in Suzhou and became a prostitute to support herself.

Pretty and bright, Chen became well known for her beauty and singing talent when she was only eighteen. She acted in the plays "The Story of the West Side Room" and "The Palace of Long Life." Whenever she came on the stage, she carried the audience away. She became very famous in Suzhou as one of the "Eight Beauties of the Qing."

Many famous prostitutes at the end of the Ming dynasty changed their status in later life by marrying. For example, Liu Ru married Qian Qianyi, the leader of the Donglin party. Chen was not so lucky. She was first bought by the son of a government official in Jiangyin as his mistress. But she was refused by his family and had to return to life as a prostitute. In 1642 A.D., Mao Xiang, a gifted scholar in South China, became acquainted with Chen when he came to watch her perform in a play. The two fell in love at first sight and planned to marry. But just when Mao Xiang went to meet Chen so that they could arrange their marriage, Tian Hongyu, a relative of the Emperor Chongzheng, abducted her and brought her to Beijing.

Tian Hongyu was the father of Emperor Chongzheng's lover. Because his daughter was favored by the emperor, Tian took liberties at court and became very cruel and domineering. He abused people and abducted women wherever he went. Tian Hongyu kept them all at home as singers.

In May 1643 A.D., the peasant rebel army led by Li Zicheng reached Beijing. Emperor Chongzheng ordered all the generals to meet him. Among the generals was Wu Sangui of Ningyuan. Originally Wu was only important in the political group in East Liaoning. Since many generals of the Ming dynasty surrendered themselves one after another to the Qing forces, the Ming court began to pay great attention to Wu Sangui and regarded him as a savior of its rule and its military backbone. Now that Wu Sangui was in Beijing, Tian Hongyu gave a dinner party in his honor and asked Chen to be his companion at the party in order to win the general over. Wu Sangui fell in love with Chen at first sight, and Tian Hongyu thereupon offered her to Wu as a present.

Soon Wu Sangui left for Shanhaiguan while Chen remained in Beijing. On March 19, 1644 A.D., peasant insurgent troops led by Li Zicheng attacked Beijing. Emperor Chongzheng committed suicide by hanging himself in the imperial gardens, ending the Ming dynasty.

This dealt a heavy blow to Wu Sangui. He had always adopted a wait-and-see attitude toward all the contending armies. Li Zicheng had hoped to win over Wu Sangui in order to conquer East Liaoning. Li promised him fame and riches and tried to persuade Wu Sangui to surrender. At first intending to surrender his troops to Li Zicheng, Wu hesitated to do so because he was concerned about his future career. Moreover, Wu Sangui's father, Wu Xiang, had been captured and tortured by Liu Zongming, a leader of the peasant rebel army, in order to get information about where Chen was living, and Wu Sangui's home and possessions were taken away. Wu Xiang told Liu that Chen had gone to Ningyuan with his son, but Liu Zongming did not believe this and therefore subjected him to more torture. Both Li Zhicheng and the peasant rebels desired to find Chen to possibly capture her and put pressure on General Wu to join them.

The pursuit of Chen by the peasant army persuaded the wealthy and cultivated Chinese general Wu Sangui that his personal interests were at stake. Li Zicheng eventually executed Wu's father, and in consideration of his personal interests and his desire to avenge his father, Wu Sangui openly opposed the peasant army and firmly went over to the Qing side, helping to ensure its success.

After seizing Beijing, Li Zicheng was so carried away by his temporary military success that he reduced his vigilance and military guard. Some leaders of his army became corrupt and indulged in luxuries. As a result, they let slip a golden opportunity and lost the political power they had just won. Because of Wu Sangui's surrender to the Qing, the peasant insurgent troops had to face an enemy attack, fighting Wu Sangui's army at Shanhaiguan. Li Zicheng's troops lost this battle and were forced to retreat first to Beijing and then to Shanxi. Afterward, the peasant forces dispersed, fleeing for the safety of the countryside.

The Qing army reached Guan in May 1644 A.D. That October, the central government of the Qing dynasty was established, to be led by Fulin, Emperor Shunzhi. Wu Sangui once again reclaimed Chen. The Qing government relied on him to suppress the remnant forces of the peasant troops and to destroy the political power of the Ming. This gave Wu Sangui a chance to enlarge and conserve his strength. After the fall of the Ming power, Wu Sangui was appointed governor of Pingxi by the new Qing emperor. He exercised control over Yunnan as well as over Guizhou. Thus he set up a separate regime by force of arms. Chen went to Yunnan with Wu Sangui and became one of his lovers.

While Wu Sangui was governor of Pingxi, Geng Jingzhong was governor of Fujian and Jingnan and Shang Kexi's son, Shang Zhixin, was governor of Dingnan in Guangdong. They all set up a separate regimes and were very powerful. This had a negative effect on the central government.

In January 1674 A.D., the Qing government decided to abolish the three independent kingdoms. Wu Sangui took the lead in revolt in Yunnan, and Gen Jingzhong and Shang Zhixin responded quickly. This conflict became known as the War of the Three Feudatories, 1673–1681 A.D. In 1678 A.D., while the Emperor Kangxi sat on the Qing throne, Wu Sangui made himself emperor in Hengzhou (now Hengyang, Hunan province). But he was killed in August of that year. His grandson, Wu Shifan, ascended the throne (claimed in opposition to the Qing ruler). In 1681 A.D., the Qing army entered Yunnan and captured Kunming at the end of the year. Wu Shifan committed suicide. The rebellion of the three governors continued for eight years and then came to an end. Having captured Kunming, the Qing army killed thirty people of Wu Sangui's family.

After Chen went to live with Wu Sangui in Yunnan, his formal wife, whose surname was Zhang, developed a jealous hatred of Chen, and Wu gradually lost interest in and finally abandoned Chen, taking new lovers. Stories, however unsubstantiated, circulated. One account said she then left Wu Sangui and followed Yu Lin, a monk, to a monastery in the suburb of Kunming. She cut her hair, changed her name to Ji Jing, and became a nun. Her formal name became Yu An. From then on, she lived a lonely and unknown life far from splendor and luxury.

Later, when Wu Sangui rose in revolt against the Qing government, and after the Qing army had captured Kunming and killed all of Wu's kin, Chen survived the massacre because no one knew where she was then living. She died a nun; according to one source, by hanging herself.

Although the history books do not indicate where she is buried, contemporary scholars have been researching the topic. It is said that, at the foot of Mount Shang in the northern suburb of Kunming, by the pond of Lian Huachi, as well as at Wacangzhang in the south part of the city, there are traces not just of places built by Wu Sangui for Chen Yuanyuan such as her Villa Anfuyuan, her dressing room, but of the dwelling called the "Temple of the Three Sages," where she lived after she left Wu Sangui and supposedly became a nun. History awaits further clarification about her burial.

The fact that Chen Yuanyuan was driven onto the streets by the destitution of her family and that she changed her status from a singer to an important general's lover are themselves of great significance and interest because her high profile life as General Wu's concubine placed her in the forefront of history and politics of the collapse of the Ming. Furthermore, she was directly involved (being sought as a hostage) in the great wave of peasant uprising at the end of the Ming dynasty. The poet Wu Meichun recounted her life in a famous poem, "The Song of Yuanyuan."

Chen collected her writings in *Poems Written After Dances*, which has not survived. Only one of her poems, "Some Meditation," has survived, as part of the collection *Poems of All Kinds*, published in 1690 A.D.

In her poem "Some Meditation," Chen wrote that she had had "more sorrows than joys." Her tragic life of poverty and prostitution and her, in the end, unhappy liaison with Wu Sangui took on importance because of her involvement in the historical events of her time. She is remembered for being one of the famous beauties who fatefully influenced the course of China's history.

Wang Xehua
Zhang Rimin, trans.

Sources

Kang Zhouyi, *Stories of Chen Yuanyuan*; Guang Xuxiu, *Record of Wujin and Yang County*, vol. 30; Mao Xiang, *Yingmei'an yiyu* (Recollections of Yingmei Temple); Zou Shu, *Poems of Ten Beauties*; Qian Shixin, vol. 8, *Biographies in the History of the Qing Dynasty*; vol. 80, "Biography of Wu Sangui"; Zhang Genpei, *Stele of the Lotus Pond*; Guo Moruo, *For the 300th Anniversary of the Year Tiashen*; See *Historical Personages*. Beijing: Xin Wenyi Press, 1959 p. 263.

Dong Bai (also known as Dong Xiaowan) (1624–1651 A.D.) was a courtesan and poet who lived during the transitional period at the end of Ming dynasty and beginning of the Qing dynasty. Born in Jinling (modern-day Nanjing, Jiangsu province), she was among some outstanding courtesans who were talented at dancing or poetry. Some courtesans, such as Chen Yuanyuan were well known for their beauty and talents. But Dong Bai, in addition, was famous for her moral character.

A pretty and clever girl, Dong Bai started reading and writing at an early age, instructed by her mother. After a few years of education, she became quite accomplished in the fields of poetry, painting, calligraphy, singing, cooking, and needlework. At thirteen, she was already a well-known singer-prostitute, admired in spite of her profession. By nature, Dong Bai was a quiet girl, and she disliked busy and noisy cities like Nanjing, where she and her mother lived. So she moved to Suzhou with her mother and stayed there for six years. She chose a secluded house near a river and closed her door to visitors. During those six years, she once traveled to Huang mountain with Qian Qianyi (a leader of the Donglin party, now composed of disgruntled ex-officials of the Ming who opposed the new Qing rulers) to take in the magnificent natural scenery.

In 1639 A.D. when she was sixteen, she met Mao Xiang, who had come to Suzhou to take a local examination. Mao Xiang (1611–1693 A.D.) by this time was already a well-known poet. Recommended by his friends—Fang Yizhi, Hou Fangyu, and Wu Yingqi—he went to visit the beautiful and talented Dong Bai.

After leaving Suzhou, Mao Xiang had become engaged to the distinguished prostitute Chen Yuanyuan (see Chen Yuanyuan). But Chen was kidnapped by Tian Hongyu, thus preventing their marriage. Mao Xiang returned to Suzhou just after these events occurred. Now, no longer having a promise of union with Chen Yuanyuan, he was free again to pursue Dong Bai.

In 1642 A.D., Dong Bai's mother died. At her sickbed, Dong Bai wrote a poem, "Luchuan oucheng" (Emotion by the Green Window), whose last sentence read:

> The oriole is so understanding,
> Singing at the willow outside.

She also composed "Shumen" (Depressed by Books) during the mourning period following her mother's death. Thus, just when Dong Bai was quite distressed and lonely, she was unexpectedly reunited with Mao Xiang. They both were very happy about their reunion and greatly enjoyed each other's company. Recovering from her sadness, she followed Mao Xiang; they took a long trip to many different places, and Dong Bai wrote of their travels:

> Climbing summits of golden mountains,
> watching boats returning from ocean.

They were joined in 1643 A.D. when she became Mao Xiang's concubine. When they started life together, Dong Bai was nineteen, and Mao Xiang thirty-two. He had been a well-known poet since his teens, but his political preferences made him a danger to those who sought to dominate the Ming court. He had joined the Donglin party and set up organizations to confront the eunuch's circle of political leaders who really controlled the Ming court. When the Ming dynasty was overthrown in 1644 A.D., Mao Xiang and a number of Ming officials faced a serious test: Should they serve the new Qing dynasty?

The Qing ruler offered Mao Xiang an appointment, but he turned it down, a decision with which Dong Bai agreed. Many former Ming intellectuals had agonized over whether to remain loyal to Ming values or accept the foreign (Manchu)

Qing rulers. Some of their friends, such as Gong Dingzi, and Qian Qianyi, had surrendered to the Qing court and received high positions. When asked about his surrender to the Qing, Gong Dingzi answered shamelessly: "I wanted to die for the Ming court, but my wife, did not." Some had compromised.

By comparison, Mao Xiang and Dong Bai were praised highly for their integrity and loyalty to the former Ming rulers. In 1645 A.D., the Qing army conquered Nanjing, and Mao Xiang and Dong Bai left to start a miserable vagrant life on the run with their family. Mao Xiang later wrote in "Yingmei an yiyu" (Memories from the Yingmei Temple):

> *We traveled on foot every day,*
> *sometimes a short distance, sometimes longer,*
> *either windy or rainy, cold or hunger.*
> *We suffered from all kinds of troubles . . .*
> *My wife looks so pale and worried*
> *and her beauty is gone.*

Dong Bai understood her husband well and fully supported him through a hard five months, even when Mao Xiang was seriously ill. It was not easy for her, since she was a prominent person, but they stuck to their principles.

They fled to Yianguan (now Haining, Zhejiang province), where Dong Bai helped her husband copy the books he borrowed. While copying, she collected all the contents regarding female clothing, dancing, singing, cooking, and so on, and later she edited the three-volume *Lianyan* (Women's Makeup). Her friends and her husband all read her book and spoke highly of it.

Dong Bai also enjoyed ancient Chinese poetry, particularly the verses written by the great poets Qu Yuan, Du Fu, Wang Jian, and Madam Huarui. She practiced writing the script of Zhong Yao (a famous calligrapher in the Three Kingdoms period) and developed her own beautiful handwriting. Dong Bai also developed into an excellent poet.

Assisting her husband in editing a chronicle of the Tang poems, Dong Bai checked history books to ensure historical accuracy. Mao Xiang later recalled: "Day and night, Dong Bai was busy with copying or checking, she worked so attentively that sometimes she had no time to talk to me even when we were facing each other. She had a very good understanding of poems and her explanations on poems were always excellent. . . . She enjoyed reading so much that her pillow-side was full of books. . . . she slept on dozens of poem books.'' In 1649 A.D., she completed a two-volume book on the best Tang poems titled *Wuqiyan jueju* for which she became well known and was highly praised.

Dong Bai died in 1651 A.D. at the age of twenty-eight. She had lived with Mao Xiang for nine years. But her life was full of turbulence caused by the transition of the Ming and Qing dynasties. She was tormented by the constant moving to escape the reprisals of the new rulers.

She was buried in Yingmei Temple in Rugao. People wrote many eulogies to express their sorrow over her early death and to show their admiration for her. Scholar Wu Weiye said in his eulogy: ''Pearl is priceless, and jade is flawless,'' comparing Dong Bai with pearl and jade. Mao Xiang's recollections of Dong Bai were preserved in ''Yingmei Temple Memories'':

> *Our affection was like a pure jade. . . .*
> *I couldn't help tearing when I recall it.*

In 1693 A.D., forty-two years after his Dong Bai's death, Mao Xiang died at the age of eighty-three. Although Dong Bai came from a lower-class background and became the concubine of Mao Xiang as a singer-prostitute, her talents in literature and personal qualities were well remembered and appreciated by later generations.

Wang Xuehua

Sources

Mao Xiang, *Yingmei'an yiyu* (Recollections of Yingmei Temple); Yu Huai, *Banqiao zaiji*, vol. 2; Qing Guan-luo, ''Mao Xiang zhuan'', in *Qingdai qibai mingren zhuan*, vol. 5; Meng Sen, *Xingshi zongkan*, vol. 3; Liang Yizhen,

Qingdai funu wenxueshi, (History of Women's Literature in the Qing Dynasty), vol. 5. Taibei: Zhonghua shuju, 1958.

Hou Zhi (ca. 1760–1829 A.D.) was a poet during the Qing dynasty. A native of Shangyuan (now Nanjing), she called herself "Xiangye ge zhuren" (The Hostess of Xiangye Mansion) and "Xiumu ge zhuren" (The Hostess of Xiumu Mansion). Her main contribution to history was her work on revising *tanci*, a literary form that resembles a long-narrative poem (ballads), usually sung with a musical accompaniment.

Her father, Hou Xueshi, became a middle-ranking official after he passed the imperial examination in 1771 A.D., holding offices in Guangdong province, such as Sanshui and Xinhui counties. He later became an official in Wuzhou, Jiangxi province. Hou Xueshi was also a poet, whose works were collected in *Bayue meihan caotang shiji* (Poems in the Hall of August Plum). His writings were typically peaceful, smooth, and earnest.

Hou Zhi was the eldest of Hou Xueshi's children. The second child was a son (Hou Yunsong), who was talented at painting and later passed the provincial examination. The third child was also a son (Hou Yunshi), who passed the imperial examination. Hou Zhi started learning to compose poetry in her early childhood. In this she was instructed by both her father and her cousin Hou Yunjin, a successful poet whose works were collected in *Tanhua shu shiju* (Poems in Epiphyllum House).

Influenced by her father and cousin, Hou Zhi had a solid foundation in poetry, which benefited her in her later work in revising *tanci*. The four *tanci* writings revised by her, beginning in 1811 A.D., were: "Jinchuan yuan" (Story of Gold Bracelets), "Zaisheng yuan" (Story of Regeneration), "Zaizaotian" (Story of Repairing Heaven), and "Jinshanghua" (Story of Brocade Flower). According to her preface to "Repairing Heaven": "In the past ten years, I did not write any poems, but concentrated on *tanci*. It is not easy to change and adapt the old versions of *tanci*. It is like weaving, very delicate and strenuous. What I am afraid of is that the original meaning has not been well expressed."

She was middle-aged and ill even before she started her work. Her family's economic circumstances had declined, and she bore the heavy burden of housework. People later found evidence of their difficult life in her son's writing. In 1810 A.D., her son, Mei Zengliang, wrote in "Ji Wang Huichuan shu" (A Letter to Wang Huichuan): "I am now twenty-four years old, young and strong, but staying at home. I feel shamed . . . I have a fifty-year-old mother; there is no father at home. . . . My job as copyist earns only a little." The following year he wrote: "My mother is troubled with her writing work; my father has not returned from official business; when I see the remote Wangong mountain, I think of going out to make money." Hou Zhi's father was an official, but he was honest and not corrupt. After he retired, he was still poor and needed final support from this grandson, who earned money mostly from writing.

Hou Zhi married Mei Chong, a poet and scholar from Shangyuan in Jiangsu Province, but his family was as financially deprived as hers. They had four sons, Mei Zhengliang, Mei Ping, Mei Zongzhao, and Mei Zengkao, and one daugher named Mei Shuyi; all were interested in poetry. Sometimes she had to pawn her clothing or jewelry to support her family. Her worries over money, about the living standard of the whole family, made her health worse. So, it was really remarkable for Hou Zhi in her fifties and sixties to revise the four *tanci* (of which yuchuanyuan was the most famous) and rewrite "Zaisheng yuan" (Story of Regeneration) as "Jingui jie" (Outstanding Maiden).

Tanci as a literary form was looked down upon by the ruling class and the so-called orthodox literary schools. Hou Zhi's work demonstrated her strong will and spirit of rebelling against old viewpoints. Her quality could be seen from the literary figures in her writings. For example, in her revised *tanci* "Story of Repairing Heaven," she bravely praised Wu Zetian (the only female emperor in China's history) (see Wu Zetian) as she had one of the characters, Madam Huangfu Feilong, comment: "Although Wu usurped power and killed too many dissenters, she was good at using personnel. She was a great leader of that generation, and no later Tang emperors could be compared with her. . . . Wu Zetian was a legend, totally different from those fatuous rulers."

Hou Zhi's husband, Mei Chong, was a fourth-generation descendent of the great Qing mathematician Mei Wending. Mei Chong passed the provincial examination and showed his ability in mathematics in his book *Gougu qianshu* (A Brief Introduction to the Pythagoream Theorem). Hou Zhi died in 1829 A.D., aged sixty-nine, but her reputation survived her as an excellent *tanci* scholar.

Wang Xuehua

Sources

Hou Zhi, "Preface to Zaisheng Yuan"; Hu Wenkai, "Lidai Funu Zhuzuo Kao," *Textual Research into Works by Women Writers in History*, vol. 12. Beijing: Commercial Publishers, 1957; Chen Zuo-lin, "Jinling Tongzhuan"; Zhang De-jun, "Guanyu Gaibian Tianci de Nushiren Hou Zhi" published in "Guanmin Ribao" May 17, 1961.

Wang Zhenyi (1768–1797 A.D.) was a famous scientist in the Qing dynasty. Her ancestral region was Sizhou, Anhui, but, since her grandfather's generation, they had lived in Jiangning (modern-day Nanjing). Her grandfather, Wang Zhefu (?–1782 A.D.), was once the governor of Fengchen county and the governor of Xuanhua prefecture. Wang Zhefu had a large collection of books—seventy-five bookcases in all. Her father was Wang Xichen, who, after failing the imperial examination, applied himself to the study of medical science and summarized his clinical experience in the four-volume *Yifang yanchao* (Collection of Medical Prescriptions).

As a child, Wang Zhenyi was fond of reading and was exceptionally clever. When her grandfather died, she was eleven years old; she went with her grandmother Dong and her father to Jiling, near the Great Wall, for his funeral. They stayed on in Jiling for five years, during which time she read many books that her grandfather had collected and gained knowledge on extensive subjects. In her own words, she once "read books at senior Madam Bo's together with Miss Bai Hexian, Miss Chen Wanyu, and Miss Wu Xiaolian, upper-class young ladies [and] learned equestrian skills and archery from the wife of a Mongolian general named Aa.'' She had a highly developed sense of horsemanship as well as archery and was able to ''hit the target with every arrow'' and ''practice martial arts while galloping on horseback.'' She was valiant and heroic in manner and bearing.

When she was sixteen years old, Wang Zhenyi returned to the southern bank of the Yangzi river and then moved again to the capital with her father. They passed through many places such as Shaanxi, Hubei, and Guangdong, which broadened her horizons and enriched her experiences. She married when she was twenty-five to Zhan Mei of Xuan cheng, Anhui. They had no children.

Though her life was short, Wang Zhenyi became very accomplished academically and made significant contributions excelling in astronomy and mathematics. In literature, she left to later generations thirteen volumes of *ci* poetry, prose, and prefaces and postscripts written for other works. One of her famous poems is ''On the Journey to Jiling,'' composed of five-character lines. ''Silkworm Breeding,'' ''Clothes Washing,'' and ''Sighs of a Withered Tree,'' poems of seven characters per line, were judged well composed and praiseworthy. Her readers considered her poetry and prose ''substantial in content and well oriented, not just flowery wording.'' In her poem ''Praise of Manly Woman,'' she wrote: ''I am for extensive traveling and reading, even greater than man's is my ambition.'' Her poetry was free of obsequiousness and appeared strong and vibrant. In ''Transiting Tong Pass,'' she wrote:

> *So important is the doorway,*
> *occupying the throat of the mountain*
> *Looking down from the heaven,*
> *The sun sees Yellow river streaming.*

In ''Climbing Tai Mountain,'' she wrote:

> *Clouds overcast the hills,*
> *The sun bathes in sea.*

As the famous Qing dynasty scholar Yuan Mei commented, Wang Zhenyi's poetry ''had the flavor of a great pen, not of a female poet.'' While in Jiling and, later, while traveling, she had opportunities to widen her acquaintance with the people. Her poems ''Woman Breeder of Silkworm'' and ''Clothes Washing'' depicted the hard life of laboring women. In other poems she denounced the polarization between rich and poor and officials' extortion through excessive taxes and levies. In ''A Poem of Eight Lines,'' composed out of despair after seeing the drought en route to Fuchun, she wrote:

> *Village is empty of cooking smoke,*
> *Rich families let grains stored decay;*
> *In wormwood strewed pitiful starved bodies,*
> *Greedy officials yet push farm levying.*

Because Wang Zhenyi was well traveled and because her own family was in decline, she gained a sense of life's deprivations and sorrows. Her poetry testified to her humanity and compassion.

Wang Zhenyi accomplished a great deal through scholarly research. In her youth she contributed to an understanding of the classics, history, poetry, and prose, in the same manner as a well-educated young lady from a wealthy family would. She also achieved great heights in astronomy, geography, mathematics, the study of the calendar, and medicine.

Wang Zhenyi's greatest contribution came as a natural scientist and astronomer. Describing her views of celestial phenomena in her article ''Dispute of the Procession of the Equinoxes,'' she gave ample proof and a simple, clear explanation of the movement of the equinoxes and methods through which their movement might be calculated. In other articles, such as ''Dispute of Longitude and Stars'' and ''The Explanation of a Lunar Eclipse,'' she expounded on the number of stars, the revolving direction of the sun, the moon, and the planets Venus, Jupiter, Mars, Mercury, and Saturn. She also described the relationship between lunar eclipses and solar eclipses. These thoughts were revolutionary in China. In several articles, she summarized the research of earlier studies in astronomy and commented on them; in other articles, she described her original research, correcting earlier views and calculations made by others. She accurately described a lunar eclipse and used the following experimental method: She placed a round table in a garden pavilion, using it as a globe; from the ceiling beam she hung a crystal lamp on a cord, using it as the sun. On one side of the table she put a big round mirror as the moon and then she moved the three objects as if the sun, earth, and moon were moving according to astronomical principles. She could see how the lunar eclipse occurred by observing the relationship of the shining lamp with the reflecting mirror. Her article ''The Explanation of the Lunar Eclipse'' was highly accurate. She understood that the earth was spherical and described it as such in ''Of the Ball-Shaped Earth.'' She attempted to describe why people would not fall off the earth, and her arguments were later improved upon with the theories of gravity. And she attempted to describe the cosmos and the relationship of the earth within.

Few women knew mathematics as well as Wang Zhenyi, as she had mastered trigonometry and understood the Pythagorean theorem. In ''The Explanation of the Pythagorean Theorem and Trigonometry,'' she explained the relationship between the shorter leg of a right triangle, the long leg, and the triangle's hypotenuse in apt detail and correct understanding. She thought very highly of Mei Wending (1633–1721 A.D.), a famous mathematician of the early Qing dynasty, mastering his book *Principles of Calculation*. Mei Wending's book was erudite, and Wang Zhenyi rewrote the text in simpler language, making it readily available to other scholars and titling it *The Musts of Calculation*. She used a simpler multiplication and division system in calculations, which made everything easier for beginners. She applied herself rigorously to the field of mathematics in *Beyond the Study of Mathematics*, a rigorous self-study of her discipline in mastering the field. She commented: ''There were times that I had to put down my pen and sighed. But I love the subject, I do not give up.'' Great concentration and perseverance resulted in her book *The Simple Principles of Calculation*, published when she was twenty-four.

The Western calendar spread to China in the Qing dynasty, but many Chinese scholars refused to accept it. Wang Zhenyi urged its adoption, saying: ''What counts is the usefulness, no matter whether it is Chinese or Western.'' She understood the sun-centered thesis and admired the Western calendar's precision, saying: "All the marrow should be absorbed" from the new ideas and calculations.

She left behind numerous books in both natural science and in poetry. Had she not died so young, no doubt she would have written many more. Among her other books were the six-volume *Denfengting zhuji* (The Preliminary Collection of Defeng Pavilon), ten-volume *Jottings, The Explanations of Constellations, Supplementary Information on Western Calculations, The Collected Verses of a Woman*, five-volume *Simple Principles of Calculation*, four-volume *Beyond the Study of Mathematics*, and ten-volume *Review of Selected Prose, Poems, and Fu*.

When she knew she was dying, she asked that her manuscripts be handed over to her best friend, Madam Kuai (Qian Yuling 1763–1827 A.D.), for preservation. But six years later, Madam Kuai gave Wang Zhenyi's manuscripts to her nephew, Qian Yiji (1783–1850 A.D.), a famous scholar who compiled the five-volume *Shusuan jiancun* (Simple Principles of Calculation) by Wang Zhenyi and wrote its preface. In this preface, he described Wang Zhenyi as the "number one female scholar after Ban Huiji" (Ban Zhao). Later her manuscripts were transferred to Zhu Xuzeng, a collector in Nanjing. Unfortunately, some of her manuscripts were lost, but what remains are the *Defengting zhuji* (Collection of the Defeng Pavilion) and the Jinling Series of her nine volumes of prose, single volume of poetry, and three volumes of *ci* poetry. This series best represents her work, as stated in her own words:

> *It's made to believe*
> *Women are same as Men;*
> *Are you not convinced*
> *Daughters can also be heroic?*

Although she lived in a feudal society, she had a progressive spirit and believed a woman could display her talents to the fullest. Happily married, she believed social feudal values to be inappropriate "when talking about learning and sciences, people thought of no women," and that "women should only do cooking and sewing, and that they should not be bothered about writing articles for publication, studying history, composing poetry or doing calligraphy.'' Wang Zhenyi advocated that within society men and women ''are all people, who have the same reason for studying.''

The idea that learning was not just for men, but for men and women was very forward looking in her day. As a woman scientist, well published and respected, she remains a role model for young people today.

Barbara Bennett Peterson

Sources

"The Preliminary Collection of Defeng Pavilion" by Wang Zhenyi; *The History of the Qing Dynasty,* the 508th vol.: The Biography of Wang Zhenyi; The Biographies of 700 Noted Personages of the Qing Dynasty, Book Four, the biography of Wang Zhenyi by Cai Guanluo; *The Supplementary Collection of Biographies on Stone Tablets*: the 59th vol.: *The Biography of Wang Zhenyi* by Min Erchang; ''The Third Edition of the Biographies, seventh vol., by Zhu Kebao; ''The Preliminary Collection of the Classified Readings of the Dynasty,'' the 228th vol.; *Textual Research into Works by Women Writers in History*, seventh vol., by Hu Wenkai.

Wang Cong'er (ca. 1777–1798 A.D.) was a military leader of the White Lotus Rebellion, which erupted at the end of the eighteenth century and extended into the nineteenth century—the first major uprising against the Qing dynasty in more than a century. Remembered in Chinese history as a heroine, Wang Cong'er was born into a peasant family in the region of Xiangyang, Hubei province. Her father died when she was young, and her mother, raising her family alone, moved about, making a living by washing clothes, sewing, and hiring herself out as a domestic servant. So scarce were family provisions that Wang Cong'er was forced to beg for food and often went without shoes.

When Wang Cong'er was still a young girl, her mother allowed her to work in a performing troupe that traveled around the country; in this way Wang Cong'er kept herself alive, fed, and clothed by performing all types of circus feats, in particular, demonstrations of dangerous fighting with guns, knives, and sticks. The troupe was thus her military training ground, and she became very skilled at such an early age out of hunger and necessity.

The troupe took her throughout Hubei and Henan provinces, allowing her to meet many people in her travels, such as Qi Lin (?–d. 1796 A.D.), who would later become rebel leaders. Once, when she was being bullied and abused, he interceded to protect her. He won her admiration and love, and eventually they were married. Qi Lin later became the leader of the White Lotus Society and generated the plan for the rebellion in Jingxiang.

Qi Lin was honored as a First Master of the White Lotus Religion and Wang Cong'er was honored with the title Second Master because she so closely assisted him in his duties.

The origins of the White Lotus Society reach back to the Yuan dynasty. Divisions among the Yuan dynasty's leadership, famine in North China, and floods and destruction had opened the way to rebellion and the Yuan downfall. Secret societies began to organize during the 1340s A.D. and 1350s A.D. aimed at accomplishing the downfall of the Yuan; one of them was the White Lotus Society, which originally was a sect of Tiantai Buddhism that traced its lore back to the first half of the twelfth century.

As a reformed group now dedicated to the overthrow of the Qing dynasty, the new White Lotus Society conducted all activities in secret and mobilized dissidents with caution. The victor among the earlier Chinese rebel "heroes" was the founder of the Ming, Zhu Yuanzhang, a humble and able commoner who rose through ability to capture the emperorship and obtain the mandate of heaven. Once in power, however, Zhu, who reigned as Emperor Hongwu, denied membership in the White Lotus Society, possibly believing it was an unwise thing to admit.

But the new leaders of the regrouped White Lotus Society attempted to emulate him and organized to overthrow the Qing using an army of commoners. The modern leaders of the White Lotus Society, including Wang Cong'er and Qi Lin, geared up for the coming rebellion by making and storing arms and food, and engaging in military preparations and training peasants, forming a citizen army. They planned an uprising to take place early in 1796 A.D. Unfortunately, someone exposed the plan, and hundreds of potential rebellion leaders were rounded up by the Qing forces. In this purge, Qi Lin was killed. But with the help of her loyal followers, Conger escaped and was protected from capture.

Wang Cong'er took refuge in a temple, where she was guarded by nuns. Wang Cong'er did not lose her spirit or will for the rebellion after her husband's death; she steeled herself to continue their work and goal of toppling the Qing dynasty. With the assistance of Yao Zhifu (?--1798 A.D.), she continued to train the peasants and to plan a second major uprising. The supporters of the White Lotus Society began to rebel in Yidu and Zhijiang, Hubei province; this became the prelude to the much larger rebellion to follow. Eventually Wang Conger's forces would fight the Qing Troops in Sichuan, Hunan, Hubei, and Shaanxi.

Wang Cong'er led her forces numbering around ten thousand, in rebellion, as they moved to capture Qing strongholds in Xiangyang. She cut her long hair and dressed in white, riding atop a large horse with a long knife in each hand, which she could wield with dexterity from the days of the traveling performing troupe. She was chosen as the general leader (zongjiaoshi) of the main force in Hubei province, her followers arising to her patriotic call. The exact site of the original uprising of Wang Cong'er and her troops created from the local peasants was on the outskirts of Xiangyang, at Huanlongdong. She moved her forces to Xiangfan in Hubei and then moved part of her force to Xiaogan in Hubei to attack Qing forces there.

At Xiaogan, her forces killed a high military official of the Qing dynasty. Then the emperor's forces sought revenge for his death. Knowing she was being pursued, she planned a diversionary move for her forces to Henan province, with the ultimate goal of linking up with all the White Lotus forces in Zhengan, Shaanxi province. In moving about the countryside, she divided her forces into even smaller units of hundreds, so that they might more easily live off the land and elude capture by the Qing. She used diversionary tactics, dispersing and then concentrating troop movements, using hit-and-run tactics of harassing the enemy.

The immediate causes of the White Lotus Rebellion in the eighteenth century were rooted in the corruption of the Qing. The Emperor Qianlong, who was over sixty-five years old when the rebellion broke out, had become dominated at court by a younger manipulative man, his bodyguard, the unscrupulous He Shen, who would plunder the imperial coffers for the next twenty years. He Shen, whose career had risen like a meteor within courtly circles, eventually amassed a fortune estimated at 900 million taels, or about half a billion dollars, plus other "trinkets," such as a solid gold dining service of 4,288 pieces and 70,000 furs. Military corruption paralleled civilian misconduct and extortion from the masses as well. When the White Lotus Rebellion broke out, it was against this type of Qing leadership that they revolted. They raided their banners supporting *guanbi minfan* (resistance against official oppression.) Further, the peasants were reacting to the plummeting living standard caused by the rise in the population, which was destroying the prosperity and peace of the country. The population had grown from 142 million in 1741 A.D. to 432 million in 1851 A.D.. At the same time, administrative efficiency had not kept pace with the population spurt. Nor was the regime making technological progress on a par with the West, then recovering from the American and French Revolutions, the Napoleonic wars, and the beginnings of the industrial revolution.

Thus the White Lotus Rebellion broke out between 1796 A.D. and 1804 A.D. in the mountainous region bounded by Hubei, Sichuan, and Shaanxi provinces, the relatively inaccessible area between the upper waters of the Han and Yangzi rivers was a manifestation of popular discontent against the government.

Religiously, the latter-day White Lotus Society that Wang Cong'er and Qi Lin had joined promised its followers "the advent of the Buddha, the restoration of the virtues of the mind, and personal salvation from suffering in this world and the next." These ideas were connecting links among the "believers," who joined the rebellious army led by Wang Cong'er in Xiangyang. One of the reasons the White Lotus Society had such a large following, of men and women alike, was that it preached equality between the sexes and between the young and the old, in the belief that their members were offsprings of deities and should share their lot. Their gains were equally divided among themselves, thus attracting a wider and wider following. The White Lotus Society was also devoted to certain martial arts, and Wang Cong'er taught many women followers what she knew.

On one day, it is retold, she killed two brilliant Qing military commanders with her own hands. On the day of her death, her forces had fought against those of the Qing for six hours. As they were outnumbered by the Qing, perhaps the outcome was inevitable. Yet she lent her strength to a cause that ultimately would come to fruition with the end of the violent and oppressive Qing later. Certainly her efforts and the entire White Lotus Rebellion weakened the Qing severely and began its cycle downward. It is a mark of Chinese history that women such as Wang Cong'er have often taken to the field of combat as military leaders, respected for their fighting skills and their idealism. Many of her military followers were women warriors.

After relinking with the entire force in Zhengan, she led the forces into Sichuan in 1797 A.D. The Qing forces pursued them there, and eventually she escaped with her band to Xiangyang. Here she lost a significant battle at Huaishugou, most of her army was killed, and she retreated with only a few remaining soldiers. She and about a dozen followers were pursued by Qing forces into hilly terrain. To elude capture they climbed a mountain peak. From this site, on the left ridge of Xiehua po they saw the Qing forces concentrated in large numbers below. Wang Cong'er, a banner in her hand jumped to her death accompanied by her loyal band, accepting death and martyrdom rather than torture and Qing persecution. Then twenty-two years old, she would be remembered for her bravery, commitment, tenacity, and courage amid hardship and reversals of fortune.

Wang Cong'er would go down in history as an exemplar of a rebel heroine. In leading her army, she risked her life to recapture her wounded soldiers; she tore her clothes for bandages for the wounded; she allowed the weak and wounded to ride on her house while she proceeded on foot; she bound up the wounds and sewed patches onto clothing; she dispensed strict discipline among her forces; and she was warmly welcomed and supported by the local peasant populations, which saw her as a liberator, offering her food and shelter.

After her courageous death, several of her loyal peasant followers retrieved her body and gave her an honorable burial in Huaishugou. There is a monument erected to her there on a large tomb. Wang Cong'er is recalled to this day in theatrical productions, songs, and stories as a heroine who led a peasant uprising in the name of justice and morality.

Barbara Bennett Peterson

Sources

Cai Lei, "An Uprising Leader of the White Lotus Religion" (translated orally by Fang Hong), in *Famous Women of Ancient Times and Today*, edited by *Chinese Woman Magazine*, Hebei: People's Publishing House, 1986. Ah Yuan, "Wang Cong'er-Leader of Peasant Uprisings," in *Women of China*, August, 1982: 20–21; "Wanger Cong'er," in *The Dictionary of Famous Women of Hua Hsia* (China) translated from Chinese by Lucia P. Ellis. Beijing: Hua Hsia Publishing House, 1988. For an excellent background of the White Lotus Society and their involvement in revolutions and rebellions against the Yuan and the Qing Dynasties see Edwin R. Reischauer and John K. Fairbank, *East Asia, the Great Tradition*. Boston: Houghton-Mifflin Company, 1960 and *East Asia: The Modern Transformation*, John K. Fairbank, Edwin R. Reischauer and Albert M. Craig. Boston: Houghton-Mifflin, 1965.

Cixi (1835–1908 A.D.), also known as Xiao Qin Xian, was empress dowager of the Qing dynasty and dominated the Chinese empire for forty-eight years after the Opium War. She was the eldest daughter of Huijeng, whose family consisted of a long line of officials; moreover, her mother came from a well-positioned official's family. She was born in Beijing of Manchu lineage. Her ancestors had come from Yehebuman; her original name was Nalalan'er. In 1852 A.D., when she was sixteen, she entered the court of Emperor Xianfeng (r. 1850–61 A.D.) as a low-ranking concubine. In March 1854 A.D., she was elevated in rank, and, in 1856, after she gave birth to the emperor's only son, Zaichun (who later reigned as Emperor Tongzhi r. 1861–

75 A.D.), she was elevated to being an imperial consort (*yi fei*). Then in January, 1857 she became (*yiguifei*) Honored Consort Yi. This allowed her a position next to the empress. In this exalted position as Honored Consort Yi, she was able to read the reports from the provinces coming to the emperor, and from this time she rose in influence and grew to love power.

The Opium Wars (1839–1842 A.D.) debilitated China and its leadership. However, the Opium Wars had forced China to open new ports to foreigners, and to pay indemnities. After the second Opium War ended, the treaties of surrender were to be signed in Beijing. But in 1859–60 A.D., the British and French representatives were refused passage to Beijing from the Dagu forts close to Tianjin. Seeking to force compliance and secure the signatures on the treaties, Lord Elgin marched on Beijing. The emperor fled to Jehol (Chengde), although Honored Consort Yi (later to be named Cixi), tried to persuade him to stay in the capital. Instead he appointed his brother Yixin, Prince Gong, to negotiate with the foreigners.

On October 8, 1860, Lord Elgin's forces ceremoniously burned the Summer Palace (Yuanmingyuan) of the Qing emperors, a complex of two hundred buildings and lavish gardens modeled after Versailles. This was to force agreement and secure signature to the original Treaty of Tianjin. Prince Gong accepted the treaties on behalf of the court. Shortly thereafter, on August 22, 1861, A.D., the emperor died. His son Zaichun succeeded him at the behest of his mother, Honored Consort Yi, reigning first as the Emperor Qixiang and later as the Emperor Tongzhi. The young emperor immediately gave honorific titles to his mother and the empress; he gave his mother the title empress dowager and named her Cixi; the widowed Empress Xiao Zhen Xian also was honored as empress dowager and called Ci'an.

Cixi and Ci'an conspired with Prince Gong to form an informal triumvirate of power against eight high-ranking officials at court who desired to halt Cixi's plans to seize power. Cixi held one seal (Ci'an holding another) of the young emperor, and any official document at court had to bear its stamp. She plotted the demise of the three leading officials—Zai Yuan, Duan Hua, and Sushun—and on November 11, 1861, A.D., forced the other five high officials to resign in a skillful coup d'état. Afterward, she elevated those who had helped her, including Prince Gong, and the two empress dowagers began to reign from behind the scenes.

After the disastrous effects of the two opium wars in China and the beginning of further foreign intrusions, "restoration" of the traditional Confucian government (and internal "self-strengthening" were the state's major goals, and absorption of Western technology in self-defense secondary to these "self-strengthening" ideals. The mind-set of the period was reflected by the Mongol scholar Wojen in 1867 A.D.: "The empire is so great that there is no need to worry about a lack of talent. If it is necessary to teach astronomy and mathematics [i.e., Western studies], an extensive search should find someone [in China] who has mastered these techniques. . . . Why must we learn from the barbarian foreigners? . . . They are our enemies." This continuing sense of nationalism, however, was complicated by the weakness, after 1860 A.D., of the central Qing government, so badly battered during the Opium Wars. At the center was Cixi, who acted as regent for Emperor Tongzhi.

Like Empress Wu (see Empress Wu) of the Tang dynasty, she learned to use the civil service examination and appointment system to her own advantage, granted promotions to loyal courtiers, and intimidated with threats, corruption, censure, punishment, and dismissal. High-positioned court eunuchs were her loyal allies and persecuted her enemies. At a time when China might have better proceeded toward modernization, she ardently desired to preserve the status quo. In fairness, she sought to do this to protect her country from foreign aggression, spoilage, and domination. "Restoration," rather than "modernization," was a policy of guile and statecraft to ward off the "barbarians," suppress local rebellions, and revive the Confucian civil service, which she hoped would restore China's strength. Her policies were adopted with an eye to securing her people's support. What foreign technology and modernization was allowed was used for the political aims and power position of the entrenched power structure under Cixi.

Until 1894 A.D. the court remained firmly in Cixi's grip. Even though Cixi had changeable and vicious moods and relied on fear and corruption, she was a woman of great accomplishment.

She ruled in one of China's most difficult periods—just after China's defeat in the Opium Wars—and, by her policies, she saved China from being colonized, divided, occupied, or torn apart by local warlords—no small feat in an era of rapid change. Her forces successfully suppressed the Taiping Rebellion which had broken out between the two Opium Wars, attempting to overthrow the Qing by recapturing Nanjing in 1864 A.D.. They also suppressed other smaller groups such as the Nian rebels on the North China Plain. In 1865, Yi Xin the Prince Regent was accused of being "presumptuous," and "a power unto himself." Cixi removed Yi Xin of his post, and she held absolute power.

Cixi also, to her credit, aided China in remaining cohesive in this troubled time by suppression of the Muslim rebellions, which had started in 1856 A.D., seeking ethnic independence. Fairbank, Reischauer, and Craig said of the central authorities' means of controlling the outbursts of violence: "In general the Ch'ing [Qing] cause seems in the end to have offered a greater degree of orderly administration and nonpartisan justice to all elements of the mixed population. . . . Even Moslem Chinese (like the general Ma Ju-Lung after 1861 A.D.) found it advantageous to take the Ch'ing sides." She swiftly had moved to protect the throne of her son in 1862 A.D. by putting down another Muslim revolt in Gansu province near Xi'an. In this ambition, Cixi successfully directed her commander Zuo Zongtang.

Thus the triumph of the "restoration" of China in the 1860s A.D. after the Opium Wars was a victory for Cixi and her policies of warfare and civil government. Her provincial leaders like Zeng Guofan, Li Hongzhang, and Zuo Zongtang acted diligently on her behalf as genuine scholar-administrators in the Confucian mold in addition to being scholar-generals. Fairbank, Reischauer, and Craig said of the success of Cixi's policies and her administrators and generals: "Their success was due not only to hard fighting but also to the application of Confucian moral and political principles, encouragement of economic recovery, effective taxation, and, in addition, some use of Western technology."

The empress dowager employed Rong Lu, an able and devoted Manchu bannerman, to command her military police at the capital, and he was also appointed commander of the new, modern-equipped Beijing Field Force. Cixi rebuilt the Summer Palace and supported Beijing Opera. In 1873, the Emperor Tongzhi became eighteen years old. According to tradition, Cixi could no longer control the affairs "behind the screen." However, she maintained most of her original power by "reviewing" imperial decisions and planting spies around the Emperor. Then in January 1875 A.D. the emperor died, at the age of nineteen. Many critics have retold tales of her encouraging his early death through excesses, so that she could act as regent for a new, young and more pliant emperor, her nephew Zaitian. Manipulating the succession, Cixi selected her younger sister's son, a first cousin of the deceased Tongzhi Emperor, and adopted him at age four as the heir of herself and the deceased Xianfeng Emperor. By this device she became the new emperor's adoptive mother. Zaitian became the Emperor Guangxu (Glorious Succession; r. 1875–1908 A.D.). Thus Cixi remained as co-regent (with Ci'an, until her death in 1881 A.D.). Cixi's own son had no male offspring. Because of her power, she was able to break the time-honored tradition of selecting the new emperor from a succeeding generation. Cixi selected the new emperor, her nephew, from the same generation as her son. Until the new emperor reached his majority in 1894 A.D., she continued to rule, even becoming strong enough by 1884 A.D. to remove her most powerful minister within the court, Prince Gong. After his removal, all court officials and provincial governors and generals fell into line with her policies. But the ethnic composition of her followers was changing slowly between 1861 and 1890 A.D.. Many more Chinese, rather than Manchu, had risen by suppressing rebellion and creating provincial military machines supported by the court.

In 1881, Cixi became sole regent for her nephew Zaitian, the Emperor Guangxu, when Ci'an died. Cixi forced the emperor to marry (1889) her niece, who became Empress Xiao Ding Jing. The young emperor faced many problems.

Guangxu was a puppet in her hands. Political control in China was becoming increasingly decentralized, and the view within the regions would slowly change to see the central leadership of the ethnic Manchu as alien by the turn of the twentieth century. Cixi was now as an advisor to Emperor Guangxu, who had turned eighteen in 1889, but the "old Buddha" as she was known still decided major court policies. She held a delicate balance in her lifetime between the forces of regional power and central, dynastic power. She cleverly manipulated the ancient symbols to her advantage, as the special stone ramp installed in the imperial palace reversed the usual pattern by having the phoenix, symbolizing the empress, placed above the dragon, symbolizing the emperor. The success of the policies of the restoration did not return China to the status quo before the Opium Wars, but to a new era of balance between the central and regional authorities. To Cixi's statecraft one may credit the leading provincial administrators' loyalty to the central state. And the dynasty's central power owed its survival to the growth and support of this loyal regionalism.

Recovery in China after the Opium Wars was not unlike the recovery of the United States after the Civil War, although in China the casualties and destruction had been greater. Cixi was able to prolong the life of the Qing dynasty amid a shortage of investment capital for industrial development to allow China to more quickly heal itself. Cixi coped with the enormous changes and problems created by Western intrusions such as the international settlement in Shanghai, the foreign operation of her postal system, and the continuation of the importation of opium under the Shanghai agreement. Her officials encouraged the extended Chinese responsibility to heal the nation's war wounds. Thus, she naturally turned to "restoration" of old ways, rather than the new, which China could not yet afford.

Cixi's actions had been to give new goals moral exhortation and direction, relief from land-tax payments in devastated areas, overall reduction of tax rates and resettlement of farmers on the land. At the heart of Cixi's problems was the fact that the central government could no longer be sustained by the traditional source of revenue—taxation. To develop new sources of revenue China needed to develop industry, but the conservative philosophy at the time saw modernization and new, Western technologies as potential avenues of Western control, perhaps correctly. Compounding Cixi's internal problems was the decline in the proportion of Manchus in high positions in Beijing compared with Chinese officials rising through merit in the examination system. Cixi herself had allowed Chinese to migrate to and settle in Manchuria; the Manchu language had no official place at court; in the long wars against the westerners, the lines dividing Manchu and Chinese were no longer visible.

Domestically, Cixi had restored the examination system to find men of talent, re-opened local schools and academies with public funds through her provincial governors, constructed and stocked libraries, established printing offices—all with the ambition of teaching the classical Confucian texts. Cixi restrained the availability of degrees by purchase so as not to pollute the talent pool. She also diminished the sales of rank and political offices. She supported an anti-Christian movement throughout China, viewing missionaries as agents of Western encroachment and competitors for the allegiance of the Chinese people. Another source of continuing antagonism between Cixi and the treaty-making powers of the Opium War days was the question of treaty revision. Revisions to the treaties were allowed ten years after the original treaty was signed. The Alcock Convention agreement (1869), which tended to put the treaty system in China on a more "equitable" and non-exploitative basis, was widely applauded in Cixi's court and approved. But the British government rejected its terms, viewed as generous to China, and did not ratify the revision. This was seen as a setback by Cixi for the policy of cooperation with the foreigners since the Opium Wars. The so-called Tianjin massacre of June 1870 A.D.—in which twenty foreigners, mainly French missionaries, were killed in an uprising of Chinese disgusted with foreign missionary activities—ended a decade of cooperation and marked the coming end of the restoration policies. Exacerbating tension further were the activities of foreign traders in the treaty ports and the foreign collection of customs revenues through the Maritime Customs Service. The Chinese populace became increasingly angry with the concessions and leases granted, under pressure, to the foreign powers operating in the fourteen treaty ports.

The foreigners, under the policy of extraterritoriality, tried their own nationals. They were free from taxation by the Chinese government in Shanghai's international settlement. However, Chinese in this area were taxed by foreigners for improvement to roads, harbors, wharves, jetties, and the like. Western law, while it favored business and investment, was slanted toward overseas nationals. That Cixi was able to balance so many conflicting interests for so long, without further full-scale civil war, is remarkable. But the price of balance was lack of modernization, democracy, industrialization, and freedom.

Cixi's juggling of internal-external affairs and regional-central authority polarities was further both complicated and aided by the Maritime Customs Service. This agency, administered by the Briton Robert Hart, functioned as a civil service and performed many functions as outlined by the terms of the Opium War treaties. The Customs Service gave Cixi a new source of revenue, as technically the customs duties were collected by the British on behalf of China. Britain, desiring to continue making money through trade and pocketing a portion of the customs revenues before passing them on to the Chinese government, was also eager to maintain peace and acted in this endeavor as Cixi's partner. Cixi, using the collected customs revenues, was able to acquit herself of all the indemnities due from the Opium Wars, which totaled 8 million taels each to Britain and France. Between 1861 and 1893 A.D., she was also able to raise foreign loans, using future customs revenues as security. Cixi's government cooperated with the Maritime Customs Service to chart and map China's coast, and she granted authority to construct lighthouses, harbor markers, and beacons to safeguard navigation. Cixi collaborated with Robert Hart and the Maritime Customs Service to regulate the traffic in legalized opium and smuggling and ensure collection of duties.

Cixi gave Macao to Portugal in 1887 A.D. in order to end corruption and smuggling there.

Her reign saw the demise of the old clipper ship, the arrival of new iron and steel ships by the 1880s, and in 1869 A.D. the opening of the Suez Canal, which greatly stimulated trade between China and Europe. Business dealings were accelerated by the telegraph cables laid in 1870–71 A.D., linking Shanghai, Hong Kong, Singapore, and Nagasaki to European and American financial centers. One of the hindrances, however, to China's financial well being was reliance throughout Cixi's reign on silver as the monetary unit. As in the United States, the value of silver on the world market fell because of overproduction. In China this caused Cixi's administration innumerable financial dilemmas, especially as other countries adopted the gold standard.

Other monetary problems faced by the empress dowager were the declining markets around the world for China's tea and, after 1900 A.D., silk. The demand for China's cotton was reduced by competition from India. Nonetheless, the system in which a native Chinese became an agent handling the Chinese side of a foreign firm's business offered local Chinese opportunities for money-making and skill-learning. Although they were criticized in some circles as being collaborators with the "foreign devils," they gained the experience to become leaders in China's later industrialization.

Cixi's government failed or defaulted in efforts to industrialize. The central government did not have the revenue to subsidize infant industries because of its antiquated tax-farming methods, allowing tax collection by provincial officials. Part of the failure can be explained by the Confucian disdain for merchants and money making. China's failure to keep pace with Japan technologically would become brutally evident in the Sino-Japanese War.

Cixi also fended off encroachment from European powers coming overland. Russia was eager to invade the Tarim Basin, but was thwarted by Chinese imperial forces. In 1884 A.D. Chinese Turkestan was further linked to the government by becoming a province, Xinjiang. Cixi's government drifted into war with France over Tonkin, or North Vietnam, during 1884–85 A.D., and her imperial forces were defeated. This was a costly defeat for Cixi's self-strengthening movement. Her losses were repeated in China's defeat in the first Sino-Japanese War of 1894–95 A.D., when China was forced to cede Taiwan (Formosa), the Pescadore islands, and the Liaodong peninsula (southern Manchuria) to Japan. Cixi also granted independence to Korea and paid an indemnity to Japan of 200 million taels of silver. Japan also received the right to open factories in all trading cities.

After these wars and setbacks, Cixi's conservative policies were opposed by supporters of reform, who popularized the slogan "Zhong xue wei ti, xi xue wei yong" (Chinese learning for the essential principle, Western learning for the practical application).

New proposals were made by scholar-reformer Kang Youwei to liberalize the domestic administration; discussions of a cabinet, parliament, and ministries with technical experts ensued. Discussion led to a reform movement whose supporters called for a democracy, a parliamentary system with representation, and a liberal constitution. Supported in the discussions by the emperor, a Hundred Days of Reform followed June 11–Sept. 21, 1898, when liberal edicts were proclaimed by Guangxu. The empress dowager Cixi now felt threatened and staged a coup d'état herself on September 21, 1898 A.D.. She and her trusted commander Rong Lu seized Emperor Guangxu, placing him under house arrest, where he would remain for the rest of his life. He died mysteriously in 1908 A.D., a day before Cixi herself died. Revolution from above had failed. When revolution came in the future, it would be launched from below.

Due to western encroachments upon China, and because of past failures such as the Opium Wars and the failed reforms, elements of society began to openly rebel against the Qing administration. The secret society *Yi he quan*, roughly translated as the "Righteous and Harmonious Fists" or "Boxers," was strongly antiforeign and anti-Qing. Their 1899 A.D. slogan was "Overthrow the Qing; Destroy the Foreigner." The Boxers also aimed to stop Christian missionary activities in China tolerated by Cixi's government. The Boxers wrote signs stating: "Catholics and Protestants have vilified our gods and sages and deceived our emperors and ministers above the oppressed the Chinese people below. . . . This forces us to practice the *Yi he* magic boxing so as to protect our country, expel the foreign bandits and kill Christian converts, in order to save our people from miserable sufferings." Compounding the circumstances that formed the backdrop of the rise of the Boxers were droughts, followed by floods, banditry in the countryside, and food riots in the cities.

Taking the reins of power, now that her nephew the Emperor Guangxu was removed, Cixi attempted to stop the rising tide of rebellion, announcing after the 1898 A.D. coup that no more foreign concessions would be granted. The court announced that it would resist foreign aggression against China by force. In the fall of 1899 A.D. an alliance gradually developed between the Boxers and the court through the machinations of Cixi, who realized that she had to support the Boxers' antiforeign attitudes or be toppled by them. Now the slogan became "Uphold the Qing; Exterminate the Foreigner." This was a deft move by Cixi. Other court factions desired to suppress the Boxers and continue the policy of collaboration with foreigners begun after the Opium Wars. The Boxers, encouraged by Cixi, burned and pillaged the countryside around Beijing, killing foreign missionaries and Christian converts. Foreign diplomats and military personnel took action to oppose the Boxers after foreign legations were threatened in Beijing. Bringing a large, multinational force from Tianjin, the foreign interests sought to protect their interests in the capital. But before they arrived in Beijing, on June 14, 1900 A.D., the foreign force was attacked along the railway line, after many foreign-owned properties had been burned in Beijing. The victorious Boxers next burst into Tianjin and burned areas of the foreign concession areas. Cixi was solidly behind the Boxer successes, especially when pro-Boxer court leaders told her that the foreigners had demanded her abdication in favor of the emperor. A fabricated story, this nonetheless spurred Cixi to push further for Boxer victory over the "foreign devils." With open fighting between Boxers and foreigners occurring in Beijing and Tianjin, on June 21, 1900, A.D., Cixi declared war on the foreign powers. Cixi's imperial troops joined the Boxers in attacking the eleven foreign legations in Beijing and other areas of the capital. By the end of the summer, after weeks of near-starvation inside the compound defended, many besieged foreigners were massacred. However, several Chinese provincial governors denounced these atrocities, repudiated the court's declaration of war, and were later able to aid peace negotiations with the foreign powers. Meanwhile, Cixi encouraged war in North China, and peace in South China, using a two-handed policy of expedience. An international foreign force raised to rescue Tianjin's foreigners proceeded from reoccupied Tianjin to Beijing, dispersing the Boxers and recapturing all legations in August 1900 A.D. Cixi and her entourage fled Beijing and retreated to Xi'an. Peace was negotiated by the imperial commander Rong Lu and court official Li Hongzhang, who propagated the fiction, adopted by the foreigners as a means to save face for the court, that war had never been declared, but that there had been a "joint" effort between Qing rulers and foreigners to suppress rebellion. Thus, in defeat the Boxers were betrayed by Cixi's representatives. Fairbank, Reischauer, and Craig described the peace terms of the so-called Boxer Protocol of September 7, 1901 A.D., that Cixi was forced later to accept:

> It required the execution of 10 high officials . . . and punishment of 100 others; formal apologies; suspension of examinations in 45 cities, half of them in Shansi, to penalize the gentry class; expansion of the Legation Quarter, to be fortified and permanently garrisoned; destruction of some 25 Chinese forts and occupation of a dozen railway posts to ensure foreign access to Peking from the sea; raising of import duties to an actual 5 per cent; and a staggering indemnity of 450 million taels (about 330 million dollars) to be paid from various customs and salt revenues in gold over forty years at interest rates which would more than double the amount.[1]

These conditions would further impede China's indigenous attempts to modernize after Cixi and her court returned to Beijing in January 1902. On a practical level, the Manchu leadership, of which Cixi was a part, could ill afford to train and educate the Chinese people for greater participation in their government, lest they educate them for their own overthrow as an alien dynasty. Hence, the step toward modernization that would have involved greater elements of democracy, popular sovereignty, and direct involvement could never be taken soon enough or convincingly enough by Cixi, who clung to "restoration" of the traditional feudal ways. This proved a tragedy of monumental proportions, necessitating violent revolution to correct and liberate China.

Sun Yat-sen's (1866–1925 A.D.) revolutionary and republican movement was growing abroad and on the periphery of power circles within China. Students returning from Western education overseas, new merchants in the treaty ports, modern soldiers trained with Western weapons all eventually turned against the Qing forces, which were too slow and antiquated. Cixi attempted to reform the public education system in China and abolished the examination system in 1905 A.D. Western learning permeated the school curriculum. A new Ministry of Finance was created. Constitutionalism was discussed, and Cixi promised a "constitutional policy" in 1906 A.D. In August 1908 A.D., the empress dowager moved further toward a nine-year program to move China toward constitutional self-government. But this did not prevent revolution.

In late 1908 A.D., Cixi named as successor to the throne the nephew of the Guangxu Emperor, her grandnephew Puyi (1906–1967; r. 1909–1912 A.D.), assisted by his father, Prince Chun, to act as regent. The next day the Guangxu Emperor died, followed a day later by Cixi. The "Old Buddha," as she was affectionately called in spite of her shortcomings, had ended half a century of power in China. Puyi and the Qing dynasty could not hold back the tide of republican, liberal, Western, and modern ideas, which would sweep Sun Yat-sen's forces to victory in 1911 A.D.

The result would have been the same had Cixi lived. Change had to come to China. Cixi had opened the door to modernization by sheltering foreign encroachment after the Opium Wars. Her Qing government was viewed by revolutionaries and critics as a "defacto foreign court." Her dilemma was how to manage modernization with obsolete dynastic frameworks and institutions. Her legacy remains mixed: a feudal ruler, who guided or misguided China into the twentieth century. She died in her palace of Zhong Nan Hai. She was buried in a tomb in Pu Tuo Valley. Three years after her death, the Qing Dynasty was overturned by the Wuchang uprising led by Sun Yat-Sen's forces.

Song Ruizhi
Trans. Ma Li

Note

1. Fairbank et al., *East Asia: The Modern Transformation.* Houghton-Mifflin Co., Boston, 1965, p. 403.

Sources

"Two Films About the Empress Dowager," Bao Wenqing, *China Reconstructs*, (December 1983), 50–51. Mary Clabaugh Wright, *The Last Stand of Chinese Conservativism The T'ung-chih Restoration, 1862–1874*. Stanford: Stanford University Press, 1957; A.W. Hummel, ed., *Eminent Chinese in the Ching Period 1644–1912*. Washington, D.C.: U.S. Government Printing Office 1943–44, 25–26. Chapter 5 titled "The Chinese Empire," in K.S. Latourette, *A History of the Expansion of Christianity*, vol. 6, *The Great Century in Northern Africa and Asia 1800–1914*. New York: Harper, 1944; Knight Biggerstaff, *The Earlier Modern Government Schools in China*. Ithaca: Cornell University Press, 1961; Paul Hibbert Clyde, *The Far East, A History of the Impact of the West on Eastern Asia*. Englewood Cliffs, N.J.: Prentice Hall, 3rd ed., 1958; Harold M. Vinacke, *A History of the Far East in Modern Times*. New York: Appleton-Century-Crofts, 6th ed., 1961; O. Edmund Clubb, *20th Century China*. New York: Columbia University Press, 1964; J.F. Fairbank, *The United States and China*. Cambridge: Harvard University Press, rev. ed., 1958. Ssu-yu Teng and John K. Fairbank, *China's Response to the West, A Documentary Survey 1839–1923*. Cambridge: Harvard University Press, 1954; C.Y. Hsu, *China's Entrance into the Family of Nations: The Diplomatic Phase, 1856–1880*. Cambridge: Harvard University Press, 1960; Paul A. Cohen, *China and Christianity: The Missionary Movement and the Growth of Chinese Anti-foreignism, 1860–1870*. Cambridge: Harvard University Press, 1963; Victor Purcell, *The Boxer Uprising: A Background Study*. Cambridge, England: Cambridge University Press, 1963; Cheng Chengzhi, *The Story of Ci Xi Finding Favor Twice*. Kunming: Yunnan People's Publishing House, 1981; Zhuan Wei, *Cixi*. Beijing: Zhonghua shuja, 1994; Wan Yi, "Titles of Ci Xi," *Document*, issue 2, 1986, 282; Zhu Jinpu, "About the Death of Dowager Ci Xi," *Journal of the Museum of the Summer Palace*, issue 4, no. 4, 1985, 3; Yu Bingkun, An Investigation of Ci Xi's Family History," *Journal of the Museum of the Summer Palace*, no. 4, 1985, 9; Feng Peilan, "Discussion About Madame Na La's Declaration of War Against Foreign Countries in Gengzi Year." *Journal of Tianjin Education Institute*, no. 2, 1987, 60; Wang Daocheng, "West Dowager Sits Behind the Curtain and Gave Orders," translated by Fang Hong in *Famous Women of Ancient Times and Today*, ed. by *Chinese Woman Magazine*. Hebei: People's Publishing House, 1986, 365–371; "Ci Xi" in *The Dictionary of Famous Women of Hua Shia* (China), Beijing: Hua Shia Publishing House, 1988, translated from Chinese by Lucia P. Ellis; Lily Xiao Hong Lee and A.D. Stefanowska, editors-in-chief, and Clara Wing-chung Ho, Qing period editor, *Biographical Dictionary of Chinese Women, The Qing Period, 1644–1911*. Armonk, N.Y.: M.E. Sharpe, 1998, 362–366; Zhao Er-yi and Yu Bin-Tun, *The Manuscript of History of the Qing Dynasty,* 3rd section. Beijing: The Central China Book Bureau, 8925–8930; Zhi Ji Cheng, *West Empress Dowager*. Beijing: China Publishing House, 11–13, 37, 82, 182, and 202.

Soong Ai-ling (Song Ailing) (1890–1973), Soong Qing-ling (Song Qingling) (1893–1981), and Soong Mei-ling (Song Mei-ling) (1897–) were the daughters of Charles Jones Soong and Ni Guizeng. Sources vary on the history of Charles Soong, whose original Chinese name was Han Jiaoshun. In any case, he went to the United States and there obtained an education as well as converting to Christianity and anglicizing his name.

With the intention of returning to China to spread the faith, he became a missionary. In 1886, he returned to China and spent time in Shanghai and Kunshan. Later, he developed a sideline as a printer and seller of Bibles in Chinese and became financially prosperous from this venture as well as other commercial ventures that followed; some of his wealth was also said to have come from his associations with anti-Manchu secret societies. His newfound wealth enabled him to contribute generously to the revolutionary movement led by a fellow secret society member, Sun Yat-sen. The two men developed a personal friendship, as Soong supported the latter's political activities.

Ni Guizeng, who was introduced to Charles Soong during his missionary days in Shanghai, was descended on her mother's side from Xu Guangqi, a famous scientist in ancient China, and from the Ming dynasty prime minister who had been converted to Catholicism by Matteo Ricci.

Soong Ai-ling, their first child, was followed by Qing-ling (see below) and Mei-ling and three sons, Ziwen (also called T.V. Soong), Ziliang, and Zi'an. All the Soong children were educated in both the Eastern and Western traditions, with a focus on religious strictures. When Ai-ling was only five years old, she was sent to the McTyeire School for Girls in Shanghai. Because she was too young to attend class, she was given special instruction by the principal, Helen Richardson. Her two sisters followed her there one after the other.

Charles Soong wanted all his children to receive an American education. An excellent student, Ai-ling went to the United States to attend college in 1904, when she was sixteen. She was admitted to the Southern Methodist-sponsored Wesleyan College in Macon, Georgia, the first female student in China to go abroad. After a year of tutoring, she started her regular courses, graduating with a bachelor's degree in 1909. Qing-ling and Mei-ling later attended the same college, having arrived in the United States in 1906 for secondary schooling in New Jersey before traveling to Georgia.

Shortly after completing her degree, Soong Ai-ling returned to China. Discarding her Western-style dresses and hats with colorful feathers, she put on the Chinese style dress, or *qipao*, adopted a Chinese hairstyle, and talked in the local dialect. She taught English to some girls who were preparing to go abroad. Assisting her father in underground revolutionary activities to overthrow the Qing dynasty, she soon became Sun Yat-sen's English secretary.

After the Qing rulers were overthrown in 1911, Sun Yat-sen was sworn in as provisional president of the Republic of China in January 1912. Soong Ai-ling and her family were invited to the inauguration. But his term in office proved short-lived. Despite his title, Sun held little authority compared to Yuan Shikai, who held the capital city of Beijing and controlled North China with his armies. After only a year, Sun resigned from office and turned his attentions to developing a democratic ideology.

After the failure of the so-called second revolution in 1913, when an attempt was made to seize power from Yuan Shikai, Sun made no secret of his opposition to Yuan—who ordered his arrest and execution—and fled to Japan; because their association with Sun placed them in danger as well, the Soong family followed him there. While working as Sun's secretary in Tokyo, Ai-ling re-encountered Kong Xiangxi (a descendant of Confucius, also called H.H. Kong), the scion of a wealthy family and now the chief secretary of the Chinese YMCA in Tokyo. She had first met him as a college student while attending a party in New York, shortly after he had received a master's degree from Yale University.

Ai-ling and Xiangxi soon fell in love, and in the spring of 1914, they were married in a church in Japan. On the morning of their wedding day, there was a heavy rain. But when the ceremony was about to start, the rain stopped and the sun came out. Xiangxi said with joy: "This must be a good omen!"

Ai-ling resigned her position as Sun's English secretary to

accompany her husband to his home town in Taigu county, Shanxi province. Qing-ling, who had left the United States in 1913, after completing her bachelor's degree, went to Japan the following year and inherited the job.

Kong Xiangxi took up his post as principal of the American-sponsored elementary school the Renming School, which later developed into a high school with some university courses. Soong Ai-ling became an English teacher there, and later the acting principal. In 1919, when the couple visited the United States, they set up some exchange programs for the school. In years to come, several excellent graduates were allowed to study in the United States, and several American graduates went there to teach.

Ai-ling was very close to her two sisters, but held different attitudes toward their marriages. When Qing-ling eloped with Sun Yat-sen in 1915, Ai-ling and the rest of the family were opposed (see below). By contrast, when Mei-ling married General Chiang Kai-shek, apparently in order to gain political power, Ai-ling fully supported it, both as a love match and as a way for the Chiang and Soong families to cement their influence over the nascent republic.

Kong Xiangxi and Soong Ai-ling benefited a great deal from Mei-ling's marriage. In 1933, H. H. Kong succeeded Soong Zi-wen as president of the central bank and in the same year he became finance minister. While still holding these two positions, he served as deputy prime minister and then prime minister of the Republic of China from the late 1930s until 1945. Although Ai-ling never held an official position in the republican government, she was a powerful figure, like a queen without a crown. She was the only person allowed to address President Chiang without calling him "Mr. President." Through her husband's position, she manipulated the national economy and the financial market from behind the scenes, as well as accumulating wealth for herself.

Soong Ai-ling made her husband the richest person in China. There are no statistics detailing Kong's wealth, but at least in the 1940s, he owned millions of dollars worth of real estate in Shanghai, such as hotels, department-store buildings, and parks. Moreover, he personally controlled the nation's four largest banks as well as some small banks, auto companies, and some big shopping markets. Hence Soong Ai-ling was recognized as one of the two richest women in China; the other one was her sister Mei-ling.

In 1937, when the anti-Japanese war broke out, the Chinese Communist Party and the Nationalist Party (Guomindang) agreed to work together to fight Japan. The three Soong sisters, after ten years separation, joined forces in one cause. Soong Ai-ling devoted herself to social work, such as helping wounded soldiers, refugees, and orphans. She donated five ambulances and thirty-seven trucks to the army in Shanghai and the air force and ordered five hundred leather uniforms for the airplane pilots. Working with the Christian Girls' Association, she set up two liaison centers to help the refugees find employment.

After the Japanese army occupied Nanjing and Wuhan, the three Soong sisters moved to Hong Kong. There Soong Ai-ling acted as the chairperson of the Association to Aid Wounded Soldiers, while Qing-ling started the China Defense League. In 1940, the three sisters returned to Chongqing in Sichuan province (the stronghold of Chiang Kai-shek) and established the Chinese Industrial Association. Their purpose was to explore more opportunities for people through setting up various small factories for weaving, sewing, and making handicrafts. It made good use of local resources and aided war-stricken people to find jobs.

During the difficult war period, the three sisters frequented schools, hospitals, orphanages, and even air raid shelters. The Chinese people will long retain the image of the three Soong sisters traveling on a simple raft along a river, walking among the refugees, and comforting the war-torn communities. Their behavior inspired the Chinese people to unite and fight against the Japanese.

On the eve of the Allied victory in World War II, Kong Xiangxi was forced to resign his positions in the Nationalist government because of financial dislocations which had destabilized the *yuan* (Chinese money system) which aroused public indignation. After that point, he never again held any important government position. The couple migrated to the United States in 1948, and maintained family connections. Kong Xiangxi died in 1967, and his wife followed him in October 1973.

Zhang Chenshu

Sources:

Kong Xiangxi qirenqishi (Beijing: Zhongguo wenshi chubanshe, 1988); Luobi Youenson, Songshi san jiemei (Beijing: Shijie zhishi chubanshe, 1988); Xing Muxuan Deng, *Diyi Furen—Soong Mei-ling xiezheng* (Hong Kong: Xianggang haixia wenhua shiye gongsi, 1987); Li Heng, *Soong Mei-ling zhuan* (Hong Kong: Xianggang haixia wenhua chubanshe, 1986).

Soong Qing-ling (1893–1981), a great patriot, democrat, and internationalist known throughout the world, was for a time honorary president of the People's Republic of China. An early supporter of Sun Yat-sen, she became his wife and at the end of her life finally joined the Chinese Communist Party. In many respects her life paralleled China's changing political situation after the democratic revolution of 1911 and the Communist revolution of 1949.

The second daughter of Charles Soong and Ni Guizeng (see Song Ai-ling), Soong Qing-ling received her early education at the McTyeire School for Girls in Shanghai; one of her favorite subjects was English. In 1908, she and her younger sister, Meiling, went to the United States to study literature at Wesleyan College, run by the Southern Methodist Church in Macon, Georgia.

After the 1911 revolution, Sun Yat-sen set up a provisional government in Nanjing. When Qing-ling, who had respected and admired Sun Yat-sen since childhood, heard the news from her father, she wrote ''The Great Event of the Twentieth Century'' for the college newspaper. In 1913, she graduated with a bachelor of arts degree. That August, she left the United States for home via Japan, where her parents and Sun Yat-sen were taking refuge after the failure of the second revolution. At that time, her older sister, Ai-ling, who was working as Sun's secretary, quit to accompany her husband, Kong Xiangxi, returning to China. Thus Qing-ling inherited the job and began her revolutionary career.

She helped Sun with his daily routine, handling secret letters, preparing speeches, drafting telegraphs, and getting in touch with revolutionaries all over China and Asia. The relationship between Qing-ling and Sun Yat-sen grew into more than friendship. Charles Soong felt that, as a someone who had been his close friend and an uncle to his children, Sun was betraying his trust by pursuing a romantic relationship. Both Soong parents objected since Sun was many years older than Qing-ling and, even more serious, was married at the time their relationship turned to romance. Against her family's wishes and the advice of friends, on October 26, 1915, Qing-ling married him in Tokyo.

Afterward, she accompanied her husband on trips between Shanghai and Guangzhou, defending the country against Yuan Shikai, who held greater control over the country because of his military strength (until Yuan's death in 1916, when Sun regained leadership). When the May Fourth movement began in 1919, Soong demonstrated her indignation over the warlords' arrests of students and supported patriotic causes. The May 4, 1919 demonstrations of students from Peking's universities protested the Versailles Treaty's terms which had given Japan control over Shandong. On June 16, 1922, the commander-in-chief of the Guangdong army turned against Sun Yat-sen and bombarded the presidential mansion, the situation became critical. Qing-ling refused to leave without her husband, insisting, "China can do without me, but not without you." She stayed in the presidential mansion as a decoy and, though pregnant, did not leave until she received the signal that Sun had been safely evacuated, and then she, escorted by guards, broke through the encirclement, escaped from the danger, and was reunited with her husband on the *Yongfeng* warship moored at Huangpu harbor. Because of her anxiety and exhaustion, she suffered a miscarriage and was unable to bear any more children.

During Sun's reshuffle of the Guomindang government, Qing-ling worked actively and effectively in the consultations on co-operation between him and representatives of the Chinese Communist Party, including Li Dazhao, and during his conversations with the special envoys such as Adolf Joffe and others sent by Lenin from the Soviet Union. Together with Liberals Liao Zhongkai, He Xiangnin, Liu Yazi, and others, she led a fierce struggle against the right wing of the Guomindang which wanted to expel the Communist members. At the first national party congress of the Guomindang in 1924, Qing-ling supported Sun Yat-sen's three policies: alliance with Russia, alliance with the Communist Party, and assistance to the peasants and workers. They both attended the memorial in Guangzhou to mourn the death of Lenin that year.

General Feng Yuxiang, a warlord in the north, invited the couple to meet with him when they traveled north to Beijing via Hong Kong, Shanghai, Japan, and Tianjin. In Japan, Qing-ling gave a speech on women's liberation at the invitation of Kobe College for Girls. At the end of December 1924, Sun arrived in Beijing; he died of liver cancer on March 12, 1925. In his will, he wrote: "I have devoted my whole life to the affairs of the state, and never cared about family property." He left Qing-ling all his books, clothes, and household items—and his legacy. She carried on with his unfinished revolutionary struggle.

In October 1925, Soong returned to Shanghai and expressed her firm support of the May Thirtieth workers' movement (Chinese workers' demonstrating against Japanese-owned textile mills and their policies during a strike) and workers' strikes breaking out in Guangzhou and Hong Kong. Having returned to Guangzhou, Qing-ling in January 1926 attended the second national party congress of the Guomindang and was one of the members of the Examination Committee reviewing reports on women's issues. Elected a member of the party central committee and the chair of the Women's Department, she firmly supported her late husband's most cherished principles—nationalism, democracy, and the people's livelihood.

After the army of Chiang Kai-shek (the Northern Expeditionary Army) captured Wuhan, the central committee of the Guomindang decided to move its headquarters there. As a member of this committee, Qing-ling was sent there and was included in the membership of a provisional joint committee, the supreme organ of the party, and the government, which was formed on

December 13. In February 1927, she ran a women's political training institute in Wuhun to train women cadres. She invited many Communists to teach at that institute and gave lectures herself, calling on women to plunge into the revolution (this was at a time when the CCP members could also join the Guomindang party).

But in April 1927, Chiang Kai-shek, leader of the Guomindang army, worked towards driving the Communists from the Guomindang party. Mei-ling still wanted to marry him, against Qing-ling's advice. Qing-ling also tried to persuade their brother Ziwen to join the revolutionary cause, but failed. When Chiang launched a coup d'Ètat in April of that year, Qing-ling denounced it, as did many members of the Guomindang's left wing and some Chinese Communists. In July, the Guomindang government, now led by Wang Jingwei, launched another military coup in Wuhan. Qing-ling refused to attend their meeting to break with the Communists. She denounced their betrayal of Sun Yat-sen's ideas and ideals and broke relations with them.

Qing-ling secretly left for Moscow in late August 1927 in fulfillment of one of her late husband's wishes. In the Soviet Union, she met with friends, made speeches and published many statements, declarations, and articles renouncing the Guomindang. She was the frequent guest of Kalinin, chairman of the Central Executive Committee of the Soviet Union. Together with political leaders Maxim Gorky, Roman Roland, and others, Qing-ling initiated and organized the Anti-Imperialist League; she attended its opening ceremony in Belgium in December 1927 and was elected honorary chairman.

In May 1929, Soong returned to China via Berlin. Chiang Kai-shek attempted to trick her into continuing to work with the Guomindang and make up with him, but she found him out. She issued a statement on her way home: "I cannot participate directly or indirectly in the work of the Guomindang until its policies are in complete conformity with the basic principles of the late Dr. Sun Yat-sen." On May 26, Soong Qing-ling, Sun Ke (Sun's son by his first wife), and others attended the burial of Sun Yat-sen's coffin, followed, on June 1, by a state funeral, after which she left for Shanghai. Chiang Kai-shek sent many of his men to persuade her to work for the Guomindang and live in Nanjing. She refused them all and drew a clear demarcation with the Guomindang, which in her mind had tarnished China.

Qing-ling traveled to Europe again in 1930, continuing her participation in international movements against imperialism and for peace. She returned to Shanghai in July 1931, after the death of Ni Guizeng. Late that year, Chiang Kai-shek murdered the democratic fighter Deng Yanda. Soong at this time was trying to rescue Deng, and she was so angry at the news that she issued a declaration condemning Chiang's actions. After fighting broke out against Japan, Soong raised money and set up a hospital for the wounded soldiers to support the Guomindang's Nineteenth Route Army and tried to arouse resistance against Japanese aggression. In December, with writers/intellectuals Lu Xun, Cai Yuanpei, and Yang Xingfo, she organized the China League for Civil Rights to oppose Chiang's violence and the activities of secret agents opposed to the Communists. The League protected and rescued many Communists, patriotic democrats such as Cheng Geng, Liao Chengzhi, and Xu Deheng, as well as foreign anti-imperialists. The Guomindang feared the League and determined to get rid of it. It accused the League of being an illegal organization, blacklisted its members, and sent threatening letters. The secretary general of the League, Yang Xingfo, was assassinated in Shanghai, for which the Guomindang was believed responsible. Nevertheless, Qing-ling declared that she would join her comrades-in-arms in continuing her struggle.

Soong supported the Chinese Communist Party's proposal of a united front against Japan. On April 20, 1934, the Six-Point Program for Resisting Japan and Saving the Nation was published, signed by Soong Qing-ling and others in the name of the Preparatory Committee of the Self-Defense Committee of Chinese National Army. And in the same year, Soong and others responded to the Chinese Communist Party's call in the August 1 Declaration, calling on the Chinese people to unite to resist Japanese aggression. In November, the Guomindang, insisting on the policy of "first pacification, then resistance," arrested the leaders of the All-China Federation of National Salvation Associations, Shen Junru and six others, who demanded that the Guomindang government stop the civil war and establish a unified government of resistance against Japan. Soong Qing-ling denounced the arrest and asked the court to imprison her with "the seven champions" who were guilty only of the "crime of patriotism." This placed the Guomindang in a most embarrassing position.

In December 1936, young Marshal Zhang Xueliang, a leader and member of Chiang's Guomindang army in Xian kidnapped Chiang Kai-shek, an event that became known as the Xian incident; Chiang was finally released after agreeing to cooperation between the Nationalists and the Communists to confront the Japanese threat. This created a "united front" between Chiang's forces and the CCP. This agreement was negotiated by Zhou Enlai.

In February 1937, at the third plenary session of the Guomindang Central Committee, Soong, along with political supporters Feng Yuxiang, He Xiangning, and ten others, proposed a law to restore Sun Yat-sen's three great policies—alliance with the Soviet Union, cooperation with the Chinese Communist Party, and assistance to the peasants and workers.

In 1937, in the face of increasing Japanese encroachment, Soong actively worked to unite people and resist the invasion. After the fall of Shanghai, she left the city for Guangzhou and then Hong Kong. In June 1938, in Hong Kong, she initiated and organized the China Defense League. Through this League, she told overseas Chinese and others about the resistance to Japanese aggression, the people's army, and anti-Japanese base areas; she also collected medical and other supplies from around the world and introduced medical teams organized by foreigners who came to help China.

In 1941, Chiang Kai-shek encircled and attacked the Communist-led New Fourth Army. Soong immediately wrote to him, accusing him of undermining the unity and resistance against the Japanese and demanding that he stop using armed forces to attack the Communist Party. At the same time, she published newspaper articles exposing the Guomindang's efforts to undermine the unified front and criticizing her brother Ziwen, the president of the China Defense League, for his withdrawal from the League.

After Japan attacked Hong Kong, Qing-ling did not leave for Chongqing until the last plane took off, six hours before the arrival of Japanese troops. Upon arrival at Chongqing, she received a warm welcome from those of like mind, but her presence worried Chiang Kai-shek. Despite close surveillance by Guomindang agents, she rallied her forces, resumed the work of the China Defense League, together with political writers George Hatem, Agnes Smedley, Edgar Snow, and other foreigners, and tried to get in touch with organizations abroad to gain support. They organized benefit performances and sports meets to collect supplies for the disaster areas and liberated areas for their resistance against Japan.

In 1945, when the Pacific war ended in victory for the Allies, including China, Qing-ling returned to Shanghai. Changing the name of the China Defense League to the China Welfare League, she also made a long-term plan for the league and sent substantial medical suppliers to the liberated areas. Soong Qing-ling also led the league in a struggle against the Relief Headquarters of the Guomindang administration. The China Welfare League regarded its own relief and welfare work as a part of the liberation cause of the Chinese people. It persistently supported democratic movements, supported liberated areas, collected large quantities of material goods, and money for the People's Liberation Army.

In 1948, some members of the Guomindang, including Li Jishen, He Xiangning, and Feng Yuxiang, set up the Revolutionary Committee of the Chinese Guomindang in Hong Kong. They unanimously elected Soong Qing-ling as its chairman. At the time, she was in Shanghai and although she supported the establishment of the committee, she thought it would be "more beneficial for me to participate in the revolutionary activities in the present status than that in the Revolutionary Committee of the Chinese Guomindang." But she was still named its honorary chairman.

In 1949, Chiang Kai-shek offered his retirement from the presidency, and Li Zongren became acting president. Li wanted to retain the southeast half of the country and planned to split the government of the country with the Yangzi river as a dividing line. He wrote to Soong Qing-ling, asking her to lead the government, leading to rumors that Soong would serve in the Guomindang government. Soong refused Li's request and issued a statement in the name of the China Welfare League that the rumors were groundless. She continued to be under the careful watch of Guomindang agents, as she witnessed the frequent arrests of communists and progressives.

On April 27, 1949, Shanghai came under Communist rule, but the city was in chaos. Former governor of Fujian and Zhejiang militarist Chen Yi sent a regiment of soldiers to guard Soong's mansion. On July 1, she gave a speech to celebrate the birthday of the CCP.

After Beijing fell to Communist forces, Soong Qing-ling, at the invitation of the Chinese Communist Party Central Committee, left Shanghai for Beijing to attend the first plenary session of the Chinese People's Political Consultative Conference (CPPCC) held as Mao Zedong was anticipating final victories. When the People's Republic of China was founded in October, she was made a vice-chairman of the central people's government, vice-chairman of the CPPCC, vice-chairman of the Standing Committee of the National People's Congress, and vice-chairman of the People's Republic of China. In these capacities she visited the Soviet Union, India, Burma, Pakistan, Indonesia, and Ceylon. In 1957, she accompanied Chairman Mao Zedong to a meeting in Moscow of representatives of the Communist and workers' parties. Chairman Mao Zedong, premier of the state council and foreign minister, Zhou Enlai, head of state Liu Shaoqi, and others often sought her views on major international and domestic issues and developed a deep friendship. Soong Qing-ling was particularly interested in issues affecting women and children's health. She presided over the work of the People's Relief Administration of China and the Red Cross of China.

She was elected a leading member of the World Peace Council in 1950 and chairman of the Peace Liaison Committee of the Asian and Pacific Regions in 1952. Soong Qing-ling was awarded the Stalin Peace Prize in 1950 and in 1981 and received an honorary law degree from the University of Victoria in British Columbia, Canada.

In May 1981, Soong Qing-ling fell ill with lymphocytic leukemia. At this juncture she asked to join the Chinese Communist Party several times. On May 15, the Politburo of the Central Committee accepted her as a full member of the Chinese Communist Party, and the next day the Standing Committee of the National People's Congress conferred on her the title of honorary president of the People's Republic of China.

A short two weeks later, Soong Qing-ling died in Beijing. The CCP Central Committee, the Standing Committee of the National People's Congress, and the State Council honored her with a state funeral. On June 4, her ashes were buried ceremoniously in the Soong family plot at Wanguo cemetery in Shanghai.

Soong Qing-ling remembered with great affection the old friends who had supported Sun Yat-sen in the early years and showed deep concern over the future of Taiwan. It was her great hope that the Guomindang and the Communist Party would hold peace talks as a prelude to reunification. For all these and more, she was respected and loved by the Chinese people throughout the country and respected throughout the world as one of the greatest women of the twentieth century.

Wu Dehua and Barbara Bennett Peterson
Fu Huisheng, trans.

Sources:

Jonathan D. Spense, *The Search for Modern China*, W. W. Norton, New York, 1999; Yansheng Ma Lum and Raymond Mun Kong Lum, *Sun Yat-sen in Hawaii: Activities and Supporters*, Hawaii Chinese History Center, 1999.

Anna Louise Strong (1885–1970) was a noted American writer and journalist who earned international fame for her unyielding pursuit of truth and firm support for progressive causes, especially in China. Anna Louise Strong was born in Friend, Nebraska, and died of a heart attack in Beijing, after a significant career to aid her adopted country. She was the eldest of three children (two daughters and a son) of a congregational minister, Sydney Dix Strong, and Ruth (Tracy) Strong. Because of her father's occupation, her family made frequent moves from one place to another—Mount Vernon, Ohio, in 1887, Cincinnati in 1891, Europe in 1896, and Oak Park, Illinois, in 1897. Strong—

the beautiful "angel" of the family—was discovered in primary school to be very bright.

Both Sydney and Ruth Strong were descendants of U.S. settlers in the 1660s, and Anna Louise inherited their pioneer spirit. She attended public and private schools and completed education through the eighth grade in four years. When her father became the pastor of an Oak Park church in 1897, she attended high school there and graduated at age fifteen. She also studied in France and Switzerland while Sidney Strong worked there. Strong attended Oberlin College in 1902 but transferred to Bryn Mawr in 1903 at her mother's request. Her mother died of typhoid fever on her way back to the United States from Africa, where she contracted the fatal disease. Strong's religious beliefs became stronger after her mother's death, and she wanted to build enthusiastic and firm ties with other people, but not rely on anyone.

Anna Louise returned to Oberlin in 1904 and received her B.A. in 1905. She entered the graduate school of the University of Chicago in March 1906 and received her Ph.D. in philosophy in 1908 after defending her dissertation, "The Psychology of Prayer."

After graduation, she went to Seattle to assist her father in organizing a successful "know your city" civic program. She also engaged in some similar programs in other northwestern cities. All these activities made Strong very popular with welfare workers, which resulted in more invitations to private homes and parties. The Russell Sage Foundation invited her to serve as an assistant director of the New York Welfare Exhibit in 1911. In late May 1914, because of her increasing popularity, Strong was invited to hold conferences on child welfare in Dublin and she distinguished herself there.

While working in Kansas City, she met Roger Baldwin. They fell in love, but did not marry because of her father's strong opposition and because of religious differences. Nevertheless, the conferences in Kansas City were successful.

After finishing her last mission in the region in 1916, Strong resigned from the National Children's Committee. She went to Seattle and was elected to the Seattle School Board. While in Seattle, Strong witnessed a famous strike by dock workers and metal workers. She supported the strike and wrote reports about it. A turning point of her life came in August 1921, when she was sent to Moscow as a journalist and decided to make her second home there, remaining until 1949. During her stay, she met some famous Soviet leaders, such as Stalin and Trotsky, whom she came to admire. In support of the Soviet revolution, Strong made regular trips to the United States to raise money. In 1932, Strong married Joel Shubin, a member of the Communist Party of the Soviet Union and editor of the Moscow Peasant's Gazette.

As a journalist, she visited collective farms, remote plateaus, and the southern frontier, making some of these visits alone, riding on horseback. Wherever she went, she took an interest in the women's movement, trade unionists' suffering, and the Soviet revolution. During the years she was resident in Moscow, she made six trips to China, the first in 1925. Arriving in Guangzhou by way of Hong Kong, she was the first Western journalist allowed to enter that city, which was then in the throes of a labor strike—the subject of her first reports from China. During her first visit, in addition to reporting, she also attended women's meetings and gave lectures on the Soviet revolution.

Strong's second trip to China was in March 1927. Her visits to Shanghai, Wuhan, and the surrounding countryside raised her awareness of the conditions there for Chinese Communists, whose annihilation had been ordered by Chiang Kai-shek. At the request of Soong Qing-ling, she went to Wuhan, then under Communist control, and was asked to work for the People's *Tribune*. Strong witnessed and reported on the state of the peasant movement.

During the anti-Japanese resistance war (1937–1945), Strong made two trips to China. In 1937, she went to the revolutionary base area of Shanxi, where she met with important military leaders including Zhu De, the chief commander of the Red Army, He Long, Liu Bocheng, Lin Biao, and Peng Dehuai. She also held talks with Zhou Enlai and his wife, Deng Yingchao, as well as Chiang Kai-shek and his wife, Soong Mei-ling. Thus the first reports to the United States from China came from Anna Louise Strong.

In December 1940, Strong returned to China once again.

Meeting with her in Chongqing, Zhou Enlai explained in detail the military conflict between Chiang's generals and the Communist-led troops and asked Strong to tell the West the situation, a story Strong was glad to report.

Two years later, she lost her husband, a loss that took some years to absorb.

Then, at the age of sixty-one, Strong made yet a fifth visit to China in July 1946, this time traveling to Yan'an. During this visit she lived in a comfortable cave and met many revolutionary leaders, as well as holding an important interview with Mao Zedong in which he first coined the phrase "paper tiger."

The ten years after she left Yan'an were the most difficult of her life. In February 1949 she was arrested in Moscow on charges of spying just as she was about to leave on yet another trip to China. She was deported to the United States and not allowed to leave. In September 1958, when she was seventy-two, she succeeded in arranging one more trip to China after a three-year struggle with the U.S. government for a passport. From then until her death in 1970, she remained in Beijing, as an old friend of the Chinese people.

Strong was treated well by the Chinese government. She had a comfortable and peaceful life and traveled widely. In 1962 she began to write her *Letters from China*, a well-received series of reports. An outstanding journalist, Anna Louise Strong devoted her life to just causes. Aside from the Soviet Union and China, she also visited Mexico, Britain, France, Germany, Poland, Spain, Yugoslavia, Laos, and Vietnam. Her objective reporting and straightforward writing style earned her great popularity among the people of China and elsewhere around the world.

Among Strong's works are *China's Millions* (originally published New York: Coward-McCann, 1928; Beijing: New World, 1965), *Red Star in Samarkand* (New York: Coward-McCann, 1929), *Road to the Grey Pamir* (Boston: Little, Brown & Company, 1931), *I Changed Worlds* (Seattle: [rev. ed. 1979] Feal Press, 1935), *I Saw the New Poland* (Boston: Little, Brown and Company, 1946), *The Chinese Conquer China* (Garden City, New York: Doubleday, 1949), *Today* (Montrose, Calif., magazine or periodical, 1950–56), *When Serfs Stood Up in Tibet* (originally published 1959; Beijing: New World, 1965), and *Let-*

ters from China (Beijing: New World, 1962–65). Other publications by Strong include *Cash and Violence in Laos* (Beijing: New World, 1961); *Why I Came to China at the Age of 72* (Beijing: Commercial Press, 1965); *The Rise of the Chinese People's Communes* (Beijing: New World, 1959); *Tibetan Interviews* (Beijing: New World, 1959).

Wang Jiyu

Sources:

Anna Louise Strong's books are the best sources for her ideas and contributions on China; Jonathan D. Spence, *The Search for Modern China*, 2nd ed., W. W. Norton & Company, New York, 1999, offers an excellent historical background.

Ding Ling (1904–1986) was the pen name of a writer who wrote passionately about women's involvement in the May Fourth movement in 1919 in which Peking University students had demonstrated against the Treaty of Versailles and about life as an intellectual during China's revolutionary struggles. Her best-selling novel was the autobiographical *Muqin* (Mother). Originally named Jiang Binzhi, she was born in Lingli county, Hunan province. Her father, Jiang Yulan, was from a land-owning family that included some imperial officials; he studied abroad in Japan and died when Ding Ling was four years old. Her mother, Yu Manzheng, worked in Changde while raising her as a single parent. Ding Ling attended a primary school in Changde that had been established by her mother.

The patriotism and intellectual fervor of the May Fourth movement, which began when she was fifteen, touched and molded her life forever. Like many young women, she and her friends Wang Jianhong and Wang Yizhi plunged into the revolutionary mainstream and called for women's liberation. She taught at a night school organized by these two women to educate the poor and then decided to advance her career through more education. With her mother's approval, Ding Ling went to Changsha to study at the Zhounan Girl's Middle School. She was inspired by the revolutionary ardor that had spread to Changsha and by the ideology of the new Marxist and Socialists ideas as analytical tools to aid China's development.

By 1915 there were approximately 4 million students attending 120,000 government schools, including universities. By 1919 half a million more were attending Catholic and Protestant schools. In short, the students—the new literati class—were becoming a force to be reckoned with. In 1915, the first women's university had opened, Jinling College, in Nanjing. Private schools were springing up all over China to grant women the education previously denied them. Intellectuals saw themselves as the leaders and saviors of the nation. Ding Ling joined this milieu and in it became a guiding force for women.

This new role for the students and the development of the New Culture movement after 1919 grew out of the students' new opportunities for contact with foreigners and for study abroad.

Before 1911, about two-fifths of the Chinese students who studied abroad went to Japan, but afterward about a third went to the United States for their education. They began to go to the United States in larger numbers because in 1908 the United States had remitted about $12 million of its share of the indemnity demanded after the Boxer Rebellion and earmarked these funds to establish Qinghua College in Beijing; from here many students went to the United States for advanced study. The United States returned the remaining third of the Boxer indemnity in installments to China to be used to establish and sustain the China Foundation for the Promotion of Education and Culture in 1924. Other students desiring to study abroad went to France, which recruited Chinese student-contract laborers on a work-study basis during the manpower shortage of World War I, especially during the years 1914 to 1918. In France, socialism was an increasingly popular doctrine, and many Chinese students first became exposed to the writings of Karl Marx there, before the creation of the Soviet Union in 1917.

At home, in China, there was a strong intellectual vanguard at Peking University, which was seen as the apex of the state education system. Its president, Cai Yuanpei, who had been a member of Sun Yat-sen's Revolutionary Alliance, then went abroad to study in Germany and France, and then returned to China, gathered around him the finest minds in China. He served first Sun Yat-sen and then Yuan Shikai as education minister in the Republican government. Cai Yuanpei encouraged open discussion of every issue and topic within the Peking University intellectual community, encouraging the professors and students to enter into the flow of politics and goals. In 1912 he called for "education above politics . . . beyond political control."

This vision of openness and freedom of dissent and discussion was short-lived, as Yuan Shikai's authoritarian rule ended Sun's dream of a republican China under parliamentary law.

The students and intellectuals of China continued to turn their eyes toward Peking University as the vanguard of new ideas and stimulus for constructive changes. After the death of Yuan Shikai in 1916, the central government's weakness and factionalism among competing warlords permitted freedom of thought throughout China's intellectual community in seeking solutions to the country's problems.

Several scholars were outstanding at the University, including Chen Duxiu (1879–1942), who advocated "Liberty, Equality, and Fraternity," the principles of freedom of the French Revolution, and was anti-Confucian because of his belief that Confucian teachings had led to the suppression of commerce and wealth and contributed to the disdain for women in China. The founder of *Xin qingnian* (New Youth) magazine—written in the new Chinese vernacular—in 1915, he called upon the youth of China to be "independent, not servile . . . progressive, not conservative, . . . dynamic, not passive . . . cosmopolitan, not isolationist, . . . utilitarian, not empty and very formalistic . . . scientific, not merely imaginative." He became the champion of Western values in China: individualism, utilitarianism, equality, and dynamism. Ding Ling and other young people in her age group read his words and dreamed of attending Peking University, where all the intellectual ferment was being generated.

The literary revolution influenced both the style and the content of Ding Ling's writing, which began to focus on the realistic and the personal. The new intellectual school at Peking University also encouraged "revolutionary" writing of "protest," a theme in which Ding Ling would excel.

During the 1920s, Ding Ling was influenced by Alphonse Daudet's *La dernier leÁon* (The Last Class), a short story which appeared in *The Works of Daudet* (1929). The story reinforced the significance of learning and appreciating one's own culture and its historical contributions. While she was based in Changsha, some of her writings were published in the *Xiangjiang Daily*. Attracted by literary developments in Shanghai, Ding Ling took up residence there in 1921 and enrolled at the People's Girls' School, administered by the Communist Party. Here she met many Party leaders, including Li Da, Qu Qiubai, and Chen Duxiu, who were active in the New Culture movement. Ding Ling was still searching for her own ideology amid the many ideas then circulating in China; she did not join the Communist Party. She ardently wanted to enroll at Peking University, but was not accepted. Nonetheless she persisted in Beijing, working at odd jobs, studying painting, and hoping to secure a place at the university in the future.

In 1925 she met Hu Yepin, a young poet who was an apprentice at a jewelry shop. He was brave, enthusiastic, strong, and optimistic, but poor. Their literary interests blended well, and so did their ambitions. In 1928 Ding Ling and Hu Yepin settled in Shanghai, which was also home to the League of Left-Wing Writers, organized by Lu Xun and his friend the novelist Mao Dun and some fifty other writers supportive of the Communist cause although they were not necessarily Communists, but rather nationalists.

Ding Ling was greatly influenced by Lu Xun, who translated books on social realism from Europe into Chinese and who was among those writers now employing the vernacular in their writings rather than formalized classical language and style. She was also influenced by Mao Dun, who in 1928 wrote *Shi* (The Eclipse), in which he illustrated the disparities between the dreams of total emancipation among his young heroines and the realities they experienced during the Northern Expedition (an attempt to recapture the northern parts of China from warlordism). Ding Ling further developed several of Man Dun's important themes of love, duty, ambition, and social responsibility.

During the Nationalists' attempt to exterminate the Communists in 1928, Ding Ling was in anguish over the death of her many friends: She wrote, "Many people whom I respected died, some persisted in hardship, some friends vacillated." That year she published *In the Dark*, a collection of short stories revealing her own thoughts in a "dark" time in the shadow of fear and terror. Over the next two years, she published "Zisha" (Suicide) and "Yi ge nuxing" (A Woman)—stories ridiculing contemporary Chinese society and expressing the disappointments felt by an impassioned woman committed to freedom, democracy, and women's equality. In "A Woman" she especially expressed spite for society and revealed "an unyielding, lonely soul."

"Shafei nushi de riji" (Miss Sophie's Diary) also won her wide acclaim. In a review, Mao Dun took notice of her: "Miss Sophie is a uniquely new and rebellious woman. She is filled with the suffering and pain of the times. Miss Sophie is an individual who rebels against outdated ethical codes. She pursues a happy and exciting life: she loves but also despises her lover, who is timid and torn by conflicts. Miss Sophie is representative of the young Chinese woman who faces contradictions in love. The male lover here is in fact only a form, the essence of the story in the internal contradictions faced by intellectual women who seek the dignity and value of humanity, and especially of women." Peking University, which had once rejected her, now turned its eyes to her, through its scholar Mao Dun, in admiration and affection.

In 1931 Ding Ling and Hu Yepin had a son. But after her work began to receive recognition, Hu Yepin was captured by the Guomindang, along with four other members of the League of Left-Wing Writers, and put to death that same year.

Ding Ling placed her three-month-old son in the care of her mother for his protection and returned to Shanghai so that she could attend to her revolutionary activities and writings. In 1932 she joined the Communist Party and published *Shui* (The Flood), which marked a turning point in her career. She now identified with the suffering peasants and their plight in the civil war then raging in China, rather than the plight of the intellectuals in the cities, which had previously concerned her. Her writings extolled communism as the solution for China's problems, styled in terms of Karl Marx's dialectical materialism.

While writing her magnum opus, *Mother*, in 1933, she was

arrested by the Guomindang. All her papers and files were confiscated. She was first placed in prison, then held under house
arrest, from which she escaped in 1936, fleeing to the protection
of the Communist revolutionary forces based in Shaanxi province. She worked alongside Mao Zedong and Zhou Enlai there
and traveled about the countryside talking to the peasants, gathering information for her novels, which inspired people to switch
allegiance from the Guomindang to the Communist Party.

In 1931, Ding Ling began to believe that the Communists held
the moral high ground, compared to the Guomindang, which
was viewed as a pawn in the hands of the foreign interests and
increasingly self-serving and corrupt, unaware of or uncon-
cerned with the masses of China. Ding Ling's popularity began
to grow, based—like the appeal of the Communist Party—on
the hard-won grass-roots contacts and aid programs among peasants in the countryside. Her stories and novels "Yi ke wei chu
tang de qiangdan" (The Unfired Bullet), "Wo zai Xiacun de
shihou" (When I Was in Xia Village), and *Taiyang zhao zai
Sanggan he shang* (The Sun Shines Over the Sanggan River)
all reflect these themes. *The Sun Shines Over the Sanggan River,*
which won the Stalin prize for literature in 1951, describes the
life of Chinese farmers during land reform in the countryside
near the Sanggan river. Like all her works, it was written in
the vernacular language so that everyone literate could read her
message.

After the Communist victory in 1949, and the creation of a
new China, Ding Ling took the lead in promoting literacy among
women. She was appointed to the posts of vice-chairman of the
Union of Chinese Writers and chief administrator of the Central
Institute of Literature. In recognition of her writings of the 1930s
and 1940s to bring the Communists to power, she was made a
deputy to the new legislature, the National People's Congress,
and a member of the National Committee of the Chinese People's Political Consultative Conference. Ding Ling stood at the
head of a group of older female authors who joined the Federation of Chinese Writers, including Cao Ming, Bai Wei, Ge Qin,
Bai Lang, and Ceng Ke. This cohort of writers set the pace for
the next generation. Although their education had been interrupted by the anti-Japanese resistance war and the civil war be-

tween the Guomindang and the Communist Party, they wrote passionately about the causes they believed in: equality for women, freedom, and democracy.

In addition to her literary activities, Ding Ling worked actively during this period for world peace, traveling to various countries to develop friendship between the people of China and those of other countries. In 1949, she also became director of the Chinese Women's Association.

During the anti-rightist campaigns of the 1950s, she was unfairly labeled a "rightist" (a reactionary). She was accused after the Hundred Flowers Campaign which had brought forth social criticism within the party. Some called her a traitor and a right-wing extremist, believing she was no longer a good Communist. All of this she denied, but was nevertheless sent to Heilongjiang province in Northeast China to work on a farm. Her books were banned, but she continued writing while working in the countryside.

In 1970, during the Cultural Revolution, she and her husband, Chen Ming, a screenplay writer and a Communist Party member, came under further suspicion and were imprisoned. Ding Ling and her husband spent five years in jail, and her health declined. She tried to regain her stamina by playing "basketball" in her cell with a homemade ball.

Ding Ling and Chen Ming were released in 1975 and took up residence in the countryside of Shaanxi province. Thousands of pages of her work had been destroyed during the Cultural Revolution, but now, her spirit unbroken, she once again took up her pen. Four years later, they returned to Beijing, where the Central Committee of the Communist Party announced their rehabilitation. Ding Ling's membership in the Chinese People's Political Consultative Conference was restored, as was her standing as a model for young members of the Federation of Chinese Writers, such as Ru Zhijuan, Wei Junyi, Yang Mo, Yuan Jing, Li Nei, Han Zi, Liu Zhen, and Bai Lang. This younger generation was less politically oriented than the earlier one. Whereas Ding Ling's generation had focused on the hardship, terror, deprivation, and humiliation of war, punctuated by poverty and fear, the younger writers were more concerned with the personal themes of love and marriage.

Ever active in advancing Chinese literature, in the fall of 1984, Ding Ling, with her friend Shu Qun, introduced a new journal—*China*. A brilliant and sensitive writer who tried to tell the world about the true China and the sufferings first of intellectuals and later of peasants in farming and New China, Ding Ling in many ways had been a "mother" to the New China, giving birth to a new sensitivity in literature and gaining world renown.

Barbara Bennett Peterson

Sources:

Yang Guixin, "Veteran Writer Ding Ling," *Women in China*, March 1986; "Ding Ling," in *Famous Women of Ancient Times and Today*, trans. Fang Hong and ed. *Women of China* (Beijing: Hebei People's Publishing House, 1986); *Dictionary of Famous Women in China* (Beijing: Huaxia, 1988).

Ming and Qing Sources

Ah Yuan. "Wang Cong'er-Leader of Peasant Uprisings." *Women of China* (August 1982): 20–21.

Bao Wenqing. "Two Films About the Empress Dowager." *China Reconstructs* (December 1983): 50–51.

Biggerstaff, Knight. *The Earlier Modern Government Schools in China*. Ithaca: Cornell University Press, 1961.

Cai Guanluo. *Qingdai qibai mingren zhuan* (Biographies of 700 Noted Personages of the Qing Dynasty). Beijing: Zhonghua shuju, 1988.

Cheng Chengzhi. *The Story of Cixi Finding Favor Twice*. Kunming: Yunnan People's Publishing House, 1981.

Cheng Shisong. "On Qin Liangyu." *Sichuan University Journal* (February 1987): 69–75.

Clubb, O. Edmund. *20th Century China*. New York: Columbia University Press, 1964.

Clyde, Paul Hibbert. *The Far East: A History of the Impact of the West on Eastern Asia*. 3rd ed. Englewood Cliffs: Prentice-Hall, 1958.

Cohen, Paul A. *China and Christianity: The Missionary Movement and the Growth of Chinese Anti-foreignism, 1860–1870*. Cambridge: Harvard University Press, 1963.

Dictionary of Famous Women of China. Beijing: Huaxia, 1988.

Der Ling, Princess. *Golden Phoenix*. New York: Dodd, Mead, 1932.

Der Ling, Princess. *Old Buddha*. New York: Dodd, Mead, 1928–1934.

Fairbank, J.K. *The United States and China*. rev. ed. Cambridge: Harvard University Press, 1958.

Famous Women of Ancient Times and Today, ed. *Women of China*. Beijing: Hebei People's Publishing House, 1986.

Fay, Peter Ward. *The Opium War 1840–1842*. Chapel Hill: University of North Carolina Press, 1997.

Feng Peilan. "Discussion About Madame Na La's Declaration of War Against Foreign Countries in the Gengzi Year." *Journal of Tianjin Education Institute*, no. 2 (1987).

Ge Zhengqi. Preface to *Zhuxizaoxan yincao* (Poems from Zhuxiaoxuan Pavilion).

———, *Qinggong mishi* (Secret History of the Qing Imperial Court), 3 vols. Taibei: Yuanliu chubanshe, 1992.

Gu Qian. "Departed but Not Forgotten." *Women of China*. (Beijing, 1984): 134–135.

Guang Xuxiu. *Record of Wujin and Yang County*.

Guo Moruo. "Matters About Qin Liangyu." *Sichuan ribao*, August 26, 1962.

He Riyu. "Anecdotes of General Qin Liangyu of the Ming Dynasty." In *Collections of Cun Chengzhai*.

Historical Personages. Beijing: Xin Wenyi Press, 1959.

History of the Ming Dynasty. Beijing: Zhonghua shuju, 1974.

History of the Qing Dynasty.

Ho, Clara Wing-chung. "Conventionality versus Dissent: Designation of the Titles of Women's Collected Works in Qing China." *Ming Qing yanjiu* 3 (1994): 46–90.

Hsu, C.Y. *China's Entrance into the Family of Nations: The Diplomatic Phase, 1856–1880*. Cambridge: Harvard University Press, 1960.

Hu Wenkai. *Textual Research into Works by Women Writers in History*. Beijing: Commercial Publishers, 1957.

Hummel, Arthur W., ed. *Eminent Chinese in the Ch'ing Period 1644–1912*. Washington, DC: U.S. Government Printing Office, 1943–1944, pp. 25–26.

Jiang Mingfang and Wang Ruifang. *Brief Biographies of Gifted Women Scholars in China*.

Kang Zhouyi. *Stories of Chen Yuanyuan*.

Latourette, K.S. *A History of the Expansion of Christianity*, vol. 6, *The Great Century in Northern Africa and Asia 1800–1914*. New York: Harper, 1944.

Liang Yizhen. *Qingdai funu wenxueshi* (History of Women's Literature in the Qing Dynasty). Taibei: Zhonghua shuju, 1958, pp. 229–33.

Lu Meiyi and Zheng Yongfu. *Zhongguo funu yundong: 1840–1921*. Zhengzhou: Henan renmin chubanshe, 1990, pp. 200–207.

Mao Xiang. *Yingmei'an yiyu* (Recollections of Yingmei Temple).

Meng Sen. *Ming Qing shi jian yi*. Beijing: Zhonghua shuju, 1981.

Meng Sen. *Xingshi zongkan*.

Meschel, S.V. "Teacher Keng's Heritage. A Survey of Chinese Women Scientists." *Journal of Chemical Education* 69, no. 9 (1992): 723–730.

New Textual Research of Novels, Dramas, Songs and Ballads. World Publishing House.

Purcell, Victor. *The Boxer Uprising: A Backgrond Study.* Cambridge: Cambridge University Press, 1963.

Qian Qianyi. *Biographies of the Poets Attached to Their Selected Poems in History—The Supplementary Section of the History of the Qing Dynasty.*

Qian Shixin. *Biographies in the History of the Qing Dynasty.*

Qiu Zongzhang. "Ji xu jichen nushi." In *Xu zihua shiwenji.* Beijing: Zhonghua shuju, 1990.

Qing Guanluo. "Mao Xiang zhuan." In *Qingdai qibai mingren zhuan.*

Reischauer, Edwin R., and John K. Fairbank. *East Asia: The Modern Transformation.* Boston: Houghton Mifflin, 1965.

Ropp, Paul S. "Dissent in Early Modern China." In *Ju-lin Wai-shih and Ch'ing Social Criticism.* Ann Arbor: University of Michican Press, 1981, pp. 120–151.

Ruan Yuan. *Lianzhe youxuan lu* (Chronicles of Travels in Zhejiang).

Shen Jianguo, ed. *Zhonghua gujin nujie pu.* Beijing: Zhongguo shehui kexue chubanshe, 1991.

Spence, Jonathan D. *The Search for Modern China.* New York: W. W. Norton, 1999.

Sun Chang, Kang-i. "A Guide to Ming-Ch'ing Anthologies of Female Poetry and Their Selection Strategies." *The Gest Library Journal* 5, no. 2 (Winter 1992): 119–160.

Tan Zhengbi. *Stories of Chinese Women Poets.*

Teng Ssu-yu and John K. Fairbank. *China's Response to the West: A Documentary Survey 1839–1923.* Cambridge: Harvard University Press, 1954.

Vinacke, Harold M. *A History of the Far East in Modern Times.* 6th ed. New York: Appleton-Century-Crofts, 1961.

Wang Daocheng. "Cixi taihou." In *Qingdai renwu zhuangao,* ed. Qingshi bianweiihui, vol. 8. Beijing: Zhonghua shuju, 1993, pp. 1–19.

Wang Shizhen. *Chibei ou tan.*

Wang Xiuqing and Hu Wenkai. *A Concise Collection of Literary Works by Famous Women in History.*

Weidner, Marsha, et al. *Views from the Jade Terrace: Chinese Women Artists, 1300–1912.* New York: Indianapolis Museum of Art, 1988.

Wright, Mary Clabaugh. *The Last Stand of Chinese Conservativism: The T'ung-chih Restoration, 1862–1874.* Stanford: Stanford University Press, 1957.

Xu Kuichen. *Collection of Poems of Women Writers in History.* Beijing: Commercial Publishing, 1969.

Xu Naochen. *Guochao gixou xiangheji.*

Xu Zihua. *Xu zihua shiwen ji.* Beijing: Zhonghua shuju, 1990.

Yang Hsien-yi and Gladys Yang, trans. *The Scholars*, 3rd ed. Beijing: Foreign Languages Press, 1973.

Yi Shaoyuan. *Complete Works of the Household of Noon Dream Hall.*

Yin Wei. *Zhonghua wuqiannian yiyuan cainu.* Zhengzhou: Zhongzhou guji chubanshe, 1992.

Yu Bingkun. "An Investigation of Cixi's Family History." *Journal of the Museum of the Summer Palace*, no. 4 (1985).

Yu DeLing. *Cixi yeshi* (Unofficial History of Cixi), trans. Qin Shou'ou. Shenyang: Liaoshen shushe, 1994. [Translated from English: Princess Der Ling. *Imperial Incense.* New York: Dodd, Mead, 1933; London: S. Paul, 1934.]

Yu Huai. *Banqiao zaiji.*

Yu RongLing. "Qinggong suoji." In *Cixi jishi congshu: Cixi yu wo*, eds. Wang Shuqing and Xu Che. Shenyong: Liaoshen shushe, 1994.

Yuan Mei. *Notes on Poetry of Siyuan.*

Zhang Dejun. "Guanyu gaibian tianci de nushiren hou zhi." *Guangming ribao*, May 17, 1961.

Zhang Genpei. *Stele of the Lotus Pond.*

Zhu Jinpu. "About the Death of Dowager Cixi." *Journal of the Museum of the Summer Palace*, no. 4 (1985).

Zhuan Wei. *Cixi*. Beijing: Zhonghua shuju , 1994.

Index

About the Editor

Barbara Bennett Peterson is the founding president of the Fulbright Association, Hawaii Chapter, an emeritus professor at the University of Hawaii, and a fellow at the East-West Center. She has been an adjunct professor at Hawaii Pacific University and a research associate at Bishop Museum. A graduate of Oregon State University, she received an A.M. from Stanford University and a Ph.D. from the University of Hawaii.

Dr. Peterson's books include *Notable Women of Hawaii* (1984); *America in British Eyes* (1988); *The Pacific Region* (with Wilhelm G. Solheim II) (1990); *American History: Seventeenth, Eighteenth, and Nineteenth Centuries* (1993); *America: Nineteenth and Twentieth Centuries* (1993); and *John Bull's Eye on America* (1995).

She has twice been a Fulbright Scholar researching in Japan at Sophia University, 1967, and teaching as a Senior Scholar at Wuhan University, China, 1988–89. While at Wuhan University, she was presented with the Teacher of the Year award in 1989. The University of Hawaii Board of Regents awarded her the Excellence in Teaching award in 1993.

She is married to Dr. Frank L. Peterson, a geologist. She supports CARE and donates part of the proceeds from this book to that international cause helping children worldwide.

In 1997, Dr. Peterson was honored with the University of Hawaii's Distinguished Alumni Award.